System Center 2012 Configuration Manager
Mastering the Fundamentals

Kent Agerlund

PUBLISHED BY

Deployment Artist
http://www.deploymentartist.com

ISBN: 978-91-979390-4-1

Warning and Disclaimer

Every effort has been made to make this book as complete and as accurate as possible, but no warranty or fitness is implied. The information provided is on an "as is" basis. The authors and the publisher shall have neither liability nor responsibility to any person or entity with respect to any loss or damages arising from the information contained in this book.

Feedback Information

We'd like to hear from you! If you have any comments about how we could improve the quality of this book, please don't hesitate to contact us by visiting www.deploymentfundamentals.com, send an email to feedback@deploymentfundamentals.com or visit our Facebook site www.facebook.com/deploymentfundamentals.

Foreword

Are you new to System Center Configuration Manager, especially System Center 2012 Configuration Manager? If the answer is a 'yes', then this book may be exactly what you need to get your feet underneath you and help you get familiar with the product and its features. Configuration Manager is an application that can complete quite a few management tasks that you need to perform to effectively manage your client computer environment. It is not just a simple—throw in the DVD, run Setup, and away you go—product. Sure, if you have experience with previous versions of Microsoft's Systems Management Server or Configuration Manager, it may be fairly easy for you to install Configuration Manager 2012 and get your environment to work as you need. However, if you are new to Microsoft systems management, then this book should help you out immensely.

Configuration Manager interacts with a number of your infrastructure components, such as Active Directory Domain Services, SQL Server, Windows Server Update Services, Windows Deployment Services, Internet Information Services, network protocols and communications. With that background information, it is very important for you to effectively plan your environment before you do attempt to install Configuration Manager. This book will help you design and deploy your environment before you attempt to install it to use for client management.

I know Kent, and know that you are in for a treat. He is one of our Microsoft Most Valuable Professionals (MVP). He is very knowledgeable on Configuration Manager, having presented at a number of Microsoft events. I'm sure that you'll enjoy the book and learn a lot about Configuration Manager. No one book can teach you all there is to know about Configuration Manager; however, this book will be a great start to your adventure with System Center 2012 Configuration Manager. Enjoy the book and your experience with Configuration Manager.

With kind regards,

Wally Mead
Senior Program Manager
Configuration Manager product group

Acknowledgements

This book would not exist without the love and support from my (very) patient family. Thank you, Nanna, Julie and Susanne. You are always in my heart.

Thank you, Johan Arwidmark, for giving me the opportunity to write this book, a challenge that I just couldn't resist.

Thanks to the System Center product team at Microsoft, and my fellow MVP mates around the globe, especially to Mr. Brian Mason for bringing me to the best steak houses in the US, and for having time to discuss ConfigMgr 2012. As always, huge thanks to my colleagues at Coretech, whom I'm proud to be associated with. These guys are by far the best and most creative team I have ever worked with. Guys, you'll Never Work Alone. Thanks to Thomas Stenby for testing all the labs in the book.

One thing I have learned from working with Configuration Manager is that the knowledge is universal. Configuration Manager really rocks the world, and administrators all over the world are often facing the same challenges. Just for fun, I made a note of the places that I visited while writing this book. While working on the book, I have also done ConfigMgr-related work in Copenhagen, Stockholm, Oslo, Trondheim, Seattle, Zürich, Minneapolis, Las Vegas, Atlanta, Orlando, Geneva, and finally London.

While I was writing the book, my good friend and colleague Michael Petersen sadly passed away. I have known and worked closely together with Michael for many years. Never before in my life have I met a guy as passionate about his work as Michael. Those thousands of readers who have been following Michael on twitter (@osdeploy) or thru his blog (blog.coretech.dk/mip) knows about his dedication and his ability to make complex challenges look easy. Working with Michael on a daily basis has been a blast.

@Michael, you will never be forgotten – thanks for everything.

Finally, a huge thanks to my Bose noise reduction headset, which has blessed my journey with tunes from Bruce Springsteen, AC/DC, John Denver, Volbeat, Toto, and the all mighty Mr. Frank "Blue Eyes" Sinatra. Trust me when I say, "a little Sinatra each day keeps the dark side away."

About the Author

Kent Agerlund

Kent Agerlund is chief system management architect and System Center specialist working as certified trainer, consultant and event speaker. Kent started his computer endeavors back in the late 80s working with databases like dBase, Paradox, and FoxPro. Almost since the beginning of his professional computer career, Kent has worked as a certified trainer and consultant. Today Kent works for Coretech, a Danish System Center house where he also contributes by writing articles and sharing tips and tricks on http://blog.coretech.dk. In recent years, Kent has travelled the globe delivering his Mastering Configuration Manager classes and speaking at various conferences like MMS and TechEd. Through the years, Kent has attained various certifications and achievements such as Windows 2008 R2 Enterprise Administrator, MCSE+A, and MCT, and has been awarded Microsoft Most Valuable Professional (MVP) in System Center Configuration Manager.

Contributing Authors

Kaido Jarvemets

A special tribute to Kaido Jarvemets, a fellow ConfigMgr MVP located in Estonia. Kaido provided the PowerShell scripts used in the book. Kaido works as an IT expert at MicroLink Eesti and is also the president at System Center User Group Estonia. Kaido also writes articles and shares tips and tricks on Depsharee.blogspot.com.

Peter Dalmanns

Huge thanks to Peter for contributing good ideas and helping out with writing some of the chapters. Peter is a fellow Microsoft MVP in ConfigMgr and lives in Breda, Netherlands. Peter works at IT-Concern, a Microsoft Gold Partner, as a Senior Technical Consultant. You can follow Peter from his blog at www.systemcenterblog.nl or on Twitter @pdaalmans.

Contents

Introduction

System Center 2012 Configuration Manager: Mastering the Fundamentals is the ultimate source for the working IT Pro who wants to design and implement System Center 2012 Configuration Manager in a in a midsize or small business environment. Enterprise administrators also will find a lot inspiration by reading the book, as many of the features and scenarios discussed fit all three environments.

Configuration Manager (ConfigMgr) is by far the most complex Microsoft product. This book focuses on HOW TO GET IT DONE RIGHT THE FIRST TIME, based on years of experience with Configuration Manager and SMS. You will not find 1,000 pages describing all the possible ways to implement ConfigMgr, but rather learn the time-tested essentials for a successful implementation, saving you many hours and headaches. After reading this book, you will have a working Configuration Manager 2012 environment with all the major features implemented. Furthermore, you will have a solid understanding of how to configure the features according to best practices and know how to troubleshoot real-world scenarios.

Say Hello (Possibly Again) to ViaMonstra Inc.

In this book, we implement ConfigMgr 2012 for the fictive ViaMonstra Inc. organization. ViaMonstra is a midsized company with 6,500 users. There is one datacenter based in New York and several remote offices in the United States and Europe. Among the users, 3,500 work in the New York office; the remote sites all have fewer than 200 users except for Liverpool, which has 750 employees.

ViaMonstra currently doesn't use any standardized system management solution. Decisions have been made to standardize and automate the company's desktop and server management. The management solution is Microsoft System Center 2012, and Configuration Manager (also known as ConfigMgr) is the first product to be implemented. The focus of the book is ConfigMgr 2012, and I do anticipate that you already have knowledge about Windows Server Update Services (WSUS), Windows Deployment Services (WDS), Domain Name System (DNS), Dynamic Host Configuration Protocol (DHCP), and Microsoft Active Directory.

BTW, the name ViaMonstra comes from *Viam Monstra*, Latin, meaning "Show me the way."

Structure of the Book

The first chapter is a concept crash course, which explains the terminology and scenarios used in the book. The second chapter describes ViaMonstra Inc. in more detail, as well as the proof-of-concept environment I use.

Chapters 3-4 explain how to install and configure ConfigMgr 2012 site server and site system server. Chapters 5-11 focus on each of the primary features in ConfigMgr. Chapter 12 covers backup and restore, and Chapter 13 is a tribute to the ConfigMgr communities.

Finally, I have the appendices, which include extra material on how to set up the related services and a tribute to the communities, blogs, and tools that I use on a daily basis.

How to Use This Book

I have packed this book with step-by-step guides, which means you can implement your solution as you read along.

In numbered steps, all names and paths are in bold typeface. I also have used a standard naming convention throughout the book when explaining what to do in each step. The steps normally are something like this:

- On the **Advanced Properties** page, select the **Confirm** check box, and then click **Next**.

Code and sample scripts are formatted like the following, on a grey background.

```
BDEInstallSuppress=NO

OSDMigrateMode=Advanced
```

The step-by-step guides in this book assume that you have configured the environment according to the information in Chapter 2, "ViaMonstra Inc. and the Datacenter."

This book is not intended as a reference volume, covering every deployment technology, acronym, or command-line switch known to man, but rather is designed to make sure you learn what you need to know to build a great deployment solution for your Windows servers.

Sample Files

All sample files used in this book can be downloaded from www.deploymentfundamentals.com.

Additional Resources

In addition to all the tips and tricks provided in this book, you will find extra resources like video recordings on the www.deploymentfundamentals.com site.

Topics Not Covered

I do not cover out of band management in this first edition of the book.

Chapter 1 Crash Course

As promised earlier, we have a concept crash course in this book, and this is it. The shorthand story: When using ConfigMgr, there are terms and services you need to know. This is a ten-minute crash course in Microsoft System Center 2012 Configuration Manager terminology.

The System Center 2012 Suite

With the release of System Center 2012 on April 17 2012, Microsoft has reached a milestone in its effort to deliver a complete set of tools to manage all aspects of the datacenter and client devices. Configuration Manager is a crucial part of the suite, and you can implement it as a standalone solution or together with the other System Center products like Operations Manager, Orchestrator, and Service Manager.

The System Center 2012 Family

Product	**Short Description**
Configuration Manager Mg deploys, updats, compliance + Inventory mgmt to servers, users +devices.	Configuration Manager, or ConfigMgr, is a systems management application providing application deployment, operating systems deployment, software update management, compliance management, and inventory management to servers, users, and their devices.
Operations Manager state, health + Performance info Proactive generate sytem alerts based on performance, availability, config Security	Operations Manager, or OpsMgr, allows management across server operating systems and hypervisors through views that show state, health, and performance information. It also allows you to be proactive by generating alerts based on factors like performance, availability, configuration, security, and much more.
Service Manager Incident + Problem resolution +Change control	Service Manager provides built-in processes for change control and incident and problem resolution. Service Manager can be integrated with the other System Center products like Orchestrator, ConfigMgr, and OpsMgr. Together they form a powerful alliance in any datacenter.

Product	Short Description
Orchestrator	I often refer to Orchestrator as the glue that enables you to convert a manual process into a fully automated process. You can use Orchestrator to grab information from one System Center product, connect to any client (or server), and then perform one or a series of tasks based on the information. At any given point during this sequence of tasks, you can configure Orchestrator to interact and deliver information to the other System Center applications.
Data Protection Manager (DPM)	DPM delivers unified data protection for Windows servers and clients. In essence, this is the backup solution you should use across the board regardless of where you store data—on tape, disk, or cloud.
Virtual Machine Manager (VMM)	VMM enables centralized management of physical and virtual IT infrastructure. It is also a platform for planning, deploying, managing, and optimizing the virtual infrastructure.
App Controller	App Controller provides a self-service experience across private and public clouds. It enables application owners to build, configure, deploy, and manage new services in the private or public cloud.
Endpoint Protection	Endpoint Protection is the successor of Forefront Endpoint Protection, an antimalware application that can be deployed and managed through Configuration Manager 2012.

Site Servers

A site server is the server you install through the System Center Installation Wizard. Without a site server in your environment, you cannot have ConfigMgr installed. It's as simple as that. When installing the site server, you also automatically install a site that is represented with a site name and a three-digit site code. Once you have the site server, you start installing site system roles. A site system role can be hosted on the site server, or you can choose to install the role on another server; one site system can even be deployed on a client operating system.

Prior to installing your environment, you need to have some basic knowledge of the three different site servers that you can install and when you need to install them. I work with enterprise, midsize, and small business customers, and what I have learned is that there is no installation scenario that fits all; but there are some questions you can ask yourself to figure out how many sites and, by extension, how many site servers you need.

Central Administration Site

A central administration site (CAS) is the top site server in the hierarchy. Unlike the other site servers, you cannot assign any clients to the CAS, nor can you install any user-facing site systems roles except from the software update point. A CAS stores client data for all clients in the hierarchy in a SQL Server database called the ConfigMgr site database. The CAS can have multiple primary child sites, all of which send data to the CAS. At the CAS, you also have the Administrator console from which you can manage hierarchy.

Question: *Do I always need a central administration site?*

Answer: No, a CAS is needed only when you have more than one primary site in the hierarchy. As a matter of fact, most readers of this book may never need to implement a CAS.

Question: *If needed, when should I install the central administration site?*
Answer: You need to install the CAS as the first site in the hierarchy. Primary sites are attached to the CAS during the installation just like backup domain controllers (BDCs) in the days of Windows NT 4.0.

Primary Site

You always need at least one primary site in the hierarchy. If you do not, there is really no reason for you to finish reading this book or any other ConfigMgr-related book. It's very simple: without a primary site, you have no working ConfigMgr environment. Clients can be assigned only to a primary site. A primary site stores client data for all clients assigned to the site in a SQL Server database called the ConfigMgr site database. Primary sites have administrative tools, such as the Administrator console, that enable an administrator to manage the site directly. Primary sites can have multiple secondary sites, all of which send data to the primary site.

Question: *When do I need more than one primary site?*

Answer: That's a good question, and I'm so glad you asked it. Unlike previous versions of ConfigMgr (and SMS), there are not many reasons why you would implement more than one primary site when using ConfigMgr 2012. The main reasons for implementing more than one primary site are:

- You have more than 100,000 users, which is the recommended maximum number for a primary site.
- For political reasons, you are required to have a primary site in each data center.

Question: *I get the point; I need an additional primary site only if I scale beyond 100,000. I have no plans for that; however, fault tolerance is really important in my organization, and we will not tolerate downtime for too long. After all, we do plan to use ConfigMgr to deploy applications and new operating systems, and also to keep our operating systems and applications up-to-date with the latest security patches. Not to mention that we plan to implement Endpoint Protection and always must have the latest definition updates applied.*

Answer: Ouch! We are just in the first chapter, and you are already asking one of the most important questions in terms of designing ConfigMgr. Well, you need to understand that a ConfigMgr site consists of different site systems and those site systems do not have to be installed on the same server. As a matter of fact, in most midsized companies, I always recommend that you remove any user-facing site system roles from the site server. When you plan for fault tolerance, you need to look at the individual role because there are individual rules for the different site system roles. Some roles support clustering (like the site system database), whereas other site systems can be hosted on several servers (e.g. distribution points and management points) and finally other site systems also support network load balancing (NLB).

Question: *OK, I understand. So, what you are saying is that I should focus on implementing multiple site system roles instead of multiple primary site servers. But what are the consequences if my boss does not understand me and still requires two primary sites?*

Answer: Well, first off, you need to implement two new sites, a CAS and one additional site. That will give you a total of three sites that you need to manage, which in my opinion makes the environment too complex and you haven't achieved much in terms of fault tolerance compared to having a single site with multiple site systems. Also, remember that whenever you start to implement a site, you say "Hello" to site replication. Replication between sites is done through SQL replication, and the old-fashioned file-based replication. One of the things that, as a consultant, I have struggled with most in the past has been replication issues, and I will go a long way to avoid that in ConfigMgr 2012.

Secondary Site

Unlike previous versions of ConfigMgr and SMS, a secondary site now also requires a SQL Server database. It doesn't have to be a Standard or Enterprise version, as the SQL Server Express edition will do just fine. If you don't have a local database, the secondary site installation can take care of that and install a version of SQL Server Express. The secondary site is always a child site of the primary site and thus managed thru the ConfigMgr Administrator console connected to the primary site. The secondary site forwards the information it gathers from clients, such as computer inventory data and system status information, to its parent site. The primary site then stores the data of both the primary and secondary sites in the site database. Secondary sites are particularly useful for remote locations where you need links where you need to control the bandwidth.

Question: *Are there any rules of thumb for when I should implement a secondary site at a remote location?*

Answer: I only recommend installing a secondary site at remote locations and only if one of the following statements is true:

- The remote location has more than 500 clients and fewer than 5000 clients.
- You need to compress traffic going to the site.
- You need to control the upward flowing traffic.
- You need a local management point.
- You need a local software update point.

Real World Note: Do not use a management point (covered in the next section) instead of a secondary site. I highly discourage configuring a management point in a remote location. It is not what I call a "site-aware site system" like a distribution point. Inevitably, some clients from the entire site will connect to and use the management point, which eventually will cause a backlog on the server.

Site Systems

As mentioned earlier in this chapter, a site is made up of a site server hosting the site *server* role and multiple site *system* roles. The site system roles can be hosted on several different servers, or you can choose to implement all site systems on the same server. I have seen several medium and small site installations where all the roles are hosted on the same server, and everything runs perfectly.

Management Point

The management point is the primary point of contact between clients and the site server. A ConfigMgr 2012 site can host ten management points, but you should not install them across a WAN link because a management point is not "site-aware." A management point provides specific client configuration details, also known as client *policies*. It receives inventory, software metering, and status information from clients and forwards it to the site server.

Software Update Point (SUP)

A software update point is a WSUS server controlled by Configuration Manager. Unlike a standalone WSUS solution, clients do not download or install updates directly from a software update point. The only data downloaded by the client from a software update point is the update metadata. There can be only one software update point per site. If you need to plan for fault tolerance, the solution is to install network load balancing. It's outside the scope of this book to describe that configuration; however, you can find information about it in this TechNet article: http://technet.microsoft.com/en-us/library/cc708533(WS.10).aspx.

Distribution Point

Whenever a client needs to install an application or a software update, the client will connect to a distribution point to fetch the software. Unlike previous versions of ConfigMgr and SMS, this version has only one distribution point type. There are no more branch distribution points or server shares. The distribution point stores packages in a new content library, which supports single instance storage for all content and thus minimizes the space required to host all packages. Another of the new cool features in this version is that you can control traffic going to the distribution point and also prestage content using any media. It's not uncommon for a distribution point to host several 100 GBs of content. So when setting up a new distribution point at a remote location, you will find the prestaging very convenient. No more sneaking along the walls when you are passing the network monitoring team office. No worries, you will not flood the network.

Distribution points can be grouped in state-based distribution point groups. The major benefit of distribution point groups is that all distribution points in the group will have the exact same content. Even if you add a new distribution point to the group, it automatically receives the same packages. (Yes, I did use the word "packages." I use that term to describe content regardless of whether it's an application, WIM file, or software update.)

Distribution Requirements

A distribution point is the only site system role that can be deployed to a client operating system and supports both x32 and x64. When you install a distribution point, you can configure the site server to install the needed IIS role and features.

Application Catalog Web Service Point

An Application Catalog web service point provides software information to the Application Catalog website from the Software Library. This site system role is installed only on the primary site.

Application Catalog Website Point

A new end-user web portal allows end users to request and install software. Applications deployed to end users are presented in the Self-Service Portal.

Site Database Server

The ConfigMgr site database server is a computer running SQL Server that stores information such as discovery data, hardware and software inventory data, and configuration and status information for the ConfigMgr sites in the hierarchy.

Fallback Status Point (FSP)

The fallback status point is used by clients when they are unable to communicate with management points. There are a few scenarios in which that can happen, such as during the client installation and assignment phase, or when a client configured to communicate using HTTPS for some reason has a problem with the certificate. Before installing the FSP, you need to be aware of the fact the non-authenticated and non-encrypted traffic is accepted by the site system.

Reporting Services Point

The SQL Reporting Services point, or reporting services point, is the only supported reporting solution in ConfigMgr 2012. You can find SQL Server Reporting Services on your SQL Server DVD and install it along with the SQL Server database.

Asset Intelligence Synchronization Point

The Asset Intelligence synchronization point is always installed at the top-most site server in the hierarchy. The site system will connect to System Center Online and synchronize updates to the Assent Intelligence.

Endpoint Protection Point

The Endpoint Protection point is a required site system when you want to install and manage Endpoint Protection clients using ConfigMgr You need to install the site system at the CAS server. When installing the site system, you won't really do much, only accept the Endpoint Protection client license information and configure the relationship with Microsoft Active Protection Service (formerly known as Microsoft Spynet).

Enrollment Point

An enrollment point is used to complete mobile device enrollment and provision AMT-based computers using PKI certificates.

Enrollment Proxy Point

An enrollment proxy point manages the enrollment requests from mobile devices.

Out of Band Service Point

An out of band service point provisions and configures AMT-based computers for out of band management. To better understand what out of band management is, think of in-band management, which is basically managing computers that are powered on and accessible. Out of band management is the opposite of that; it's managing computers that are not powered on.

Configuration Manager Related Services

One of the real powers of ConfigMgr is that it often uses services already implemented in the network. For most organizations, no new network services have to be implemented in order to service ConfigMgr. Having said that, you still need to ensure that you have good knowledge of the following:

- Active Directory
- Dynamic Host Configuration Protocol (DHCP)
- Domain Name System (DNS)
- Internet Information Server (IIS)
- Key Management Service (KMS)
- Public key infrastructure (PKI)—if you choose to let site systems and clients communicate using HTTPS
- Windows Deployment Services (WDS)
- Windows Management Instrumentation (WMI)
- Windows Server Update Services (WSUS)

That wraps up the elementary school. Now you know what a site and a site system are and what services you rely on when implementing ConfigMgr 2012.

Chapter 2 ViaMonstra Inc. and the Datacenter

As you remember from the first chapter, ViaMonstra Inc. is the fictive company I use throughout this book. In this chapter, I describe the company in more detail, as well as the management solution I have built for that company. I also provide details about the proof-of-concept (datacenter) environment I use in our step-by-step guides.

In addition to the information in this chapter, you can find detailed instructions on how to install and configure the servers in Appendix A. If you want to follow all the step-by-step guides in this book, you need to have your environment setup as described in Appendix A.

ViaMonstra Inc.

ViaMonstra Inc. was invented for the very purpose of having a "real" company for which to build a deployment solution. In the real world, these deployment solutions come from multiple consulting engagements I have done. For purposes of this book, I have consolidated them into a single generic scenario.

As mentioned in Chapter 1, ViaMonstra has a single datacenter, which is described in the following sections.

Hardware

ViaMonstra Inc. knows that the key factors involved in developing any good performing ConfigMgr site server is choosing the correct disk layout, combined with lots of memory for SQL Server and the appropriate CPUs. With that in mind, ViaMonstra has decided to install a storage area network (SAN) with the storage of five RAID 10 LUNs with separate spindles.

The site server and disk layout for a midsized installation like ViaMonstra looks like this:

- **Server.** HP ProLiant DL380p Gen8
- **Memory.** 16 GB RAM (You will do just fine with 4 or 8 GB RAM to finish all the exercises in this book.)
- **CPU.** 2 * Intel® Xeon® E5-2630 with six cores

Drive	**Usage**	**Disk Size**
C:\	Operating system	72 GB
D:\	Program files	100 GB
E:\	Content library	300 GB

Drive	Usage	Disk Size
F:\	SQL Server TempDB system database (TempDB)	50 GB (Estimated TempDB size is 35% of total database size.)
G:\	SQL Server database (.db) files	100 GB (Estimated database size is 30 GB.)
H:\	SQL Server transaction log files	75 GB (Estimated log size is 11 GB.)

Software

Like most companies, ViaMonstra has some core desktop applications and some custom made lines of business applications. The following list describes ViaMonstra's deployed roles, features, and applications related to our ConfigMgr project:

- Domain Controller
- DNS
- DHCP
- Exchange 2010
- Hyper-V
- SQL Server 2008 R2
- Microsoft Office 2010
- 7-Zip
- WinRAR

Servers

In the step-by-step guides, what we call Build-While-Reading, we use the following servers.

> **Real World Note:** The servers can very well be virtual machines, but as in any production-like environment, make sure that at least one of the domain controllers runs on a physical machine. Please don't make the mistake of running all the domain controllers as virtual machines, at least not when your Hyper-V hosts are members of the domain they host.

- **DC01.** A **Windows Server 2008 R2** machine, fully patched with the latest security updates, and configured as Active Directory Domain Controller, DNS Server, and DHCP Server in the **corp.viamonstra.com** domain.
  - Server name: **DC01**
  - IP Address: **192.168.1.1**
  - Roles: **DNS**, **DHCP** and **Domain Controller**

- **CM01.** A **Windows Server 2008 R2** machine, fully patched with the latest security updates, and configured as a member server in the **corp.viamonstra.com** domain. The server has been configured with the WDS and WSUS roles; it has SQL Server 2008 R2 Standard installed.
  - Server name: **CM01**
  - IP Address: **192.168.1.2**
  - Roles: **Management Point**, **Software Update Point**, **Distribution Point**, **Application Catalog Web Service Point**, and **Application Catalog Website Point**
  - Software: **SQL Server 2008 R2 Standard**, **Configuration Manager 2012 Site Server**, and **Microsoft Deployment Toolkit 2012**

  For detailed, step-by-step guidance on how to configure the CM01 server, please review Appendix A, "Using the Hydration Kit to Build the POC Environment."
- **PC001.** A **Windows 7 x64 client**, fully patched with the latest security updates, and configured as a member server in the **corp.viamonstra.com** domain.
  - Client name: **PC001**
  - IP Address: **DHCP client**
  - Roles: **Client**
- **PC002.** A **Windows XP x86 client**, fully patched with the latest security updates, and configured as a member server in the **corp.viamonstra.com** domain.
  - Client name: **PC002**
  - IP Address: **DHCP client**
  - Roles: **Client**
- **CM02.** A **Windows Server 2008 R2** machine, fully patched with the latest security updates, and configured as a member server in the **corp.viamonstra.com** domain. This server represents our remote distribution point that we have in our remote locations. The site system roles all are installed as part of the book.
  - Server name: **CM02**
  - IP Address: **192.168.3.3**
  - Roles: **Remote PXE-enabled Distribution Point**
- **CM03.** A **Windows Server 2008 R2** machine, fully patched with the latest security updates, and configured as a member server in the **corp.viamonstra.com** domain. This is our secondary site server in Liverpool. The site server and site system roles all are installed as part of the book.
  - Server name: **CM03**

- IP Address: **192.168.3.3**
- Roles: Secondary **Site Server with Management Point**, **Remote PXE-enabled Distribution Point**, and **State Migration Point**

- **EX01.** A **Windows Server 2008 R2** machine, fully patched with the latest security updates, and configured as a mail server in the **corp.viamonstra.com** domain. This server is not required in order to complete the exercises.
  - Server name: **EX01**
  - IP Address: **192.168.1.3**
  - Roles: **Exchange 2010**

Real World Note: For a standalone lab or test environment, two single disks are just fine. For production use, a distribution point should have two separate disk sets for OS and data (RAID 1 for the OS disk set, and RAID 5 for the data disk set).

Software Requirements

In addition to the configuration and software needed for servers CM01, CM02 and CM03 (see Appendix A), you need the following software to be able to perform all the step-by-step guides in this book:

- Windows Server 2008 R2 media and product key (the product key is used differently depending on whether you use Multiple Activation Keys [MAKs] or Key Management Service [KMS] for activation).
- System Center 2012 Configuration Manager
- Office 2010 Professional Plus x86 (volume license) and product key
- The following free software downloaded from microsoft.com:
  - System Center Updates Publisher (SCUP) 2011
  - Microsoft Deployment Toolkit (MDT) 2012
  - Configuration Manager 2012 Toolkit
  - Scriptomatic from Microsoft's Scripting Guys
- The following software from downloaded from rarlabs.com:

  WinRAR
- The following software from downloaded from 7-Zip.org:

  7-Zip

Chapter 3 Installing and Configuring ConfigMgr 2012

In this chapter, you learn to install ConfigMgr. As mentioned in Chapter 2, the step-by-step guides in this and the following chapters assume that you have installed and configured the servers as described in Appendix A.

Installing ConfigMgr 2012 is not in itself a difficult task, at least not if you know what you want to install and why. In ViaMonstra, I have decided to install the following ConfigMgr servers:

- In the datacenter, a primary site server
- In Liverpool, a secondary site server
- In each of the remote locations, a remote PXE enable distribution point

Before you start installing any site servers, you first need to prepare Active Directory and install SQL Server.

> **Real World Note:** The reason for selecting a secondary site in Liverpool is due to the number of supported users in that location. The magic number is 500 users. Above that you should consider adding a site server in the location.

Active Directory Prerequisites

Before implementing ConfigMgr, you need to make a decision whether you want to extend the Active Directory schema. It is not a requirement, but it is a very good idea that will make your life as administrator somewhat easier. After you have extended the schema, clients will be able to query the global catalog and get information about site systems and command-line installation properties. As part of preparing Active Directory, you complete the tasks covered in the following sections.

Extend the Active Directory Schema

1. Log on to **DC01** as **Administrator** in the **VIAMONSTRA** domain.
2. Ensure that you have access to the **ConfigMgr 2012 DVD** (or other medium).
3. Open a command prompt as **Administrator**, navigate to **.\SMSSETUP\BIN\X64** on the **ConfigMgr DVD**, and run **extadsch.exe**.
4. Verify that the schema extension was successful by reviewing the **extadsch.log** located in the root of **C:**.

Real World Note: There are no Active Directory schema changes like those with Configuration Manager 2007. For that reason, if the schema is already extended, you do not have to extend it again.

Create the System Management Container

The System Management container is a folder below the System folder in Active Directory used by the site server and the management points to store published data like boundaries and certificates. The site server can create the container during the installation, but that requires full administrator permissions for the site server computer account on the System Management container. For security reasons, I prefer to add all site servers and management points to a local security group and create the container manually using adsiedit.msc. That way I do not have to grant the site server computer account unnecessary permissions.

1. Create the **ConfigMgr_Servers AD** group:
    a. Log on to **DC01** as **Administrator** and open **Active Directory Users and Computers**.
    b. Create an organizational unit called **Service Accounts**.
    c. In the **Service Accounts** OU, create a domain local security group with named **ConfigMgr_Servers**.
    d. Add the **CM01** and **CM02** computers to the **ConfigMgr_Servers** group.
    e. Restart both the **CM01** and **CM02** servers. Restarting the servers is needed to update the group membership for a computer account.
2. On **DC01**, open the **ADSI Edit MMC console**.
3. Right-click **ADSI Edit**, and then click **Connect to** and **OK**.
4. In the console pane, expand **Default naming context[DC01.corp.viamonstra.com]**, expand **DC=corp,DC=viamonstra,DC=com**, and right-click **CN=System**.
5. On the context menu, click **New** and then click **Object**.
6. In the **Create Object** dialog box, select **Container** and click **Next**.
7. In the **Value** field, type **System Management** and click **Next**.

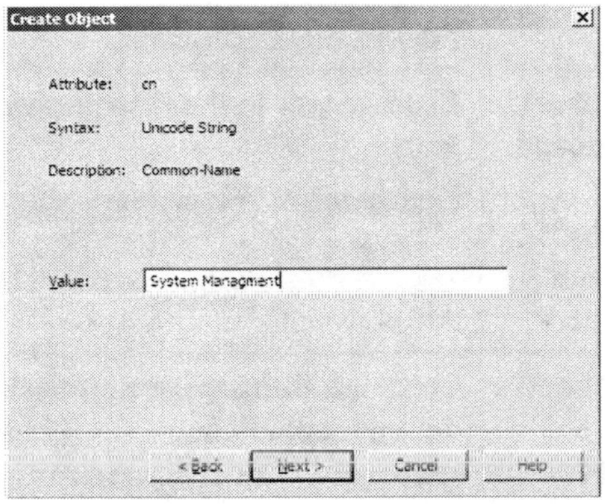

Creating the System Management container.

8. Click **Finish**.
9. Expand the **CN=System** container, right-click **CN=System Management**, and select **Properties**.
10. In the **CN=System Management Properties** dialog box, click the **Security** tab.
11. Click **Advanced**, and click **Add.** In the **Enter object name** box, enter **ConfigMgr_Servers**; then click **OK** and grant the account **Full Control** permissions.
12. In the **Apply onto** list, select **This object and all descendant objects**.
13. Click **OK** three times, and then close the **ADSI Edit console**.

Users, Groups, and Group Policy Objects

Both ConfigMgr 2012 and SQL Server 2008 R2 can run under the context of the local system account. However, for SQL Server, it is considered a best practice to create a user account with limited permissions and use that as the service account. For ConfigMgr, the number of user accounts needed depends on the features you wish to implement. In order to use some features, you also need to configure some Group Policy objects (GPOs). You use the GPOs to configure the Windows firewall, add the client push account to the local Administrator group, and configure the local WSUS settings.

The following table includes the different accounts, short descriptions of their purposes, and required permissions.

Account	Description	Permissions Required
Network access	Used whenever a client needs access to the ConfigMgr infrastructure and can't use the logged on user credentials. Two commonly used scenarios are OS deployment and supporting workgroup clients.	Read access to the distribution point. One account per primary site.
Client push	Used in conjunction with the client push installation method. This account connects to the admin$ share on the client, copies the needed client bootstrap files, and creates the ccmsetup service.	Local administrative permissions on the local client. Multiple accounts per site.
Exchange connector	Used to synchronize information from Exchange Server 2010.	Read and modify access to Exchange Server 2010 active sync. One account per hierarchy.
Discovery	Used when the site server computer account does not have access to read information about user, computer, and group objects in Active Directory.	Read access to the needed objects in Active Directory. One account per discovery LDAP path.
Join domain	Used during a task sequence to join the computer account to a domain.	A domain user account with permissions to create and modify computer accounts in a specified OU. Multiple accounts per hierarchy.
SQL Reporting Services dataset authentication	Used whenever you access a SQL Reporting Services report. During the installation of the Reporting Services site system, ConfigMgr will automatically grant the account the needed permissions in SQLServer.	A domain user account. One account per Reporting Services site system.
SQL Server service	Used to start and run the required SQL Server services.	A local system account or a user account. One account per SQL installation.

For ViaMonstra, you need six accounts: a Network Access Account, a client push account, a join domain account, a SQL Service account, a SQL Reporting Services dataset authentication account, and finally an Exchange connector account.

Create the Required Accounts

1. On **DC01**, open **Active Directory Users and Computers**.
2. In the **Service Accounts** OU, create an Active Directory user account called **CM_NA** with **Configuration Manager Network Access** as the description.
3. In the **Service Accounts** OU, create an Active Directory user account called **CM_JD** with **Configuration Manager Join Domain** as the description.
4. In the **Service Accounts** OU, create an Active Directory user account called **CM_CP** with **Configuration Manager Client Push** as the description.
5. In the **Service Accounts** OU, create a domain local group called **LocalCorpAdmins** and add **CM_CP** to the group.
6. In the **Service Accounts** OU, create an Active Directory user account called **CM_SR** with **Configuration Manager SQL Reporting** as the description.
7. In the **Service Accounts** OU, create an Active Directory user account called **CM_EX** with **Configuration Manager Exchange Connector** as the description.
8. In the **Service Accounts** OU, create an Active Directory user account called **CM_SQ** with **Configuration Manager SQL Service** as the description.

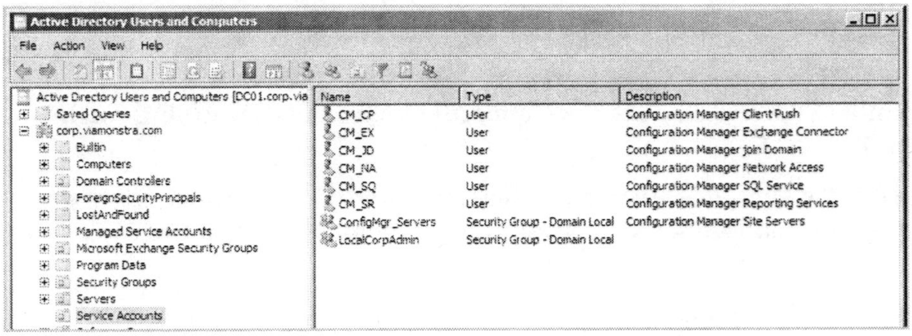

Creating the required accounts.

Configure Group Policy Objects

1. Add the client push account **CM_CP** to the local administrators group:
   a. On **DC01**, open the **Group Policy Management console**.
   b. Expand **Forest: corp.viamonstra.com**.

   c. Expand **Domains**.
   d. Right-click the **corp.viamonstra.com** domain and select **Create a GPO in this domain and link it here**.
   e. Create a new Group Policy object called **Add Client Push to Local Admin** and click **OK**.
   f. Right-click **Add Client Push to Local Admin GPO** and select **Edit**.
   g. Expand **Computer Configuration**, expand **Policies**, expand **Windows Settings**, and then expand **Security Settings**.
   h. Right-click **Restricted Groups** and select **Add Group**.
   i. Browse to the **LocalCorpAdmin** account you created, add it to **Restricted Groups**, and click **OK**.
   j. In the **This group is a member of** box, click **Add**. Then, in the **Group** box, type **Administrators** and click **OK** twice.

2. Configure the Windows Firewall:
   a. In the **Group Policy Management console**, expand **Forest: corp.viamonstra.com**, expand **Domains**, and then expand **corp.viamonstra.com**.
   b. Right-click the domain and select **Create a GPO in this domain and link it here**.
   c. Create a new **Group Policy object**, and name the object **Configure Firewall**.
   d. Right-click the **Configure Firewall** policy and select **Edit**.
   e. Expand **Computer Configuration\Policies\Administrative Templates\Network\Network Connections Windows Firewall\Domain Profile**.
   f. Enable the **Windows Firewall: Allow inbound file and printer sharing exception** and **Windows Firewall: Allow inbound remote administration exception** policies.
   g. Close the **Group Policy** dialog box.

3. Configure local WSUS policies:
   a. In the **Group Policy Management console**, expand **Forest: corp.viamonstra.com**, expand **Domains**, and then expand **corp.viamonstra.com**.
   b. Right-click the domain, and select **Create a GPO in this domain and link it here**.
   c. Create a new **Group Policy object**, and name the object **Configure WSUS**.

   d. Right-click **Configure WSUS** and select **Edit**.
   e. Expand **Computer Configuration\Policies\Administrative Templates\Windows components\Windows Update**.
   f. Configure **Allow signed content from Intranet Microsoft Update service location** to **Enabled**.
   g. Configure **Configure Automatic Updates** to **Disabled**.
4. Close the **Group Policy Management console**.

Configure Join Computer Permissions

1. On **DC01**, open **Active Directory User and Computers**.
2. Right-click the domain and select **New, Organizational Unit.**
3. Type **Workstations** and click **OK**. Notice that this OU already exists if you used the hydration kit to create the lab environment, as described in Appendix A.
4. In the **View** menu, select **Advanced Features**.
5. Right-click the **Workstations** OU, select **Properties**, select the **Security** tab, and then click the **Advanced** button.
6. In the **Advanced Security Settings for Workstations** window, click **Add**, type **CM_JD**, and click **OK**.
7. In the **Permissions Entry for Workstations** window, verify that **Apply to** is set to **This object and all descendant objects**. Then select the following permissions:
   a. **Create Computer objects**
   b. **Delete Computer objects**
8. Click **OK**.
9. In the **Advanced Security Settings for Workstations** window, click **Add** once more, type **CM_JD**, and click **OK**.
10. In the **Permissions Entry for Workstations** window, set **Apply to Descendant Computer objects**, and select the following permissions:
    a. **Read All Properties**
    b. **Write All Properties**
    c. **Read Permissions**
    d. **Modify Permissions**
    e. **Change Password**
    f. **Reset Password**

g. **Validated write to DNS host name**
h. **Validated write to service principal name**

11. Click **OK** twice.

SQL Server

There are some facts that you need to be aware of before installing and some post configuration tasks you need to perform to ensure maximum performance. First, the table contains some facts you need know.

Setting	Value
Recommended SQL Server version	SQL Server 2008 R2 with SP1 and CU6.
SQL Server edition	For a hierarchy with more than 50,000 clients, SQL Server Enterprise Edition at the CAS and Standard Edition at the primary sites. For hierarchies with fewer than 50,000, always SQL Server Standard Edition.
Installation directory	Same drive as ConfigMgr 2012, e.g. D:\Program Files\.
Database directory	Dedicated drive.
Database files	Equal to the number of cores in the server.
Log directory	Dedicated drive.
Log files	One file per database.
TempDB directory	Dedicated drive.
TempDB files	Equal to half the number of CPUs.
TempDB log directory	Dedicated drive. (If this is not possible, place it on the same drive as TempDB.)
TempDB log file	One file.
Memory	A minimum of 8 GB reserved on CAS and primary sites and 4 GB on a secondary site server.
Collation	SQL_Latin1_General_CP1_CI_AS. (Notice that this, along with Chinese, is the only supported collation orders.)

Setting	Value
Service account	Can be the local system or a user account. Using a domain user account is considered to be more secure, but it also requires more work, as you have to manually register the service principal names (SPN). When using a user account, you must register the SPN (service principal name) in Active Directory manually. Registering NetBIOS syntax: Setspn -A MSSQLSvc/<SQL Server name>:1433 <domain>\<user> Registering FQDN syntax: Setspn -A MSSQLSvc/<FQDN SQL Server name>:1433 <domain>\<user>

Real World Note: Often you'll find it easier to install SQL Server 2008 R2 using a scripted installation. When doing that, remember to specify the collation order as it will default to the server's local settings.

Local vs. Remote SQL Installation

This must be one of the most commonly asked questions when starting a new project: shall I configure a local SQL Server or a remote SQL Server? I always go a very long way to argue for a local installation. *Why?* You might ask:

- **Saves time in the project.** Often I find that DBAs (database administrators) try to configure a ConfigMgr SQL Server database like any other SQL Server database, and it's not like any of the other databases.
- **Simplifies permissions.** The site server requires the installer to be a member of the local Administrator group on SQL Server and the person installing Configuration Manager must have sysadmin permissions.

One thing you should be aware off is the limitation on the number of clients you can have when using a local SQL Server. The supported number of clients is limited to 50,000. If you have more than that, you should consider a remote SQL Server installation.

When installing SQL Server, you are required to select only the **Database Engine Services** service. Even if you have multiple sites (which requires SQL Server replication), you're not required to install any replication services. In this installation, you will install SQL Server, SQL Server Reporting Services, Business Intelligence Development Studio (BIDS), and the management tools. The installation properties are stored in a file called configurationfile.ini that you can find in the book sample files.

Install SQL 2008 R2

Before you start the installation, make sure that you have installed all the required components described in Appendix A. In these steps I assume you have downloaded SQL Server 2008 R2, SQL Server 2008 R2 SP1, SQL Server 2008 R2 SP1 CU6, and the book sample files to D:\Setup\ on CM01.

1. Open a command prompt with administrative permissions.
2. Navigate to **D:\Setup\SQL 2008 R2** and type the following:

   setup.exe /Configurationfile=D:\Setup\Scripts\SQLConfigurationfile.ini

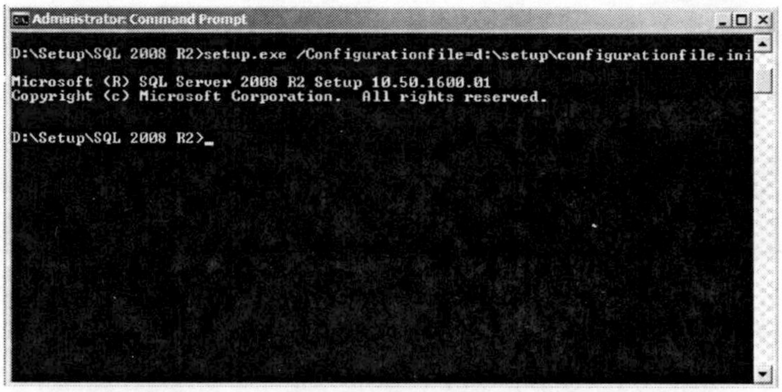

Installing SQL Server 2008 R2.

Install SQL Server 2008 R2 SP1

While still at the command prompt, type:

"D:\Setup\SQL 2008 R2 SP1\SQLServer2008R2SP1-KB2528583-x64-ENU.exe" /IAcceptSQLServerLicenseTerms /AllInstances /Quiet

The command prompt might return before the upgrade is complete. If it does, monitor the installation process using Task Manager.

Install SQL Server 2008 R2 SP1 CU6

While still at the command prompt, type:

"D:\Setup\SQL\SQL 2008 R2 SP1 CU6\SQLServer2008R2-KB2679367-x64.exe" /Action=Patch /IAcceptSQLServerLicenseTerms /AllInstances /Quiet

The command prompt might return before the upgrade is complete. If it does, monitor the installation process using Task Manager.

Verify SQL Server Installation Success

1. Open **SQL Server Management Studio**, and connect to the local host.
2. Click **New Query** and ensure that the **Master** database is selected.
3. Type the following statement and then press **F5**:

   SELECT SERVERPROPERTY('productversion'), SERVERPROPERTY ('productlevel'), SERVERPROPERTY ('edition')

   With SP1 and CU6 installed, you should have a product version of **10.50. 2811.0** and product level of **SP1**.

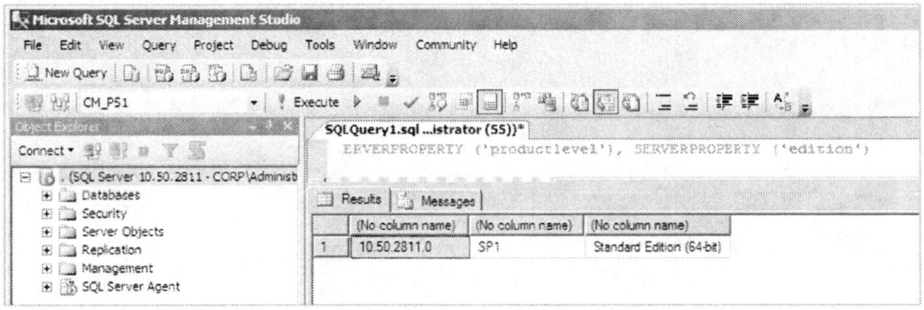

Checking the SQL Server version.

Configure SQL Server Memory

SQL Server likes memory. As a matter of fact, SQL Server likes memory so much that it will take all available memory, leaving very little to other applications and the operating system. For that reason, you should limit the amount of memory allocated to SQL Server. There are a lot of best practices when it comes to allocating SQL Server memory, my rule of thumb is:

- 2 GB for the operating system
- 2 GB for other applications running on the server
- 4 GB for ConfigMgr
- 8 GB or more for SQL Server 2008 R2

Real World Note: The memory calculation assumes you have 16 GB of memory. ConfigMgr can run with less memory, however, and there is no fixed limit. If you have a small environment, like a lab environment or fewer than 500 users, then ConfigMgr will likely perform well with as little as 4–8 GB RAM. In those scenarios, you should limit the SQL memory to a maximum of 50 percent of the physical memory.

Perform the following steps to configure SQL Server memory:

1. Open **SQL Server Management Studio**.
2. Connect to the local SQL Server.
3. Right-click **SQL Server** and select **Properties**.
4. Select the **Memory** page and configure these settings (provided that you have 16 GB of RAM):
    a. Minimum server memory (in MB): **8192**
    b. Maximum server memory (in MB): **12228**

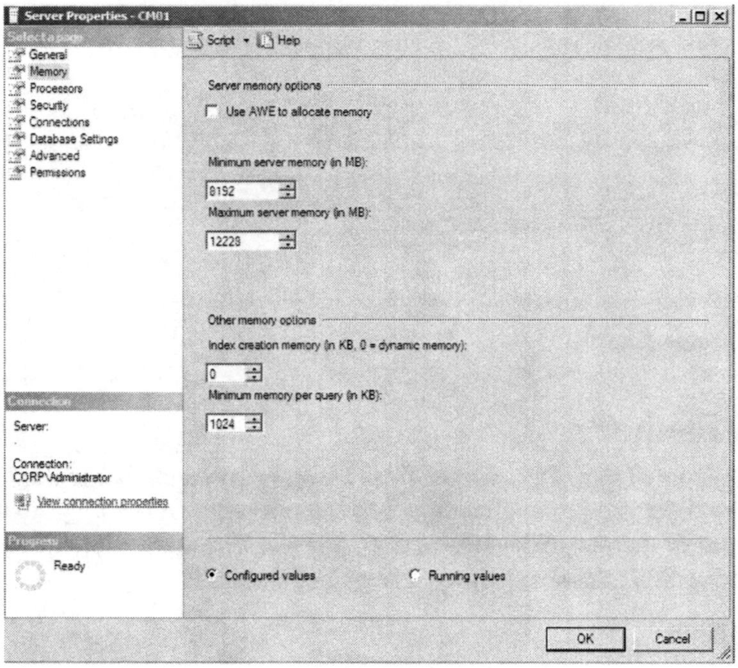

Configuring SQL Server memory.

5. Click **OK** to save the changes.

Configure the SQL Server Service Account

To follow best practices, ViaMonstra uses a domain user account for all of its SQL Server service accounts.

1. From the **Start** menu, select **Administrative Tools**, **Services**.
2. Select **SQL Server (MSSQLSERVER)** and open the properties.
3. Select the **Log On** tab, click **This account,** click **Browse**, and find the **CM_SQ** account for the **CORP** domain.

4. Type the password and click **OK**.
5. Notice the message in the two dialog boxes, and click **OK** for each.
6. Restart the **SQL Server (MSSQLSERVER) service**.
7. Repeat steps 1–6 for the **SQL Server Reporting Services** service and **SQL Server Agent** service.
8. Open a command prompt with administrative permission, and type and execute these two commands one at the time:
    a. **setspn -A MSSQLSvc/CM01:1433 CORP\CM_SQ**
    b. **setspn -A MSSQLSvc/cm01.corp.viamonstra.com:1433 CORP\CM_SQ**

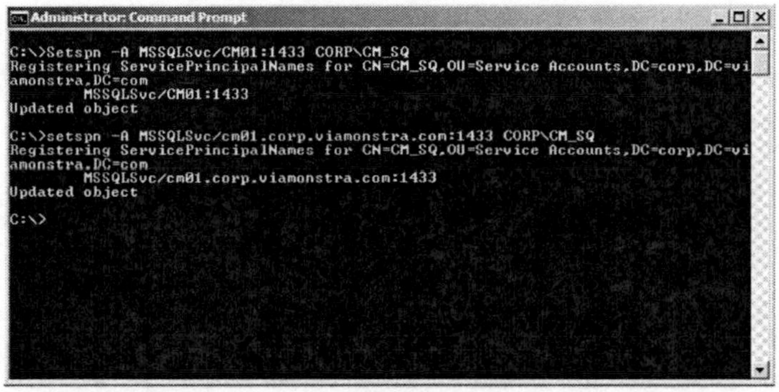

Registering service principal names SPN.

Real World Note: You can change the service account back to use the local system account. This can be very useful when troubleshooting SQL Server problems. That way you will very quickly figure out whether your problems are related to the SQL Server service. You also can run setspn -L CORP\CM_SQ to verify that the principal names are correctly registered.

Installing the Site Server

Installing the ConfigMgr primary site server is a fairly straightforward operation. But, before you start, you need to know what the final hierarchy will look like. After you have installed a primary site server, you are not able to move it to another hierarchy.

Install the Site Server

For ViaMonstra, you already know that you need only one primary site server. In this guide, I assume you have downloaded ConfigMgr 2012 to D:\Setup\CM2012.

1. Log on to **CM01** with a domain account that has local administrative permissions—you can use **CORP\Administrator**.
2. Open a command prompt with administrative privileges.

3. Navigate to **D:\Setup\CM2012** and type **splash.hta**.
4. Click **Install**.
5. On the **Before You Begin** page, read the notes and click **Next**.
6. On the **Getting Started** page, select **Install a Configuration Manager primary site** and click **Next**.

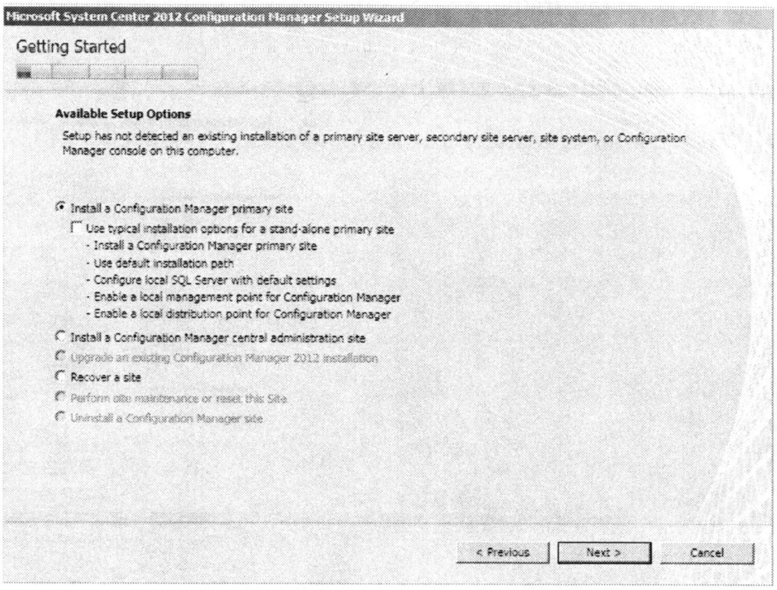

Installing a primary site server.

7. On the **Product Key** page, enter your 25-character product key, or select **Install this product as an evaluation** if you don't have the key at the present time, and click **Next**.
8. On the **Microsoft Software License Terms** page, click **I accept these license terms**, and then click **Next**.
9. On the **Prerequisite Licenses** page, accept the prerequisite license terms and click **Next**.
10. On the **Prerequisite Download** page, click **Download required files**; use the **Browse** button to create the **D:\Setup\CM2012DL** folder, select it, and then click **Next**.
11. On the **Server Language Selection** page, ensure that **English** is the only selected language and click **Next**.
12. On the **Client Language Selection** page, select the client languages you wish to support in your environment. In ViaMonstra, English is the only supported language. You can always rerun setup and add additional client languages. The client will apply the language along with the client installation. For that reason, you have to reinstall the client to reflect any new language settings.

13. On the **Site and Installation Settings** page, enter the following settings and click **Next**:

a. Site code: **PS1**

b. Site name: **ViaMonstra HQ**

c. Installation folder: **D:\Program Files\Microsoft Configuration Manager**

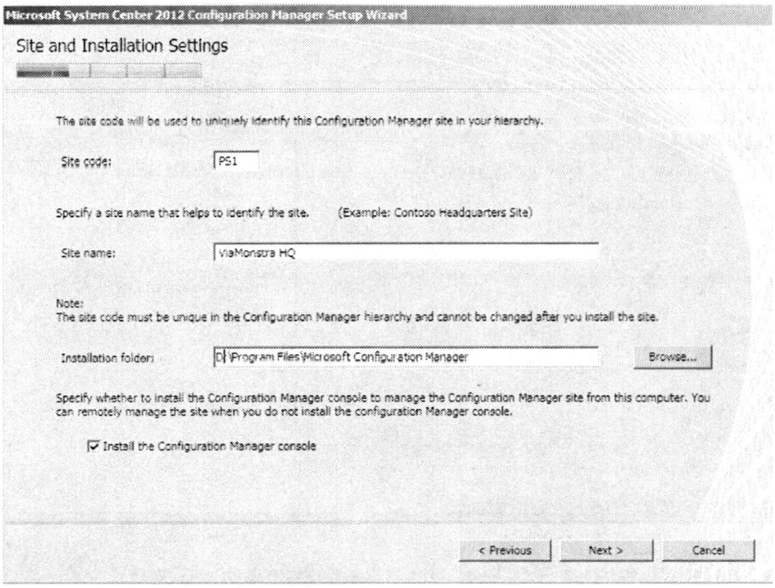

Specifying the site code.

14. On the **Primary Site Installation** page, select **Install the primary site as a standalone site** and click **Next**.

15. Click **Yes** in the warning dialog box. In ConfigMgr RTM, you are not able to join a standalone primary site to an existing CAS.

16. On the **Database Information** page, accept the default SQL Server information and click **Next**. This performs the installation as a default instance.

17. On the **SMS Provider Settings** page, click **Next**.

18. On the **Client Computer Communication Settings** page, select **Configure the communication method on each site system role** and click **Next**.

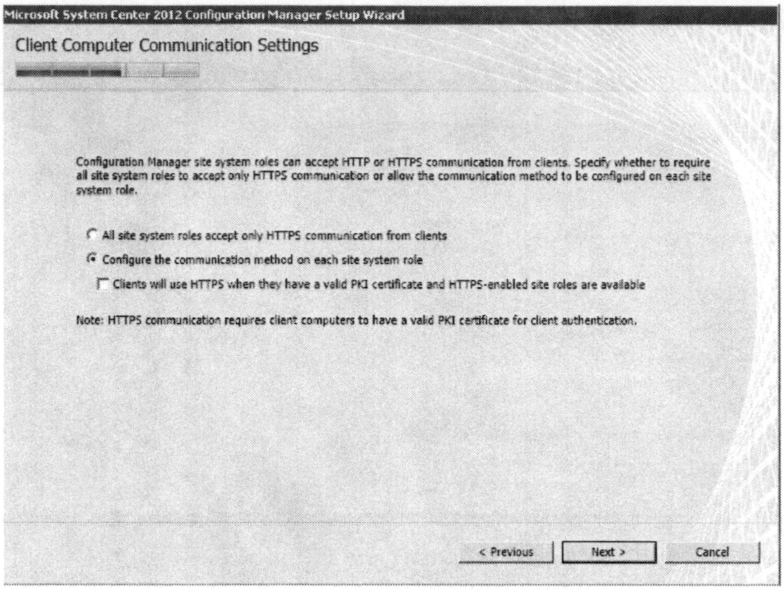

Configuring a client communication protocol.

19. On the **Site System Roles** page, ensure that both the management point and distribution point roles are selected and click **Next**.

20. On the **Customer Experience Improvement Program Configuration** page, select **Join the Customer Experience Improvement Program** and click **Next**.

21. On the **Settings Summary** page, review the summary and click **Next**.

22. On the **Prerequisite Checker** page, click **Begin Install** to start the installation. You might receive three warnings about WSUS, Firewall exceptions and SQL. For now you can safely ignore those warnings, we will configure those settings later.

23. Open **D:\Setup\CM2012\SMSSetup\Tools\CMTrace.exe** and accept it as the default log viewer.

24. Pin **CMTrace.exe** to the Start menu and Windows taskbar.

25. Check **C:\ConfigMgrSetup.log** and monitor the installation.

26. While waiting for the installation to finish, open **D:\Setup\CM2012\SMSSetup\TOOLS** and investigate the tools:

    a. **CMtrace.exe** is used to make your daily life easier.

    b. Navigate to **.\Tools\Portconfiguration**:

Portswitch.vbs is a script to modify the port used by the client when communicating with the management point.

c. Navigate to **.\Tools\ConfigMgrADMTemplates**:

- **ConfigMgrAssignment.adm** is a Group Policy template that can be used to control the site assignment.
- **ConfigMgrInstallation.adm** is a Group Policy template that can be used to add the client installation properties to the registry.

Verify the ConfigMgr Installation

After the core ConfigMgr services installation is finished, you still have a lot going on in the background, like configuring, installing, and configuring components. I usually monitor the following two log files to verify that everything is all right. Both are server log files and found in D:\Program files\Microsoft Configuration Manager\Logs:

- **Sitecomp.log.** This log file is for the Site Component Manager, the component responsible for installing most of the ConfigMgr components.
- **hman.log.** This is the log file for the Hierarchy Manager who is responsible for updating Active Directory, handling certificates, the site control file(s) and much more.

Furthermore, I perform a simple check against the management point. To do that, open **Internet Explorer** and go to **http://cm01/SMS_MP/.sms_aut?MPLIST**. This should give you a list of the management points installed in the site.

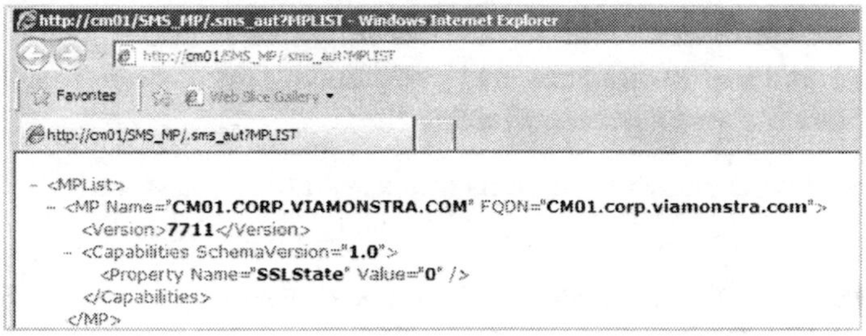

Verifying the management point.

Create a ConfigMgr Package Source Directory

A package source directory is used to store source files for all your packages. The term *packages* is used for all content like drivers, software updates, applications, and so forth. I usually recommend that you locate the package source directory on a remote server like a file server. That way you do not have to worry about the original source files in the event of a hardware failure on the site server.

1. On **CM01,** create a directory on **D:** named **Sources**.
2. Share the directory as **Sources$**.

3. Allow the **Everyone** group **Change** permissions on the share.
4. Create the following directory structures:
    a. **D:\ Sources\Updates\2012-1**
    b. **D:\ Sources\Updates\2012-2**
    c. **D:\Sources\Updates\Definitions**
5. Create the following directory structure:

    D:\Sources\Software
6. Create the following directory structure:

    D:\ Sources\OSD

Post SQL Configuration

One of the recommended post installation tasks is to create additional ConfigMgr database files. You most likely can find different best practices when searching the Internet, but ViaMonstra has decided to create one file per core. Since the server has two CPUs with six cores each, you will create 11 additional files. With 6,500 clients in the database, the estimated size of the database is 30 GB. When creating the files, you can configure them to the estimated size of the database, or configure a lower value and let them autogrow when needed. Since 30 GB is not that big of a database, ViaMonstra has decided to create 11 database files of 3 GB each. As needed, the files will autogrow 1 GB at the time. Those settings match ViaMonstra, but will not match a larger enterprise installation.

Before you create the additional files, a short introduction to the files might be in order. The ConfigMgr database is called CM_PS1 and was created automatically during the installation. The database consists of two files, a *database* file and a *transaction log* file:

- The database file *.mdf stores database objects, such as indexes, table, and stored procedures.
- The log file *.ldf is a transaction log file. Every single database transaction is written to the log file that is committed to the database.

Create Additional Files

You can configure the additional SQL files manually in SQL Server Management Studio, or by running the script below (also in SQL Server Management Studio) as described in the following steps:

1. Start **SQL Server Management Studio** and connect to the **local SQL Server**.

2. Click **New Query,** type the text below, and click **Execute**. (You also can copy and paste the query. You can find it in the Add SQL files.txt file with the companion content for this book.)

```
Use master
ALTER DATABASE CM_PS1
ADD FILE (NAME = CM_PS1_2, FILENAME = 'G:\msSQLdb\CM_PS1_2.mdf',
SIZE = 3072MB, MAXSIZE=UNLIMITED, FILEGROWTH = 1024MB)
ALTER DATABASE CM_PS1
ADD FILE (NAME = CM_PS1_3, FILENAME = 'G:\msSQLdb\CM_PS1_3.mdf',
SIZE = 3072MB, MAXSIZE=UNLIMITED, FILEGROWTH = 1024MB)
ALTER DATABASE CM_PS1
ADD FILE (NAME = CM_PS1_4, FILENAME = 'G:\msSQLdb\CM_PS1_4.mdf',
SIZE = 3072MB, MAXSIZE=UNLIMITED, FILEGROWTH = 1024MB)
ALTER DATABASE CM_PS1
ADD FILE (NAME = CM_PS1_5, FILENAME = 'G:\msSQLdb\CM_PS1_5.mdf',
SIZE = 3072MB, MAXSIZE=UNLIMITED, FILEGROWTH = 1024MB)
ALTER DATABASE CM_PS1
ADD FILE (NAME = CM_PS1_6, FILENAME = 'G:\msSQLdb\CM_PS1_6.mdf',
SIZE = 3072MB, MAXSIZE=UNLIMITED, FILEGROWTH = 1024MB)
ALTER DATABASE CM_PS1
ADD FILE (NAME = CM_PS1_7, FILENAME = 'G:\msSQLdb\CM_PS1_7.mdf',
SIZE = 3072MB, MAXSIZE=UNLIMITED, FILEGROWTH = 1024MB)
ALTER DATABASE CM_PS1
ADD FILE (NAME = CM_PS1_8, FILENAME = 'G:\msSQLdb\CM_PS1_8.mdf',
SIZE = 3072MB, MAXSIZE=UNLIMITED, FILEGROWTH = 1024MB)
ALTER DATABASE CM_PS1
ADD FILE (NAME = CM_PS1_9, FILENAME = 'G:\msSQLdb\CM_PS1_9.mdf',
SIZE = 3072MB, MAXSIZE=UNLIMITED, FILEGROWTH = 1024MB)
ALTER DATABASE CM_PS1
ADD FILE (NAME = CM_PS1_10, FILENAME =
'G:\msSQLdb\CM_PS1_10.mdf', SIZE = 3072MB, MAXSIZE=UNLIMITED,
FILEGROWTH = 1024MB)
ALTER DATABASE CM_PS1
ADD FILE (NAME = CM_PS1_11, FILENAME =
'G:\msSQLdb\CM_PS1_11.mdf', SIZE = 3072MB, MAXSIZE=UNLIMITED,
FILEGROWTH = 1024MB)
ALTER DATABASE CM_PS1
ADD FILE (NAME = CM_PS1_12, FILENAME =
'G:\msSQLdb\CM_PS1_12.mdf', SIZE = 3072MB, MAXSIZE=UNLIMITED,
FILEGROWTH = 1024MB)
GO
```

3. All additional files are now created with an autogrowth value of 1 GB. However, the initial database created during ConfigMgr setup is not yet configured with the same autogrowth settings. While still in SQL Server Studio Management, select **Database**, right-click the **CM_PS1** database, and open the **Properties**.
4. Select the **Files** tab; notice all the files you just created. (If you didn't use the script, you can always create the files manually by clicking the **Add** button and completing the **Add File** dialog box.)
5. Look at the File Growth setting for the first file; it's configured to grow by 2 percent at the time. Change the setting from In Percent to **In Megabytes** and enter **1024**.

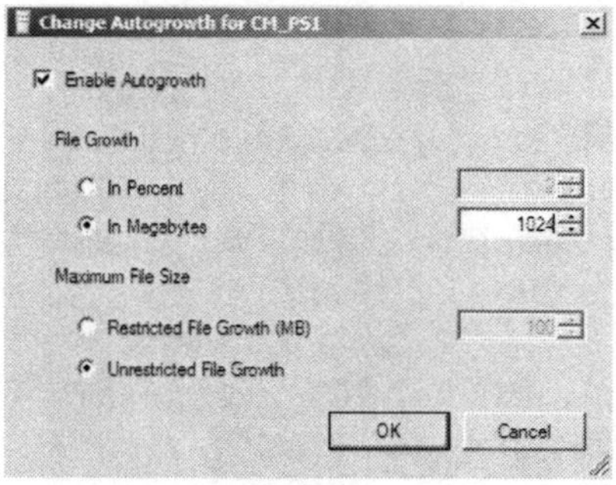

Configuring autogrowth for the SQL Server database files.

6. Click **OK** and then close **SQL Management Studio**.

Installing and Configuring WSUS 3.0 SP2

Even though you configure and control all aspects of the software update process from within the ConfigMgr console, you still need to install a WSUS server in each primary site and in the CAS site. In this section, you install the core WSUS service.

Install WSUS 3.0 SP2

To perform these steps, you need to have Internet access on CM01.

1. On **CM01**, using **Server Manager**, click **Add Roles**.
2. In the **Select Server Roles** page, select the **Windows Server Update Services** role.
3. In the **Add Roles Wizard** dialog box, select **Add Required Role Services**, and then click **Next**.
4. On the **Web Server (IIS)** page, click **Next**.
5. On the **Select Role Services** page, accept the default settings, and click **Next**.
6. On the **Windows Server Update Services** page, click **Next**.

7. On the **Confirm Installation Selections** page, click **Install.**
8. On the **Welcome to the Windows Server Update Services 3.0 SP2 Setup Wizard** page, click **Next**.

Real World Note: In Windows Server 2008 R2, the Welcome to the Windows Server Update Services 3.0 SP2 Setup Wizard is hidden behind the Add Roles Wizard. Check the Taskbar for a new item.

9. On the **License Agreement** page, accept the license terms and click **Next**.
10. On the **Select Update Source** page, accept the default settings, and click **Next**.
11. On the **Database Options** page, select **Use an existing database server on this computer** and click **Next**.
12. On the **Connecting to SQL Server Instance** page, click **Next**.
13. On the **Web Site Selection** page, select **Create a Windows Server Update Services 3.0 SP2 Web site** option, and click **Next**.
14. On the **Ready to Install Windows Server Update Services 3.0 SP2** page, click **Next**.
15. On the **Completing the Windows Server Update Services 3.0 SP2 Setup Wizard** page, click **Finish.**
16. Cancel the Windows Server Update Services Configuration Wizard, and then close the Add Roles wizard as there is no reason to configure any settings in the WSUS console.

Configuring SQL Reporting Services

In these steps, you configure SQL Reporting Services 2008 R2 (SSRS). It's a very good idea to configure and verify that the service is running before adding the Reporting Services site system role.

1. On **CM01**, from the **Start** menu, select **Microsoft SQL Server 2008 R2**, **Configuration Tools**, **Reporting Services Configuration Manager**.
2. Click **Connect** and connect to the local report server instance.
3. Verify that the report service status is **Started**. If it isn't, click **Start**.
4. Select the **Web Service URL** page and click **Apply**.

5. Select the **Database** page and click **Change Database**. This starts the Report Server Database Configuration Wizard. Complete the following pages:
   a. On the **Action** page, select **Create a new report server database** and click **Next**.

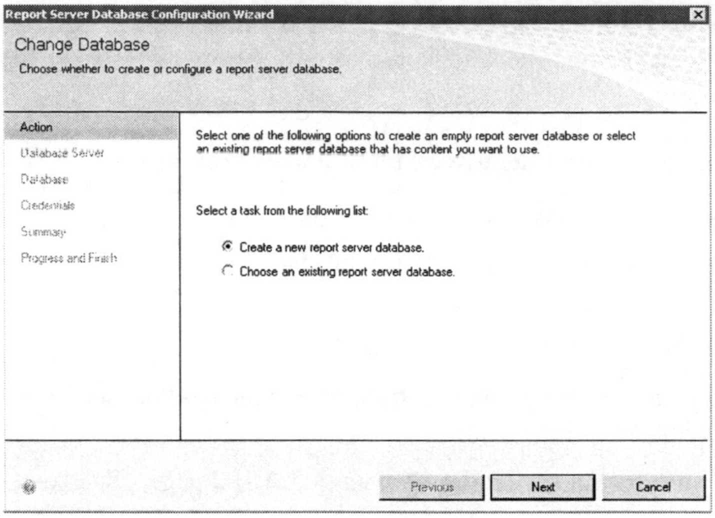

Creating the SQL Reporting Services database.

   b. On the **Database Server** page, click **Test Connection** to verify that the security credentials are okay and click **Next**.
   c. On the **Database** page, ensure that **Native Mode** is selected and click **Next**. This is the only supported reporting server mode in ConfigMgr.
   d. On the **Credentials** page, click **Next**.
   e. On the **Summary** page, click **Next**.
   f. On the **Progress and Finish** page, click **Finish**.

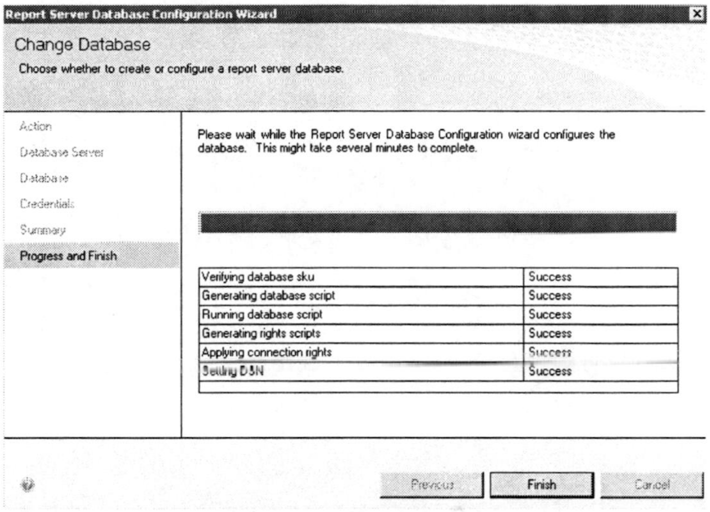

Finishing the database creation process.

6. Select the **Report Manager URL** page and click **Apply**.
7. Click **Exit** to close the **Reporting Services Configuration Manager**.

Chapter 4 Configuring the Site Server

Installing a site server is the easy part. Configuring the server often requires a little more planning and thinking. There are some basic things you need to plan before you start working with each of the features:

- What features do you want to work with and what are the dependencies?
- Where do you want to install your site system roles?

Different features have specific site system role dependencies that you have to consider when deciding on which features you will use. In ViaMonstra, you start out with these features and site system roles:

- **Client Management**: Requires a management point.
- **Application Management**: Requires a distribution point, an application web service point, and an application web catalog point.
- **Software Updates**: Requires a distribution point and a software update point.
- **Operating System Deployment**: Requires a distribution point and perhaps a state migration point if user state migration is used.
- **Endpoint Protection**: Requires a distribution point, software update point, and endpoint protection point.
- **Inventory Management**: Requires a management point and Asset Intelligence synchronization point. The last role is not a requirement for inventory management, but it allows you to synchronize new Asset Intelligence software catalogs from Microsoft.

It's very common for midsize and enterprise installations to offload all user-facing site system roles from the primary site server for performance reasons. I also believe that's a very good idea but not necessarily a rule in every environment. ViaMonstra sees itself as a midsize business with average system management needs. You are not supporting 40,000–60,000 clients and will not upgrade 1,000 machines with new images every single week. For that reason, ViaMonstra decided to go ahead with all site systems on the same server. However, if performance-related issues were to arise in the future, you would start by offloading the user-facing site system roles in this order:

- Distribution point
- State migration point
- Management point
- Software update point

Installing the Site System Roles

In this section, you walk through the installation of the needed site system roles. As mentioned earlier in this book, you do not have to install all site systems on the primary site server. For performance reasons, enterprise companies often choose to offload the site server and install "user-facing" site system roles on other servers.

Install the Roles

Use the steps below to install a software update point, Application Catalog web point, Application Catalog web service point, Asset Intelligence synchronization point, and reporting services point. You will install the Endpoint Protection point later after you have your software update point running.

1. On **CM01**, open the **ConfigMgr console** (from the **Start** menu, select **All Programs**, **Microsoft System Center 2012**, **Configuration Manager Console**).
2. Select the **Administration** workspace.
3. Navigate to **Overview**, **Site Configuration**, **Servers and Site System Roles**.
4. Select **CM01**, click **Home** on the ribbon, and then click **Add Site System Roles**.

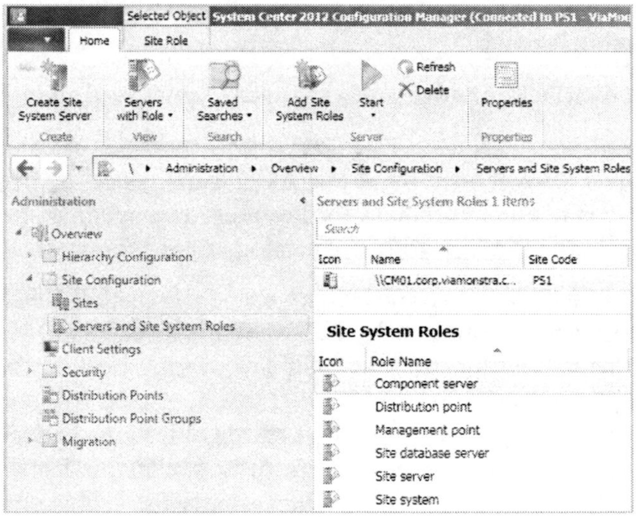

Adding site system roles.

5. On the **General** page, click **Next**.
6. On the **System Role Selection** page, select the following site system roles and click **Next**:
   a. **Application Catalog Web Service Point**
   b. **Application Catalog Website Point**

c. **Asset Intelligence synchronization point**

d. **Reporting services point**

e. **Software update point**

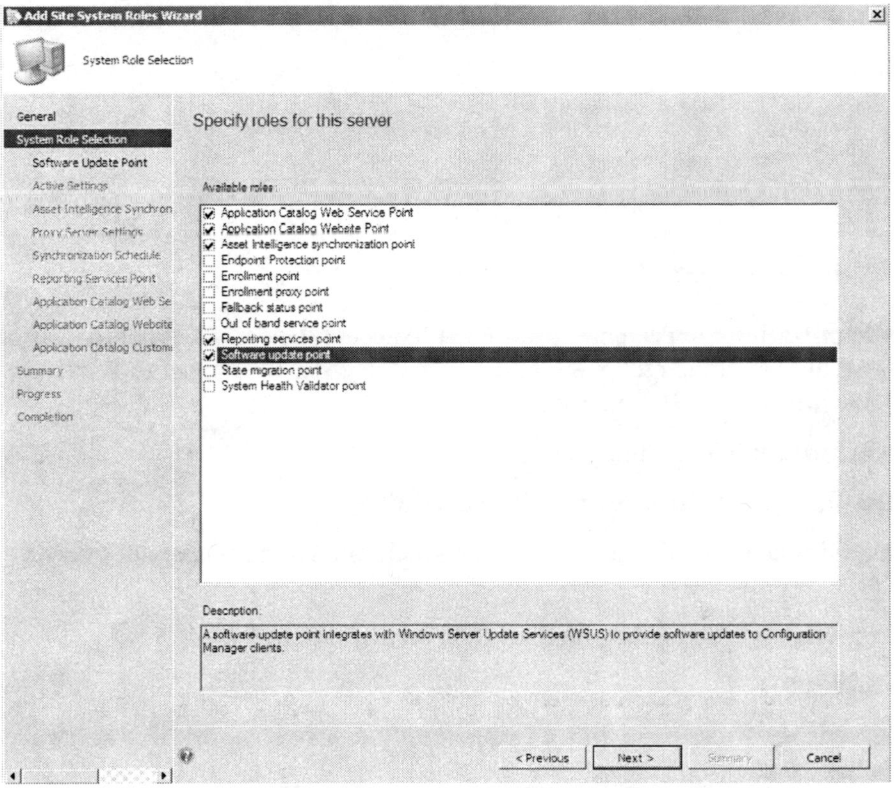

Selecting the site system roles.

7. On the **Software Updates Point** page, click **Next** and do not configure any proxy settings.

8. On the **Active Settings** page, select **Use this server at the active software update point** and **WSUS is configured to use a custom website**. Click **Next**.

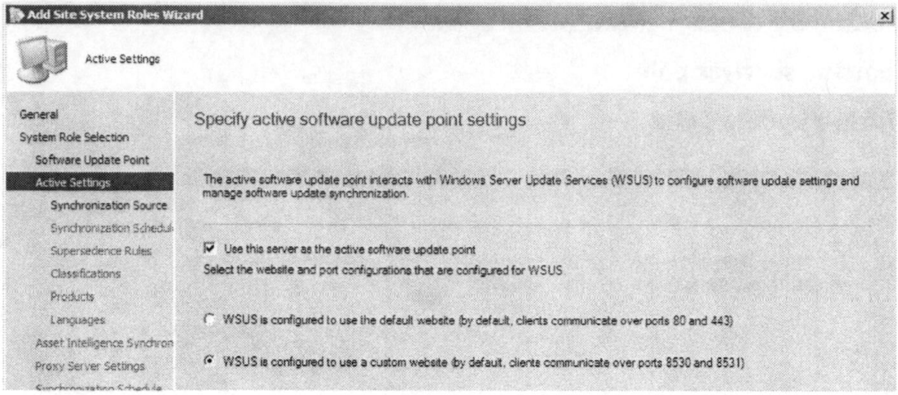

Configuring the software update point custom web site.

9. On the **Synchronization Source** page, click **Next** to accept the default synchronization settings. Note that this setting requires Internet access in order to connect to Windows Update and download the WSUS metadata.
10. On the **Synchronization Schedule** page:
    a. Select **Enable synchronization on a schedule.**
    b. Select **Simple schedule** and configure a synchronization schedule of every **8** hours.
    c. Select **Alert when synchronization fails on any site in the hierarchy**.
    d. Click **Next.**
11. On the **Supersedence Rules** page, select **Immediately expire a superseded software update** and click **Next.**
12. On the **Classifications** page, select these update classifications and click **Next**:
    a. **Critical Updates**
    b. **Definition Updates**
    c. **Security Updates**
    d. **Service Packs**

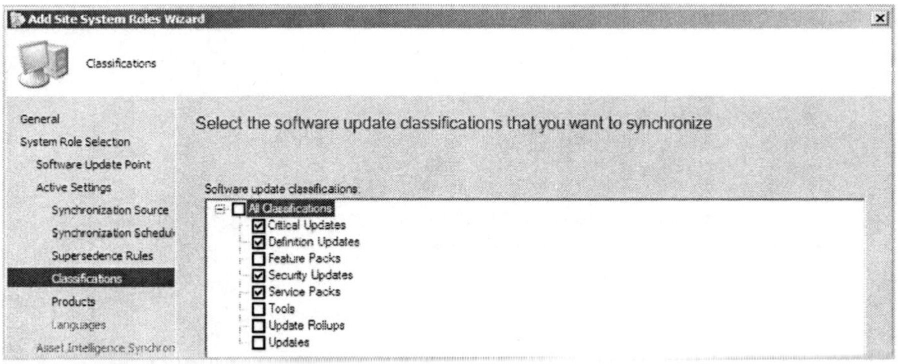

Selecting software update classifications.

13. On the **Products** page, ensure that these products are all selected and click **Next**:

a. **Office 2010**

b. **Windows 2008 R2**

c. **Windows 7**

d. **Forefront Endpoint Protection 2010**

Real World Note: After the initial synchronization, you can add more products. To do that, navigate to the **Administration** workspace, select **Site Configuration**, **Sites**, and select **Configure Site Components**, **Software Update Point** from the ribbon.

14. On the **Languages** page, deselect all languages except for **English** and click **Next**.

15. On the **Asset Intelligence Synchronization Point** page, click **Next** three times to accept the default settings. You will be asked about a certificate for System Center Online, proxy settings, and a synchronization schedule. There is no requirement for specifying a certificate, as one is already exists in ConfigMgr 2012.

16. On the **Reporting Services Point** page, do the following:

a. Click **Verify** to verify your site database connection settings.

b. In **Reporting Services Point Account**, click **Set** and **New Account**. Then click **Browse** and find the **CM_SR** account in the CORP domain. Assign the password and click **OK**, and then click **Next**.

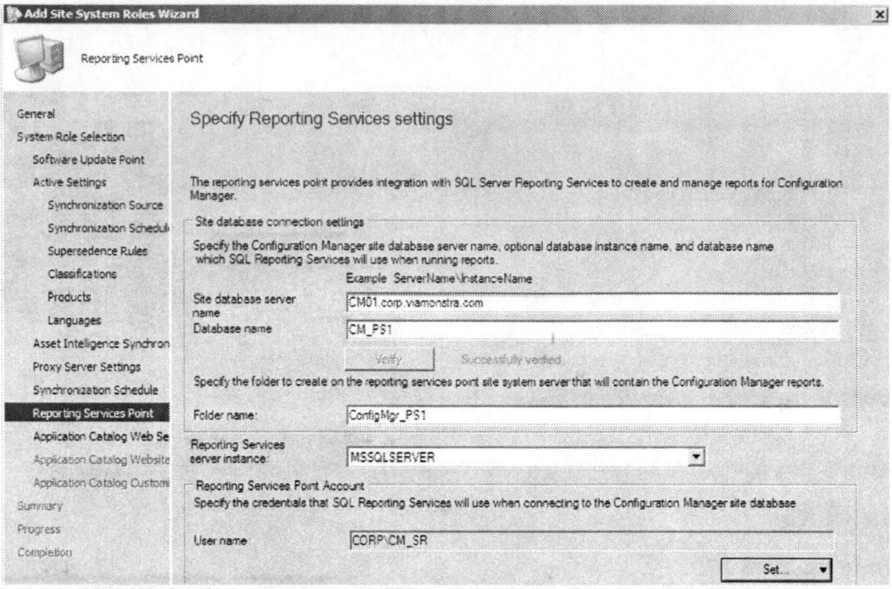

Configuring the reporting services point.

17. On the **Application Catalog Web Service Point** page, keep the default settings and click **Next**. This configures the web service to use HTTP and port 80.
18. On the **Application Catalog Website Point** page, keep the default settings and click **Next**.
19. On the **Application Catalog Customization** page, type **ViaMonstra**, select a website theme, and click **Next**.
20. On the **Summary** page, verify that the all roles are listed and click **Next**.
21. Click **Close**.

What Happens Behind the Scenes

ConfigMgr has many components that are involved in the process of installing and configuring site system roles. The main component is the Site Component Manager, and by reading the corresponding log file (sitecomp.log), you'll learn a lot about what's going on and which commands are used to install each of the site system roles. The following figure contains a snippet that shows a successful installation of the reporting services point. By reading each of the individual log files, you can get important information about the needed prerequisites and verify a successful installation.

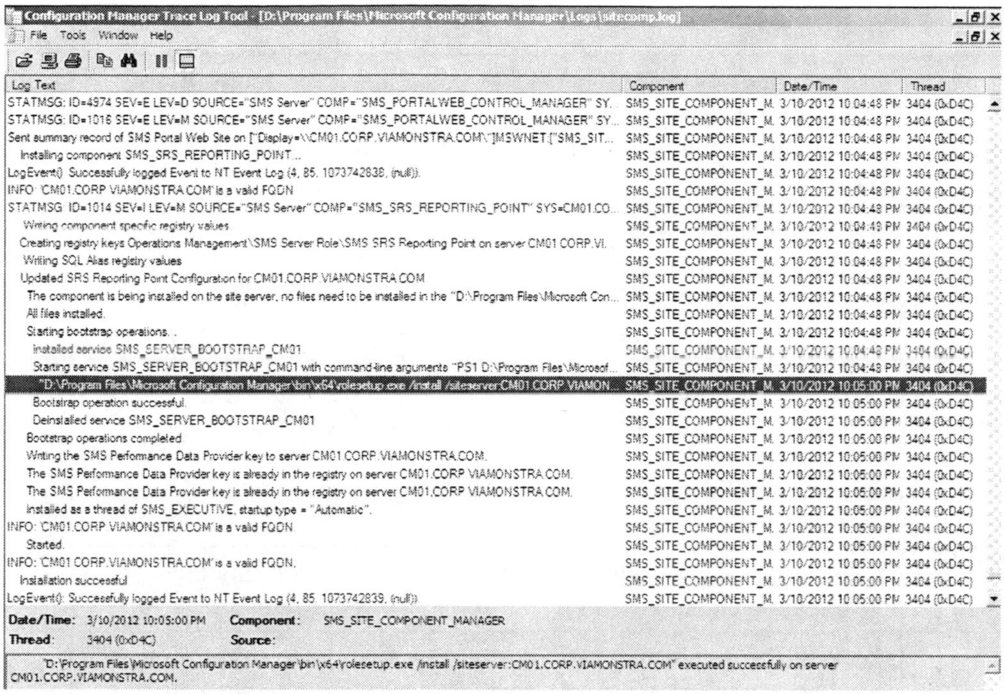

The sitecomp.log file.

Useful Log Files

The log files in the following table can be used to track your site system role installations.

Log File	Description
sitecomp.log	Records activity on the Site Component Manager.
srsrpsetup.log	Records activity on the SQL Reporting Services setup. In this log file, you see whether the needed prerequisites are present and whether the srsrpmsi installation process completes successfully.
srsrpmsi.log	Records activity on the SQL Reporting Services setup.
srsrp.log	Records activity on the SQL Reporting Services in terms of configuring security and copying reports. In this log file, you see information about the reports being imported, security being added, and the style being applied to the reports.
wcm.log	Records activity on WSUS configuration for subscribed update categories, classifications, and languages.

Log File	Description
wsusctrl.log	Records activity on WSUS configuration, database connectivity, and health of the WSUS server. If you see errors in wsyncmgr.log, most likely you will find an explanation to the problem in this log file.
wsyncmgr.log	Records activity on WSUS synchronization. The initial synchronization between WSUS and ConfigMgr can easily take more than 30 minutes. This log file is especially useful for monitoring detailed information about the synchronization process like duration, time left, and so forth.
smsawebsvcsetup.log	Records activity on installing the Application Catalog web service. In this log file, you see whether the needed prerequisites are present and whether the awebsvcmsi installation process completes successfully.
awebsvcmsi.log	Records detailed installation information about installing the Application Catalog web service point site system role.
awebsctl.log	Records the monitoring activities for the Application Catalog web service point site system role, including certificate maintenance.

The Basic Site Server Configuration

The next logical step is to perform the basic configuration of the site server. Basic configuration includes:

- Backup and other site maintenance tasks
- Discovery of resources from Active Directory

Configure Site Maintenance Tasks

ConfigMgr provides a graphical interface for managing site maintenance properties and maintaining the SQL Server database. The benefit of the site maintenance tasks is that administrators do not have to use any native SQL Server configuration tools to manage the database. There are many different tasks, but not all of them need to be configured. ViaMonstra requires a daily backup of ConfigMgr, a weekly update of the SQL Server indexes, and the cleanup of inactive and obsolete clients.

1. On **CM01**, open the **ConfigMgr console**.
2. Select the **Administration** workspace.
3. Navigate to **Overview**, **Site Configuration**, **Sites**.
4. Select **Settings**, **Site Maintenance** from the ribbon.

5. A list of predefined maintenance tasks is shown; select **Backup site server**, click **Edit**, and then click **Enable this task**.
6. Click **Set Paths** and configure the backup files to be stored in **D:\CM2012.BCK** and click **OK** (the folder is created automatically by the backup process). Make sure that you do not select a drive where you also store the site database. (We cover backup and recovery later in this book.)
7. Configure the backup process to generate an alert if the site backup task fails by selecting the **Enable alerts for backup task failures** check box and clicking **OK**.
8. Select **Delete Inactive Client Discovery Data**, click **Edit**, and select **Enable this task.**
9. Configure the task to delete all records **older than 60 days** and click **OK.**
10. Select **Delete Obsolete Client Discovery Data** and click **Edit**.
11. Configure the task to delete all records **older than 1 day** and **run the task daily**, and then click **OK.**
12. Select **Rebuild Indexes** and click **Edit** and then click **Enable this task**
13. Configure the task to start every **Sunday after 12:00 AM** and no later then **3:00 AM**, and then click **OK.**
14. Click **OK** to close the Site Maintenance dialog box.

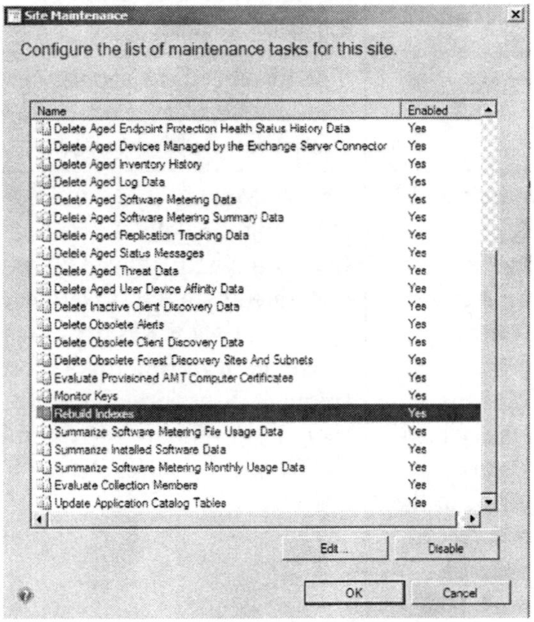

Configuring site maintenance tasks.

Configure Discovery

Discovery is a process by which ConfigMgr queries a predefined source and searches for basic information about a given object. The source and object are configured in the properties of each discovery method. Discovery comes in different "flavors." Different discovery methods are used for different purposes. For ViaMonstra, you will configure the Active Directory discovery methods in the following table.

Discovery Method	What the Method Does	Why You Use the Method
Active Directory Forest	Discovers Active Directory sites and IP ranges.	You use it to automate the creation of boundaries, thus minimizing your own manual work and eliminating typos.
Active Directory System	Discovers computer objects and adds information like basic computer information, information about the OU, and System group membership.	For ViaMonstra, you want to see all your computer objects before you start installing clients. That way can create collections based on the operating system and location.
Active Directory User	Discovers user objects.	You need the user information to support your user-centric application strategy.
Active Directory Group	Discovers Active Directory security groups.	You also need the security group information to support our user-centric application strategy.
Heartbeat	Discovers a variety of data that will be cover later in Chapter 6, "Inventory Management and Reporting." This is the only method enabled by default. This method also is the only one initiated by the client and thus works only for existing clients. The heartbeat discovery also is listed as the Discovery Data Collection Cycle when looking at the client properties. Data in this record includes computer name, domain name, operating system name, last logged on user, and so forth.	For ViaMonstra, you will be changing the default interval from 7 days to 1 day. The traffic generated by a data discovery cycle is about 8 KB per client. The benefit of running a more frequent discovery is getting more up-to-date information in the ConfigMgr console.

Even though it might be tempting to discover the entire domain, that's really not a good idea. It might work in a lab environment or in a small business installation. But for midsize and enterprise scenarios, it's really important that you specify the exact LDAP path to the location of the objects.

For ViaMonstra, you want to use the discovery methods in the following list to discover resources in the indicated organizational units and paths:

- **Active Directory Forest** (OUs: N/A)

  DC=corp,DC=viamonstra,DC=com

- **Active Directory System** (OUs: Workstations, Domain Controllers, Servers)
  - LDAP://OU=Domain Controllers,DC=corp,DC=viamonstra,DC=com
  - LDAP://OU=Workstations,DC=corp,DC=viamonstra,DC=com
  - LDAP://OU=Servers,DC=corp,DC=viamonstra,DC=com
- **Active Directory User** (OUs: Users, VIM Users)
  - LDAP://CN=Users,DC=corp,DC=viamonstra,DC=com
  - LDAP://OU=VIM Users,DC=corp,DC=viamonstra,DC=com
- **Active Directory Security Group** (OU: Software Groups)

  LDAP://OU=Software Groups,DC=corp,DC=viamonstra,DC=com

Follow these steps to configure discovery:

1. On **DC01**, using **Active Directory Users and Computers**, create the following organizational units:
   - **VIM Users**
   - **Software Groups**
2. In the **VIM Users** OU, create the following user accounts:
   - BOP, full name Bob Paisly
   - JAP, full name Julie Petersen
   - MAC, full name Mark Carragher
   - MLG, full name Michael L Gerrad
   - NEP, full name Nanna E Petersen
   - SAN, full name Suzanne Angelhart
   - SMA, full name Sofie M Andersen
   - WKO, full name Wally König
3. Log on to **CM01**, open the **ConfigMgr console**.
4. Select the **Administration** workspace.
5. Navigate to **Overview**, **Hierarchy Configuration**, **Discovery Methods**.
6. Right-click **Active Directory Forest Discovery** and select **Properties**.

7. Select **Enable Active Directory Forest Discovery**, **Automatically create Active Directory site boundaries when they are discovered**, and **Automatically create IP Ranges when they are discovered.**

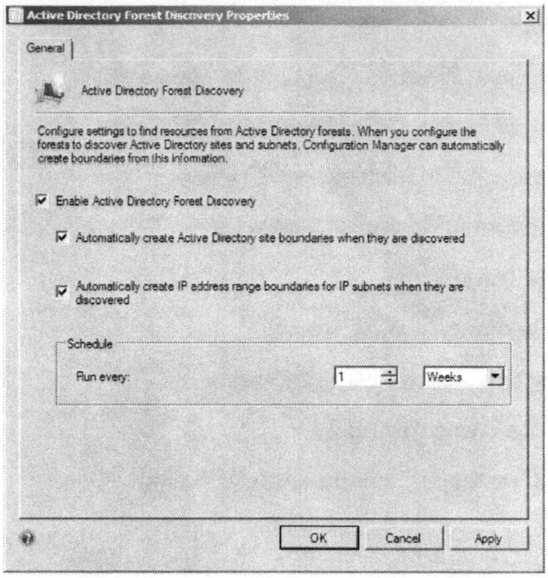

Configuring Active Directory Forest Discovery.

8. Click **OK** and **Yes** to close the dialog box and run the Active Directory Forest Discovery method.
9. Select **Active Directory System Discovery** and click **Properties**.
10. In the **General** tab:
    a. Select the **Enable Active Directory System Discovery** check box.
    b. Click **New**, click **Browse**, and then select this path: **LDAP://OU=Domain Controllers,DC=corp,DC=viamonstra,DC=com.**
    c. In the **Search options** area, select **Recursively Search Active Directory child containers**.
    d. Click **OK.**
    e. Repeat steps B–D for these two LDAP paths:
        i. **LDAP://OU=Workstations,DC=corp,DC=viamonstra,DC=com**
        ii. **LDAP://OU=Servers,DC=corp,DC=viamonstra,DC=com**

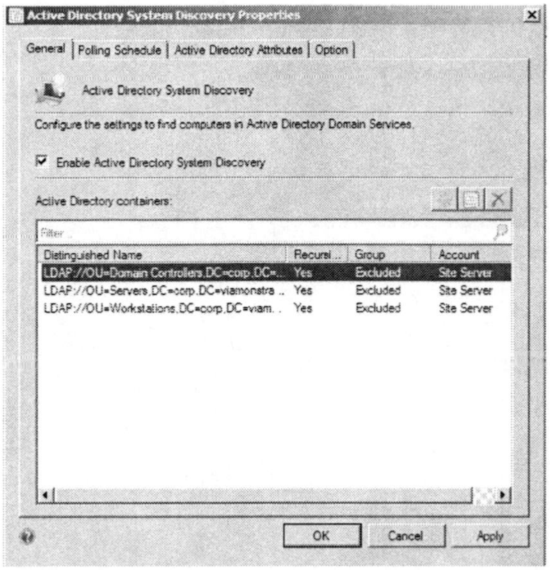

Active Directory System Discovery.

11. In the **Option** tab:

a. Enable **Only discover computers that have logged on to a domain in a given period of time** and select **30**.

b. Enable **Only discover computers that have updated their computer account password in a given period of time** and keep the default settings.

12. Click **OK** to save the settings and **Yes** to run a full discovery.

13. Right-click **Active Directory User Discovery** and click **Properties**.

14. In the **General** tab:

a. Select the **Enable Active Directory User Discovery** check box.

b. Click **New**, click **Browse**, and then select this path: **LDAP://CN=Users,DC=corp,DC=viamonstra,DC=com**.

c. In the **Search options** area, select **Recursively Search Active Directory child containers**.

d. Click **OK**.

e. Click **New**, click **Browse**, and then select this path: **LDAP://OU=VimUsers,DC=corp,DC=viamonstra,DC=com**.

f. In the **Search options** area, select **Recursively Search Active Directory child containers**.

g. Click **OK** twice and **Yes** to run a full discovery.

15. Right-click **Active Directory Group Discovery** and click **Properties**.
16. Select the **Enable Active Directory Group Discovery** check box.
17. Click **Add Location**.
18. In the **Name** field, type **Software Groups**.
19. For **Location**, click **Browse**, select **LDAP://OU=Software Groups,DC=corp,DC=viamonstra,DC=com**, and then click **OK**.

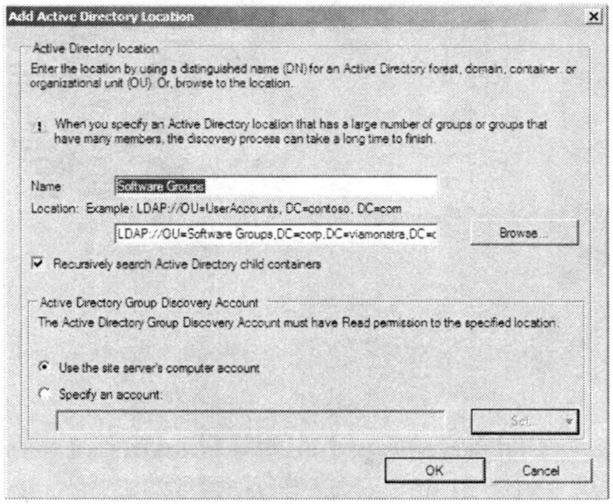

Specifying the LDAP path.

20. In the **Option** tab, configure these options:
    a. Enable **Only discover computers that have logged on to a domain in a given period of time**. Time since last logon: **30**
    b. Enable **Only discover computers that have updates their computer account password in a given period of time** and leave the default settings.
21. Click **OK** to save the settings and **Yes** to run a full discovery.

Verifying the Discovery Process

The discovery process runs in the background and should by now have generated multiple data discovery records in the ConfigMgr console. Go thru these checks to verify that the process ran successfully.

Verify Active Directory Forest Discovery

Navigate to the **Administration** workspace, and to **Overview\Hierarchy Configuration\ Boundaries**. You should see three IP ranges and an Active Directory site. Unlike in previous versions of ConfigMgr, a boundary in ConfigMgr 2012 has no real value until it's added to a boundary group. By default, ConfigMgr queries only objects from Active Directory Sites and

Services in the local forest. You can add additional forest support by creating a new forest object in **Hierarchy Configuration\Active Directory Forests**. From this view, you can verify the discovery and publishing status. From the publishing status, you can tell whether ConfigMgr can successfully write data to Active Directory (the system management container).

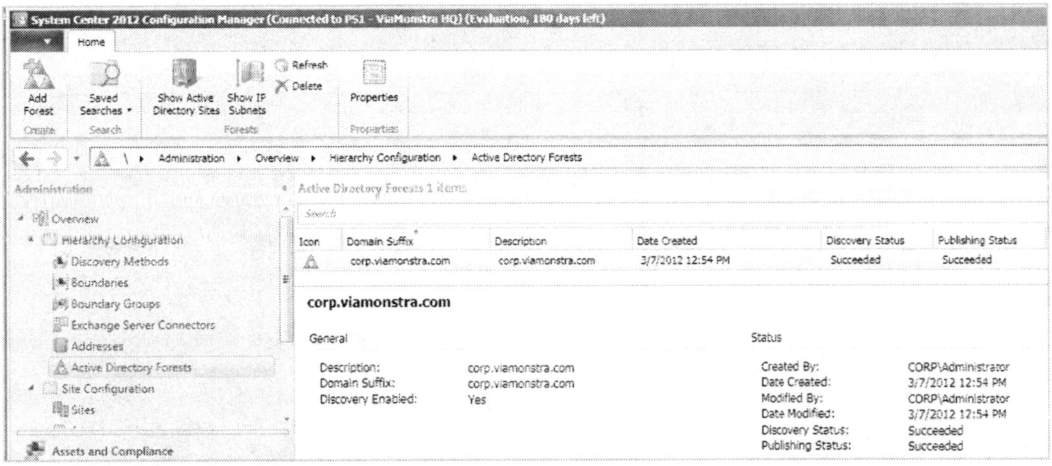

Verifying Forest discovery.

Verify Active Directory System Discovery

Navigate to the **Assets and Compliance** workspace, and to **Overview\Devices**. You should see a list of the devices that are created in the domain. You can right-click each of the computers to see the discovery information generated by the process. The discovery data is not as rich as the data produced by the hardware inventory process, but the data can still be used later when you want to create queries, reports, or collections.

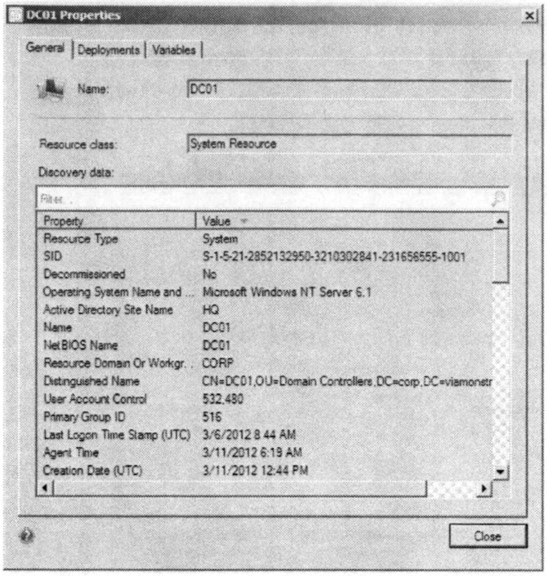

Device discovery information.

Verify Active Directory User Discovery

Navigate to the **Assets and Compliance** workspace, and to **Overview\Users**. You should see a list of the users that are created in the domain.

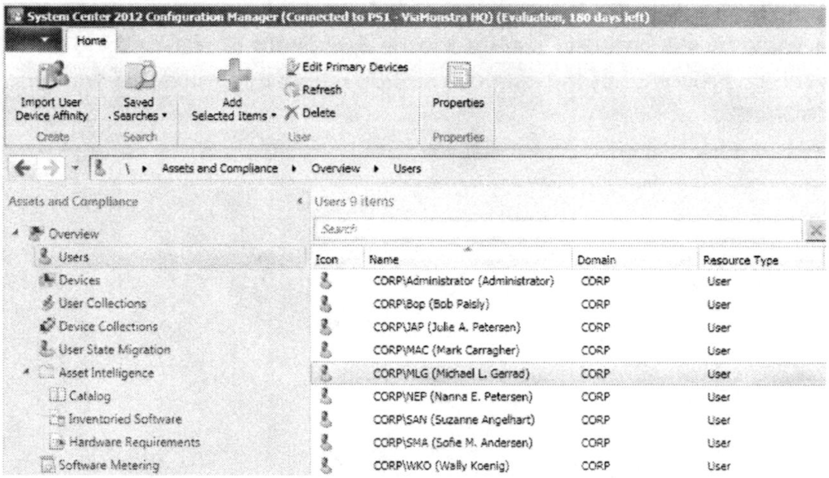

Viewing users in the domain.

Verify Active Directory Security Group Discovery

Navigate to the **Assets and Compliance** workspace, and to **Overview\User Collections**. Right-click the **All Users Group** collection and click **View Members**. As this point in the book you have not created any groups in the **Software Groups** OU so the member count should be 0.

What Happens Behind the Scenes

When you are initiating a discovery process, the site server automatically queries Active Directory for the resources that you have specified in the LDAP path. There are two different discovery schedules, a Full discovery and the Delta discovery process. The full will by default run once a week and do a complete scan for all objects unlike the delta process that will only find objects added, removed or modified since the last full cycle. This process by default runs every five minutes:

1. The site server queries Active Directory.
2. For each resource, a data discovery record (ddr) is created and written to D:\Program files\Microsoft Configuration Manager\Inboxes\Auth\ddm.box.
3. From there, the data are processed and added to the database by the data loader component.

Collections

A collection is a logical grouping of one or multiple objects grouped to serve a specific purpose. A very commonly seen error is starting to use the main features of ConfigMgr without first designing the collections. I cannot stress the importance of designing a reasonable hierarchy as one of the very first things after installing the primary site server. You create collections for several reasons like these:

- To control security
- To support the way to control you features
- To minimize the needed SQL code in your reports

In ViaMonstra, I have decided to create the high-level collection design outlined in the following table.

Collection Purpose	Collection Prefix	Created in Folder
Used to define the role-based security in ViaMonstra and reflect the physical infrastructure of the company.	VM	ViaMonstra
Used to control the Endpoint Protection feature. The collection is used to control the Endpoint Protection agent installation and the applying antimalware policies.	EP	Endpoint Protection
Used to control the application deployment. There will be two Software folders in ViaMonstra, one for Users and one for Devices. You create software collections for most applications and	SW	Software

packages, one collection to control the install process, and one collection to control the uninstall process.		
Used to control the compliance settings. There will be two Settings Management folders in ViaMonstra, one for Users and one for Devices. You create settings management collections to control deployment of the company baselines.	SM	Settings Management
Used to control the operating system deployment process. During the operating system installation, you are able to read data and variables from a collection.	OSD	Operating System Deployment
Collection Purpose	**Collection Prefix**	**Created in Folder**
Used to control the software update patching process.	SUM	Software Updates

Create Folders

1. Log on to **CM01**, open the **ConfigMgr console**.
2. Select the **Asset and Compliance** workspace.
3. Right-click **User Collections** and select **Folder**, **Create Folder**.
4. Type **Software** as the folder name and click **OK**.
5. Repeat steps 3–4 and create the following folders:
    a. **ViaMonstra**
    b. **Settings Management**
6. Right-click **Device Collections** and select **Folder**, **Create Folder**.
7. Type **Software Updates** as the folder name and click **OK**.
8. Repeat steps 6–7 and create the following folders:
    a. **Endpoint Protection**
    b. **Settings Management**
    c. **Software**
    d. **ViaMonstra**
    e. **Operating System Deployment**

Real World Note: You might find it easier to use a scripted solution when building the initial collection design.

Automate Creating Folders Using PowerShell

The following scripts create two folders, a device folder called **Endpoint Protection** and a user folder called **Software**. (It's the -Type value that determines whether it's a device or user folder.)

1. Open **PowerShell** as **Administrator**.
2. Navigate to the folder containing the scripts.
3. Type **. .\CM12_Function_Library.ps1** (note the space between the two dots) and press **Enter**.
4. Type **Add-CMFolder -SiteCode PS1 -SiteServer CM01 -FolderName "Endpoint Protection" -Type 5000**; then press **Enter**.
5. Type **Add-CMFolder -SiteCode PS1 -SiteServer CM01 -FolderName "Software" -Type 5001**; then press **Enter**.

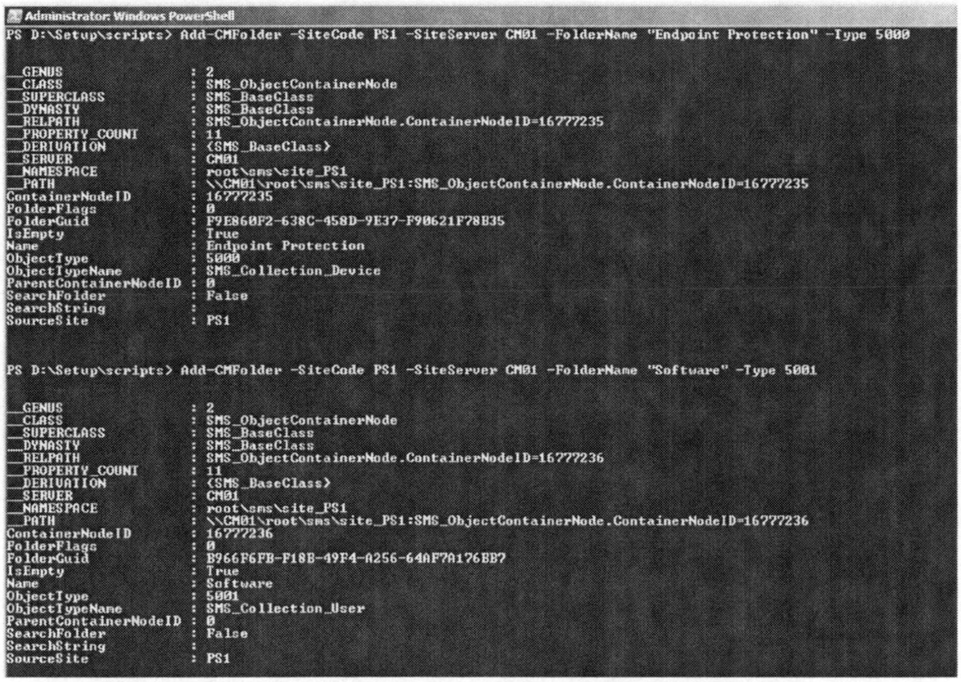

Creating user and device folders using PowerShell.

Role-Based Administration (RBA)

RBA goes hand in hand with defining collections. Before you start planning security, you need to know the basics and also have knowledge about the way you want to control your own environment. For ViaMonstra, you have several ConfigMgr administrators but all with different tasks to perform and responsibilities.

Defining the Support Model

ViaMonstra knows the importance of defining the support model that will maintain ConfigMgr. Even though ConfigMgr might only be a "single" application, it is by far the most complex application currently shipped out of Microsoft in Redmond. No other application requires that a single administrator is a master of software deployment, Active Directory, operating system deployment, security processes, update management, SQL Server, antimalware management, and on top of that know everything there is to know about the infrastructure. If you are tired after a hard day's work, it's fully understandable and, yes, you do deserve that big bowl of ice cream.

In ViaMonstra, I have decided to use security roles in the following table.

Security Role	Responsibility
Full Administrator	Overall responsible for ConfigMgr; must have full access to every single object in the ConfigMgr console.
Server operators	Must have full access to manage all server objects, including creating applications, operating system images, and applications.
Workstation operators	Must have full access to manage all workstation objects, including creating applications, operating system images, and applications.
Endpoint Protection manager	Responsible for managing everything related to Endpoint Protection.
Reporting users	Read-only access; for users who can only read reports and not access any object in the ConfigMgr console.

Security Objects in ConfigMgr

Before you start defining security there are a few objects you need to understand.

Object	Purpose
Security Role	A role defines the actions a user can perform in the ConfigMgr console. ConfigMgr ships with several built-in security roles and also enables you to create custom roles.
Scope	Most objects in the console can be configured to belong to one or more scopes. When importing users or groups, you can limit them to work only with objects from one or more scopes. For ViaMonstra, have applications and images that are meant to be used only by the server administrators and/or the workstation administrators. Those objects will be assigned to either the Server or the Workstation scope. Objects that can be shared between the two groups will be added to both scopes.

Object	Purpose
Collections	Look at a collection like a security boundary where you are limited to work only with those objects in that specific collection. For ViaMonstra, you will create specific collections containing servers only and workstations only. That way you ensure that server operators can't work with workstations and vice versa. All collections are limited to objects in a parent collection, and collections are always divided between users or devices. At the top of the hierarchy, you find the default collections All Systems and All Users. In ViaMonstra, only the Full Administrator group will have access to members in these collections. The other teams will get access only to a subset of devices and users.

Create the Collections to Support Your Security Model

1. Log on to **CM01**, open the **ConfigMgr console**.
2. Select the **Assets and Compliance** workspace.
3. Select **Device Collections**, right-click the **ViaMonstra** folder, and select **Create Device Collection**.

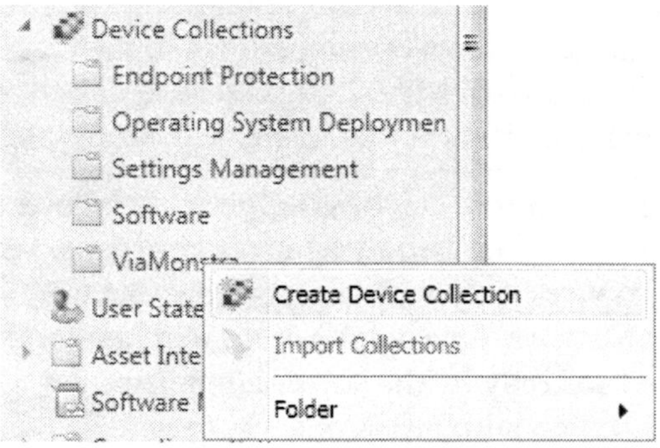

Creating a device collection.

4. On the **General** page, enter the following details:
   a. Name: **VM All Servers**
   b. Comment: **Top level collection for all company servers**
   c. Limiting Collection: Click **Browse** and select **All Systems**.

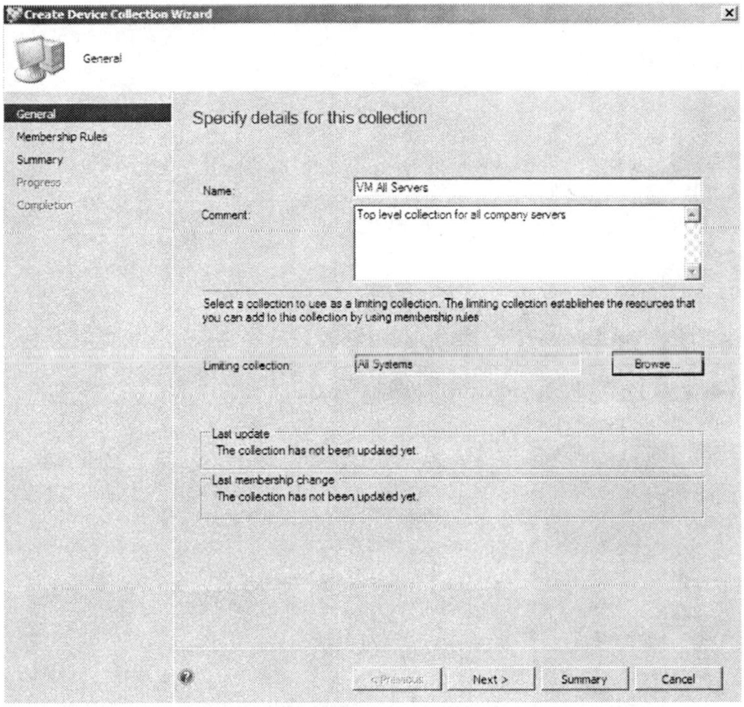

Creating a collection.

5. Click **Next**.
6. Click **Add Rule**, **Query Rule**.

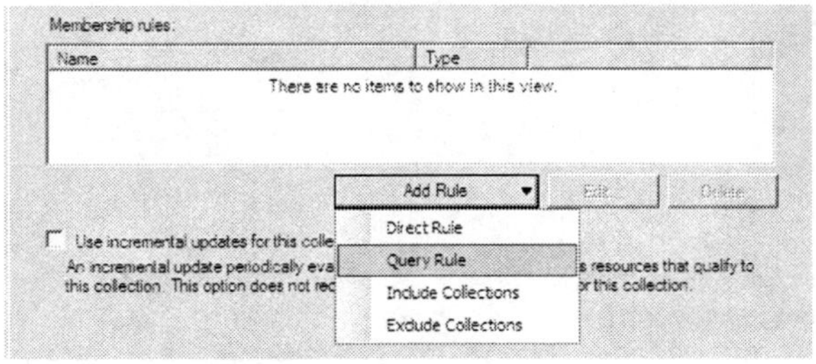

Adding a query rule.

7. Name the rule **All Servers** and click **Edit Query Statement**.
8. Select the **Criteria** tab.
9. Click the **yellow icon** and click **Select** to create the criteria.
10. Select **System Resource** as the **Attribute class** and **Operating system name and version** as the **Attribute**.

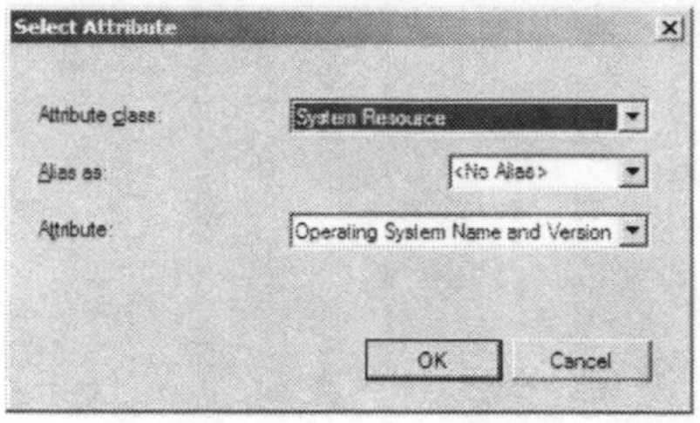

Creating the All Servers collection.

11. Click **OK** to return to the Criterion Properties dialog box.
12. In **Operator**, select **is like**, and in **Value**, type **%Server%**.

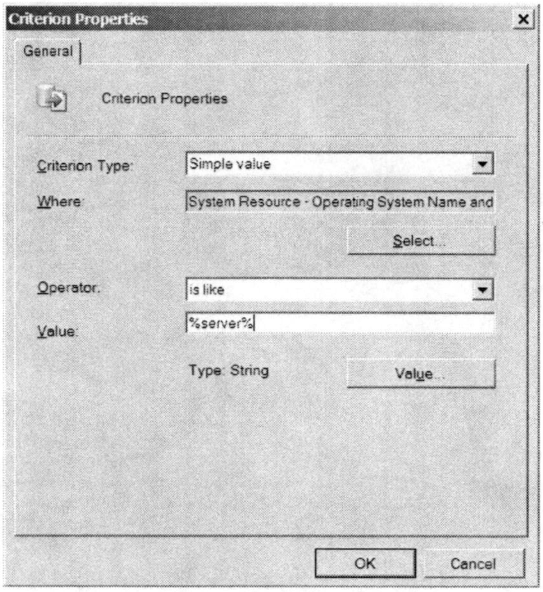

Creating a query using wildcards.

13. Click **OK** three times and return to the Memberships Rules page.
14. Enable **Use incremental updates for this collection**, click **Summary**, click **Next**, and then click **Close** to close the wizard.

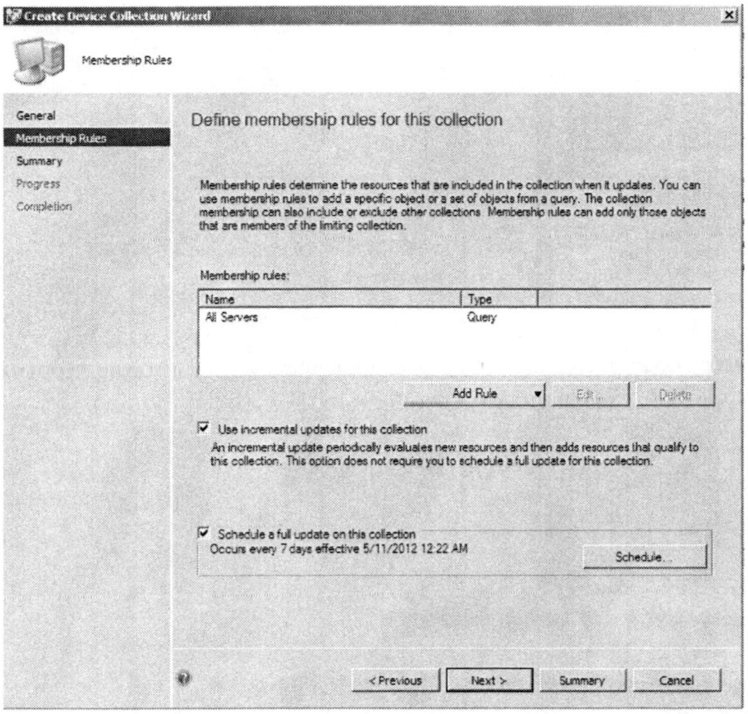

Using incremental updates for a query based collection

15. Create a new device collection called **VM All Workstations** using the same methodology as the VM All Servers collection (steps 3–13):
    a. For step 10, use the following criteria and then click **OK**:
        i. Attribute Class: **System Resource**
        ii. Attribute: **Operating system name and version**
    b. In **Operator**, select **is like**, and in **Value**, type **%Workstation%**.

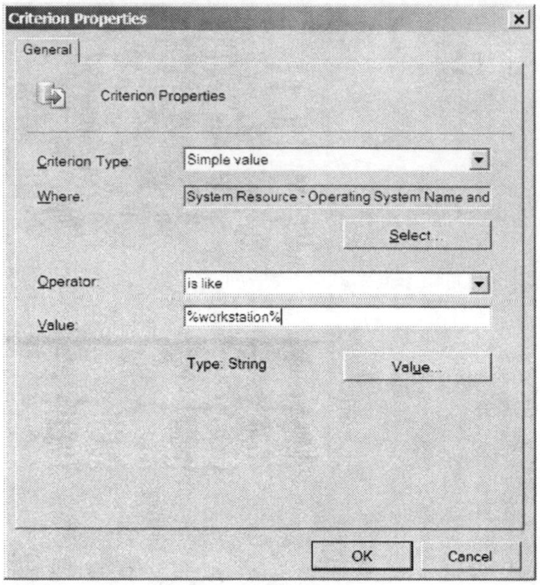

Creating a collection query with all workstations.

16. Click **OK** three times and return to the **Memberships Rules** page.
17. Enable **Use incremental updates for this collection**, click **Summary**, click **Next**, and then click **Close** to close the wizard.

Automate Creating Collections Using PowerShell

Below are a few examples showing you how to automate the process of creating collections. These are only command examples and the **All HR Users** collection is not required for any of the guides in this book.

1. Open **PowerShell** as **Administrator**.
2. Navigate to the folder containing the scripts.
3. Type **. .\CM12_Function_Library.ps1** and press **Enter**.
4. Create a user collection:
   a. Type **Add-CMCollection -SiteCode PS1 -SiteServer localhost -Name "All HR Users" -Type User -LimitToCollectionID SMS00002**.
   b. Press **Enter**.
5. Create a user collection with full collection update schedule every second Saturday and incremental updates:
   a. Type **Add-CMCollection -SiteCode PS1 -SiteServer localhost -Name "All HR Users" -Type User -LimitToCollectionID SMS00002 -Day Saturday -NumberOfWeeks 2 –Incremental**.
   b. Press **Enter**.

6. Create a user collection in a folder called Software with a comment:
    a. Type **Add-CMCollection -SiteCode PS1 -SiteServer localhost -Name "All HR Users" -LimitToCollectionID SMS00002 -Folder "Software" -Type user -Comment "Mastering ConfigMgr 2012 Fundamentals"**.
    b. Press **Enter**.

Create the Security Roles

Create the Administrative Groups in Active Directory

1. Log on to **DC01** as **Administrator**.
2. Start **Active Directory Users and Computers**.
3. Create an organizational unit called **Security Groups**.
4. In the **Security Groups** OU, create two domain local security groups:
    a. **Server Admins**
    b. **Workstation Admins**
5. In the **WIM Users** OU, create two user accounts and add them to the corresponding groups:
    a. Account **SrvAdmin**: add to **Server Admins**.
    b. Account **WrkAdmin**, add to **Workstation Admins**.

Assign Security Roles

1. Log on to **CM01**, and open the **ConfigMgr console**.
2. Navigate to the **Administration** workspace, and open **Security**, **Administrative Users**.
3. Click **Add User or Group** on the ribbon.
4. Click **Browse** and add the **Server Admins** group.
5. In **Assigned Security roles**, click **Add**, select these roles, and click **OK**:
    a. **Application Administrator**
    b. **Asset Manager**
    c. **Compliance Settings Manager**
    d. **Operating System Deployment Manager**
    e. **Remote Tools Operator**
    f. **Software Update Manager**

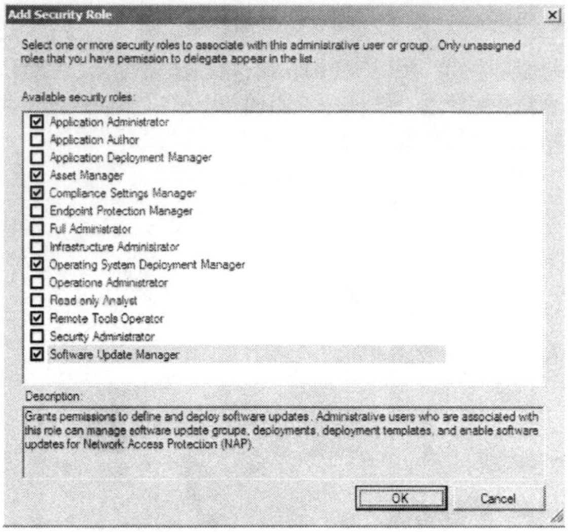

Adding security roles.

6. In **Assigned security scopes and collections**, select the **All Systems** collection and **All Users and User Groups** collection, and then click **Remove**.
7. Click **Add Collection**.
8. Select **Device collections**.
9. Select **ViaMonstra\VM All Servers** and click **OK**.
10. Click **OK** to close the **Add User or Group** window.
11. Click **Add User or Group** on the ribbon.
12. Click **Browse** and add the user to the **Workstation Admins** group.
13. In **Assigned roles**, click **Add**, select these roles, and click **OK**:
    a. **Application Administrator**
    b. **Asset Manager**
    c. **Compliance Settings Manager**
    d. **Operating System Deployment Manager**
    e. **Remote Tools Operator**
    f. **Software Update Manager**
14. In **Assigned security scopes and collections**, select the **All Systems** collection and **All Users and User Groups** collection, and then click **Remove**.
15. Click **Add Collection**.
16. Select **Device collections**.

17. Select **ViaMonstra\MW All Workstations** and click **OK**.
18. Click **OK** to close the **Add User or Group** window.
19. Click **Add Collection**.
20. Select **Device collections**.
21. Select **MW All Workstations** and click **OK**.

Test the New Server Administrator Role

Testing security roles is an important step. In this section, you verify that the SrvAdmin user (who is a server administrator) can see only objects related to security role. You can easily perform the test by creating a new collection containing one or more servers. The SrvAdmin should not be able to see or work with any workstation computers.

1. Open a new instance of the **ConfigMgr console** (Shift+right-click and select **Run as a different user**).
2. Log in as **CORP\SrvAdmin** and navigate to the **Asset and Compliance** workspace.
3. Select **Device Collections** and the **ViaMonstra** folder.
4. Click **Create Device Collection** on the ribbon.
5. Create a new collection named **VM All Domain Controllers** limited to the **VM All Servers** collection.
6. Click **Next** and create a new **Direct** rule.
7. Click **Next.**
8. Type **DC01** in the **Value** field and click **Next**.

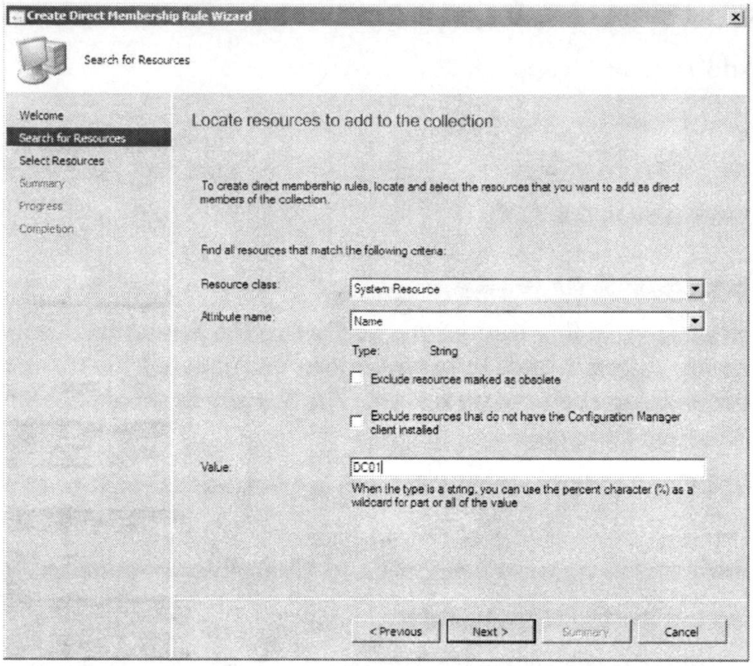

Creating a collection with a direct membership rule.

9. Select **DC01**, click **Summary**, click **Next**, and then click **Close**.
10. Finish the wizard, accepting the defaults for the remaining pages.
11. Close the ConfigMgr console.

Automate Creating Collection Direct Rules Using PowerShell

This is an example of how to create a direct collection rule using PowerShell:

1. Open **PowerShell** as **Administrator**.
2. Navigate to the folder containing the scripts.
3. Type **. .\CM12_Function_Library.ps1** and press **Enter**.
4. Type **Set-CMCollectionDirectRule -SiteServer Localhost -SiteCode PS1 -ResourceName DC01 -CollectionName "VM All Domain Controllers"**; then press **Enter**.

Work with Scopes

1. Ensure that you are logged in to **ConfigMgr console** as **Full Administrator**.
2. Select the **Administration** workspace and navigate to **Security**, **Security Scopes**.
3. Click **Create Security Scope** on the ribbon.

4. Create these two scopes:
    a. **Servers**
    b. **Workstations**
5. Navigate to **Administrative Users**. Right-click **CORP\Server Admins** and select **Properties**.
6. In the **Security Scopes** tab, select **Default** and then click **Remove**.
7. Click **Add, Security Scope**. Then select **Servers** and click **OK**.

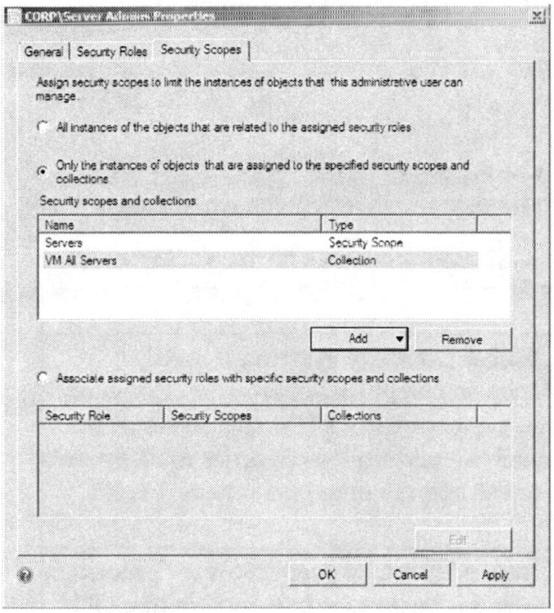

Creating a security scope.

8. Click **OK** and repeat the steps with **CORP\Workstation Admins** (limit the scopes to Workstation).

Audit Administrative Users

1. Open the **ConfigMgr console** as **Administrator** and navigate to the **Monitoring** workspace.
2. Select **Reporting, Reports**, and type **Security** in the **Search** field.
3. Select the report **Administration Activity log** and click **Run** on the ribbon. Notice that all the administrative changes in the console are written to the report.
4. Close the report.

5. Run the report **Security roles summary**. This report will list all the security roles and any user or group associated with the role.
6. Close the report.
7. Run the report **Security for a specific or multiple Configuration Manager objects**.
8. In **Administrative User**, select **CORP\Server Admins** and click **View Report**.
9. Close the report.
10. Type **Audit** in the **Search** field (make sure to have the **Reports** node selected when searching) and run the report **All audit messages for a specific user**.
11. In **SMS User Name**, select **CORP\SrvAdmin** and click **View Report**.
12. Close the report.

Useful Log Files

You can use the log files in the following table to track your site maintenance, discovery, and collection updates.

Log File	Description
Adsysdis.log	Records activity about the Active Directory system discovery process. The record includes basic computer information. Common errors in this process are missing permissions (the site server or the discovery account must have Read permissions in order to discover objects) and missing DNS registration (a client must have a valid DNS record).
Adusrdis.log	Records activity about the Active Directory user discovery process. The user discovery record contains basic user information like OU and user name. Common errors in this process are missing permissions (the site server or the discovery account must have Read permissions in order to discover objects) and misconfigured LDAP paths.
Adforestdisc.log	Records activity about the forest discovery process. A common error in this process is missing permissions (the site server or the discovery account must have Read permissions in order to discover objects). By default, ConfigMgr only has permission to discover objects from the local forest.
Adsgdis.log	Records activity about the security group discovery process.
InventoryAgent.log	Records activity about the local heartbeat discovery process. This log file is only on the client.
SMSdbmon.log	Records activity about processing the site maintenance tasks.
Colleval.log	Records activity about the collection updates process. This is a

	commonly used log file whenever you are troubleshooting why collections are not being refreshed.

Chapter 5 Installing and Managing ConfigMgr Clients

The first requirement for managing a client is to install the ConfigMgr client. In most scenarios, that is a pretty straightforward process, and you will find that 95% of all your client deployments succeed with very little effort. Before deploying clients, however, you need to know which features you want to enable on the different clients. In ViaMonstra, I have decided to use the features in the following table.

Feature	Environment
Hardware Inventory	Servers and workstations
Software Inventory	Servers and workstations
Software Metering	Workstations
Power Management	Workstations
Remote Control	Servers and workstations but with different security settings
Endpoint Protection	Servers and workstations but with different policies

Configuring Client Settings

Client features and settings are controlled through an object called *Default Client Settings*. By default, all clients automatically download and apply all settings. Whenever you have to apply settings that differ from the default settings, you should create custom client settings and deploy those to a collection. In the event of a conflict, the client agent will apply the setting with the lowest priority.

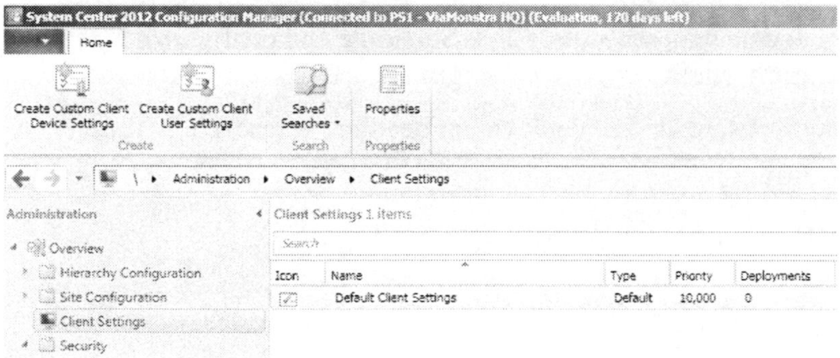

Default Client Settings.

Complete the following steps:

1. Log on to **CM01**, and open the **ConfigMgr console**.
2. In the **Administration** workspace, select **Client Settings**, **Default Client Settings** and click **Properties** on the ribbon.
3. Modify these settings:
   a. Client Policy

      Client policy interval (in minutes): **30**
      (This setting will fit a midsized environment like ViaMonstra's.)

   b. Compliance Settings

      Schedule compliance evaluation: **Daily check**

   c. Computer Agent

      Organization Name displayed in Software Center: **ViaMonstra**

   d. Hardware Inventory

      Schedule hardware inventory: **Simple schedule daily**

   e. Power Management

      Allow power management of devices: **False**.

   f. Software Inventory

      i. Select **Inventory these file types** and click **Set Types**.
      ii. Click the **yellow icon**, type ***.EXE**, and click **OK** twice.

   g. Software Metering

      Enable software metering on clients: **False**

   h. Software Updates

      i. Software update scan schedule: Click **Schedule** and configure a **Simple schedule daily check**.
      ii. When any software Update deployment deadline is reached...: **True**

   i. User and Device Affinity

      Allow user to define their primary devices: **True**.

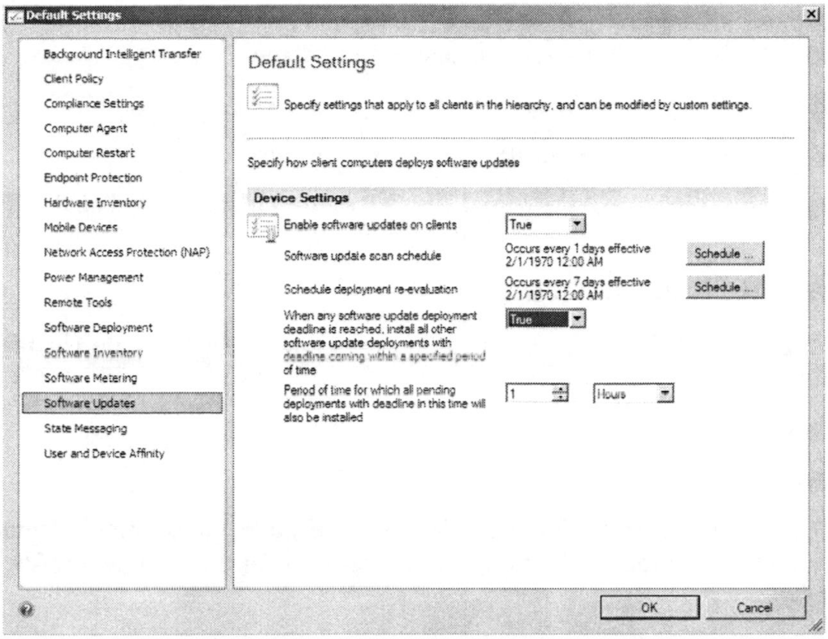

Configuring the default client settings.

4. Click **OK** to close the Default Settings dialog box.

Create Custom Settings for Workstations

1. Click **Create Custom Client Device Settings** on the ribbon, and select **Create Custom Device Settings**:
    a. Name: **Workstation**
    b. Select **Remote Tools**, **Software Metering**, **Power Management**, and **User and Device Affinity**.
    c. In the left pane, click **Remote Tools** and click **Configure**. Then click **Enable Remote Control client computers**, enable the Firewall Settings for the Domain profile, and click **OK**.
    d. In **Permitted viewers of Remote Control and Remote Assistance**, click **Set Viewers**.
    e. Click the **yellow icon**, specify the **CORP\Workstation admins** group, and click **OK**.
    f. In the left pane, click **Software Metering**, and configure **Enable software metering on clients** to **True**.
    g. In the left pane, click **Power Management**, and configure **Allow power management of devices** to **True**.

   h. In the left pane, click **User and Device Affinity**, and configure **Automatically configure user device affinity from usage data** to **True**.
   i. Click **OK** to close the dialog box.
2. Right-click the new Workstation device settings and click **Deploy**.
3. Deploy the settings to the **ViaMonstra\VM All Workstations** collection and click **OK**.

Create Custom Settings for Servers

1. Click **Create Custom Client Device Settings** on the ribbon, and select **Create Custom Device Settings**:
   a. Name: **Servers**
   b. **Select Remote Tools**.
   c. In the left pane, click **Remote Tools**, and click **Configure**. Click **Enable Remote Control client computers**, enable the firewall settings for the Domain profile, and click **OK**.
   d. In **Permitted viewers of Remote Control and Remote Assistance**, click **Set Viewers**.
   e. Click the **yellow icon**, specify the **CORP\Server admins** group, and click **OK**.
   f. Click **OK** to close the dialog box.
2. Right-click the new server settings and click **Deploy**.
3. Deploy the settings to the **ViaMonstra\VM All Servers** collection and click **OK**.

Client Installation Methods

As mentioned previously, ConfigMgr does support the use of different client installation methods. Not all environments are alike, and you need to know the different client deployment alternatives and their requirements before installing the first client. The table below is a list of the most commonly used deployment methods, along with short descriptions.

Regardless of the selected installation method, a client installation sequence always goes through these three phases:

1. Starting the client installation, deploying the needed bootstrap files to the client, and downloading the prerequisites.
2. Installing the client by running the client.msi file.
3. Approving and assigning the client to a site.

Method	Description and Requirements	Used in ViaMonstra
Client push	Client push is an often used deployment method and can be initiated manually or automatically from the ConfigMgr console. The Client Configuration Manager component on the site server connects to the local client, pushes the needed files (ccmsetup.exe and mobileclient.tcf), and starts the installation service (ccmsetup service). This method requires an account with local administrative privileges on the client. The local firewall must be configured to enable file and printer sharing and allow access to the administrative shares like IPC$ and Admin$.	Yes
Logon script	Welcome to the 90s and logon scripts! This requires that the end user is a local administrator on the client, and there is no way I would allow that in ViaMonstra.	No
Software update	This installation method will publish the ConfigMgr client as a required infrastructure update in WSUS. You can the leverage the existing WSUS infrastructure to deploy the client. This installation method will bypass any local firewall rules and will run in the context of the local system account.	No
Group policy	This method uses an Active Directory software group policy installation policy. ConfigMgr ships with a ccmsetup.msi file that you can use to create the package. The reason why I have chosen this as the primary installation method for workstations is that all workstations perform a daily restart and will then install the ConfigMgr client.	Yes
Manual	The manual installation method is often used when installing clients that reside in a workgroup, or when testing client installation command-line properties. In order to run a manual installation, you need to have local Administrator permissions on the server or workstation.	Yes

Client Command-line Properties

The list of supported command-line properties is long, and I will not cover all the properties in this book. For a full list, open your favorite search engine and search for "Configuration Manager 2012 ccmsetup.exe" and open the link for "About Client installation properties in Configuration Manager." Notice that you can specify command lines for the CCMSetup.exe process and for the client.msi process. CCMSetup.exe will be processed first and then call Client.msi to finish the installation.

In ViaMonstra, you will use command lines to control the assigned site and the initial management point. For servers, you will also disable Silverlight (Silverlight is a required component when using the Application Web Catalog Point). The default command lines can be published to Active Directory and used by the client by running CCMSetup.exe without specifying any command lines.

The CCMSetup.exe process is able to use command lines from several places. Knowing how command lines are applied can help you tailor the different scenarios. The following sequence is the order used by the CCMSetup process:

1. Command line specified manually.
2. Registry specified by the ConfigMgrInstallation.adm and written to \HKLM\SOFTWARE\Policies\Microsoft\ccmsetup\SetupParameters.
3. Lookup in Active Directory and search for any command lines that are specified in the properties of the Client Push feature, as explained later in this chapter.

Boundaries and Boundary Groups

As explained previously, all client installation sequences go through three phases, in which the third phase is the site assignment phase. During that phase, the client searches Active Directory for any site that has a boundary group configured for site assignment matching the local IP information.

What Is a Boundary?

A boundary is an IP scope that you create manually, or that is discovered and created automatically using the Active Directory forest discovery method. Boundaries come in four flavors:

- IP ranges
- IP subnets
- AD sites
- IPV6

I always recommend that you use IP ranges, as they always work as intended. IP subnets and AD sites do not always work, especially if you are working with IP subnetting and IP supernetting in your environments. In ViaMonstra, I have decided to support the use of IP ranges and AD sites (since ViaMonstra is not using IP supernetting).

Automate Creating Boundaries Using PowerShell

In this example, you create Boundary AD HQ and the value is Active Directory Site name. Parameter Type can be AD, IPv6, IPSubnet, or IPRange. Again, this is just example syntax; you have already created the following boundary since you configured Active Directory Forest Discovery previously in this book.

1. Open **PowerShell** as **Administrator**.
2. Navigate to the folder containing the script.
3. Type **. .\CM12_Function_Library.ps1** and press **Enter**.
4. Type **Add-CMBoundary -Name "AD HQ" -Value "HQ" -Type AD -SiteCode PS1 -SiteServer Localhost**; then press **Enter**.

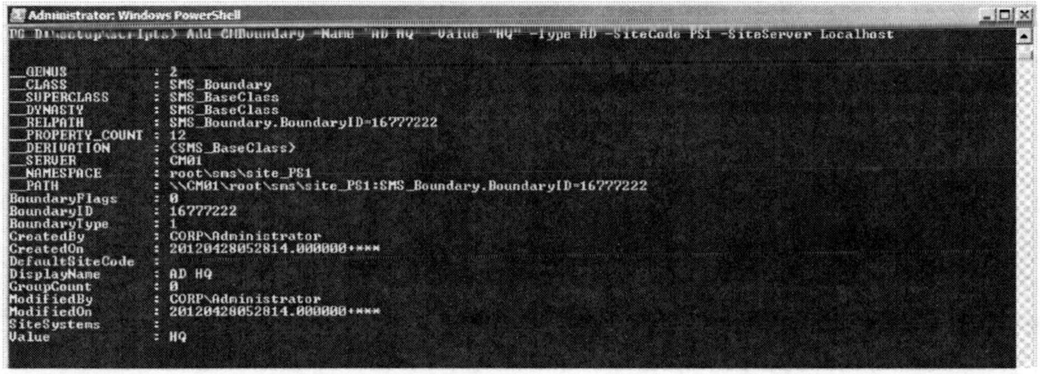

Creating a boundary using PowerShell.

What Is a Boundary Group?

A boundary group is essentially a group of boundaries created for the following purposes:

1. To assign the client to a site during the third phase of the client installation. In ViaMonstra, you have only one primary site, and for that reason, you need only one *site assignment* boundary group.
2. To locate distribution points when installing images, applications, packages, or software updates. In ViaMonstra, you do have several remote locations that will host a local distribution point. For each of those locations, you will create a unique *content location* boundary group.

Create a Site Assignment Boundary Group

1. Navigate to the **Administration** workspace; select **Hierarchy Configuration**, **Boundary Groups**, and click **Create Boundary Group** on the ribbon.
2. In the **Name** field, type **VM Assignment** and click the **References** tab.
3. In **Site assignment**, select **Use the boundary group for site assignment** and click **OK**.

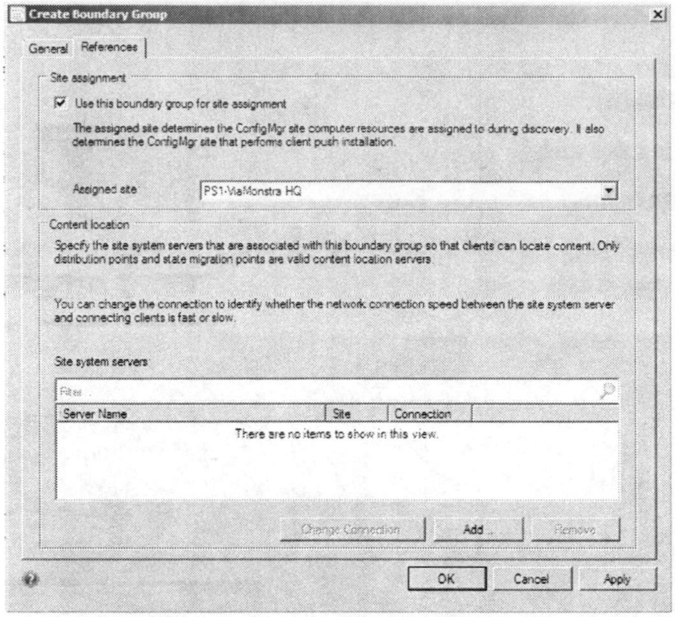

Creating a site assignment boundary group.

4. Select **Boundaries**.
5. Right-click the Active Directory site boundary and select **Add Selected Items**, **Add Selected Items to Existing Boundary Groups**.
6. Select the **VM Assignment** boundary group and click **OK**.

Automate Creating Boundary Groups Using PowerShell

In this example, you create a boundary group called **HQ Assignment**, add the HQ boundary to the group, and add the site server to the HQ Assignment group. Again, these are just sample commands; you don't need to do this configuration for the setup in this book.

1. Open **PowerShell** as **Administrator**.
2. Navigate to the folder containing the script.
3. Type **. .\CM12_Function_Library.ps1** and press **Enter**.
4. Type **Add-CMBoundaryGroup -SiteServer Localhost -SiteCode PS1 -Name "HQ Assignment"**; then press **Enter**.

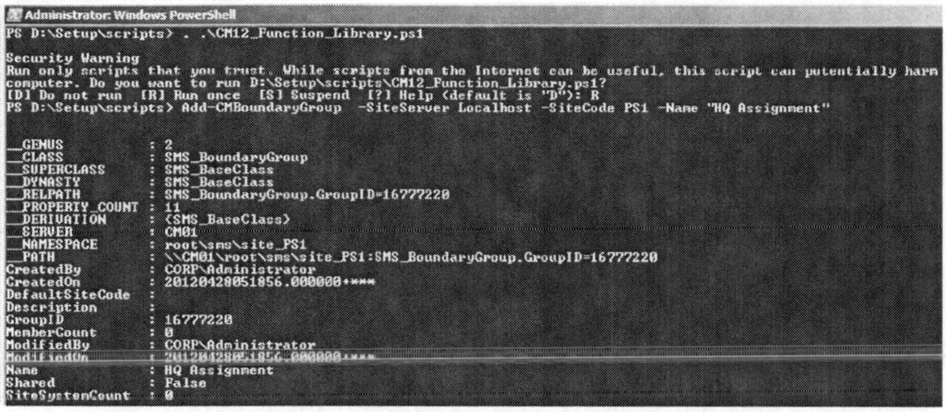

Creating a boundary group with PowerShell.

5. Type **Add-CMBoundaryToGroup -SiteServer Localhost -SiteCode PS1 -BoundaryGroup "HQ Assignment" -Boundary "AD HQ"** and press **Enter**.

Adding the HQ boundary to the new boundary group.

6. Type **Add-CMSiteSystemToBoundaryGroup -SiteServer Localhost -SiteCode PS1 -SiteSystem "CM01.corp.viamonstra.com" -BoundaryGroup "HQ Assignment"** and press **Enter**.

Configure Client Push Installation Properties

Before installing a client, you should start by configuring the client push installation properties. These properties are automatically replicated to Active Directory and will be used by different installation methods without specifying any command lines. The PC001 client machine needs to be started before doing these steps.

1. On **CM01**, open the **ConfigMgr** console, select the **Administration** workspace, and navigate to **Site Configuration**, **Sites**.
2. Click **Settings** on the ribbon, and select **Client Installation Settings**, **Client Push Installation**.
3. In the **Accounts** tab, click **New** and then **New Account**.
4. Click **Browse,** find the user **CORP\CM_CP**, and specify the password.
5. Click **Verify**; then in **Network share**, type **\\PC001\Admin$** and click **Test Connection**. If the Test connection fails, you may need to run **gpupdate /force** on **PC001** to force a group policy update.

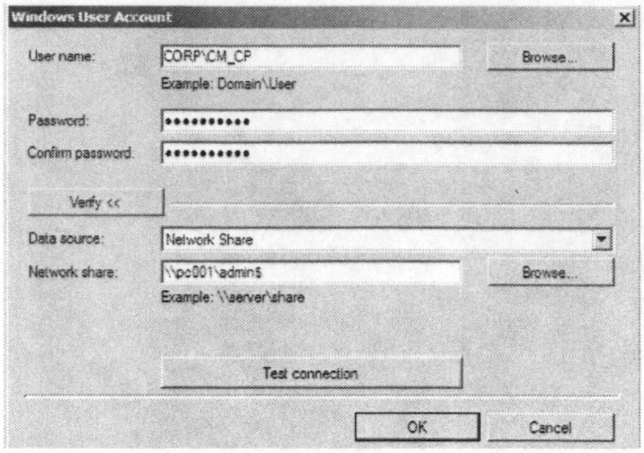

Verifying the client push account.

6. Click **OK**.

> **Real World Note:** ConfigMgr will try to connect to the client using each of the accounts. If no connection is successful, the site server computer account will be used. Usually you are required to create a specific account for servers and one for workstations.

7. In the **Installation Properties** tab, configure properties to **SMSSITECODE=PS1 SMSMP=CM01.corp.viamonstra.com** and click **OK**.

8. Start **CMTrace** and open **D:\Program Files\Microsoft Configuration Manager\Logs \CCM.log**.

   Notice that the values you have configured in the client push properties are written to the CCM.log file. When you start a client push installation, all activities are written to this log file.

Install Clients Using Client Push

1. Navigate to the **Assets and Compliance** workspace and select **Devices**.
2. Select **CM01, CM02** and click **Install Client** on the ribbon.
3. On the first page, read the information and click **Next**.
4. Select the following settings and click **Next**:
   - **Always install the client software**
   - **Install the client software from a specified site**

> **Note:** The preceding settings are not required in this specific scenario but can be very useful when redeploying clients and/or controlling the site used to download the client installation files.

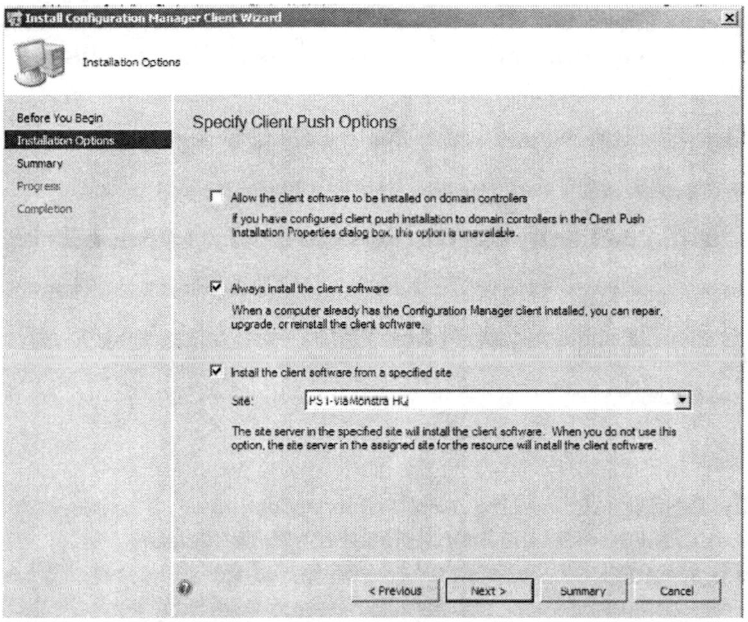

Starting the client push installation.

5. On the **Summary** page, read the summary and click **Next**.
6. On the **Completing the Client Push Installation** page, click **Close**.

   You can monitor the client push process by reading the **ccm.log** with **CMtrace.exe** and by opening the folder **D:\Program Files\Microsoft Configuration Manager\inboxes \ccr.box\InProc** in **Windows Explorer**. When the client push process begins, you can see activity in the log file and also see an object created in the inproc folder. The object created in the folder will be processed quickly and removed from the folder.

Real World Note: The good thing about using the client push installation method is that you can control exactly when the installation starts. The downside is that the site server needs to connect to the Admin$ share on the client. If the client configuration manager component can't connect, then it will retry the attempt once an hour for a week. This can potentially generate a lot of warning and error messages in the ConfigMgr console.

Verify the Client Installation

1. Log on to **CM01** as **Administrator** and open the **%windir%\ccmsetup** folder.
2. In the folder, you will find several files; among those files is the **ccmsetup.cab** file, which contains a list of prerequisites along with other information.
3. Open **client.msi.log** and search for **Installation operation completed successfully**.

4. On **CM01**, open **D:\Program Files\SMS_CCM\Logs**. This is the location of the client log files for a client that also has a management point role installed. Other clients will have the CCM folder created in %windir%.
5. Open the **ClientIDManagerStartup.log** and verify that the client is registered correctly.
6. Open the **Clientlocation.log** and verify that you can locate a management point.
7. Open the **LocationServices.log** and verify that the client can find the current AD site.
8. Open the **ConfigMgr console,** and navigate to the **Assets and Compliance** workspace.
9. Select **Devices** and verify that the client is installed on **CM01** (you might have to refresh the console view).

Install a Client Manually

When installing a client manually, local administrative permissions are required. You can copy the entire .\Client folder to the local machine or start the installation through the default SMS_Sitecode share. This share is automatically created when you install the site server. When running CCMSetup.exe without any command lines, the installation automatically uses the MSI command lines specified in the client push properties.

1. Log on to **DC01** as **CORP\Administrator**.
2. From the **Start** menu, select **Run** and type **\\CM01\SMS_PS1\Client\ccmsetup.exe SMSSITECODE=PS1 /MP:CM01 /skipprereq:Silverlight.exe**

   The installation will run without any user intervention. You can monitor the process by opening **Task Manager** and monitoring the **CCMSetup.exe** process.
3. Open **C:\Windows\ccmsetup\ccmsetup.log** and monitor the installation process using **CMTrace.exe**.

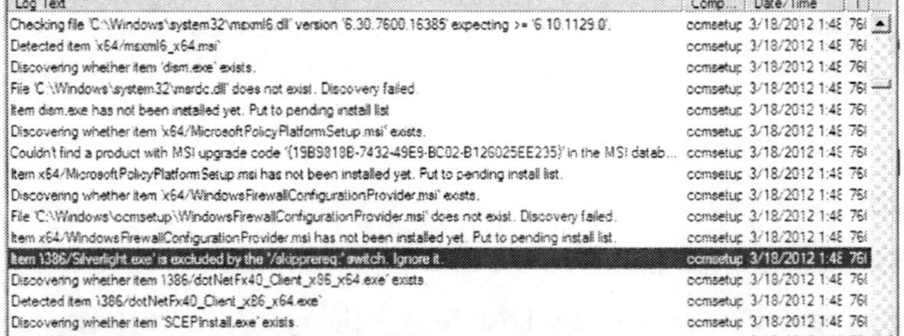

Excluding Silverlight from client installation.

Install a Client Using a Group Policy

Installing clients manually is too time-consuming for any company and using the client push method will not guarantee that all clients will start an installation attempt. By default ConfigMgr ships with an .msi version of ccmsetup.exe that is found in .\Program files\Microsoft Configuration Manager\bin\i386\ccmsetup.msi.

1. On **CM01**, open **Explorer** and create a subfolder called **ClientGPO** in **D:\Sources\Software**.
2. Copy **D;\Program files\Microsoft Configuration Manager\bin\i386\ccmsetup.msi** to the newly created **ClientGPO** folder.
3. Log on to **DC01** as **Administrator** and open the **Group Policy Management console**:
   a. Expand **Forest: corp.viamonstra.com**.
   b. Expand **Domains**.
   c. Right-click the **Workstations** OU and select **Create a GPO in this domain and Link it here**.
   d. Create a new Group Policy object called **Install WRK CM12 Client Agent** and click **OK**.
   e. Expand the **Workstations** OU, right-click the **Install WRK CM12 Client Agent** GPO and select **Edit**.
   f. Select **Computer Configuration\Policies\Software Settings\Software Installation**.
   g. Right-click **Software Installation** and select **New**, **Package**.
   h. For **File name**, type **\\CM01\Sources$\Software\ClientGPO\ccmsetup.msi** and click **Open**.
   i. Select **Assigned** and click **OK**.
   j. Close the GPO.
4. Start or restart **PC001** to apply the new computer-based GPO. After restarting, you can verify the client installation process by opening **Computer Management\Event Viewer \Windows Logs\System Log**.

Real World Note: Because of the way software installation policies are applied in Windows, you most likely will need to restart PC001 twice. One restart is for the policy to apply, and the other is for the actual install.

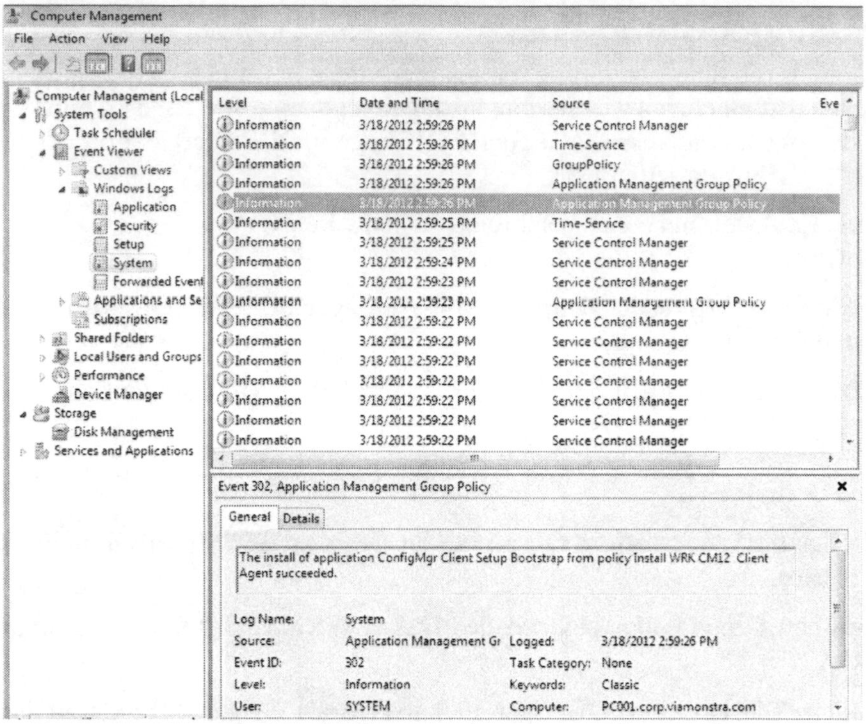

Verifying the GPO installation.

Software GPOs always attempt to install the ConfigMgr client even if it is installed by another client installation method. To prevent that from happening, create a WMI filter and apply that to the GPO. The GPO will be applied only if the WMI filter evaluates to True.

Create a WMI Filter to Exclude All Existing ConfigMgr 2012 Clients

1. Log on to **DC01** as **Administrator** and open the **Group Policy Management console**.
2. Expand **Forest\Domains** and select **WMI Filters**.
3. Right-click **WMI Filters** and click **New**.
4. In the **Name** field, type **Any installed ConfigMgr 2012 client** and click **Add**.
5. For **Namespace**, type **root\ccm**.
6. For **Query**, type **Select * from SMS_Client where NOT ClientVersion like "5.%"** and click **OK**.

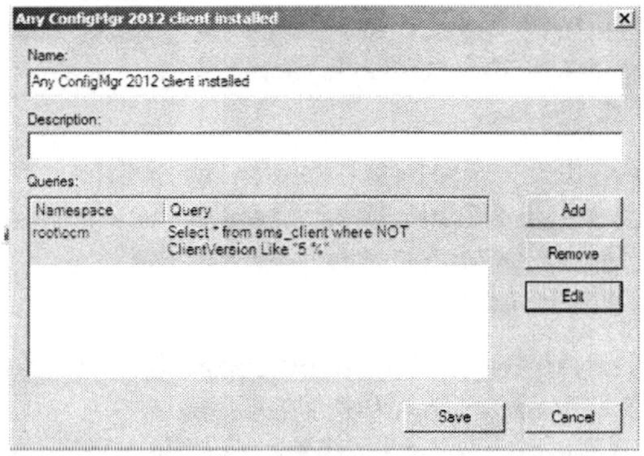

Creating a WMI filter.

7. Click **Save.**
8. Select the **Install WRK CM12 Client Agent** GPO.
9. In the **Scope** tab, select the newly created WMI filter and click **Yes** in the dialog box.
10. Close the GPO.

There will be scenarios in which you do not want to apply the published client command lines. In those scenarios, you can tattoo the CCMSetup command lines to the registry either manually or by applying the command lines in the group policy. ConfigMgr ships with two ADM files both found on the installation media in .\SMSSetup\Tools\ConfigADMTemplates. ConfigMgrAssignment.adm can be used to assign the client to a specific site, and ConfigMgrInstallation.adm will tattoo CCMSetup command lines to the registry.

Real World Note: Using the ConfigMgrAssignment.adm template can be very useful when installing clients in an untrusted forest or if you didn't extend the active directory schema.

Create a GPO to Tattoo CCMSetup Command Lines to the Registry

Log on to **DC01** as **Administrator** and open the **Group Policy Management console.**

a. Expand **Forest: corp.viamonstra.com.**
b. Expand **Domains.**
c. Right-click the **Servers** OU and select **Create a GPO in this domain and Link it here.**
d. Create a new Group Policy object called **ConfigMgr command lines** and click **OK.**
e. Expand the **Servers** OU, right-click the **ConfigMgr command lines** GPO, and select **Edit.**
f. Navigate to **Computer Configuration\Policies\Administrative Templates,** right-click **Administrative Templates,** and select **Add/Remove Templates.**

g. Click **Add**; browse to your ConfigMgr 2012 installation folder on **CM01**, and then to **\SMSSetup\Tools\ConfigMgrADMTemplates**; then select **ConfigMgrInstallation.adm** and click **Open**.

h. Back in the **Add/Remove templates** dialog box, click **Close** to import the template. Importing the template adds a new folder called **Classic Administrative Templates (ADM)**. As child nodes, you will find the **Configuration Manager 2012 Client** settings.

i. Browse to **Classic Administrative Templates (ADM)\Configuration Manager 2012\ Configuration Manager 2012 Client**, right-click **Configure Configuration Manager 2012 Client Deployment Settings**, and then click **Edit**.

j. Enable the policy, and in the **CCMSetup** text box, type **SMSSITECODE=PS1 /MP:CM01 /skipprereq:Silverlight.exe**; then click **OK** and close the GPO.

With the new GPO, all servers will load the CCMSetup command lines into the registry and use those settings when installing the client. Information is written to HKLM\Software\Policies\Microsoft\ccmsetup\.

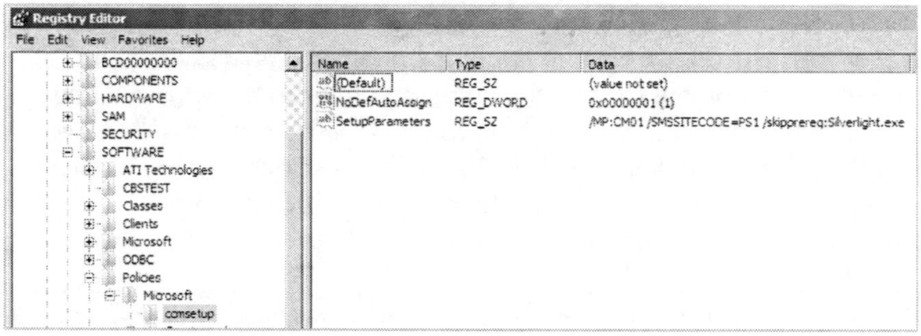

Client command lines in the registry.

The Client Interfaces

With the client installation you also get the Software Center installed. From the Software Center, the logged on client can easily see a status of installed applications along with information about upcoming installations. Software Center also allows the user to control settings like Working Hours, Power Management, and Remote Control. All of those settings can naturally be controlled by the ConfigMgr administrators, or left in the hands of the user.

The Configuration Manager Client properties can be launched from System and Security in the Control Panel. With the properties, a user can manually launch one of the enabled client agent actions like running the hardware inventory cycle or download new policies from the management point.

Modify the Local Working Hours in the Software Center

Business hours define when the user is working on the device. When software or updates are deployed to the user, the user can postpone the installation so it takes place outside the defined business hours. A deployment can be postponed only until the defined deadline for the deployment.

1. Log on to **PC001**.
2. From the **Start** menu, select **All Programs**, **Microsoft System Center 2012, Configuration Manager**, **Software Center**.
3. Click **Options** and customize the **Business hours** from **7:00 AM** through **6:00 PM**.
4. Click **Apply**.

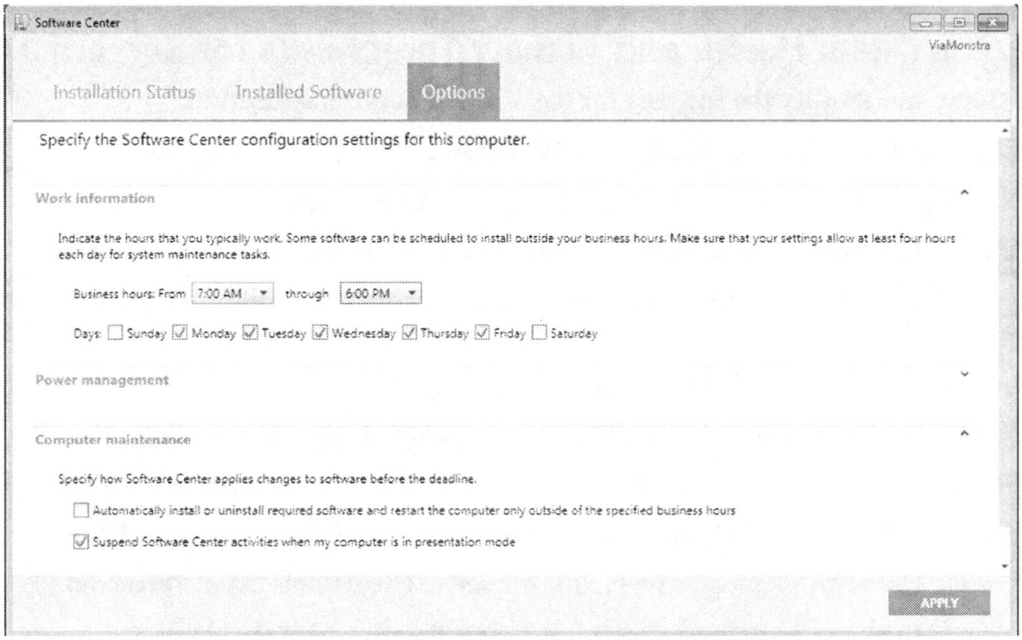

The client Software Center.

Manually Refresh the Machine Policies

1. Log on to **PC001**.
2. Open the **System and Security** category in **Control Panel**.
3. Open the **Configuration Manager** applet.
4. Select the **Actions** tab, select **Machine Policy Retrieval & Evaluation Cycle,** and click **Run Now**.

Working with Client Health

It is one thing to install the client; it is another thing to ensure that all clients stay healthy. Unhealthy clients are unmanaged and can potentially harm your infrastructure. Client remediation is built into the client installation through a Windows task that performs a series of different checks and remediates if any of the checks fails. The process is called ccmeval and can be manually launched by running ccmeval.exe from C:\windows\ccm\ or running the Windows task.

Besides keeping the clients healthy, it's also beneficial to know how many of your clients are active on the network. In ViaMonstra, you support workstations, laptops, and servers clients. Those have different behaviors: for instance, the laptops can be disconnected from the office for days or even weeks. In order not to receive too many alerts in the ConfigMgr console, ViaMonstra has decided to modify the client activity thresholds and create custom alert settings for servers.

Modify the Client Health and Activity Thresholds for Servers

In these steps, you modify the settings for the VM All Servers collection:

1. Log on to **CM01** and start the **ConfigMgr console**.
2. Navigate to the **Monitoring** workspace and select **Client Status**.
3. Click **Client Status Settings** on the ribbon (in the **Home** tab).
4. In the **Evaluation periods to determine client activity** area, modify the five values from 7 to **21**.
5. In **Retain client status history**, type **60**.
6. Navigate to the **Assets and Compliance** workspace and select **Device Collections**.
7. Select the **ViaMonstra / VM All Servers** collection and click **Properties** on the ribbon.
8. Select the **Alerts** tab, click **Add**, enable the following settings, and then click **OK**:
   a. **Client check pass or no results for active clients falls below threshold (%)**
   b. **Client remediation success falls below the threshold (%)**
   c. **Client activity falls below the threshold (%)**
9. Configure these thresholds:
   a. Client check: **ALERT Severity, Critical 95%**
   b. Client remediation: **ALERT Severity, Critical 99%**
   c. Client activity: **ALERT Severity, Critical 95%**

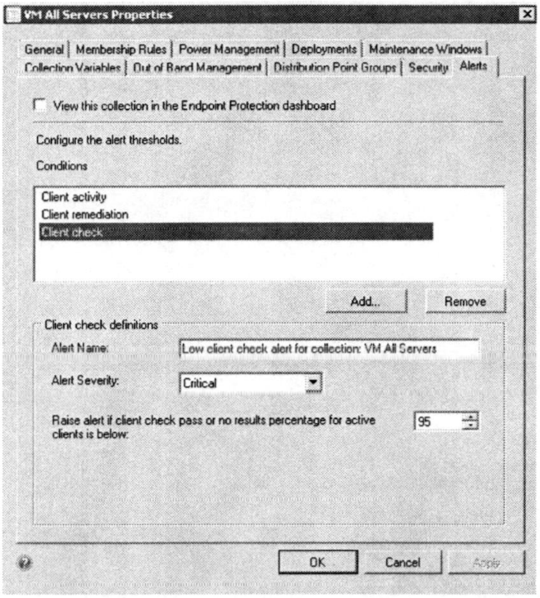

Client status settings.

10. Click **OK** to save the settings.
11. Navigate to the **Monitoring** workspace, and expand **Client Status**.
12. Click **Client Check** and monitor the dashboard. You might not have that much information yet, but you will in a few days when you have some more client history.

Modify the Client Health and Activity Thresholds for Clients

In these steps you modify the settings for the VM All Workstations collection:

1. Navigate to the **Assets and Compliance** workspace and select **Device Collections**.
2. Select the **ViaMonstra\VM All Workstations** collection and click **Properties** on the ribbon.
3. Select the **Alerts** tab, click **Add**, enable the following settings, and click **OK**:
   a. **Client check pass or no results for active clients falls below threshold (%)**
   b. **Client remediation success falls below the threshold (%)**
   c. **Client activity falls below the threshold (%)**
4. Configure these thresholds:
   a. Client check: **ALERT Severity, Critical 95%**
   b. Client remediation: **ALERT Severity, Critical 99%**
   c. Client activity: **ALERT Severity, Critical 95%**

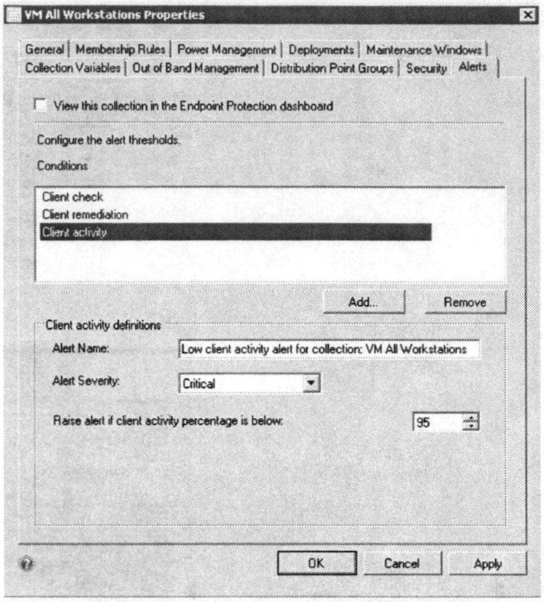

Defined client alert settings.

Manually Start the Client Health Check

1. Log on to **PC001** as **CORP\Administrator**.
2. Open a command prompt with administrative privileges.
3. Navigate to **C:\Windows\CCM** and run **ccmeval.exe**.

Monitor Client Health

You can monitor client health information in at least three different places. In the ConfigMgr console, you have two options. You can either look at an individual client, or get the overview from the Client Status dashboard in the Monitoring workspace.

1. Log on to **CM01** and start the **ConfigMgr console**.
2. To view the dashboard:

   In the **Monitoring** workspace, select **Client Status**. Client Activity presents you with the activity status, and Client Check provides you with remediation data.

3. To view individual client data:

   In the **Assets and Compliance** workspace, select **Overview, Devices.** Select any client and notice the Client activity tabs at the bottom of the console.

4. To view data in a report:
    a. In the **Monitoring** workspace, select **Reporting**, **Reports.** Then, in the search box, type **Client Status**.
    b. Select **Client Status Summary** and click **Run** on the ribbon.
    c. Click **Values**, select **All Systems**, click **OK**, and then click **View Report** to run the report.

Useful Log Files

The log files in the following table can be used to track client installation and evaluation.

Log File	Description	Location
ccm.log	Records activity about client push attempts and publishing installation properties to Active Directory.	Server default
ccmsetup.log	Records information about downloading the client, installing the prerequisites, and installing the client. This log is the first one you should look at when troubleshooting client installations.	Client %windir%\ccmsetup
Client.msi.log	Records information about installing client.msi. This log file is useful to read when you have WMI-related errors in the installation.	Client %windir%\ccmsetup
ClientIDManagerStartup.log	Records information about the client approval process.	Client default
Clientlocation.log	Records information about finding the assigned management point.	Client default
Locationservices.log	Records information about finding local user-facing site system roles like distribution points, management points, and software update points.	Client default
Policyagent.log	Records information about downloading user and machine policies.	Client default
Ccmeval.log	Records information about the evaluation process and the individual rules.	Client default
Ccmsetup.eval.log	Records information about the evaluation process. Check this log file to verify that all needed prerequisites are still installed.	Client %windir%\ccmsetup

Chapter 6 Inventory Management and Reporting

Working with inventory has long been one of the strengths in previous ConfigMgr versions and this version is no different. All companies need to know what hardware and software assets are "out there," and guessing is not an option. ViaMonstra has certain requirements when it comes to asset management. For example, management requires that you have the following reporting capabilities:

- Being able to generate a complete list of all computers, with a count for each hardware model, including serial numbers.
- Being able to list all the software installed on a specific computer.
- Being able to tell the specific number of computers that have a specific application installed.
- Being able to collect a custom ViaMonstra registry key.

The data needs to be as up-to-date as possible, while still minimizing network traffic and not causing any performance issues when gathering the data.

Inventory

ConfigMgr basically offers two different inventory processes, one for hardware inventories and one for software. A hardware inventory queries WMI on the client for all information defined in the client agent settings. A software inventory should really be called *software file scanning*, as that is what the agent does: scans for files in the locations that you have defined.

The first questions you always have to answer when working with inventory data are *What?* and *Why?*

- What kind of inventory data do you really need?
- Why do you need the inventory data? Is it just because some wise guy in the company requires them or just because you can get them? I have always found that the small word *"why"* often gets people who have been asking the wrong questions to rethink what they are really asking for. Asking for unnecessary and unrealistic reporting can easily flood the network with data or bring the client computer to its knees due to uncontrolled inventory scanning.

ViaMonstra has already answered these questions, so you know both what you need and why. You need the hardware inventory report to keep track of the computers and the software reports for licensing purposes and to keep track of installed software.

> **Note:** One of the most commonly used types of inventory information is the applications listed in Add/Remove programs. That information is gathered as part of the hardware inventory process.

Configuring Hardware Inventory Data

In Chapter 5, you already configured a daily hardware scan and a weekly software scan. Before you start working with the features, you just need to verify that the settings are correct and that you have inventory data in the database.

Verify Inventory Settings

1. Log on to **CM01**, and open the **ConfigMgr console**.
2. In the **Administration** workspace, in **Client Settings**, **select Default Client Settings** and click **Properties** on the ribbon.
3. Verify these settings:
    a. Enable Hardware Inventory on clients: **True**
    b. Hardware Inventory, Schedule hardware inventory: **Simple schedule**, **Every 1 day(s)**
    c. Collect MIF Files: **None**
    d. Enable Software Inventory on clients: **True**
    e. Software Inventory, Schedule software inventory: **Simple schedule**, **Every 7 day(s)**
    f. Inventory these file types: ***.EXE**

> **Real World Note:** ConfigMgr creates new tables or modifies existing tables in the site database to accommodate the properties in IDMIF and NOIDMIF files. However, IDMIF and NOIDMIF files are not validated, so they could be used to alter tables that you do not want altered. Valid data could be overwritten by invalid data. Large amounts of data could be loaded, causing delays in all ConfigMgr functions. To mitigate this risk, you should enable IDMIF and NOIDMIF collection only when absolutely necessary (as in *never at all*).

Verify That Inventory Settings Are Working

1. On **CM01**, in the **Control Panel**, open the **Configuration Manager** applet; in the **Actions** tab, select **Hardware Inventory Cycle** and click **Run Now**.

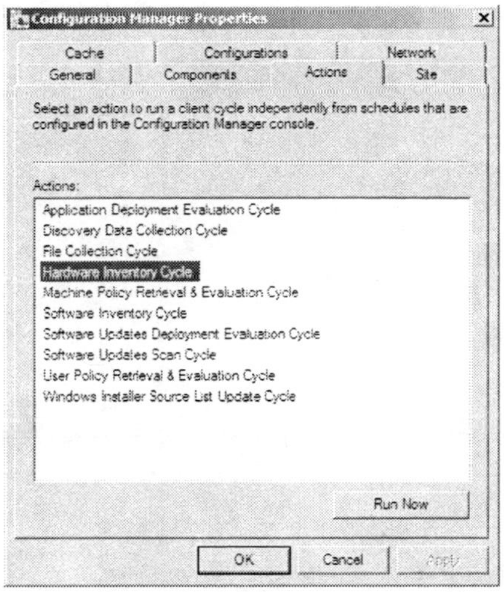

Initiating the hardware inventory action.

2. A message box displays stating that the action was triggered but could take several minutes to complete. Click **OK** and then click **OK** again to close the properties dialog box.
3. Back in the **ConfigMgr console**, select the **Assets and Compliance** workspace and click **Devices**.
4. In the **Search** box, click **Criteria**, select **Name**, type **CM01**,and click **Search**.
5. In the **Home** tab, select **Start**, **Resource Explorer** from the ribbon.
6. Expand the **Hardware** node, and browse through the default set of inventoried items.

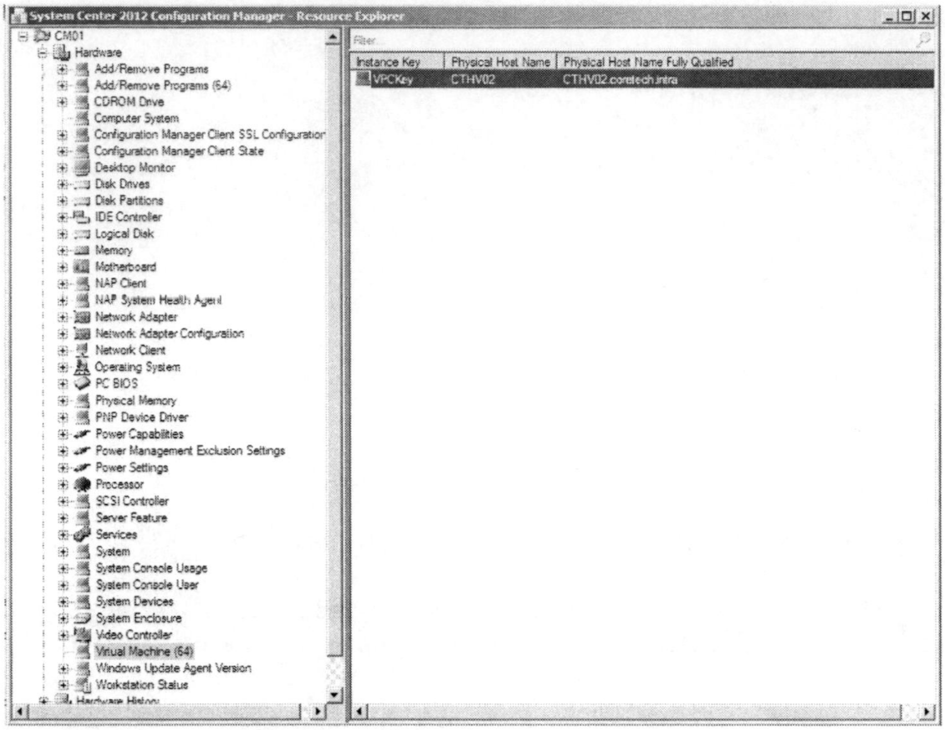

Viewing data in Resource Explorer.

Extending Hardware Inventory

How you extend hardware inventory data depends on what you want gather. If the clients already have the data stored in WMI, all you need to do is add that custom class to the client agent settings. If the data is not yet stored in WMI, then you'll have to add the data to the Configuration.mof file and then add the custom class to the client agent settings. Data added to the Configuration.mof file is automatically added to WMI on the client. You can edit the Configuration.mof file using Notepad. Because there is only one Configuration.mof file per Hierarchy, backing up the file prior to making any changes is highly recommended.

In ViaMonstra, it has been decided to work with two different types of managed devices. Type 01 is fully managed devices and Type 02 is only receiving basic inventory management. For ViaMonstra, I have decided to tattoo the management type in the registry and gather the information as part of the hardware scanning. To achieve this, you need to perform a few things:

1. Add the custom registry information.
2. Add the registry information to Configuration.mof. You will do this with a free community tool called RegKeyToMOF, written by Mark Cochrane. Mark was also gracious enough to allow me to add his tool to the sample files of this book (I tip my hat).
3. Add the newly created WMI class to the client agent settings.

4. Scan and collect the data.

Add Custom Registry Information

In these steps, I assume that you have downloaded the book sample files to C:\Setup on PC001. (Copying them from \\CM01\D$\Setup works great too. ☺)

1. Log on to the **PC001** computer as **Administrator**.
2. In the **Start** menu, type **Regedit.**
3. Navigate to **HKLM\SOFTWARE**.
4. Right-click **SOFTWARE** and select **New, Key.**
5. Type **ViaMonstra** and click **OK**.
6. Right-click **ViaMonstra** and select **New, String value**.
7. Type **ComputerType** as the value and click **OK.**
8. Right-click **ComputerType** and select **Modify.**
9. Type **01**, which is the value for a fully managed device, and click **OK**. Then close the Registry Editor.

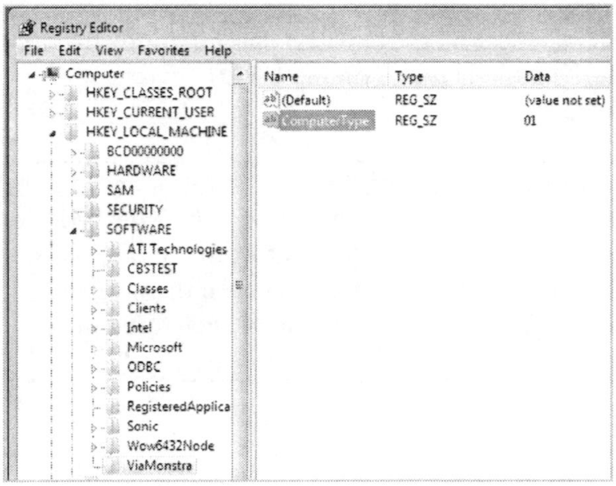

Creating a custom registry key.

10. Run **C:\Setup\RegKey\RegKeyToMofV3.exe**, navigate to **SOFTWARE\ViaMonstra**, and then select **SOFTWARE\ViaMonstra\ComputerType** in the right pane.

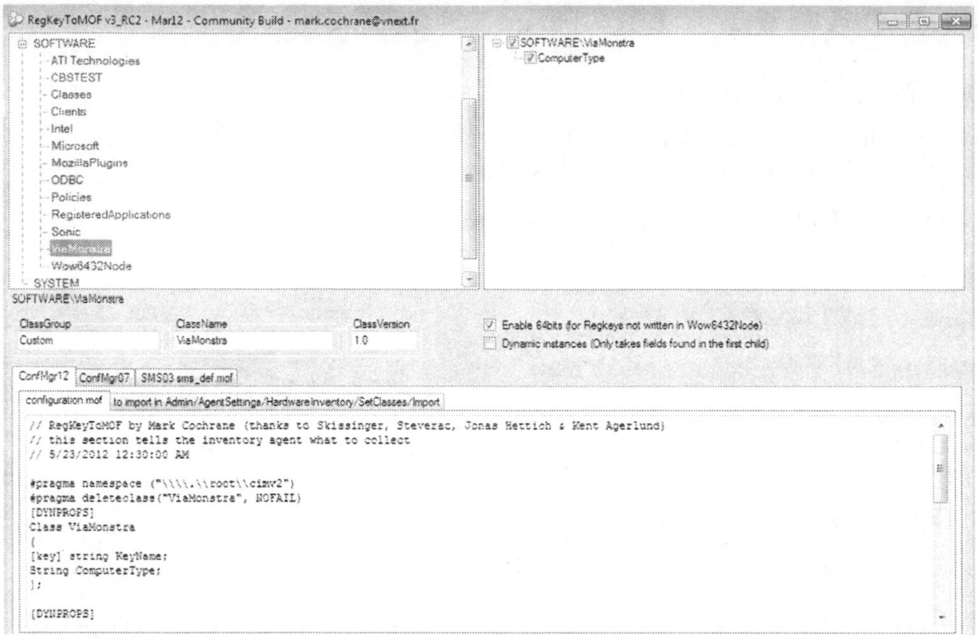

Using RegKeyToMOF.

11. From the lower pane in **RegKeyToMOF**, select all the text and paste the information at the end of the **Configuration.mof** file. The file is found on the **CM01** server in **\\CM01\SMS_PS1\inboxes\clifiles.src\hinv**.

> **Real World Note:** It's always a good practice to make a copy of the Configuration.mof file before editing it. ConfigMgr will also make a copy of the file and store it in D:\Program Files\Microsoft Configuration Manager\data\hinvarchive. Furthermore, when adding entries to the file, make sure you add those entries at the end of the file. That way it's easier for you to keep track of any custom changes. The information in the Configuration.mof file is compiled and stored in the database as soon as you save the file.

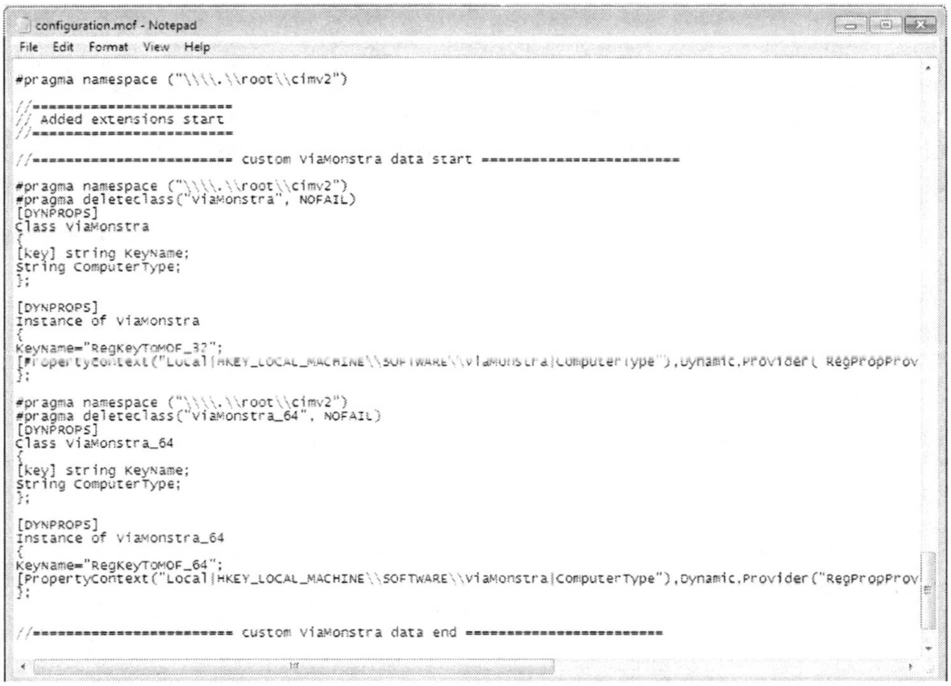

The Configuration·mof file·

12. You can (read SHOULD) monitor the activity in the **Dataldr.log** file on the server.

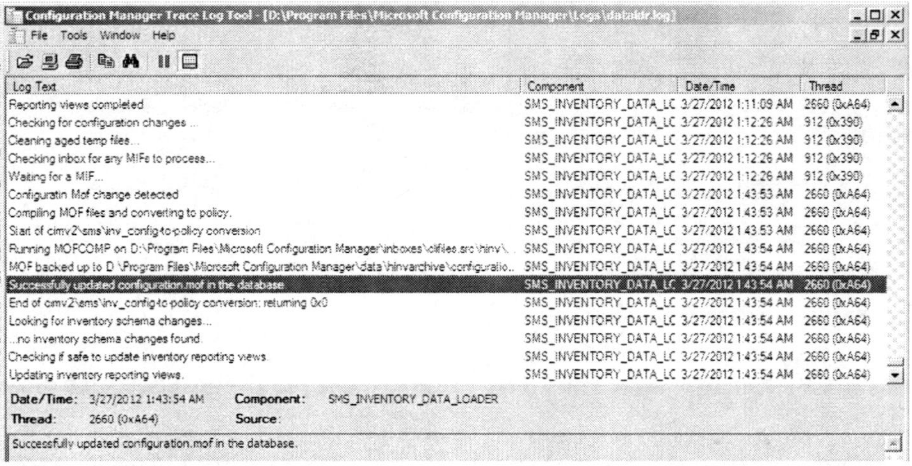

Monitoring the Dataldr·log file on the site server·

13. Clients will read the new settings and add the custom ViaMonstra registry date to WMI after the machine policies have been downloaded and applied. By default, that will happen based on the computer client settings defined in the previous chapter. In order to force a machine policy download, on **PC001**, open the **Configuration Manager** applet from the **Control Panel**; then in the **Action** tab, select **Machine policy retrieval and evaluation cycle** and click **Run Now**.

14. Log on to **CM01**, navigate to the **Administration** workspace, and select **Client settings**.

15. Open the properties for the **Default Client Settings**.

16. Select **Hardware Inventory** and click **Set Classes**.

17. Click **Add**, **Connect**, and connect to **PC001**.

18. Select the **ViaMonstra** classes and click **OK**.

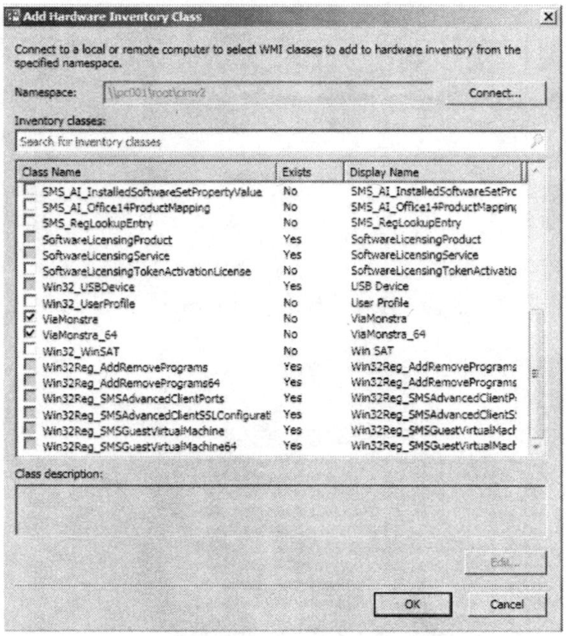

Modifying hardware inventory classes.

19. This enables the ViaMonstra class. Click **OK** twice to close the **Default Settings** dialog box.

20. Log on to **PC001**, and from the **Control** Panel, open the **Configuration Manager** applet. From the **Actions** tab, perform a **Machine policy refresh and evaluation cycle** and wait a few seconds.

21. Start a **Hardware Inventory Cycle** action. This will trigger a hardware scan, using all the new information that you have just added to the client agent settings.

22. You can monitor the inventory process by reading **InventoryAgent.log** on the local client.

23. On **CM01**, in the **ConfigMgr console**, open the **Resource Explorer** for **PC001**. You should be able to find the newly created custom class. If the data is not yet to be found - NO PANIC - it will appear shortly.

Viewing hardware information using Resource Explorer.

Monitor the Sizes of the Inventory Process Files

One of the important things to know when implementing any inventory solution is the load on the network generated by the client actions. When working with ConfigMgr, at least three different files are generated and uploaded to the management point (hardware, software, and the heartbeat data files). You can monitor the sizes of the files by creating a *"secret"* file called *archive_reports.sms* and storing that in the inventory temp folder on the client. I always select a group of pilot machines and store the file on those for a few weeks. That way I can easily calculate the average file size for each inventory action.

1. Log on to the **PC001** computer as **Administrator**.
2. Open **%systemroot%\CCM\Inventory\Temp**.
3. Create a file called **archive_reports.sms** (make sure that you do not create a .txt file).
4. Open the **Configuration Manager** applet from the **Control Panel** and perform these actions one at the time:
    a. Initiate a **Discovery Data Collection Cycle.**
    b. Initiate a **Hardware Inventory Cycle.**
    c. Initiate a **Software Inventory Cycle.**
5. Open the **%systemroot%\CCM\Inventory\Temp** folder. You should be able to see three XML files, each containing the data from the three cycles. The files can be deleted any time.

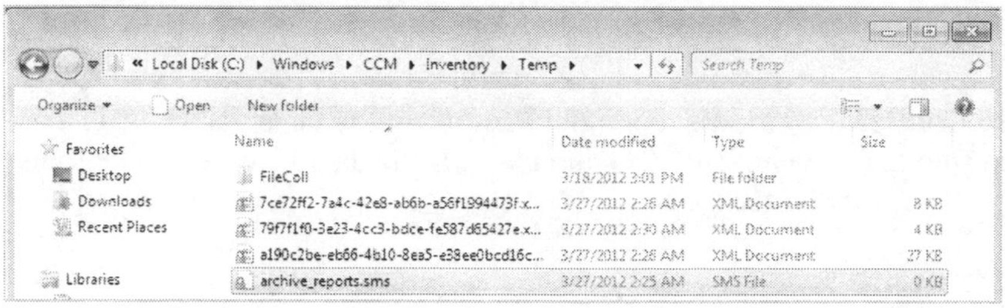

Traffic generated by the inventory actions.

Software Metering

Besides gathering basic inventory information, ViaMonstra also wants to track the usage of a few predefined applications. To do this, you need to create a software metering rule for each of the applications. For the sake of simplicity, I have decided that software metering will be tested using Notepad. That way you do not have to install any other application in your lab environment.

Create a Software Metering Rule

1. Log on to **CM01**, and open the **ConfigMgr console**.
2. In the **Assets and Compliance** workspace, select **Software Metering**.
3. Right-click **Software Metering**, and select **Folder**, **Create Folder**.
4. Type **Microsoft** and click **OK**.
5. Expand **Software Metering**, select the **Microsoft** folder, and click **Create Software Metering Rule**.
6. In the **Name** box, type **Notepad.**
7. In the **File Name** box, type **notepad.exe**.
8. In **Original File Name**, type **notepad.exe**.
9. The **Version** box should have the * (asterisk) character in it.
10. **Language** should be set to **- Any -**.
11. Click **Next** twice.
12. Click **Close**.

Generate and Review Software Metering Data

1. Log on to **PC001**.
2. In the **Control Panel**, launch the **Configuration Manager** applet.

3. In the **Actions** tab, select **Machine Policy Evaluation and Retrieval Cycle** and click **Run Now**. This action triggers the client to download new policies including the software metering rules.
4. Start **Notepad**.
5. Type **Learning about System Center 2012 Configuration Manager is a blast!**
6. Close **Notepad**.
7. In **Control Panel**, launch the **Configuration Manager** applet.
8. In the **Actions** tab, select **Software Metering Usage Report Cycle** and click **Run Now**. This uploads a report containing all the software metering recorded activity. At the site server, the data is processed by the site maintenance rules. After the processing is done, the usage data will be available in the software metering reports.

Working with Queries

When working with any database, you always need to create queries. In ConfigMgr, the user creating the query needs access to the administrator console and have at least read permissions to the objects retrieved. Queries often are used for personal ad-hoc purposes, in which a report is created for presenting data to other users in the organization. In ViaMonstra, you start by creating three basic queries using the GUI and one more advanced query using the WMI Query Language (WQL) interface.

Create a Dynamic Query Collection

The first collection you create is a collection that lists all your fully managed clients. You can go through the following steps only if you extended the hardware inventory with the ViaMonstra class as described earlier in this chapter.

1. Log on to **CM01**, and open the **ConfigMgr console**.
2. Select the **Assets and Compliance** workspace.
3. Select **Device collections**, right-click the **ViaMonstra** folder, and select **Create Device Collection**.
4. Complete the following settings:
    a. Name: **VM All Managed Clients**
    b. Comment: **All ConfigMgr managed client devices**
    c. Limiting Collection: Click **Browse** and select **All Systems**.
5. Click **Next**.
6. Click **Add Rule**, **Query Rule**.
7. Name the rule **All Managed Clients** and click **Edit Query Statement**.

8. Select the **Criteria** tab.
9. Click the **yellow icon** and click **Select** to create the criteria.
10. Select **ViaMonstra** as the **Attribute class** and **ComputerType** as the **Attribute**.

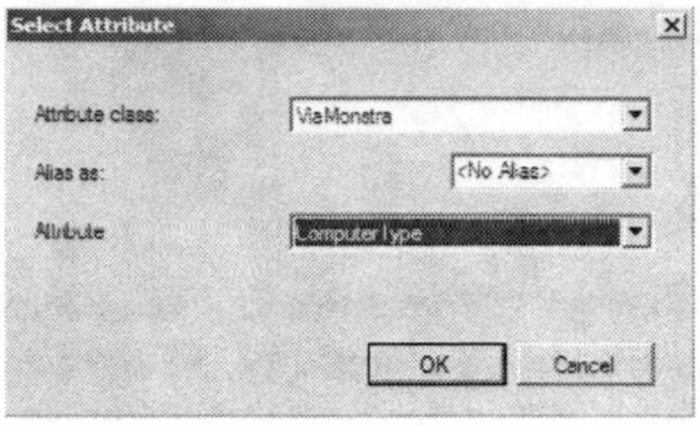

Querying for custom data.

11. Click **OK** to return to the Criterion Properties dialog box.
12. In **Operator**, select **is equal to**, and in **Value**, type **01**.
13. Click **OK** three times and finish the wizard using the default settings.

Create a Query to List Installed Software

Another commonly used query is one that lists all computers with a specific application installed. The following steps guide you through the creation of a query that lists all SQL 2008 R2 servers installed in the company:

1. Open the **ConfigMgr console**, select the **Monitoring** workspace and select **Queries**.
2. Click **Create Query** on the ribbon.
3. Type **All Servers with SQL installed** as the query name.
4. Click **Edit Query Statement**.
5. In the **General** tab, click **New**.
6. Click **Select** and select the **NETBIOS Name** attribute from the **System Resource** class.
7. Click **OK** twice.
8. Select the **Criteria** tab.
9. Click **New**.
10. Click **Select**.
11. In **Attribute Class**, select **Add/Remove Programs (64)**; and in **Attribute**, select **Display Name**.
12. Click **OK**.
13. Click **Values**.

14. The values include all software products installed. Scroll down to **Microsoft SQL Server 2008 R2 (64 bit)** and click **OK** twice. This returns you to the Criteria tab.
15. Click **OK, Next** twice, and then click **Close** to create the query.
16. Select the **All Servers with SQL installed** query and click **Run** on the ribbon. (Note that you might get duplicate entries, but don't worry as those will be fixed later.)

Create a SubSelected Query

A subselected query is one that you use from time to time, such as whenever you need to find objects that do *not* meet a certain criterion, e.g. all servers that do not have SQL Server installed, or all workstations without Office 2010 installed. This query will list the NETBIOS names for all servers without SQL Server 2008 installed.

1. Still in the **Monitoring** workspace, select **Queries** and click **Create Query** on the ribbon.
2. Type **All Servers without SQL installed** as the query name.
3. Click **Edit Query Statement**.
4. In the **General** tab, add this display attribute: **System Resource, NETBIOS Name**.
5. Click **OK**.
6. Select the **Criteria** tab.
7. Click **New**, select **SubSelected values** as the criterion type.
8. Click **Select** and select **System Resource, NETBIOS Name**.
9. Click **OK**. This returns you to the **Criterion Properties** dialog box.
10. In **Operator**, select **is not in**.
11. Click **Browse** and select **All Servers with SQL installed**.

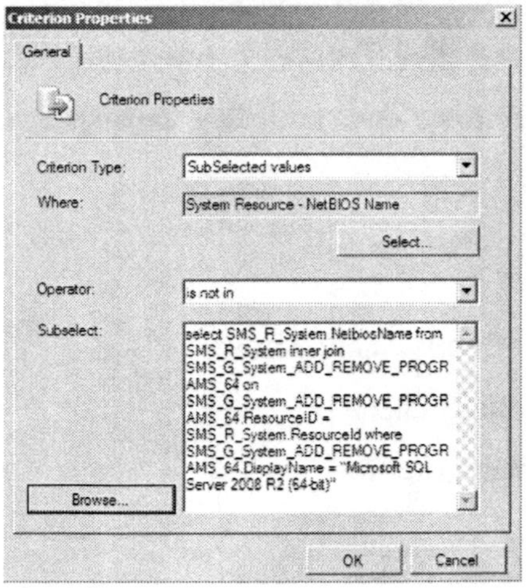

Creating the subselected query.

12. Click **OK**. This returns you to the Criteria tab.
13. Click **New** to build the next criterion.
14. Click **Select**.
15. For **Attribute Class**, select **System Resource**; and for **Attribute**, select **Operating System Name and Version**. Click **OK**.
16. In **Operator**, select **is like**, and in **Value**, type **%Server%**.
17. Click **OK** twice, click **Next** twice, and then click **Close**.
18. Select the query and click **Run** on the ribbon.

The Subselected WQL Code

The statement that you created in the wizard is similar to what you see below. If you know you way around WQL, then there is no need to use the GUI to create the queries.

```
select SMS_R_System.NetbiosName from SMS_R_System where
SMS_R_System.NetbiosName not in (select SMS_R_System.NetbiosName
from  SMS_R_System inner join SMS_G_System_ADD_REMOVE_PROGRAMS_64
on SMS_G_System_ADD_REMOVE_PROGRAMS_64.ResourceID =
SMS_R_System.ResourceId where
SMS_G_System_ADD_REMOVE_PROGRAMS_64.DisplayName = "Microsoft SQL
Server 2008 R2 (64-bit)") and
SMS_R_System.OperatingSystemNameandVersion like "%Server%"
```

Create a Query Using Functions()

The third query you create for use in ViaMonstra uses one of the famous Date() functions that has existed in SQL since the dawn of time. In this section, you create a query that returns all workstations that haven't had their hardware inventories reported for seven days.

1. Still in the **Monitoring** workspace, select **Queries** and click **Create Query** on the ribbon.
2. Name the query **Computers with no HW inventory for 7 days** and click **Edit Query Statement**.
3. In the **General** tab, add these display attributes:
    a. System Resource: **NETBIOS Name**
    b. Workstation Status: **Last Hardware Scan (Client Local Time)**
    c. Select the **Omit duplicate rows (select distinct)** check box.
4. Select the **Criteria** tab and click **New** to build the next criterion.
5. Click **Select**.
6. For **Attribute Class**, select **System Resource**; and for **Attribute**, select **Operating System Name and Version**. Click **OK**.

7. In **Operator**, select **is like**, and in **Value**, type **%Workstations%**.
8. Click **OK** and **Show Query Language**, and then type (at the end of the statement)

   and (DateDiff(day, SMS_G_System_WORKSTATION_STATUS .LastHardwareScan, GetDate()) > 7)
9. Save the query and run the query to view the result.

Working with Reports

Reporting is a huge part of working with ConfigMgr, which is why you need to have some basic knowledge of SQL Reporting Services. All data that is gathered in the SQL Server database is shown in either a canned report or a custom report that you create. ViaMonstra has a few requirements for reporting, such as being able to automatically mail some reports on a monthly basis, brand the report with company data, add chart objects, and finally create some custom reports.

Changing the Logo on All Canned Reports

When you enable a SQL Reporting Services point, ConfigMgr automatically imports the reports from **D:\Program Files\SMS_SRSRP\reports and** applies the style and logos to all the reports. You can manually start the process by modifying a registry key as described in the following steps. Before you go through the steps, ensure that you have a custom logo called Report_Header_Right.png.

1. On **CM01**, open the **D:\Program Files\SMS_SRSRP\style** folder.
2. Make a backup of the existing **Report_Header_Right.png** file and copy your custom logo to the **Style** folder.
3. Open the registry by clicking the **Start** menu, selecting **Run**, and entering **Regedit**.
4. Navigate to **HKLM\SOFTWARE\Microsoft\SMS\SRSRP**.
5. Right-click **SRSInitializeState**, click **Edit**, and change the value to from 1 to **0**.

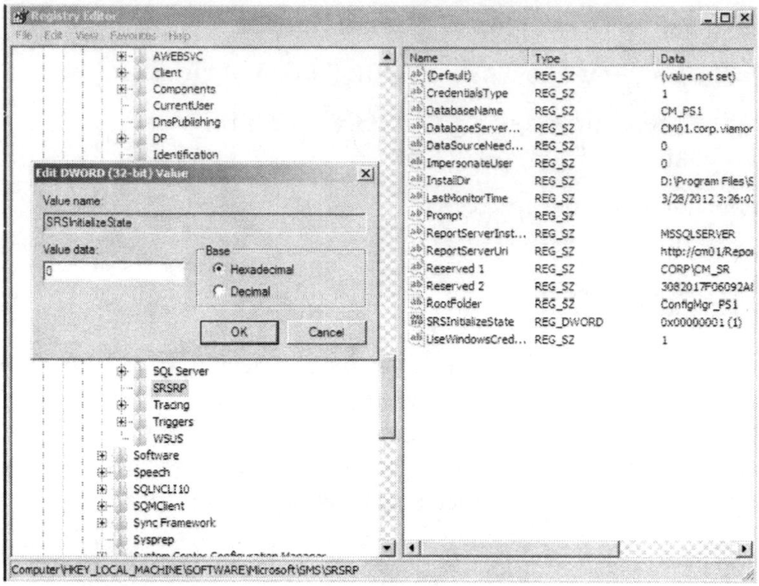

Changing the logo on all reports.

6. Click **OK** and monitor the activity in the **srsrp.log** file on the site server.
7. Wait a few minutes and open any of the canned reports. You should be able to see the new default logo.
8. Open **Internet Explorer** and go to the following URL: **http://CM01/Reports**.
9. In the **Content** tab, click **ConfigMgr_PS1** to view available reports.
10. Click **Administrative Security** and run the **Administration Activity Log** report.
11. Select **CORP\Administrators**. Notice the logo in the canned report. (Depending on your screen resolution, you may need to scroll to the right in the report to see it.)
12. Close Internet Explorer.

Creating an Email Subscription

When working with subscriptions, you have two options: creating a file-based subscription which stores the report in a shared folder, or creating an email subscription that renders the report and stores it as an attachment to the email. In order to create an email–based subscription, you need to have a working mail server and also configure SQL Reporting Services to support emailed subscriptions. ViaMonstra has a Microsoft Exchange 2010 server. Installing the server is outside the scope of this book.

1. From the **Start** menu, select **All Programs**, **Microsoft SQL Server 2008 R2**, **Configuration Tools**, and start **SQL Reporting Services Configuration Manager**.

2. In the left pane, click **E-mail Settings**. Configure **CM_SR@CORP.local** as the sender address and **EX01.CORP.Viamonstra.com** as the SMTP server. Then click **Apply**.

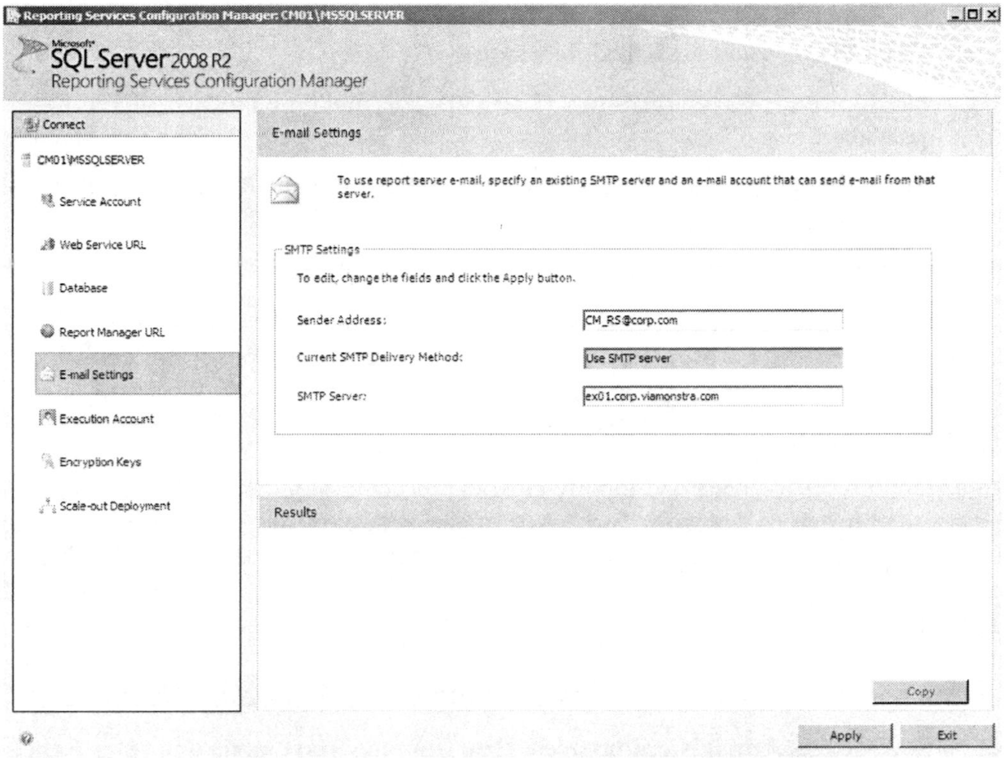

Configuring email support in SQL Server Reporting Services.

3. Click **Exit** to close the reporting configuration tool.

4. Open **Internet Explorer** and connect to **http://CM01/Reports**.

5. Select **ConfigMgr_PS1**, and open the **Client Status** category.

6. Move the mouse over the **Client Status Summary** report until you see a drop-down menu. In the drop-down menu, select **Manage**.

7. In the left pane, click **Subscriptions**.

Note: You also can create subscriptions in the ConfigMgr console.

8. Click **New Subscription**. You can choose between E-mail and Windows File share. Select **E-mail** and configure these settings:

    a. To: **administrator@corp.com**

    b. Render Format: Click the drop-down box, make a note of the different supported formats, and select the **MHTLM** format.

   c. Comment: **Latest client status report**
   d. Click **Select Schedule** and create a weekly new schedule of **every Monday at 6:00**.
   e. Click **OK** to close the Schedule window.
   f. Configure the **Credentials** to **CORP\CM_SR**, and type **Password01** as the password.
   g. Select **All Desktops and Servers** as the collection and **All Configuration Manager Client** versions.

9. Click **OK** to close the New Subscription window.

One of the benefits of using the web interface to create the schedule is the ability to see whether something went wrong during the process. That's not possible from the ConfigMgr console.

Modifying Reports

You can use different tools to create and modify custom reports in SQL Server Reporting Services. Most use either SQL Reporting Builder or Business Intelligence Development Studio (BIDS). In the following sections, you add a custom logo, modify the layout, and add a chart object to an existing report. First you configure ConfigMgr to launch SQL Reporting Builder 3.0 instead of Reporting Builder 2.0.

Configure Configuration Manager 2012 to Launch SQL Reporting Builder 3.0

1. Log on to **CM01** as **Administrator**; select **Run** from the **Start** menu and enter **Regedit** to open the registry.
2. Navigate to **HKLM\SOFTWARE\WoW6432Node\Microsoft\ConfigMgr10 \AdminUI\Reporting**.
3. Edit the **ReportBuilderApplicationManifestName** string from ReportBuilder_2_0_0_0.application to **ReportBuilder_3_0_0_0.application** and click **OK**.

Modify an Existing Report

1. Log on to **CM01** as **Administrator**, and open the **ConfigMgr console** as **Administrator**.
2. Navigate to the **Monitoring** workspace, and select **Reporting**, **Reports** and then the folder **Operating Systems**.
3. Select **Count operating system versions** and click **Edit** on the ribbon. This launches SQL Reporting Builder 3.0. After you select **Run** (only the first time), it will open the report in edit mode.

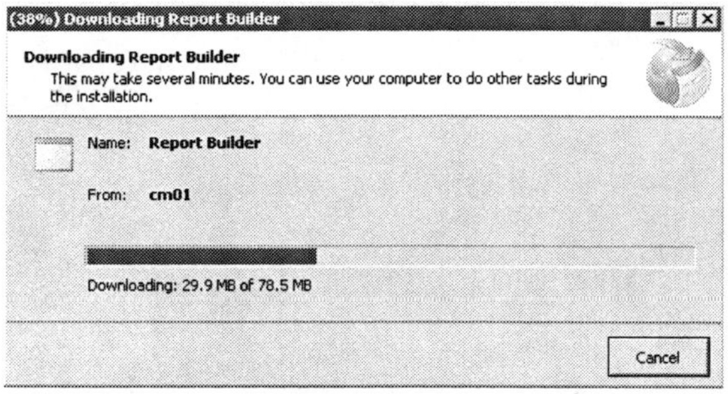

SQL Reporting Builder 3.0 is being installed on the server.

4. Delete the default heading and the expressions in the header.
5. Click **Insert** on the ribbon. Click **Text Box** and add a new heading called **Count of Operating Systems in ViaMonstra**.
6. Click **Insert** on the ribbon, and select **Chart**, **Insert Chart**.
7. Insert the chart under the expressions.
8. Select **Shape** and a **3D pie**.

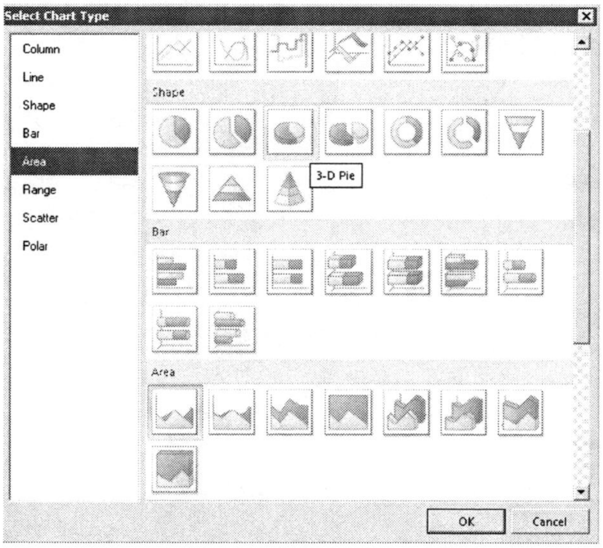

Selecting the 3-D Pie chart.

9. Click **OK**.
10. From **Datasets**, drag and drop **C0** to the **Series Group**.
11. From **Datasets**, drag and drop **Count** to the **Values group**.

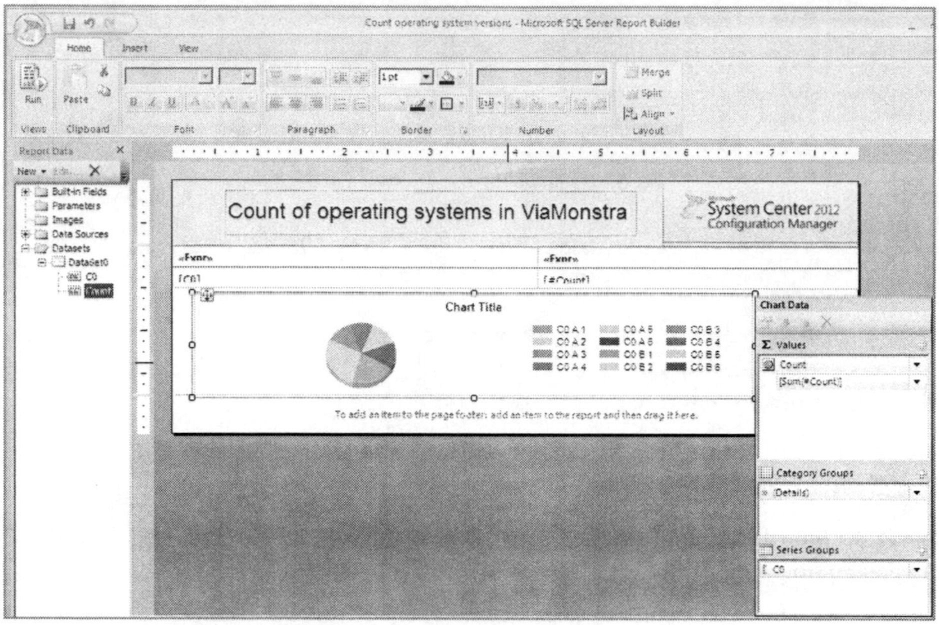

Adding a chart to an existing report.

12. Right-click the pie and select **Show Data Labels**.
13. Select and delete the **Chart Title**.
14. Right-click the lower left footer and select **Insert Textbox.**
15. Right-click the text box and select **Expression**.
16. Type **"Page " &**, and select the built-in field **[PageNumber]**; then type **& " of " &**, and select the built-in field **[TotalPages]**.

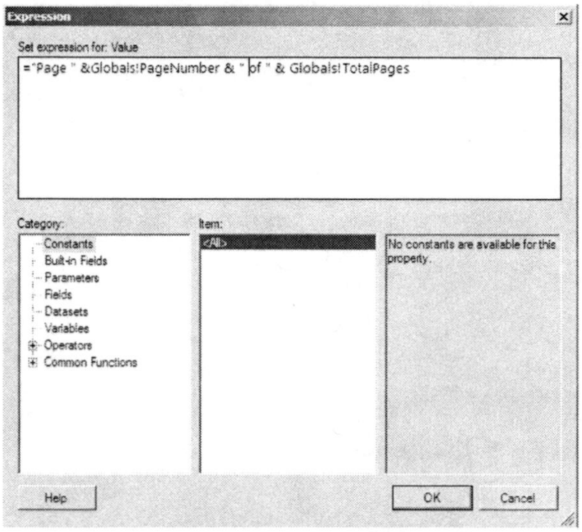

Creating an expression.

17. Click **OK** to close the expression, and then click **Run** on the ribbon.
18. Select the **Reporting Builder** logo in the upper left corner and click **Exit Report Builder**.
19. Save the changes and close SQL Report Builder.

Create a Custom Report

You can use SQL Reporting Builder or BIDS to create custom reports. Usually I prefer BIDS because it gives me a few more choices, like a full development environment. Management wants to see a report with fully managed devices and inventory managed devices. To solve the challenge, you must create a custom report based on the registry information gathered previously in this chapter.

1. Start **SQL Server Business Intelligence Development Studio** as **Administrator** from **Start**, **All Programs, Microsoft SQL Server 2008 R2.**
2. Select **File, New, Project.**
3. Select **Report Server Project Wizard**, name the project **ViaMonstra reports**, and click **OK**.
4. In the **Report Wizard**, click **Next.**
5. You need to add a data source to the project. A data source is the connection to the data along with the needed credentials.
    a. In **Name**, type **CM2012** and click **Edit**. Use the following settings:
        i. Server name: **CM01**
        ii. Database: Click the drop-down box and select **CM_PS1**.
        iii. Click **OK** to return to the Report Wizard.
    b. Select **Make this a share data source** and click **Next.**

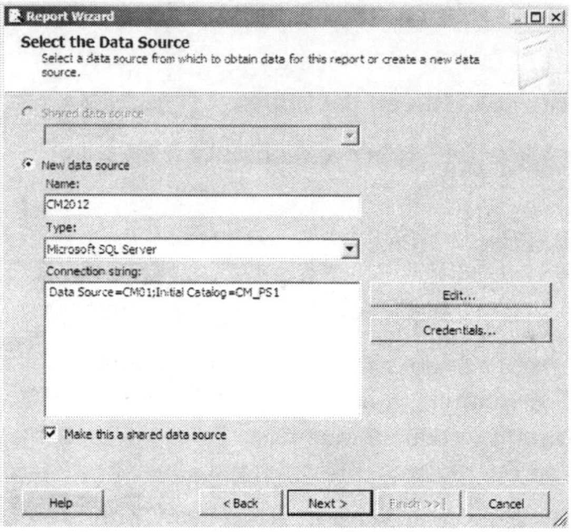

Creating a shared data source.

6. Click **Query Builder** to create the query.
7. In the **Query Designer**, click **Add Table** on the ribbon and select **Views**.
8. Select **V_GS_Viamonstra, V_R_System** (pressing **Ctrl** to select multiple items) and click **Add**.
9. From **V_R_System**, drag and drop **ResourceID** on to **ResourceID** in the **V_GS_Viamonstra** view. This creates an Inner Join between the two views.
10. From **V_GS_Viamonstra**, select **ComputerType()**, and from **V_R_System**, select **Netbios_Name()**.
11. Click **Use Group by** on the ribbon.
12. From **V_GS_Viamonstra**, drag another instance of **ComputerType()** to the **Criteria** pane (the second pane from the top that looks like Excel ☺).
13. In **Alias**, type **Total** and then select **Count** in the **Group by** drop-down list.
14. Click **Run** on the ribbon.

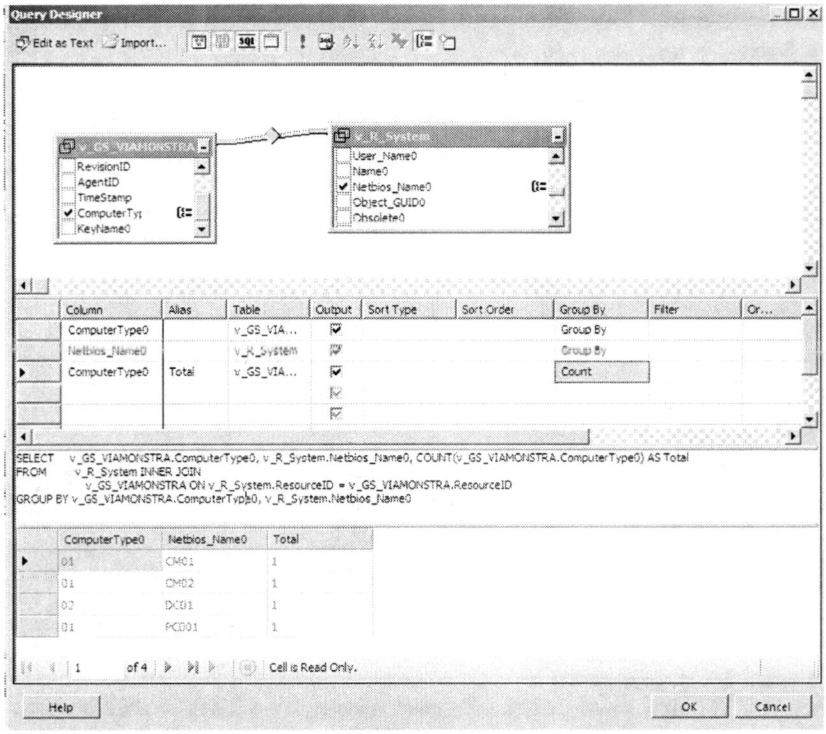

Creating a SQL statement in the Query Designer.

15. Click **OK** and return to the Report Wizard.
16. Click **Next**.
17. On the **Select Report Type** page, ensure that **Tabular** is selected and click **Next**.
18. On the **Design the Table** page, move **ComputerType()** to **Group**, move Netbios_Name(), Total() to Details(), and click **Next**.
19. On **Choose the Table Layout** page, use the following settings and click **Next**:
    a. Ensure that **Stepped** is selected.
    b. Select **Include subtotals**.
    c. Select **Enable drilldown**.
20. Select any style and click **Next**.

21. On the **Choose the Deployment Location** page, type **ViaMonstra** in **Deployment folder** text box, and click **Next**.

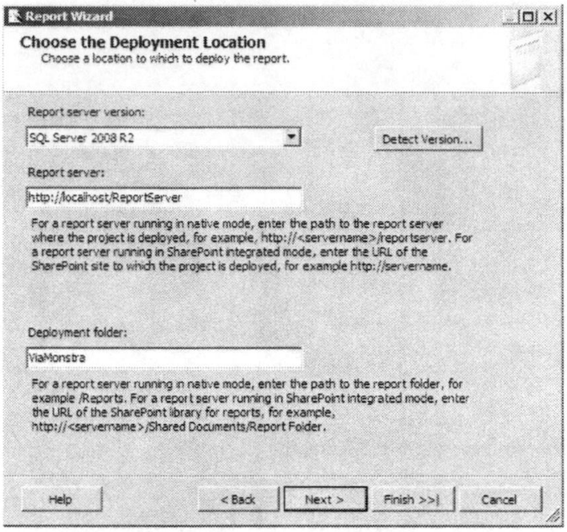

Specifying the report folder.

22. On the **Completing the Wizard** page, for the **Report name**, type **Total Fully Managed and Inventory Managed Clients**.

23. Click **Finish**.

24. From the **Report** menu, select **Add Report Header** and drag the report title to the **Report** header. Notice that the option to select a report header depends on the report style you selected in step 20.

25. Right-click the **CM2012.rds** shared date source in the **Solution Explorer** and click **Deploy**.

26. Right-click the **Total Fully Managed and Inventory Managed Clients** shared report in the **Solution Explorer** and click **Deploy**.

27. Close BIDS, save the project, and open **Internet Explorer**. Go to **http://cm01/reports**. Notice the new ViaMonstra folder, which contains the newly deployed report.

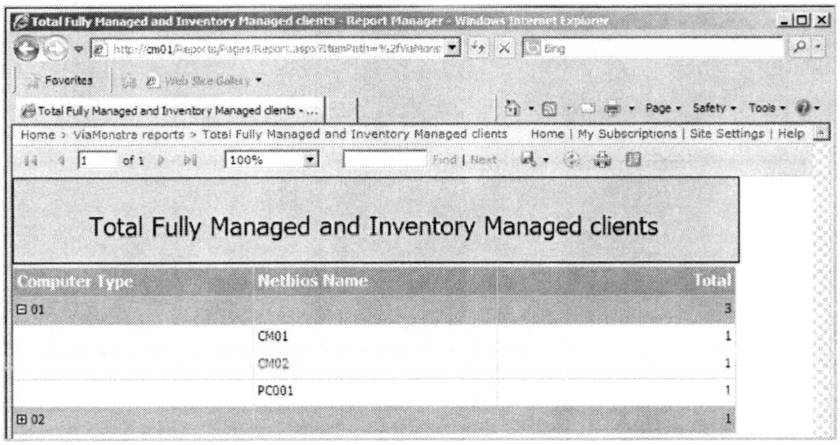

The custom report.

Useful Log Files

You can use the log files in the following table to track inventory and reporting activity.

Log File	Description	Location
InventoryAgent.log	Records activity about inventory and heartbeat discovery.	Server default
FileSystemfile.log	Records activity about software inventory. This log files is especially useful when you want to track which folders and partitions are not part of the software inventory scanning.	Client default
MP_hinv.log	Converts inventory data from XML to MIF clients and copies them to the site server.	Management point
Dataldr.log	Records activity about adding inventory and discovery data to the database (among other things).	Server default
mtrmgr.log	Records activity about processing software metering rules.	Client default
SWMTRReportGen.log	Records activity about generating software metering reports and uploading them to the management point.	Client default
Srsrp.log	Records activity involving report copies, logos, styles, and applying security.	Server default

Chapter 7 Application Deployment

Like many other companies, ViaMonstra needs to deliver applications to end users. In this chapter, you learn about applications and packages, as well as the deployment process and how to uninstall applications. Working with applications is not just about creating an application and a deployment. You need to have a strategy for how the applications should be made available for the users. Some applications are suitable for device targeting while others are for user targeting. ViaMonstra is very user centric and has a requirement to publish applications to users in a web portal and let them decide when the applications should be installed. Being user centric lowers the burden on your helpdesk due to fewer end-user calls and also assists ViaMonstra in becoming a more agile company.

Content Management Objects

Before going into detail about how you create and deploy applications, I want to take a moment to define processes, describe packages and applications, and ensure the content deployment infrastructure is configured correctly.

Distribution Points

A distribution point is the site system role where all content—packages, applications, software updates, drivers, and images—are stored and downloaded by the client. You can install a distribution point on a server operating system or a client operating system. ViaMonstra has decided to install all distribution points on Windows 2008 R2 servers. By doing that, you will have full support for local PXE services, which is a business requirement. A client OS does not have support for PXE. Besides that a client OS can service all other content.

Create a New Distribution Point

In all remote locations except Liverpool, you will install a local distribution point. The distribution points will be configured to support local clients.

1. Log on to **CM02** as **Administrator**. Open **Server Manager**, **Configuration**, **Local Users and Groups**, **Groups**.
2. Right-click the **Administrators** group and select **Add to Group**.
3. Click **Add**, select **Object Types**, **Computers**, and then click **OK**.
4. Type **CM01** and click **OK** twice to add the primary site server computer account to the local Administrators group.
5. Reboot **CM02**, and do not continue until it is fully restarted
6. Log on to the **CM01** primary site server as **Administrator** and start the **ConfigMgr console**.

7. Navigate to the **Administration** workspace, and select **Site Configuration**, **Servers and Site System Roles**.
8. In the **Home** tab, click **Create Site System Server** on the ribbon.
9. Click **Browse**, type **CM02**, and click **OK**.
10. In **Site code**, select **PS1 - ViaMonstra HQ** and click **Next**.
11. On the **System Role Select** page, select **Distribution Point** and click **Next**.
12. On the **Distribution Point** page, enable **Install and configure IIS if required by Configuration Manager** and click **Next**.

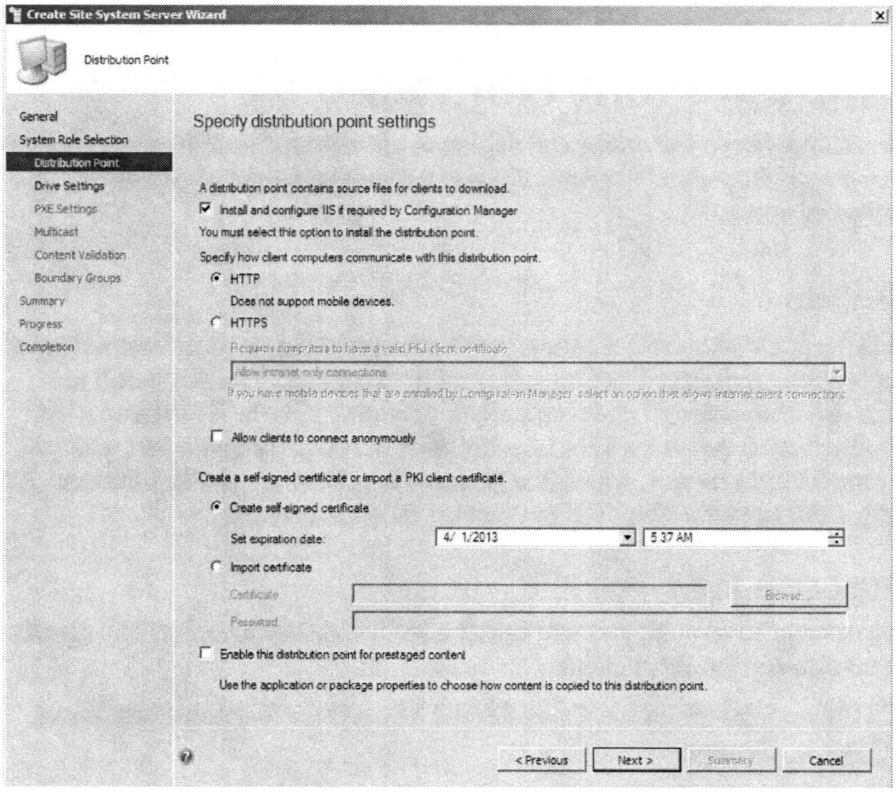

Creating a remote distribution point.

13. On the **Drive Settings** page, configure these settings and click **Next**:
    a. Drive space reserve (MB): **1024**
    b. Primary content library location: **D:**
    c. Secondary content library location: **Automatic**
    d. Primary package share location: **D:**

   e. Secondary package share location: **Automatic**

14. On the **PXE Settings** page, leave everything unselected and click **Next**.
15. On the **Multicast** page, leave everything unselected and click **Next**.
16. On the **Content Validation** page, enable **Validate content on a schedule**. Click **Schedule, Custom interval** and configure a daily schedule starting at 04:00 AM. Click **OK** to close the **Custom Schedule** dialog box and click **Next**.
17. On the **Boundary Groups** page, deselect **Allow fallback source location for content** and click **Next**.
18. On the **Summary** page, read the summary and click **Next** to start the installation.
19. Click **Close**.

Monitor the Installation of the Remote Distribution Point

You can monitor the installation and configuration process three different ways:

- Log on to **CM02**, open **Windows Explorer**, and monitor the process:
  a. Open **D:** in Windows Explorer.
  b. Navigate to **SCCMContentLib**. After a while you should see three subfolders. Notice that the subfolders are created when the first content is deployed to the distribution point. It can easily take a few minutes.
     - **Datalib.** Contains all metadata for the library.
     - **FileLib.** Single Instance Storage, contains all the files.
     - **PkgLib.** Contains information about each of the packages deployed to the distribution point.
  c. Navigate to **D:\SMS_DP$**. This folder and its subfolders contain the needed binaries and log files; and in the Tools folder, you'll find the ExtractContent.exe file. This file is used to extract compressed files that you have chosen to precache on the remote distribution point.
  d. From the **Start** menu, select **All Programs, Accessories, System Tools, Task Scheduler**. Click **Task Scheduler Library, Microsoft, Configuration Manager**. Select **Content validation** and the **Actions** tab. Notice the program **\\CM02\sms_dp$\sms\bin\smsdpmon.exe**. This is the scheduled content validation task that you enabled in the wizard. Again, it can take a few minutes before the scheduled task is created.
  e. Open **Server Manager**, select **Roles** and notice that the IIS role is installed.

- Log on to **CM01**, open the **ConfigMgr console**, and navigate to the **Monitoring** workspace:
  a. Select **Distribution Status, Distribution Point Configuration Status**.
  b. Select **CM02** and click the **Details** tab. It will take some minutes until all the steps are finalized and configured correctly.

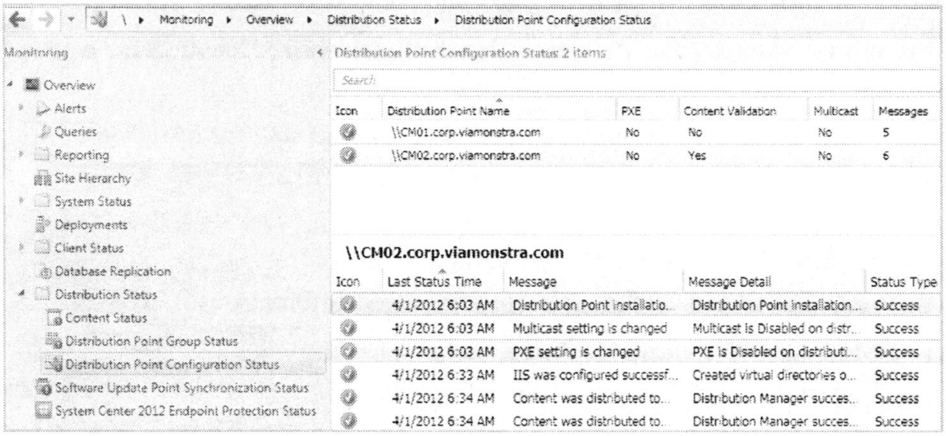

Monitoring the remote distribution point.

- The third way to monitor the process is by reading the **distrmgr.log** file on the site server. Among other things, the log file gives you information about how IIS was installed on the remote server.

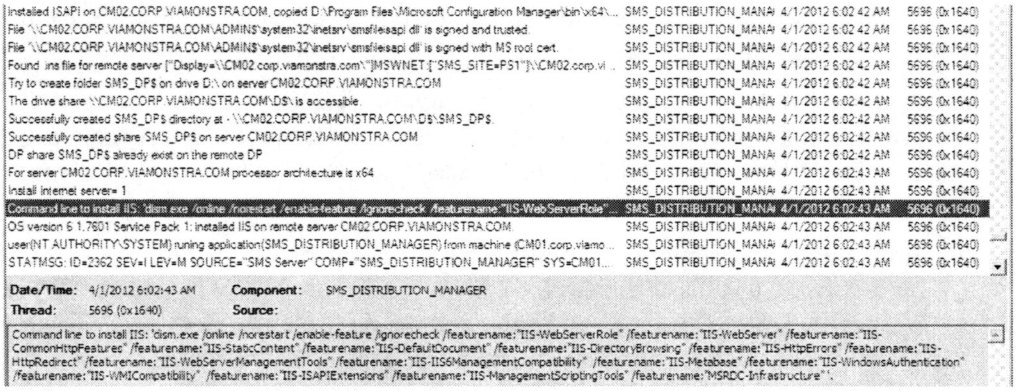

Monitoring the remote distribution point in the distmgr.log file.

Control Bandwidth on Remote Distribution Points

Prestaging content and controlling bandwidth has long been one of the reasons why you would select a secondary site in ConfigMgr 2007 and SMS 2X. This has changed in ConfigMgr 2012 where you can now control bandwidth and hours of operations. ViaMonstra has decided to control all traffic going from the primary site server to all remote site systems, but not to control the upward floating traffic.

1. Navigate to the **Administration** workspace, and select **Distribution Points**.
2. Select **CM02** and click **Properties** on the ribbon.
3. Select the **Schedule** tab and configure daily traffic between **06:00 AM – 08:00 PM** to allow only medium and high priority.
4. Select the **Rates Limits** tab and configure the limit to be **50%** for business hours (06:00 AM – 08:00 PM) and **75%** during non-business hours. (To set the limits, you select the **Limited to specified maximum transfer rates by hour** option, select the blocks on the timeline you want to modify, and then type the percentage number in the **Limit available bandwidth (%)** field.)

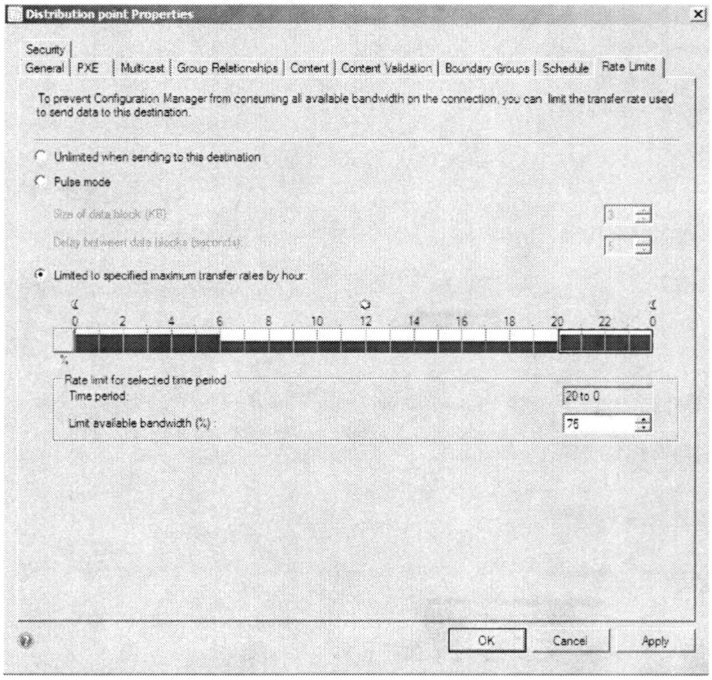

Controlling bandwidth on a remote distribution point.

5. Click **OK** to close the Distribution point Properties dialog box.

Distribution Point Groups

A distribution point group allows you to manage the same content on multiple distribution points. When you distribute content to a group, all members of that group automatically receive the content. If you add a distribution point to an existing group, that distribution point automatically receives the same content as the rest of the group members. A distribution point can be a member of multiple groups.

1. Log on to **CM01** and open the **ConfigMgr console**.
2. Navigate to the **Administration** workspace and select **Distribution Point Groups**.
3. Click **Create Group** on the ribbon.
4. In **Name**, type **All Content**.
5. Select the **Members** tab, click **Add**, select **CM01** and **CM02**, and click **OK**.

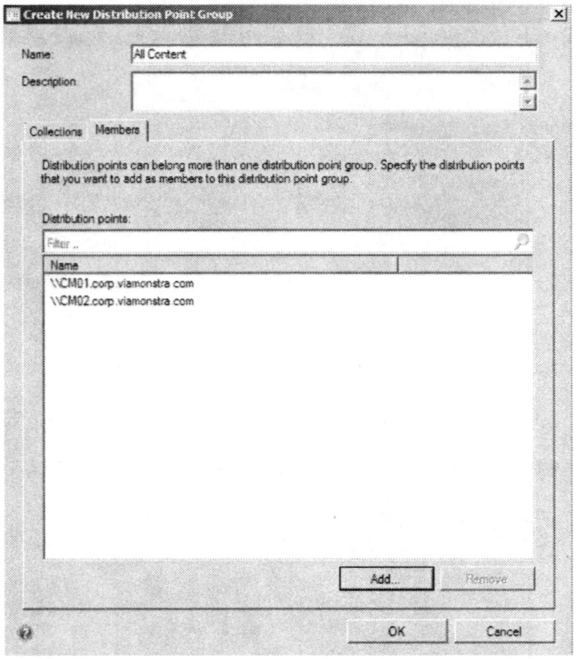

Creating the distribution point group.

6. Click OK.

> **Real World Note:** You should always create a distribution point group even if you have a small environment with just a single distribution point. Chances are that you will add a new distribution point in the future. With a distribution point group, it will be easy for you to add the same content to the new distribution point.

Content Boundary Groups

Boundary groups control assignment and content location. In ViaMonstra, the strategy is to allow all clients to fall back to the HQ for content location, but they should always use any local distribution point first. With this strategy, you have to create a unique content lookup boundary group for each remote distribution point.

Create Content Location Boundary Groups

1. Log on to **CM01** and open the **ConfigMgr console**.
2. Navigate to the **Administration** workspace, and select **Hierarchy Configuration, Boundary Groups**.
3. Click **Create Boundary Group** on the ribbon, type **CL HQ** as the name, and click **Add**.
4. Select the IP range **192.168.1.1 - 192.168.1.254** and click **OK**.
5. Select the **References** tab. In **Content location**, click **Add** and select **CM01**.
6. Click **OK**.
7. Click **Create Boundary Group** on the ribbon, type **CL Orlando** as the name, and click **Add**.
8. Select the IP range **192.168.2.1 - 192.168.2.254** and click **OK**.
9. Select the **References** tab. In **Content location**, click **Add** and select **CM02**.
10. Click **OK**.

Packages

If you are familiar with previous versions of the ConfigMgr, you most likely already have knowledge about packages. Although packages haven't changed in recent versions of ConfigMgr, there are nevertheless still many scenarios where you can benefit from creating a package instead of an application.

When to Use a Package

I often use packages for trivial tasks like running a maintenance script, copying files or other tasks that are machine based. Later in this book, you will learn how to create a package to copy the needed System Center Updates Publisher certificates to all computers. In previous versions of ConfigMgr, it also was very common to create packages to modify registry keys. That is still possible although you might find it easier to solve those challenges using the new Settings Manager feature. Other very useful examples of packages are the packages created using the MDT 2012 task sequence (toolkit, settings, and USMT packages).

Default Packages

By default, ConfigMgr ships with two packages. One is the Configuration Manager Client package, which is located in Software Library, Application Management, Packages. The second package is a Configuration Manager Client Upgrade package. That package is not exposed in the Software Library. Navigate to the Monitoring workspace, Distribution Status, Content Status, and you will be able to see both ConfigMgr client packages. The Configuration Manager Client Upgrade package is used to keep clients up-to-date on the latest version.

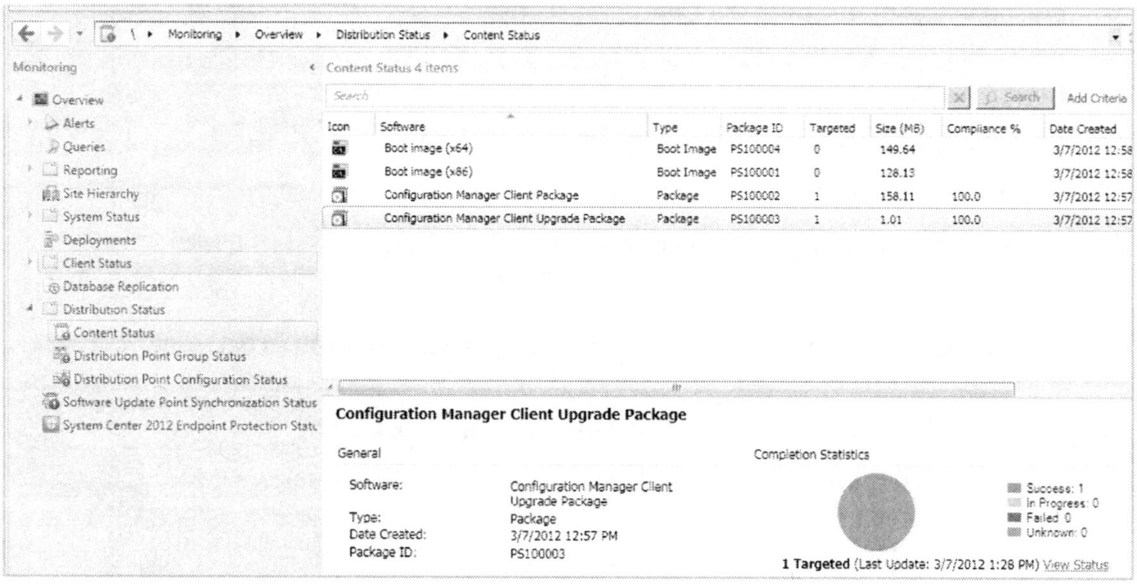

The ConfigMgr client packages.

Automate the ConfigMgr Client Upgrade Process

1. Open the **ConfigMgr console** and navigate to the **Administration** workspace.
2. Select **Site Configuration**, **Sites** and then click **Hierarchy Settings** on the ribbon.
3. Select the **Client Installation Settings** tab.
4. Select **Upgrade client automatically when new updates are available** and click **OK**.

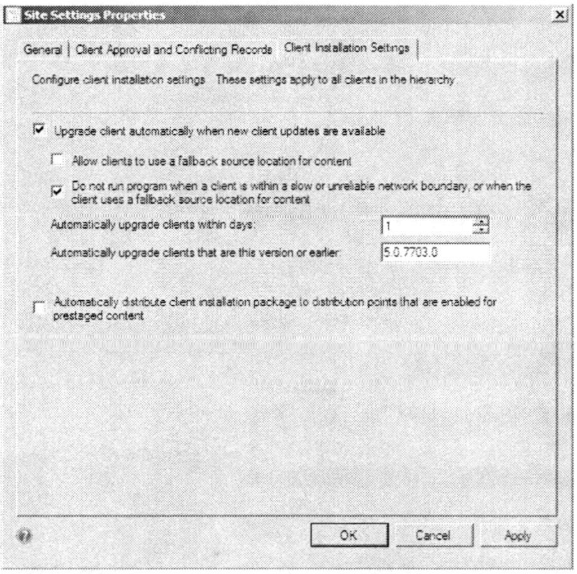

Configuring the automatic client upgrade.

5. Click **OK** to close the Site Settings Properties dialog box.

Creating and Deploying a Package

The first package that you create is a VBScript that copies CMtrace.exe to %windir%\system32 on all clients. In order to create the package, you need to place CMtrace.exe and the script in the same folder and use the folder as the source location for the software package. For these steps I assume you have downloaded the book sample files to D:\Setup on CM01.

Create the Package Source

1. Log on to **CM01**, open **Explorer**, and create the folder **CopyCMTrace** in **D:\Sources\Software**.
2. Create the folder **BusinessHours** in **D:\Sources\Software**.
3. Copy **CMtrace.exe** from D:\Setup\CM2012 \SMSSetup\Tools\ to **D:\Sources\Software\CopyCMTrace**.
4. Copy **Get-CMClientBusinesshours.ps1** and **Set-CMClientBusinessHours.ps1** from **D:\Setup\Scripts** to **D:\Sources\Software\BusinessHours**.

Create the Copy CMTrace Package

1. Open the **ConfigMgr console** and navigate to the **Software Library** workspace.
2. Select **Application Management**, **Packages**, and then select **Folder**, **Create Folder** from the ribbon.

3. Name the folder **Utilities**.
4. Expand **Packages**, right-click the **Utilities** folder, and select **Create Package**.
5. On the **Package** page, type these settings and click **Next**:
    a. Name: **VM_CopyCMTrace**
    b. Description: **Copy CMTrace to C:\Windows\System32**
    c. Manufacturer: **ViaMonstra**
    d. Version: **1.0**
    e. This packages contains source files**: Enable**
    f. Source folder: **\\CM01\Sources$\Software\CopyCMTrace**

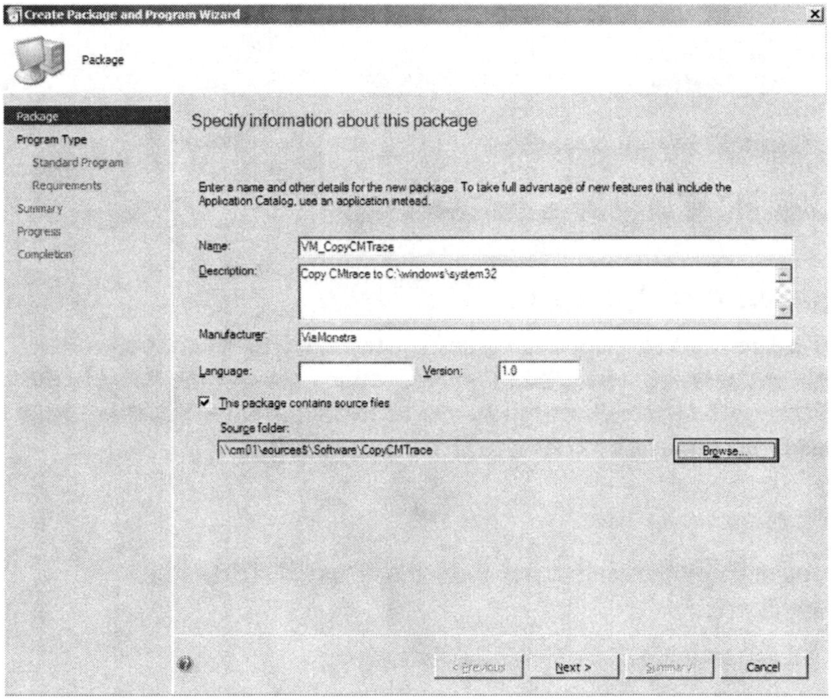

Creating a package.

6. On the **Program Type** page, ensure **Standard program** is selected and click **Next**.
7. On the **Standard Program** page, type these settings and click **Next**:
    a. Name: **CMTrace_Install**
    b. Command line: **powershell.exe -ExecutionPolicy Bypass –Command Copy-Item CMTrace.exe –Destination C:\Windows**
    c. Program can run: **Whether or not a user is logged on**

8. On the **Requirements** page, leave the default settings and click **Next**.
9. On the **Summary** page, read the summary and click **Next** to start the package creation.
10. After the package is created, click **Close** to finish.

Distribute the Package to the Distribution Point Group

1. Select the **VM_CopyCMTrace** package and click **Distribute Content** on the ribbon.
2. On the **General** page, click **Next**.
3. On the **Content Destination** page, click **Add**, **Distribution Point Group**.
4. Select the **All Content** distribution point group, and click **OK** and **Next**.
5. On the **Summary** page, read the summary and click **Next** to start the content distribution.
6. Close the wizard.

Deploy the Package

Unlike many other applications, this package is deployed as a required package to all computers with a ConfigMgr agent installed. Usually a software deployment requires you to create a collection, but this time you use the default **All Desktop and Server Clients** collection.

1. Select the **VM_CopyCMTrace** package and click **Deploy** on the ribbon.
2. On the **General** page, click **Browse**, select **All Desktop and Server Clients** collection, and click **Next**.
3. On the **Content** page, verify that the content is distributed to all distribution points and click **Next**.
4. On the **Deployment Settings** page, verify that **Purpose** is **Required** and click **Next**.
5. On the **Scheduling** page, click **New** and click **Assign immediately after this event**. Verify that **As soon as possible** is selected for the event, and click **OK** and **Next**.

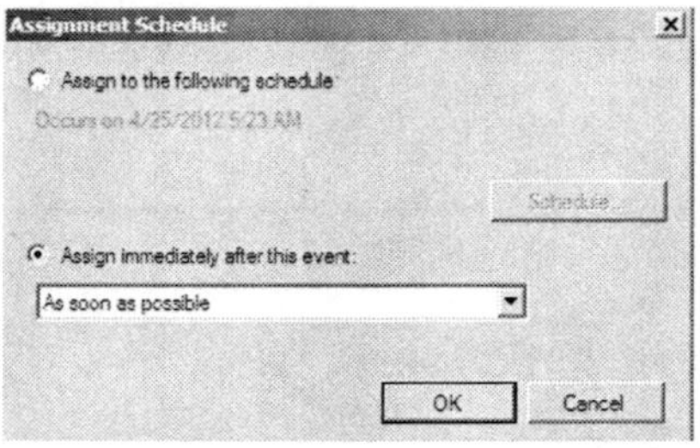

Configuring a deployment to run as soon as possible.

6. On the **User Experience** page, keep the default settings and click **Next**.

7. On the **Distribution Points** page, enable **Allow clients to use a fallback source location for content** and click **Next**.
8. On the **Summary** page, read the summary and click **Next** to start the deployment.
9. Close the wizard.

Create the Configure Business Hours Package

1. In the **Software Library** workspace, select **Application Management**, **Packages**.
2. Right-click the **Utilities** folder and select **Create Package**.
3. On the **Package** page, use these settings and click **Next**:
    a. Name: **Configure Business Hours**
    b. Description: **Define local client business hours**
    c. Manufacturer: **ViaMonstra**
    d. Version: **1.0**
    e. This packages contains source files**: Enable**
    f. Source folder: **\\CM01\Sources$\Software\BusinessHours**
4. On the **Program Type** page, ensure **Standard program** is selected and click **Next**.
5. On the **Standard Program** page, use these settings and click **Next**:
    a. Name: **Default Client Business Hours**
    b. Command line: **powershell.exe -ExecutionPolicy Bypass -File .\Set-CMClientBusinessHours.ps1 -StartTime 08 -EndTime 17 -WorkingDays 62**
    c. Program can run: **Whether or not a user is logged on**
6. On the **Requirements** page, leave the default settings and click **Next**.
7. On the **Summary** page, read the summary and click **Next** to start the package creation.
8. After the package is created, click **Close** to finish.

Note: The values used to calculate the weekdays in the PowerShell script are:

1 Sunday, 2 Monday, 4 Tuesday, 8 Wednesday, 16 Thursday, 32 Friday, 64 Saturday

If you want to configure business hours for Friday only, you should specify -WorkingDays 32. If you want to specify Friday and Monday, it is 32 + 2 like this: -WorkingDays 34.

Distribute the Business Hours Package to the Distribution Point Group

1. Select the **Configure Business Hours** package and click **Distribute Content** on the ribbon.
2. On the **General** page, click **Next**.
3. On the **Content Destination** page, click **Add**, **Distribution Point Group**.
4. Select the **All Content** distribution point group, and click **OK** and **Next**.
5. On the **Summary** page, read the summary and click **Next** to start the content distribution.
6. Close the wizard.

Deploy the Business Hours Package

You deploy this package to all workstations. You can create additional programs with other business hour values and deploy those programs to other collections.

1. Select the **Configure Business Hours** package and click **Deploy** on the ribbon.
2. On the **General** page, click **Browse**; then, in the **ViaMonstra** folder, select the **VM All Workstations** collection, and click **Next**.
3. On the **Content** page, verify that the content is distributed to all distribution points and click **Next**.
4. On the **Deployment Settings** page, verify that Purpose is **Required** and click **Next**.
5. On the **Scheduling** page, click **New** and click **Assign immediately after this event**. Verify that **As soon as possible** is selected for the event, and click **OK** and **Next**.
6. On the **User Experience** page, keep the default settings and click **Next**.
7. On the **Distribution Points** page, enable **Allow clients to use a fallback source location for content** and click **Next**.
8. On the **Summary** page, read the summary and click **Next** to start the deployment.
9. Close the wizard.

Verify the New Business Hours on the Client

1. Log on to **PC001** as **CORP\Administrator** and launch the **Software Center** from the **Start** menu.
2. Click **Options**, and notice the business hours.
3. Without closing the Software Center, open the **Control Panel**, select the **System and Security** category, and open the **Configuration Manager properties**.
4. In the **Actions** tab, select the **Machine Policy Retrieval & Evaluation Cycle** and click **Run Now**.
5. Close the Configuration Manager properties and the Control Panel.

6. Back in the Software Center, select the **Options** tab again and press **F5** to perform a refresh. If the deployment has been executed, you will see the new business hours.

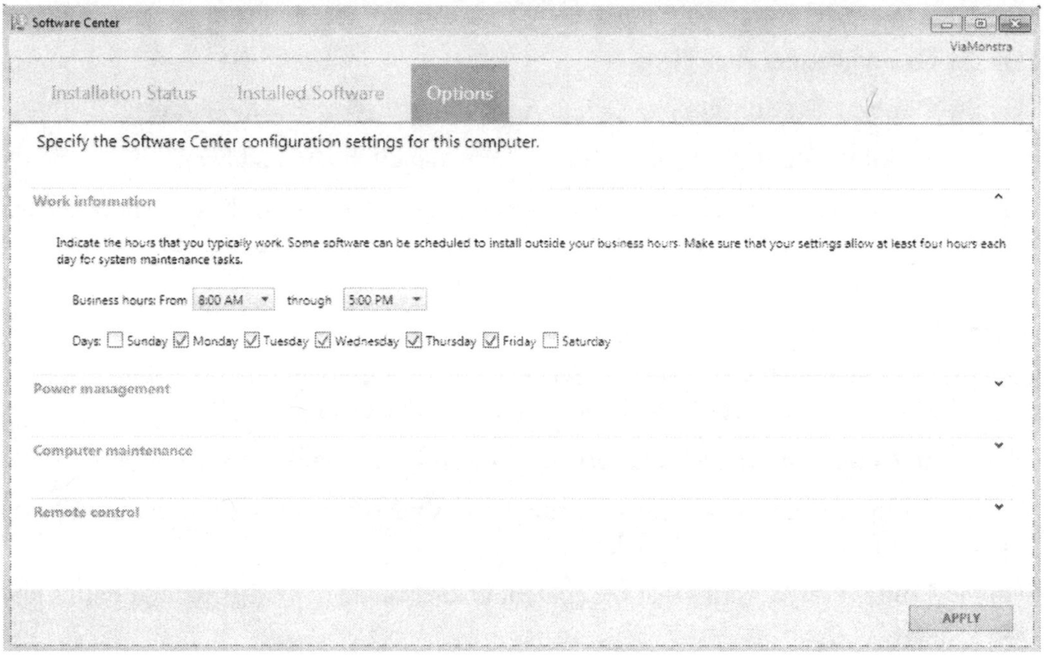

Controlling business hours with PowerShell.

Monitor the Deployment

There are several ways you can monitor the deployment.

Use the ConfigMgr Console and the Monitoring Workspace

1. Navigate to the **Monitoring** workspace and select **Deployments**.
2. Click **Run Summarization** on the ribbon and then click **Refresh**.

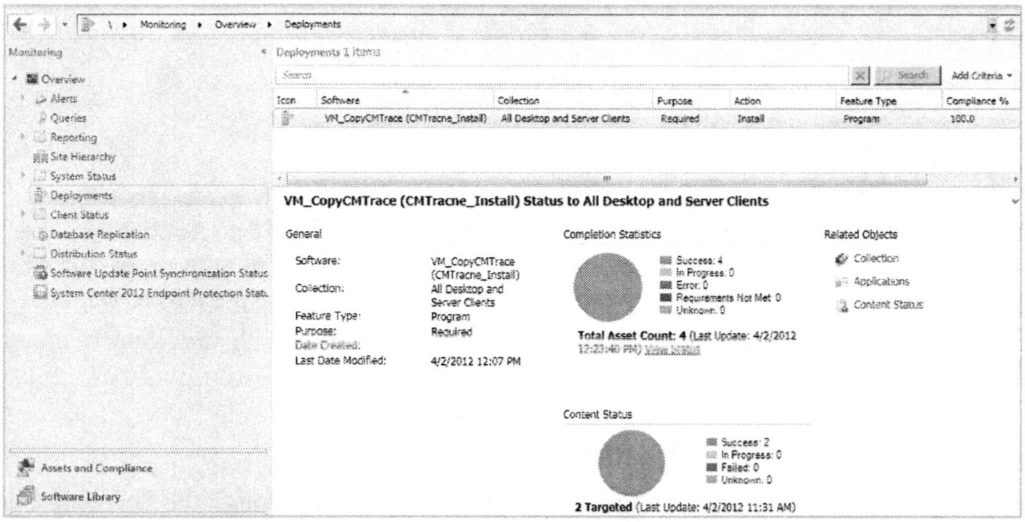

Monitoring the deployment.

Use the Reports

1. Open **Internet Explorer** and go to **http://cm01/reports**.
2. Select the **ConfigMgr_PS1** folder.
3. Select the **Software Distribution - Package and Program deployment** folder.
4. Run the report **All deployments for a specified package and program.**
5. From the **Package (program)** drop-down list, select **VM CopyCMTrace (CMTrace_Install)** and click **View Report.**
6. The report lists all deployments for that specific package or program. Click the deployment name to drill into the statistics.

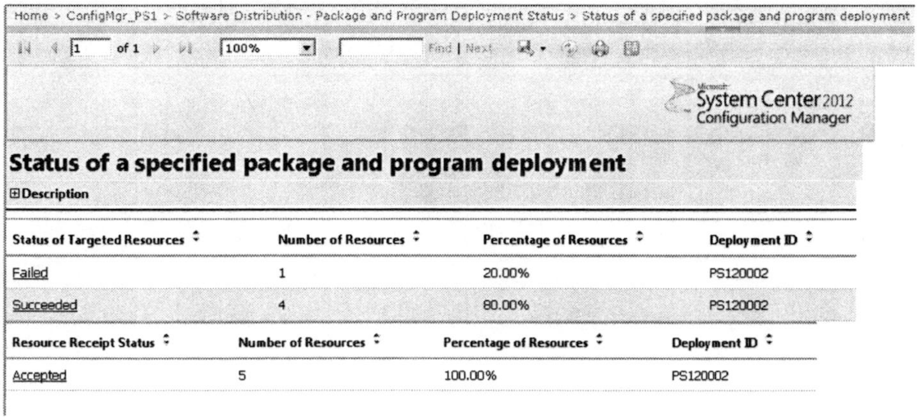

Monitoring the deployment using a standard report. Notice the failed deployment; that is Windows XP not liking PowerShell.

Applications

I often refer to applications as one of the more "sexy" objects of ConfigMgr. Applications are much more intelligent than packages and allow you as the administrator to gain more control over what happens. Applications are also much more user-centric compared to packages. With the correct requirement rules, you control if and which deployment type is installed to a device. Before creating the applications, you need to understand the basics.

How Applications Are Installed

Applications can be installed automatically without user intervention through the Software Center or from the Application Catalog website point. It's essential that you know when to use the different options. When deploying an application, the deployment can either be required or available (optional):

- A *required* deployment is a deployment that is installed based on either an event or a schedule. The logged on user might have the option to install the application prior to the scheduled deadline.
- An *available*, or optional, deployment requires user interaction and must be started by a logged on user.

Where the Application Will Be Presented	Required Deployment	Available Deployment
User targeted	Software Center	Application Catalog website point and Software Center (once installed)
Device targeted	Software Center	Software Center

The Application

To understand applications, you first need to learn the high-level overview. An application is not a MSI package, nor is it an .exe file. Instead an application represents all possible deployment types for a specific software package. For example, Adobe Reader is one application containing multiple deployment types like App-V, .msi, and .exe. All these different deployment types are all child objects to the same application, but only one of the deployment types will be installed on device. Which one depends on the requirement rules and order of the deployment types.

The following table describes the pages you'll complete when creating your application using the Create Application Wizard.

Application Tab	**Description**
Application Properties	The first information you have to worry about when creating a new application. The properties should all follow the same naming standard and that way make it easier for the administrators to work with the application in the ConfigMgr console.
Application Catalog	The end-user metadata. The values in the Application Catalog are used by end users when searching for applications or viewing additional information about the application.
References	Information about links between this application and other applications. On this page, you can see whether the application is superseded by another application and whether other applications have dependencies on this application.
Deployment Type	A list of the associated deployment types and their priorities. Keep in mind that only one of the deployment types is installed on the device. The first deployment type matching all the requirements is installed, and the remaining deployment types are not applied.
Content Locations	A list of the distribution point(s) and distribution point group(s) where the content can be located. You select each distribution point(s) or group(s) and redistribute the package, remove the package from distribution points, and validate the package. The package validation verifies that all the files used by the package are present in the content library and that all HASH values are correct.
Supersedence	Used to create a supersedence relationship between this application and the application you want to supersede.
Security	Security information for the application.

The Deployment Type

Later in this chapter, you configure the deployment types represented by your application. The following table lists and describes the tabs in the Deployment Type properties.

Deployment Type Tab	Description
General	Deployment type properties like name, technology, comments, and language.
Content	Source location and information about Microsoft Branch cache support (which allows clients to share content with other clients on the same subnet). Allowing clients to use a fallback source location for content enables them to use another distribution point as a fallback source for the package in the event that the local distribution point is unavailable. On the Content tab, you also can configure whether the client will be allowed to download the package from a slow connection. A "slow connection" is not based on a real time evaluation, but rather on a setting configured in the boundary group.
Programs	Allows you to specify the install and uninstall program.
Detection Method	Needed for every deployment type. The detection method is used by the client to determine whether that specific deployment type is already present on the device. You can create multiple detection methods like MSI product code, registry, file based, or a custom script.
User Experience	Can be used to configure whether the end user should be able to interact with the installation and whether the installation is intended for a user or device.
Requirements	Also known as *global conditions*. Requirements are evaluated in real-time before the application is downloaded and installed. You can create device, user, and custom requirement rules based on registry values, WMI queries, and much more.
Return Codes	Allows you to specify the return code that the specific deployment type returns in the event of a successful installation, restart required, or failure. I have a dream that one day all software developers start reading the same book and come to a mutual agreement on which return codes to use.

Deployment Type Tab	Description
Dependencies	List of other deployment types that this deployment type depends on. One example is that a virtual App-V application depends on the App-V client being installed on the device.
Publishing	Only available for App-V deployment types and defines the icons that are published when "installing" this deployment type. I have "installing" in quotation marks because we are not installing a virtual application like a traditional application.

The Deployment

The settings you can configure on a deployment depend on how and to whom you target the deployment. As mentioned earlier, a deployment can be targeted to a user or device collection, and it can be either available or mandatory (have a deadline for the installation). This table describes the pages you use to configure your deployment.

Deployment Tab	Description
General	Deployment information like software used, collection, and optional comments.
Content	List of the distribution point(s) and distribution point group(s) where the content is available.
Deployment Settings	Information about the deployment action, Install or Uninstall; the purpose of the deployment, Available or Required; and the setting to control whether administrator approval is required in order to install the application. If the deployment has a deadline, you also can configure ConfigMgr to send a wakeup package prior to running the deployment. This setting requires that Wake On LAN has been configured.
Scheduling	Defines the application availability time. If none is specified, the application becomes available as soon as possible. If the deployment is required, you also have the option to configure the installation deadline. When specifying the installation deadline, you have the option to configure whether the time is based on client local time or UTC.

Deployment Tab	Description
User Experience	Defines how the deployment interacts with the logged on user. If the deployment is required, you have the option to completely hide all notifications, as well as not displaying anything in the Software Center. For available deployments, you can specify the level of notifications shown, but the deployment is always visible in the Software Center. This is also the page where you can choose to ignore maintenance windows for the deployment. By ignoring maintenance windows, you allow the application to be installed outside of any defined maintenance window.
Alerts	Allows you to set alerts for your deployment. The alerts depend on the deployment purpose. For required deployments, you can specify when alerts are created (that being created in the ConfigMgr console) for failed and missing deployments. If you have OpsMgr 2012 installed, you also can place the OpsMgr 2012 client in maintenance mode and thus not generate any alerts in the OpsMgr console.

The Collections

For every application, there must be at least two collections. For your Microsoft Office 2010 application, for example, you will have these collections:

- SW_Office_2010_Pro_X64_Install
- SW_Office_2010_Pro_X64_Uninstall

The collections are query based and look for members of the corresponding Active Directory user or computer group.

The Application Catalog website point is the site system role that users will connect to when they are "shopping" for software. All user-targeted applications without a deadline will be available in the web catalog.

Create the Active Directory Groups

1. Log on to **DC01** as **Administrator** and open **Active Directory Users and Computers**.
2. Right-click the **Software Groups** OU and select **New**, **Group**.
3. Create a new security group with these settings:
    a. Group Name: **SW_Office_2010_Install**
    b. Group scope: **Domain local**
    c. Group type: **Security**

4. Create a new group in the same OU with these settings:
   a. Group Name: **SW_Office_2010_Uninstall**
   b. Group scope: **Domain local**
   c. Group type: **Security**
5. Right-click **SW_Office_2010_Install** and click **Properties.**
6. Navigate to the **Members** tab, click **Add**, and add the users **JAP**, **NEP** and **MLG** as members to the group.
7. Click **OK** and close the group properties.
8. Repeat the preceding steps and create the following groups (add the same users to the new Install groups):
   a. **SW_WinRAR_Install**
   b. **SW_WinRAR_Uninstall**
   c. **SW_7-Zip_Install**
   d. **SW_7-Zip Uninstall**

Create the Uninstall Collection(s)

1. Log on to **CM01** as **Administrator** and open the **ConfigMgr console.**
2. Select the **Assets and Compliance** workspace.
3. Select **User collections**, right-click the **Software** folder, and select **Create User Collection.**
4. Use these settings:
   a. Name: **SW_Office_2010_Uninstall**
   b. Comment: **All groups and users in this collection will automatically have Microsoft Office uninstalled.**
   c. Limiting Collection: Click **Browse** and select **All Users and User Groups.**
5. Click **Next.**
6. Enable **Use incremental updates for this collection.**
7. Click **Add Rule, Query Rule.**
8. Name the rule **Office 2010 Uninstall**, ensure **User Group Resource** is selected in the **Resource class**, and click **Edit Query Statement.**
9. Select the **Criteria** tab.
10. Click the **yellow icon** and click **Select** to create the criteria.
11. Select **User Group Resource** as the **Attribute class** and **Name** as the **Attribute.**

12. Click **OK** to return to the Criterion Properties dialog box.
13. In **Operator**, select **is equal to**, and in **Value**, type **CORP\SW_Office_2010_Uninstall**. (You also can click Value and select the group name from a list of groups.)
14. Click **OK** three times and return to the Memberships Rules page.
15. Finish the wizard.
16. Repeat the preceding steps and create a collection called **SW_WinRAR_Uninstall**. The dynamic collection query will look for all members in the **CORP\SW_WinRAR_Uninstall** security group.

Note: You will only be able to see the list of groups that have had a user resource as a member during the User discovery. If you are unable to find a group, like SW_Office_2010_Uninstall, just type the group name and resources will be added when they fall into the scope of the criteria.

Create the Install Collection

1. Select **User collections**, right-click the **Software** folder, and select **Create User Collection.**
2. Use these settings:
    a. Name: **SW_Office_2010_Install**
    b. Comment: **All groups and users in this collection will automatically get a version of Microsoft Office installed.**
    c. Limiting Collection: Click **Browse** and select **All Users and User Groups**.
3. Click **Next**.
4. Enable **Use incremental updates for this collection**.
5. Click **Add Rule**, **Query Rule**.
6. Name the rule **Office 2010 Install**, ensure **User Group Resource** is selected in the **Resource class**, and click **Edit Query Statement**.
7. Select the **Criteria** tab.
8. Click the **yellow icon** and click **Select** to create the criteria.
9. Select **User Group Resource** as the **Attribute class** and **Name** as the **Attribute**.
10. Click **OK** to return to the Criterion Properties dialog box.
11. In **Operator**, select **is equal to**, and in **Value**, type **CORP\SW_Office_2010_Install**. (You also can click Value and select the group name from a list of groups.)
12. Click **OK** three times and return to the Memberships Rules page.
13. Click **Add Rule**, **Exclude Collections**.

14. Select **Software**, **SW_ Office_2010_Uninstall**, and click **OK**.
15. Finish the wizard.
16. Repeat the preceding steps and create the following collections (add the related security group via a dynamic collection query):
    a. **SW_WinRAR_Install**
    b. **SW_7-Zip_Install**

Automate Creating Dynamic Queries to User Collections Using PowerShell

This example shows you how to automate the process of creating a dynamic query on a user collection. Again this is just a sample command, and this action is not needed for the other guides in this book. (You already created the queries in the previous guide.)

1. Open **PowerShell** as **Administrator**.
2. Navigate to the folder containing the scripts.
3. Type **. .\CM12_Function_Library.ps1** and press **Enter**.
4. Create a user collection:
    a. Type **Set-CMCollectionQueryRule -SiteServer Localhost -SiteCode PS1 -Query 'select * from SMS_R_User where SMS_R_User.UserGroupName = "CORP\\SW_7-Zip_Install "' -QueryName "7-Zip Install" -QueryType User -CollectionName "SW 7-Zip Install"**.
    b. Press **Enter**.

Work with Applications

In ViaMonstra, you are supporting both the x32 and x64 editions of Microsoft Office. The installed edition is based on the operating system. All Windows 7 x64 computers must have the x64 edition of Microsoft Office installed. In order to control the process, configure Microsoft Office as explained in Appendix D.

The steps in this section guide you through the creation of one application with two deployment types. The wizard takes you through some basic steps before you are asked to create the first deployment type.

Create the Microsoft Office 2010 Application

In these steps, I assume you have created the **D:\Sources\Software\MS_Office_2010_Pro_X86** and **D:\Sources\Software\MS_Office_2010_Pro_X64** administrative setups of Office 2010 described in Appendix D.

1. Log on to **CM01** as **Administrator** and open the **ConfigMgr console**.
2. In the **Software Library** workspace, select **Application Management**, **Applications**.

3. Right-click **Applications** and select **Folder**, **Create Folder**; then type **Required User** as the folder name.
4. Expand **Applications**, select the **Required User** folder, and click **Create Application** on the ribbon.
5. On the **General** page, select **Manually specify the application information** and click **Next**.
6. On the (second) **General** page, specify these application properties and click **Next**:
    a. Name: **Microsoft Office 2010**
    b. Administrator comments: **All Microsoft Office 2010 editions**
    c. Manufacturer: **Microsoft**
    d. Software Version: **2010**
    e. Optional reference: **POmsOff2010** (This is a custom attribute that you can use for whatever purpose. In ViaMonstra, I have decided to type the internal PO number for the software.)
    f. Administrative Categories: Click **Select**, **Create**; then type **Core Office application** and click **OK**.
    g. Enable **Allow this application to be installed from the Install Application task sequence instead of deploying it manually**.

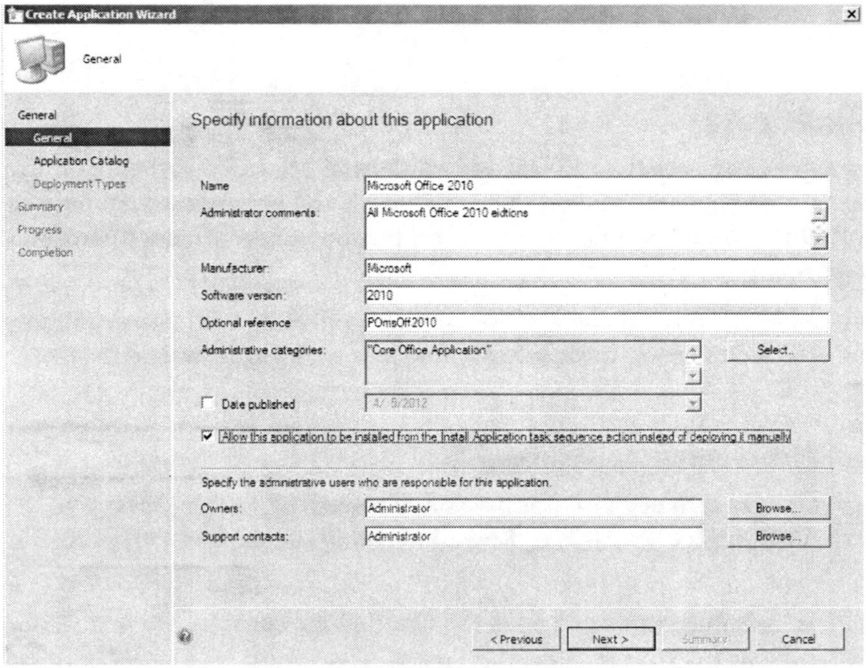

Specifying the application properties.

7. On the **Application Catalog** page, fill out these metadata and click **Next**:

   a. User categories: Click **Edit, Create**; then type **Office Applications** and click **OK** twice.

   b. User documentation: **http://office.microsoft.com/en-us/office-video-FX102493438.aspx** (This is a link to the official Microsoft Office tutorial videos.)

   c. Localized description: **Microsoft Office 2010 is our standard Office platform with tools like Word, Excel, OneNote, PowerPoint.**

   d. Keywords: **Office, Word, Excel, OneNote, PowerPoint**

   e. Icon: Click **Browse** and search for the Office icon file. (In my example, I used the utility from **Nirsoft**—see the Real World Note later in this guide—to find all Office-related icons and store them in D:\Sources\Software\Icons.)

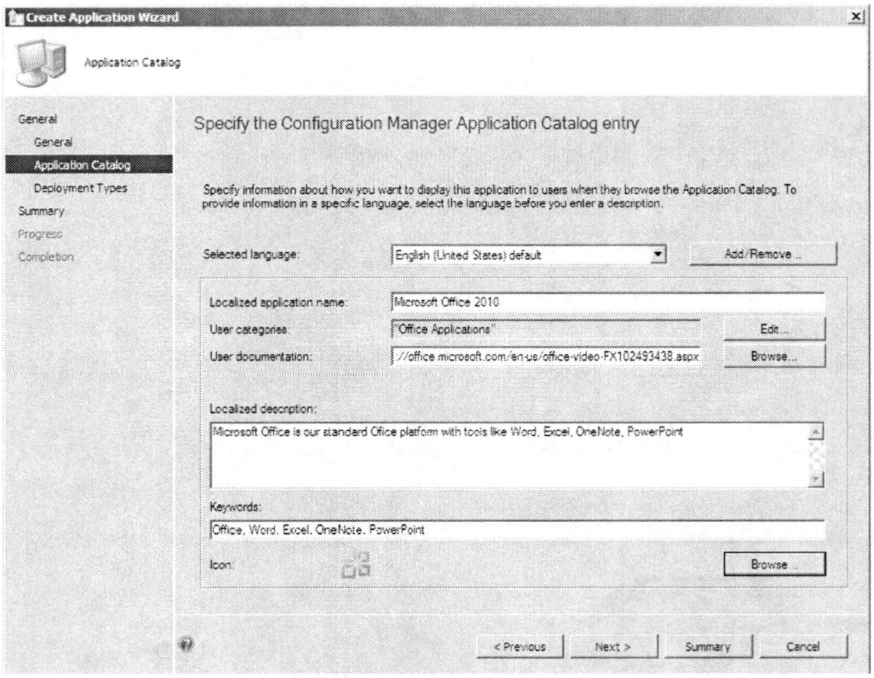

Specifying the application end-user metadata.

> **Real World Note:** Filling out the metadata is a very important step in going user centric. Users can use all the information when searching for applications. One of the metadata is specifying the icon. In ViaMonstra, I use Icon Extractor, which is an application from http://www.nirsoft.net/utils/iconsext.html.

Create the x64 Deployment Type

1. In **Deployment Types**, click **Add** to begin creating the Office 2010 x64 deployment type.
2. On the **General** page, in **Type**, select **Script Installer (Native)** and then click **Next**.
3. On the **General Information** page, use this setting and click **Next**:

   Name: **Microsoft Office 2010 x64 MSI**
4. On the **Content** page, specify these settings and click **Next**:
   a. Content location: **\\CM01\Sources$\Software\MS_Office_2010_Pro_X64**
   b. Installation program: **setup.exe**
   c. Uninstall program: **setup.exe /uninstall ProPlus /config .\ProPlus.WW\config.xml**

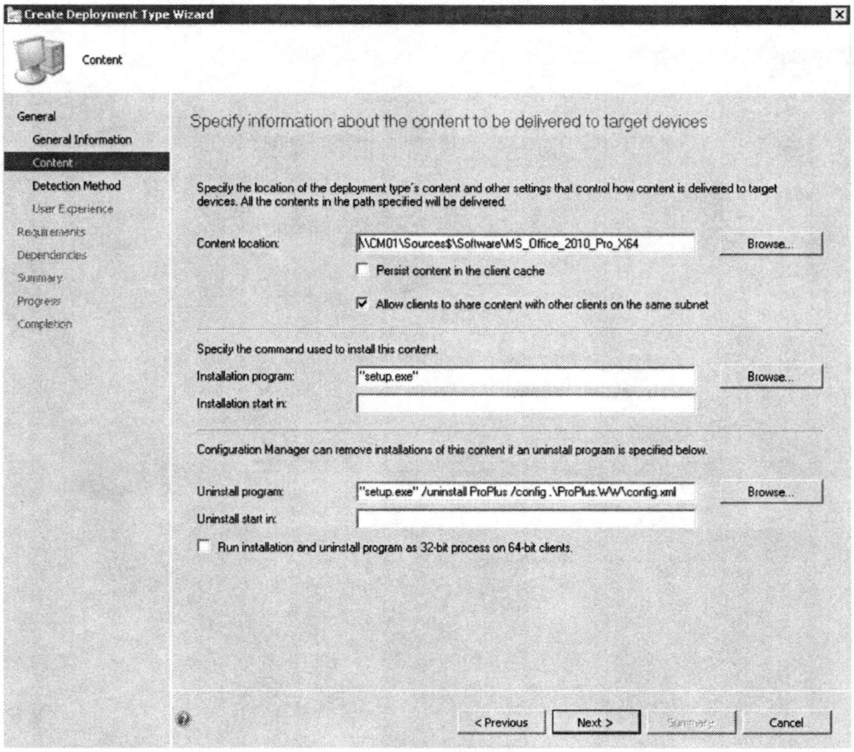

Specifying the install and uninstall commands.

5. On the **Detection Method** page, specify these settings and click **Next**:
   a. Click **Add Clause**, and select **Windows Installer** as the **Setting Type**.
   b. Click **Browse**, navigate to the **ProPlus.WW** folder, select **ProPlusWW.msi**, and click **Open**.
   c. Click **OK** to close the Detection Rule page.

6. On the **User Experience** page, specify these settings and click **Next**. (The settings for this deployment type are for a user-targeted installation in which the end user is able to follow the installation progress on the monitor.)
    a. Installation behavior: **Install for system**
    b. Logon requirement: **Only when a user is logged on**
    c. Installation program visibility: **Normal**
7. On the **Requirements** page, specify these settings and click **Next**:
    a. Click **Add**.
    b. Category: **Device**
    c. Condition: **Operating System**
    d. Operator: Select **One of**; then select **Windows 7, All Windows (64 bit)**, and click **OK**.
    e. Click **Add**.
    f. Category: **User**
    g. Condition: **Primary device**
    h. Operator: **Equals**
    i. Value: Select **True** and click **OK**.
8. On the **Dependencies** page, click **Next**.
9. On the **Summary** page, read the summary and click **Next** to start the creation of the deployment type.
10. On the **Completion** page, click **Close** to return to the Create Application Wizard.

Create the x86 Deployment Type

1. Click **Add** to start creating the x86 deployment type.
2. On the **General** page, in **Type**, select **Script Installer (Native)** and then click **Next**.
3. On the **General Information** page, use this setting and click **Next**:

    Name: **Microsoft Office 2010 x86 MSI**
4. On the **Content** page, specify these settings and click **Next**:
    a. Content location: **\\CM01\Sources$\Software\MS_Office_2010_Pro_x32**
    b. Installation program: **setup.exe**
    c. Uninstall program: **setup.exe /uninstall ProPlus /config .\ProPlus.WW\config.xml**

5. On the **Detection Method** page, specify these settings and click **Next**:
    a. Click **Add Clause**, and select **Windows Installer** as the **Setting Type**.
    b. Click **Browse**, navigate to the **ProPlus.WW** folder, select **ProPlusWW.msi**, and click **Open**.
    c. Click **OK** to close the Detection Rule page.
6. On the **User Experience** page, specify these settings and click **Next**:
    a. Installation behavior: **Install for system**
    b. Logon requirement: **Only when a user is logged on**
    c. Installation program visibility: **Normal**
7. On the **Requirements** page, specify these settings and click **Next**:
    a. Click **Add**.
    b. Category: **Device**
    c. Condition: **Operating System**
    d. Operator: Select **One of**; then select **Windows 7, All Windows (32 bit)**, and click **OK**.
    e. Click **Add**.
    f. Category: **User**
    g. Condition: **Primary device**
    h. Operator: **Equals**
    i. Value: Select **True** and click **OK**.
8. On the **Dependencies** page, click **Next**.
9. On the **Summary** page, read the summary and click **Next** to start the creation of the deployment type.
10. On the **Completion** page, click **Close** to return to the Create Application Wizard.
11. On the **Deployment Types** page, note your two deployment types and click **Next**.
12. On the **Summary** page, read the summary and click **Next** to start creating the application.
13. On the **Completion** page, click **Close** to return to the ConfigMgr console.

Distribute the MS Office 2010 Application

1. Select the **Microsoft Office 2010** application and click **Distribute Content** on the ribbon.
2. On the **General** page, click **Next**.
3. On the **Content** page, click **Next**.

4. On the **General Destination** page, click **Add**, **Distribution Point Groups**. Select **All Content**, and click **OK** and **Next**.
5. On the **Summary** page, read the summary and click **Next** to start distributing the content.
6. On the **Completion** page, click **Close** to return to the ConfigMgr console.

Create the WinRAR Application

Usually you should go a long way to ensure that applications can be installed silently without any user interaction. But you will most likely run into scenarios in which you can't (or won't) spend the time needed to repackage the application. The steps below take you through the creation of a WinRAR application. You configure only the most basic application properties and allow the user to interact with the installation. If you have the time, I encourage you to fill out the application metadata just like you did for Microsoft Office 2010.

In these steps, I assume you have downloaded the x86 version of WinRAR 4.11 to D:\Sources\Software\WinRAR on CM01.

1. Log on to **CM01** as Administrator and open the **ConfigMgr console**.
2. In the **Software Library** workspace, select **Application Management\Applications**.
3. Right-click **Applications** and select **Folder, Create Folder**. Type **Optional User** as the folder name.
4. Select the **Optional User** folder and click **Create Application** on the ribbon.
5. On the **General** page, configure this setting and click **Next**:

   Type: Select **Manually specify the application information**.
6. On the **General Information** page, specify these application properties and click **Next**:
   a. Name: **WinRAR**
   b. Administrator comments: **Our only company supported ZIP application**
   c. Manufacturer: **Rarlab**
   d. Software Version: **4.11**
   e. Optional reference: **POWR**
   f. Administrative Categories: Click **Select**, **Create**; then type **Utility** and click **OK**.
7. On the **Application Catalog** page, specify these properties and click **Next**:
   a. Localized description: **Company Zip application**
   b. Keywords: **Zip, WinRAR, Compress, RAR**
   c. Icon: Click **Browse** and navigate to the **WINRAR icon** file.
8. Click **Add** to start creating the deployment type.
9. On the **General** page, in **Type**, select **Script Installer (Native)** and then click **Next**.

10. On the **General Information** page, use this setting and click **Next**:

Name: **Rarlab WinRAR 4.11 x86 EXE**

11. On the **Content** page, specify these settings and click **Next**:

a. Content location: **\\CM01\Sources$\Software\WinRAR**

b. Installation program: **wrar411.exe -s**

c. Uninstall program: **Uninstall.exe /s**

d. Uninstall start in: **C:\Program Files(x86)\WinRAR**

12. On the **Detection Method** page, click **Add Clause** and specify these settings; then click **OK** and **Next**.

a. Setting Type: **File System**

b. Type: **File**

c. Path: **C:\Program Files(x86)\WinRAR**

d. File or folder name: **WinRAR.EXE**

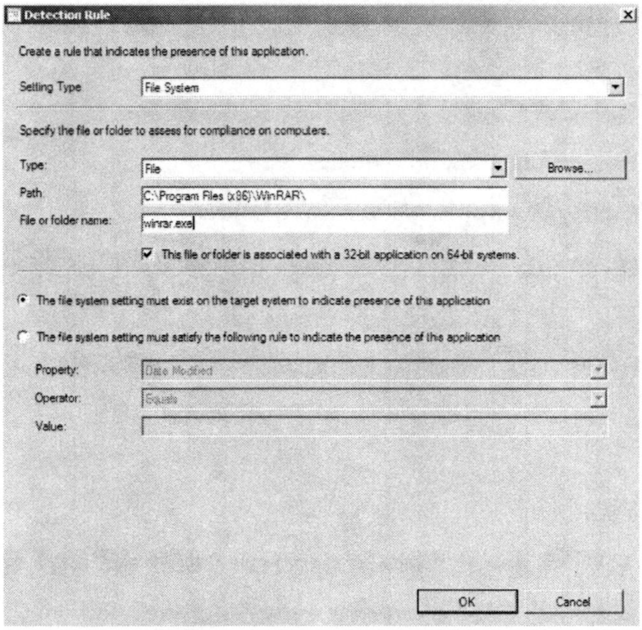

Specifying a detection method.

13. On the **User Experience** page, specify these settings and click **Next.**:

a. Installation behavior: **Install for system**

b. Logon requirement: **Only when a user is logged on**

c. Installation program visibility: **Normal**

14. On the **Requirements** page, specify these settings and click **Next**:
    a. Click **Add**.
    b. Category: **Device**
    c. Condition: **Operating System**
    d. Operator: Select **One of**; then select **Windows 7**, **All Windows (64 bit)** and click **OK**.
15. On the **Dependencies** page, click **Next**.
16. On the **Summary** page, read the summary and click **Next** to start the creation of the deployment type.
17. On the **Completion** page, click **Close** to return to the Create Application Wizard.
18. Select the new **Deployment Type** and click **Edit**.
19. Select the **Return Codes** tab, and notice that there is no return code for a successful uninstall.
20. Click **Add**, configure these settings, and click **OK**:
    a. Return Code Value: **1**
    b. Code Type: **Success (no reboot)**
    c. Name: **Uninstall Success**
    d. Description: **Successfully uninstalled WinRAR**

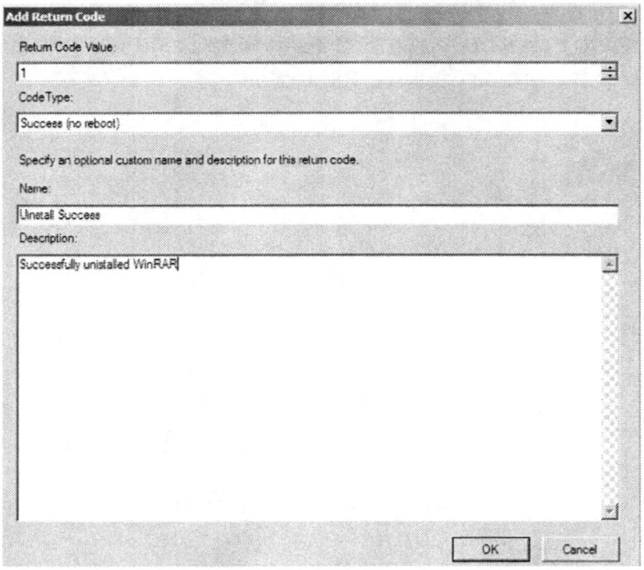

Creating a custom return code.

21. On the **Deployment Types** page, click **Next**.
22. On the **Summary** page, read the summary and click **Next** to start the creation of the application.
23. On the **Completion** page, click **Close** to return to the ConfigMgr console.

User Device Affinity (UDA)

User Device Affinity or UDA is a major part of going user centric for ViaMonstra. It is company policy that all users have at least one device selected as their primary device. In ConfigMgr, you can specify the primary device in several ways:

1. Automate the process in the client agent settings.
2. Let the end user specify their primary device in the Application Catalog website point.
3. Manually specify the device in the ConfigMgr console.
4. Define the primary user when installing the operating system.
5. Import a CSV file with information about users and devices.
6. Write a custom script to define the relationship.

Specify the Primary Device in the Application Catalog

1. Log on to **PC001** as **CORP\JAP**.
2. Start **Internet Explorer** and open **http://CM01/CMApplicationCatalog**.
3. Select the **My Devices** tab and enable **I regularly use this computer to do my work**. This option configures the device as the primary device for JAP.

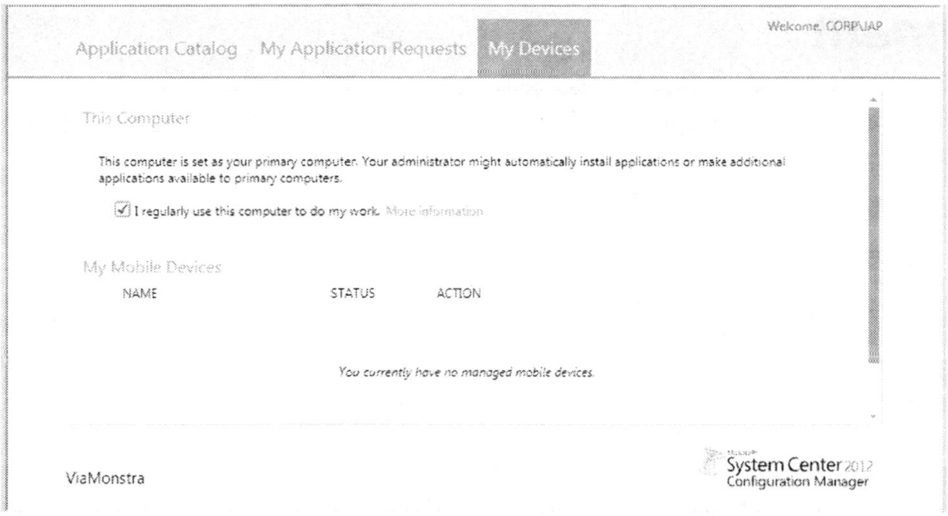

Specifying the primary user in the Application Catalog.

4. Log on to **CM01**, and in the **ConfigMgr console**, navigate to the **Assets and Compliance** workspace.
5. In **Devices**, right-click **PC001** and select **Edit Primary Users**. You should now be able to see the JAP.

   In the Affinity Type, notice that two users are listed. One is Usage Agent Defined (by the client agent settings) and the other one is Catalog Defined.

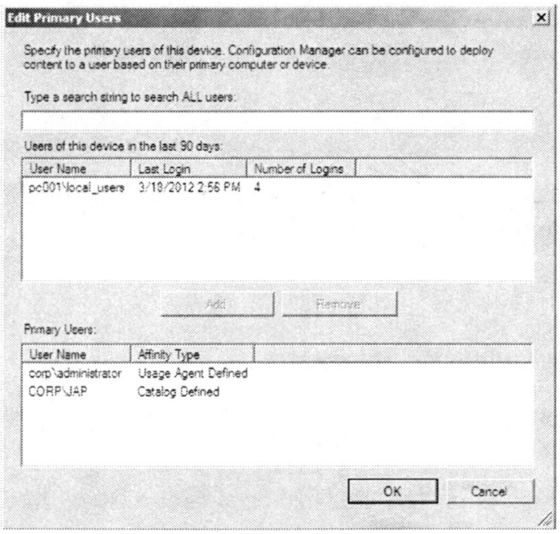

Viewing the primary user for a device.

Deployment

A deployment is the process of offering the user or device an application (and sometimes requiring it). Before deploying any application, it's always a very good idea to follow these simple rules:

1. Never deploy any application before you have tested the command line.
2. Never deploy any application to All Systems or All Users except in lab environments.
3. When in doubt, always create a simulated deployment first.

Simulated Deployments

A simulated deployment is almost like a real deployment except that the application is never installed on any device. The purpose of the simulated deployment is to test the requirement rules, dependencies, and detection methods. The simulated deployment will also give you information about how many of each deployment type will be installed.

Create the Simulated Deployment of Microsoft Office 2010

1. Log on to **CM01** as **Administrator** and open the **ConfigMgr console**.
2. Navigate to **Software Library**, **Application Management**, **Applications**, **Required User**.
3. Select the **Microsoft Office 2010** application, and then select **Deployment**, **Simulate Deployment** from the ribbon.
4. On the **Simulate Application Deployment** page, in **Collection**, click **Browse**; then select **User Collections, Software, SW Microsoft Office 2010 Install**, and click **OK**. Verify that the Action is **Install** and click **Next**.
5. On the **Summary** page, read the summary and click **Next** to start creating the simulated deployment.
6. On the **Completion** page, click **Close** to return to the ConfigMgr console.

Monitor the Simulated Deployment

1. Navigate to the **Monitoring** workspace and select **Deployments**.
2. Right-click the column header (any column) and select **Group By, Purpose**. This creates a group for each deployment purpose, like simulated, required, and so forth.
3. Notice the **Completion Statistics** for the Microsoft Office 2010 application (most likely the statistics are not updated yet). You can update the statistics by running **Run Summarization** from the ribbon.

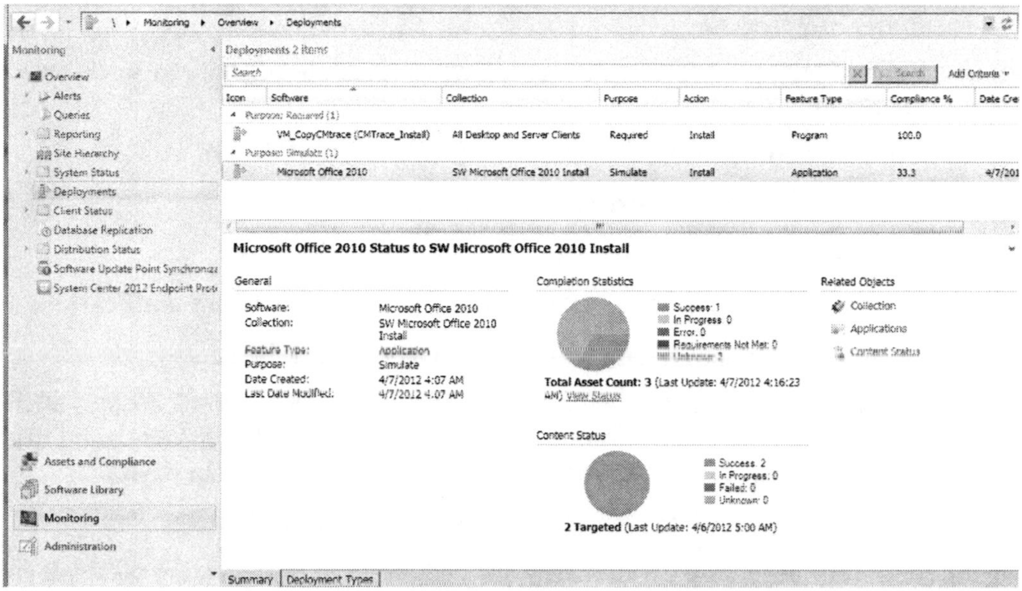

Viewing the simulated deployment status.

4. On the **Summary** tab, click **View Status**. In this view, you get a list of user simulated deployment statuses: succeeded, in progress, error, and requirements not met. You also get a list of users for whom a status is unknown. Users listed in the Unknown tab are users who have not uploaded any states messages about the deployment.
5. Select the deployment again and click the **Deployment Types** tab. In this view, you get a nice chart illustrating the progress of the simulated deployment.

Deploy a Required Application

1. Select the **Software Library** workspace, and then select **Application Management, Applications, Required User**.
2. Select the **Microsoft Office 2010** application. Click the **Deployments** tab, right-click the simulated deployment, click **Delete**, and then click **Yes** in the dialog box. The reason for doing this is that ConfigMgr does not allow you to deploy the same application to the same collection twice.
3. Click **Deployment, Deploy** on the ribbon.
4. On the **General** page, in **Collection**, click **Browse**; then select **User Collections, Software, SW Microsoft Office 2010 Install,** and click **OK**. Click **Next**.
5. On the **Content** page, verify that the content is distributed and click **Next**.
6. On the **Deployment Settings** page, configure these settings and click **Next**:
   a. Action: **Install**

   b. Purpose: **Required**
   c. Enable **Deploy automatically according to schedule whether or not a user is logged on.**

7. On the **Schedule Settings** page, configure this setting and click **Next**:

   Installation Deadline: **Current time + 3 days**

8. On the **User Experience** page, configure this setting and click **Next**:

   User Notifications: **Display in Software Center and show all notifications**

9. On the **Alerts Settings** page, configure these settings and click **Next**:
   a. Threshold for successful deployment: Configure a value of **90%** success after **4days** from now. (This setting should trigger a console alert if Microsoft Office is not installed on at least 90% of the primary devices within four days.)
   b. Threshold for failed deployment: Configure a failed value of **5%**.

10. On the **Summary** page, read the summary and click **Next** to start creating the deployment.
11. On the **Completion** page, click **Close** to return to the ConfigMgr console.

Install the Required Application

1. Log on to **PC001** as **CORP\JAP**.
2. From the **Start** menu, select **All Programs**, **Microsoft System Center 2012**, and **Software Center**.
3. The application will become available after the next user policy update cycle.
4. Select the **Microsoft Office 2010** application and click **Install**.

Deploy an Optional User Application

1. Log on to **CM01** as **Administrator** and open the **ConfigMgr console**.
2. Select the **Software Library** workspace, and then select **Application Management**, **Applications**, **Optional User**.
3. Select the **WinRAR** application.
4. Click **Deployment**, **Deploy** on the ribbon.
5. On the **General** page, in **Collection**, click **Browse**; then select **User Collections**, **Software**, **SW WinRAR Install**, and click **OK** and then **Next**.
6. On the **Content** page, click **Add, Distribution Point Group**. Select **All Content**, and click **OK** and then **Next**.
7. On **Deployment Settings** page, configure these settings and click **Next**:
   a. Action: **Install**

   b. Purpose: **Available**
   c. Enable **Require administrator approval if users request this application**.
8. On the **Schedule Settings** page, click **Next**.
9. On the **User Experience** page, configure this setting and click **Next**:

   User Notifications: **Display in Software Center and show all notifications**
10. On the **Alerts Settings** page, configure this setting and click **Next**:

    Threshold for failed deployment: Configure a failed value of **5%**.
11. On the **Summary** page, read the summary and click **Next** to start creating the deployment.
12. On the **Completion** page, click **Close** to return to the ConfigMgr console.

Install the Optional Application

1. Log on to **PC001** as **CORP\JAP**.
2. Open **Internet Explorer** and go to **http://cm01/cmApplicationCatalog**.

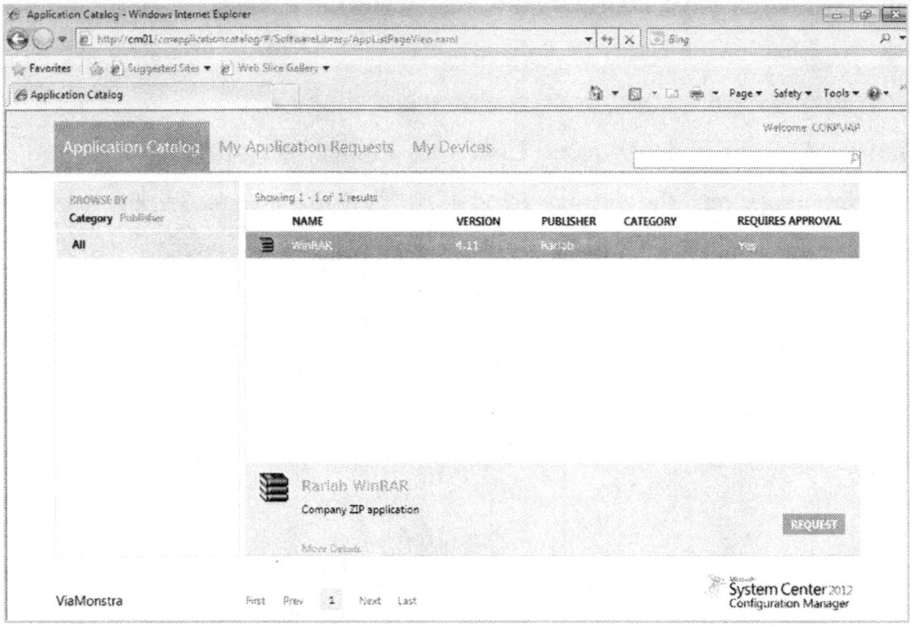

Requesting approval.

3. Select the **WinRAR** application and click **Request**.
4. In the text box, type a message to the administrator like **I really need WinRAR to do my work** and click **Submit**.

   The approval request is written to the ConfigMgr console.
5. Log on to **CM01**, open the **ConfigMgr console**, and navigate to **Software Library**, **Application Management**, **Approval Requests**.
6. Select the request from **CORP\JAP** and click **Approve** on the ribbon.
7. Type a comment and click **OK**.

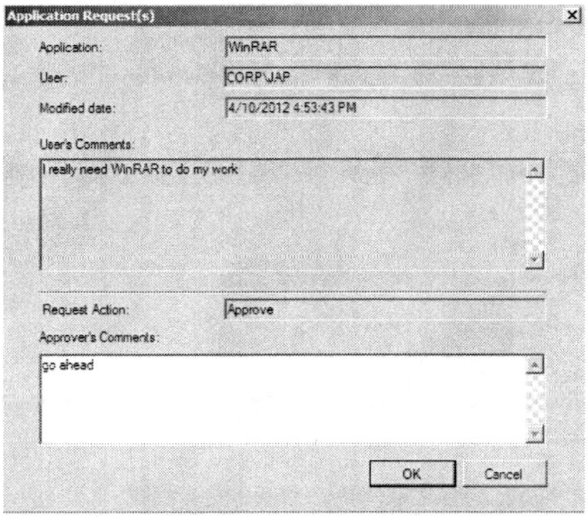

Accepting the approval request.

8. Log on to **PC001** as **CORP\JAP** and open **http://cm01/cmApplicationCatalog**.
9. Select the **WinRAR** application and click **Install.**
10. Click **Yes** and start the installation.

Uninstalling Applications

As a natural part of any application life cycle is the decommissioning phase where the application is either superseded with a new version or uninstalled. You can supersede any application with another application as long as both applications are created as applications in the ConfigMgr console.

Create 7-Zip and Supersede WinRAR

The following steps take you through the creation of a 7-Zip application. You configure only the most basic application properties. If you have the time, however, I encourage you to fill out the application metadata just like you did for Microsoft Office 2010.

In these steps, I assume you have downloaded 7-Zip 9.20 x64 to **D:\Sources\Software\7-Zip** on **CM01**.

1. Log on to **CM01** as **Administrator** and open the **ConfigMgr console.**
2. In the **Software Library** workspace, select **Application Management**, **Applications**.
3. Select the **Optional User** folder and click **Create Application** on the ribbon.
4. On the **General** page, configure these settings and click **Next**:
    a. Type: **Windows Installer (Native)**
    b. Location: **\\CM01\Sources$\Software\7-Zip\7z920-x64.MSI**

   c. Click **Yes** when asked about importing this file.

5. On the **Import Information** page, read the information about the imported application and deployment and click **Next**.
6. On the **General Information** page, specify these application properties and click **Next**:
   a. Name: **7-Zip**
   b. Administrator comments: **Our only company supported Zip application**
   c. Manufacturer: **7-zip.org**
   d. Software version: **9.20**
   e. Optional reference: **PO7Z**
   f. Administrative Categories: Click **Select,** select **Utility**, and click **OK**.
7. On the **Summary** page, click **Next**, and then click **Close**.
8. Select the **7-Zip** application and click **Properties** on the ribbon.
9. Click the **Supersedence** tab.
10. Click **Add**, configure these settings, and click **OK**:
    a. Superseded Application: Click **Browse**, select **Optional User**, **WinRAR**, and then click **OK**.
    b. New Deployment Type: **7-Zip 9.20 (x64 edition)**
    c. Uninstall: Enable **uninstall**.

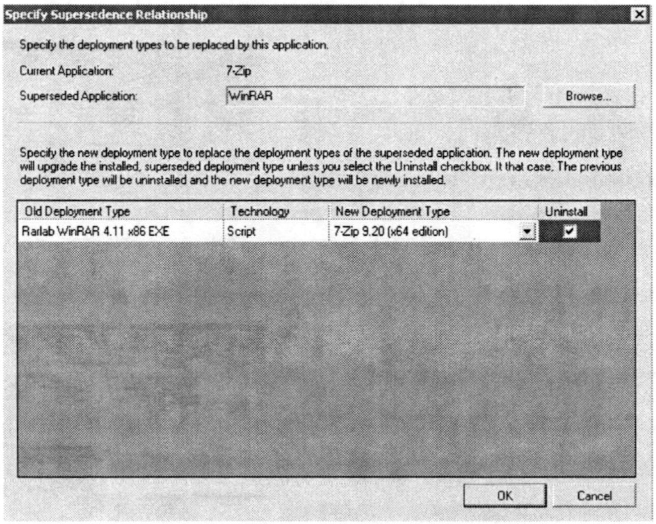

Configuring a supersedence relationship.

11. Click **OK** and close the properties.

12. Select the **7-Zip** application and click **Deployment**, **Deploy** on the ribbon.
13. On the **General** page, click **Browse** and select **Software\SW_7-Zip_Install** as the collection; then click **OK** and **Next**.
14. On the **Content** page, click **Add**, **Distribution Point Group**, and select the **All Content** distribution point group; click **OK** and **Next**.
15. On the **Deployment Settings** page, configure these settings and click **Next**:
    a. Action: **Install**
    b. Purpose: **Available**
    c. Automatically upgrade any superseded versions of this application: **Enabled**

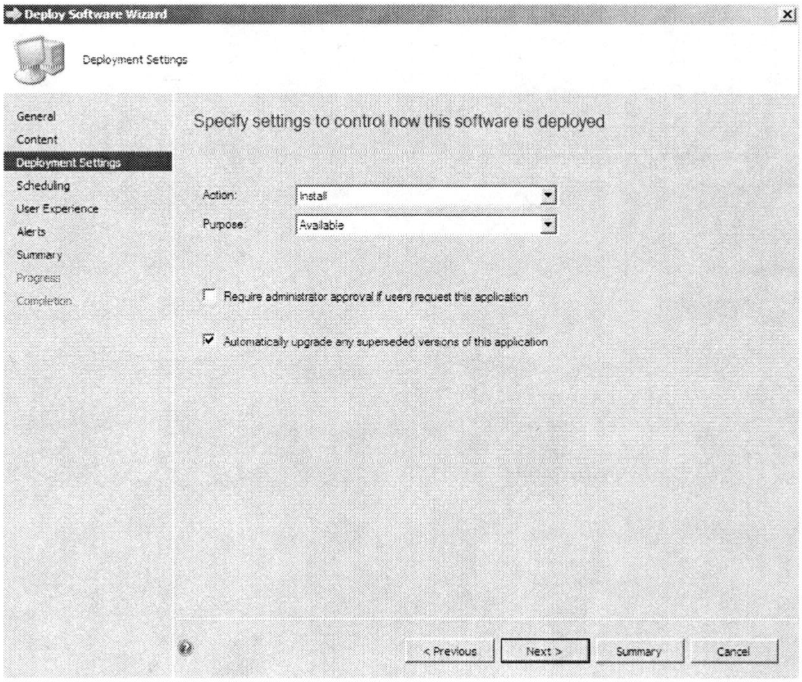

Creating an optional deployment.

16. Finish the Deploy Software Wizard using the default settings.
17. Log on to **PC001** as **CORP\JAP**, open **Software Center**, and monitor the upgrade process. (You can speed up the process by refreshing the User policy.)
18. Log on to **PC001**, start **Internet Explorer**, and open **http://CM01/CMApplicationCatalog**. You should be able to see the 7-ZIP application.

Uninstall 7-Zip

1. Log on to **CM01** as **Administrator** and open the **ConfigMgr console**.
2. Navigate to the **Software Library** workspace, and select the **7-Zip** application.
3. In the **Home** tab, click **Deployment**, **Deploy**, select the **SW_7-Zip_Uninstall** collection, and click **Next** twice.
4. On the **Deployment Settings** page, configure the Action to **Uninstall** and click **Next**.
5. On the **Schedule** page, click **Next**:
6. On the **User Experience** page, select **Software Uninstall**.

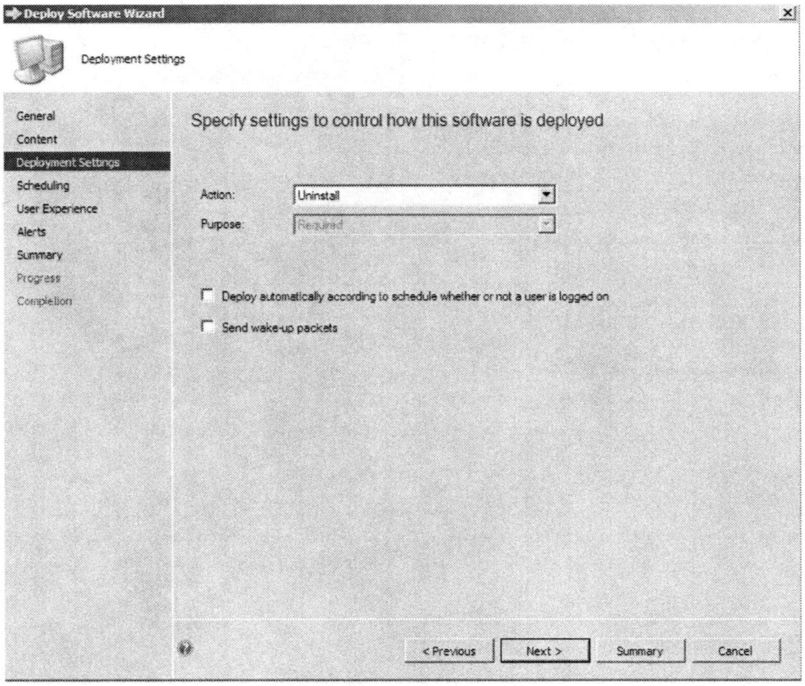

Creating an uninstall deployment.

7. Finish the Deploy Software Wizard using the default settings.
8. Log on to **DC01**, and open **Active Directory Users and Computers**.
9. Navigate to the **Software Groups** organizational unit. Right-click the **SW_7-Zip_Uninstall** group, select **Properties**, and click the **Members** tab.
10. Click **Add** and add **JAP** as a group member. By adding JAP to the uninstall group, you automatically add her to the corresponding SW_7-Zip_Uninstall collection. Members of that collection are automatically excluded from the SW_7-Zip_Install collection.

> **Note:** If you target an install and an uninstall deployment to the same collection, the install deployment always takes precedence over that uninstall deployment. This is the main reason for always creating an Exclude collection rule in the SW Install collection.

Remove Applications from the ConfigMgr Console

After applications have been uninstalled and are no long supported in ViaMonstra, the policy is to first retire the application and then delete it completely from the ConfigMgr console after 3 months. After an application is retired, no new deployments are available. The application is not automatically uninstalled from any device as a consequence of retiring it in the console. The retirement action is simply to prevent any new installations. After the application is retired, you can always reinstate it and start creating new deployments if needed.

Retire an Application

1. Log on to **CM01** as **Administrator** and open the **ConfigMgr console.**
2. Navigate to the **Software Library** workspace, and select the **WinRAR** application in the **Optional User** folder.
3. Right-click **WinRAR** and select **Retire.**

   To make the application "active" again, right-click the application and select **Reinstate.**

Deleting the application removes it from the ConfigMgr console and also deletes all entries of the application from the database. After it is deleted, there is no way to get the application back, except by recreating it manually or restoring a backup. A restore in ViaMonstra will never be started just to restore a single object from the database. Before you delete an application, you need to ensure that all deployments are deleted.

Export an Application

1. Log on to **CM01** as **Administrator** and open the **ConfigMgr console.**
2. Navigate to the **Software Library** workspace, and select the **WinRAR** application in the **User Optional** folder.
3. Right-click **WinRAR** and select **Export.**
4. On the **General** page, in **File**, click **Browse**; then navigate to **D:\Setup\Exported Software\WinRAR** (the folder must be manually created), type in **WinRAR**, and click **Next**.

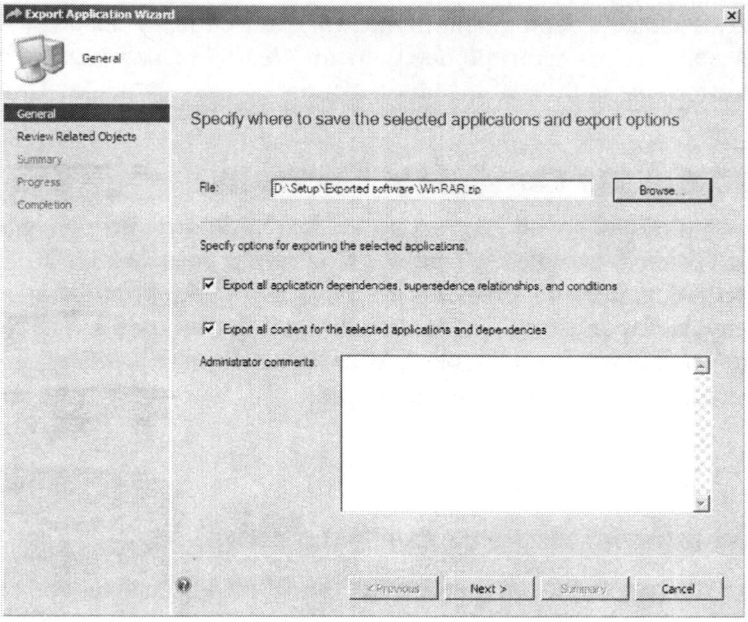

Exporting an application.

5. On the **Review Related Objects** page, notice that only WinRAR is listed and click **Next**.
6. On the **Summary** page, read the summary and click **Next** to start exporting the application.
7. On the **Completion** page, click **Close** to return to the ConfigMgr console.

Delete an Application

1. Go to the **Software Library** workspace, and select the **WinRAR** application.
2. Right-click **WinRAR** and select **Delete**. Notice the warning that you cannot delete an application that has one or more deployments.

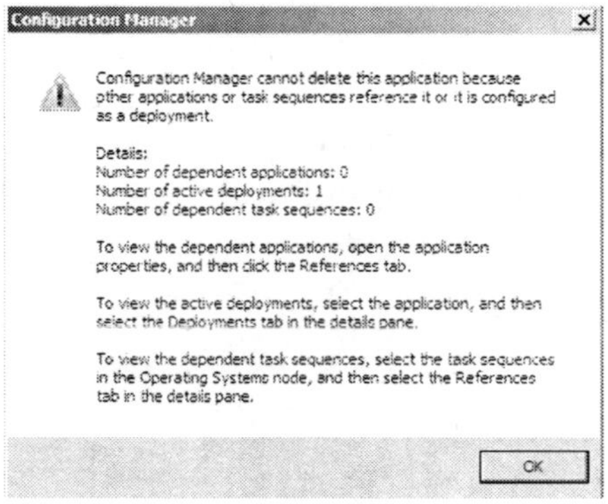

The cannot delete application warning message.

3. Click **OK** in the warning dialog box and select the **Deployments** tab.
4. Right-click the **SW_WinRAR_Install** deployment and click **Delete.**
5. Click **OK** in the Delete warning dialog box.
6. Right-click **WinRAR** and select **Delete**. Notice the warning about permanently deleting the application from ConfigMgr. Click **Yes** to delete the application.

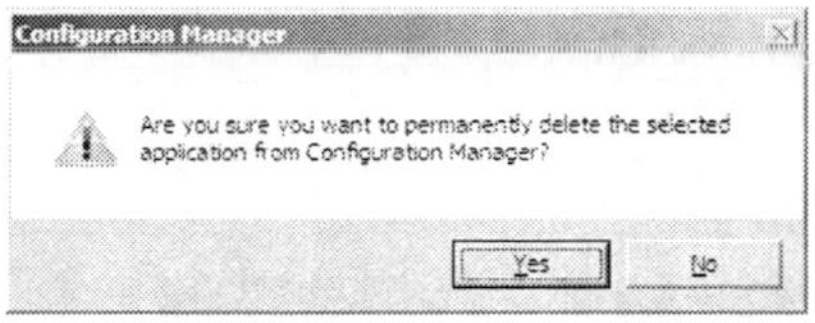

The delete the application warning.

Import an Application

1. Log on to **CM01** as **Administrator** and open the **ConfigMgr console**.
2. Navigate to the **Software Library** workspace, right-click the **User Optional** folder, and click **Import Application**.
3. On the **General** page, in **File**, click **Browse**: then navigate to **\\CM01\D$\Setup\Exported Software\WinRAR**, select the **WinRAR.zip** file, click **Open**, and click **Next**.
4. On the **File Content** page, click **Next**.
5. On the **Summary** page, read the summary and click **Next** to start the import.
6. On the **Completion** page, click **Close** to return to the ConfigMgr console.

Useful Log Files

This table includes log files you can use to track activity related to your applications and packages.

Log File	**Description**	**Location**
execmgr.log	Records information about classical packages and task sequences	Client default
AppIntentEval.log	Records information about the current and intended state of applications, their applicability.	Client default

AppDiscovery.log	Records information about install and uninstall attempts and detection method evaluations.	Client default
Log File	**Description**	**Location**
ConfigMgrSoftwareCatalog .log	Records the information of the Application Catalog, which includes its use of Silverlight	Client default
SoftwareCenterSystemTasks .log	Records the activities for Software Center prerequisite component validation. This log files is mainly used if Software center is causing problems.	Client default
SoftwareCatalogUpdateEndpoint.log	Records the activities for managing the address for the Web Application Catalog shown in Software Center.	Client default
CAS.log	Records the activities for managing the client cache.	Client default
SCClient_<domain>@ <username>_1.log	Records the activity in Software Center for the specified user on the client computer	Client default
SCNotify_<domain>@ <username>_1.log	Records the activity for notifying users about software for the specified user	Client default
UserAffinity.log	Records details about user device affinity.	Client default
LocationServices.log	Records information about which distribution point used for downloading packages,	Client default
DataTransferService.log	Records all BITS communication for policy and package access.	Client default
ContentTransferManager.log	Records information about BITS and SMB in regards to downloading and accessing packages	Client default
SMSdpmon.log	Records information about the health monitoring scheduled task that is configured on a distribution point	Distribution point .\SMS_DP$\SMS\ Logs
smsdpprov.log	Records information about injecting packages into the content library	Distribution point .\SMS_DP$\SMS\ Logs

Chapter 8 Software Update Deployment

Keeping Windows and third-party software up-to-date with the latest security updates is a discipline that requires planning and testing. When you plan for software updates, it's very important that you take these factors into consideration:

- It must be easy to approve and deploy new updates.
- No updates must be installed without proper testing.
- All devices must be part of the update plan.
- There must be a plan for the least acceptable compliance level.

Understanding the Update Components

Server Components

The software update solution consists of two components, an active software update point with WSUS installed and the ConfigMgr client. An active software update point is configured on the top level site hosted on a server with Internet access. Some of the software update's synchronization settings are configured at the CAS and are not available at child sites. All primary sites in the ConfigMgr hierarchy must have an active software update point unlike secondary sites that do not require a software update point.

A High-Level Overview of the Software Update Process

1. The WSUS server synchronizes software update metadata from Windows Update. No binaries will be downloaded as part of this process.
2. The active software update point synchronizes metadata from the WSUS server.
3. The ConfigMgr client performs scanning using metadata from the WSUS server. Compliance state messages are uploaded to the ConfigMgr server through the management point.
4. From the ConfigMgr server, updates are approved and content distributed to distribution point(s).
5. The ConfigMgr client receives the deployment policies, starts downloading required updates from the distribution point to the cache, and installs the updates according to the deadline.

Server Requirements for the Software Update Point

- WSUS 3.0 SP2 locally installed
- WSUS administrator console installed on the site server if WSUS 3.0 SP2 is installed remotely
- Available disc space of 1 GB on the system drive

Client Requirements

- Clients must be running Windows Update Agent 3.0 or above.
- The Automatic Updates service must be running.
- There are no group policies pointing to other WSUS server. Configure the client to turn off any automatic updates.

Real World Note: If you have a proxy server, ensure that the software update point can access these sites:

http://windowsupdate.microsoft.com
http://*.windowsupdate.microsoft.com
https://*.windowsupdate.microsoft.com
http://*.update.microsoft.com
https://*.update.microsoft.com
http://*.windowsupdate.com
http://download.windowsupdate.com
http://download.microsoft.com
http://*.download.windowsupdate.com
http://test.stats.update.microsoft.com
http://ntservicepack.microsoft.com

WSUS Group Policies

The ConfigMgr client receives information about the active software update point as part of the machine policy. The information is merged into local policies as a local WUAU policy. If domain policies for Windows Update are defined, they override the ConfigMgr policies and can cause the clients not to scan correctly.

Real World Note: It's highly recommended to configure a WSUS group policy where the setting "Enable Automatic Updates" is disabled. That way, if for any reason you disable the software update client agent setting, clients will fall back to the group policy and the agent will be disabled. A disabled agent is so much better than having thousands of clients automatically downloading and installing updates using the default Windows settings.

Software Update Point Components

When working with a software update point, you have three components that are very interesting to monitor and know about.

WSUS Control Manager

The WSUS Control Manager is responsible for checking the health of the WSUS server. The check is performed once an hour, and you can monitor it by reading the WSUSctrl.log file on the WSUS server.

WSUS Configuration Manager

The WSUS Configuration Manager component initially configures the WSUS settings. You can change these settings any time from the Software Update Point Component properties in ConfigMgr. Most WSUS settings should be configured in the ConfigMgr console. If settings are changed from the WSUS console, they might overwritten by the settings found in ConfigMgr. When I write "might," it is because not all settings can be controlled from the ConfigMgr console.

WSUS Synchronization Manager

The WSUS Synchronization Manager handles the synchronization process between Microsoft Windows Update and the WSUS server and between the WSUS server and the ConfigMgr server. When synchronization is initiated at the top-level site, the software updates metadata is synchronized from Microsoft Update. After a complete synchronization, the WSUS Synchronization Manager synchronizes the software updates metadata from the WSUS database to ConfigMgr. After that process is complete, software updates metadata will be replicated to any child sites.

Planning for Software Updates

Approving and installing updates can be a very easy process when you have some basic understanding of the software update components.

Software Update Collections

Like with any other feature, it is important that your software update solution has a collection design that allows you to ease the administrative work while keeping complete control of the feature. When designing a collection, it's important that you know exactly how you want to control the deployments.

Create Software Update Management Collections

This section guides you through creating the needed software update collections. With those collections, you can create a software update solution where you can minimize the number of deployments and yet still be able control different deployment times.

- **Pilot 1.** A collection used for a simple test to see whether the updates can install and restart the computers without breaking anything.
- **Pilot 2.** A test collection that runs after pilot 1 is accepted. In pilot 2, ViaMonstra will have a subset of computers from different departments. All users are informed about their membership to this group.
- **WRK Production.** The workstation production collection. After pilot 1 and pilot 2 are accepted, members not part of the Excluded collection have the updates installed.
- **WRK Excluded.** The workstation collection for members that for any reason must be excluded in any software update deployment.
- **SRV Automatic.** The collection containing servers where updates are automatically installed and servers restarted in a maintenance window. The collection will only have Include Collection rules, one rule for each of the SRV MW collections.
- **SRV MW.** There will be multiple SRV MW collections, one for each unique maintenance window. ViaMonstra will have four collections, where the first is named SRV MW1. The maintenance windows are used to control when software updates are installed and the servers restarted. For each collection, you create a unique maintenance window.
- **SRV Manual.** The collection containing servers where updates must be manually installed and the server manually restarted.

Create the Active Directory Groups

1. Log on to **DC01** as **Administrator** and open **Active Directory Users and Computers**.

   You must create the domain local security groups in the **Software Groups** OU; otherwise, they will not be discovered by the Security Group discovery process.

2. Create the domain local security groups in the following table and add the listed computer accounts as members.

Active Directory Security Group	Add These Computers to the Active Directory Group
SUM_Pilot_1	PC001
SUM_Pilot_2	
SUM_WRK_Excluded	
SUM_MW1	DC01
SUM_MW2	EX01 (only if you have set up an Exchange Server)
SUM_MW3	CM02
SUM_SRV_Manual	CM01

Create the Pilot 1 and Pilot 2 Collections

1. Log on to **CM01** as **Administrator** and open the **ConfigMgr console**.
2. Navigate to the **Assets and Compliance** workspace, select **Device Collections** and the **Software Updates** folder.
3. Click **Create Device Collection** on the ribbon.
4. On the **General** page, define these settings and click **Next**:
    a. Name: **SUM Pilot 1**
    b. Comment: **All computers that are part of the first update pilot deployment**
    c. Limiting Collection: Click **Browse** and select **All Systems**.
5. On the **Membership Rules** page, define these settings:
    a. Enable **Use incremental updates for this collection.**
    b. Click **Add Rule, Query Rule**.
    c. Name the rule **SUM Pilot 1** and click **Edit Query Statement**.
    d. Select the **Criteria** tab.
    e. Click the **yellow icon** to build the criteria, and then click **Select**.
    f. Select **System Resource** as the **Attribute class**.
    g. Select **System Group Name** as the **Attribute**.
    h. Click **OK** to return to the Criterion Properties dialog box.
    i. Click **Operator** and select **is equal to**; in **Value**, type **CORP\SUM_Pilot_1**. (You also can click Value and select the group name from a list of groups.)

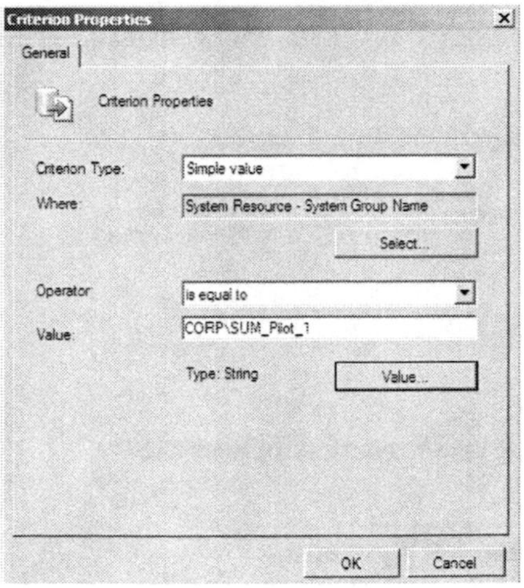

Creating a device collection based on AD group membership.

   j. Click **OK three times** to return to the Memberships Rules page.

6. Click **Next** twice, and then click **Close**.
7. Repeat the preceding steps to create the **SUM Pilot 2** collection.

Create the Workstation Collections

1. Still in the **Software Updates** folder, click **Create Device Collection** on the ribbon.
2. On the **General** page, define these settings and click **Next**:
   a. Name: **SUM WRK Excluded**
   b. Comment: **All workstation computers that are excluded from software updates**
   c. Limiting Collection: Click **Browse** and select **All Systems**.
3. On the **Membership Rules** page, define these settings and then click **OK**:
   a. Enable **Use incremental updates for this collection**.
   b. Click **Add Rule**, **Query Rule**.
   c. Name the rule **SUM WRK Excluded** and click **Edit Query Statement**.
   d. Select the **Criteria** tab.
   e. Click the **yellow icon** to build the criteria.
   f. Select **System Resource** as the **Attribute class**.
   g. Select **System Group Name** as the **Attribute**.
   h. Click **OK** to return to the Criterion Properties dialog box.
   i. Click **Operator** and select **is equal to**; in **Value**, type **CORP\SUM_WRK_Excluded**. (You also can click Value and select the group name from a list of groups.)
   j. Click **OK** three times to return to the Memberships Rules page.
4. Click **Next** twice, and click **Close**.
5. Click **Create Device Collection** on the ribbon.
6. On the **General** page, define these settings and click **Next**:
   a. Name: **SUM WRK Production**
   b. Comment: **All workstation computers that are included in update management**
   c. Limiting Collection: Click **Browse** and select **All Systems**.

7. On the **Membership Rules** page, define these settings and :
    a. Enable **Use incremental updates for this collection**.
    b. Click **Add Rule, Query Rule**.
    c. Name the rule **SUM WRK Production** and click **Edit Query Statement**.
    d. Select the **Criteria** tab.
    e. Click the **yellow icon** to build the criteria.
    f. Select **System Resource** as the **Attribute class**.
    g. Select **Operating System Name and Version** as the **Attribute**.
    h. Click **OK** to return to the Criterion Properties dialog box.
    i. Click **Operator** and select **is like**; in **Value**, type **%Workstation%**.
    j. Click **OK** three times to return to the Memberships Rules page.
8. Click **Add Rule, Exclude Collections**.
9. Click the **Software Updates** folder, select **SUM WRK Excluded**, and click **OK**.
10. Finish the wizard using the default settings.

Create the Server Collections

1. Click **Create Device Collection** on the ribbon.
2. On the **General** page, define these settings and click **Next**:
    a. Name: **SUM SRV MW1**
    b. Comment: **All Servers in Maintenance group 1**
    c. Limiting Collection: Click **Browse** and select **All Systems**.
3. On the **Membership Rules** page, define these settings:
    a. Enable **Use incremental updates for this collection**.
    b. Click **Add Rule, Query Rule**.
    c. Name the rule **SUM MW1** and click **Edit Query Statement**.
    d. Select the **Criteria** tab.
    e. Click the **yellow icon** to build the criteria, and then click **Select**.
    f. Select **System Resource** as the **Attribute class**.
    g. Select **System Group Name** as the **Attribute**.
    h. Click **OK** to return to the Criterion Properties dialog box.

i. Click **Operator** and select **is equal to**; in **Value**, type **CORP\SUM_MW1**. (You also can click Value and select the group name from a list of groups.)

j. Click **OK** three times to return to the Memberships Rules page.

4. Click **Next** twice, and then click **Close**.
5. Repeat the steps to create the two additional collections for **SUM SRV MW2** and **SUM SRV MW3.**
6. Click **Create Device Collection** on the ribbon.
7. On the **General** page, define these settings and click **Next**:
   a. Name: **SUM SRV Automatic**
   b. Comment: **All servers where updates can be installed according to maintenance windows**
   c. Limiting Collection: Click **Browse** and select **All Systems**.
8. On the **Membership Rules** page, define these settings:
   a. Enable **Use incremental updates for this collection.**
   b. Click **Add Rule**, **Include Collections**; then navigate to the **Software Updates** folder, select the three **SUM SRV MW** collections, and click **OK**.

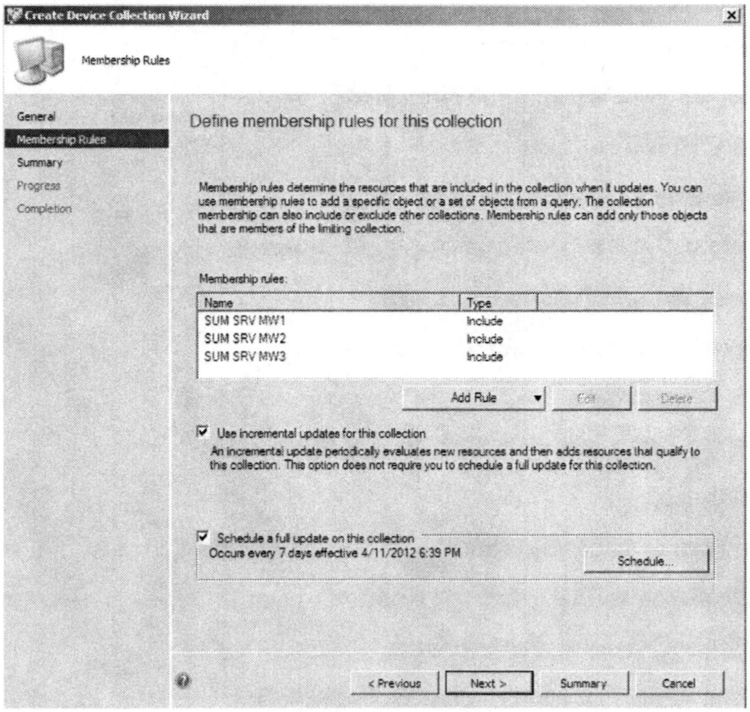

Creating include rules for servers.

9. Finish the wizard using the default settings.
10. Click **Create Device Collection** on the ribbon.
11. On the **General** page, define these settings and click **Next**:
    a. Name: **SUM SRV Manual**
    b. Comment: **All servers where updates must be manually installed.**
    c. Limiting Collection: Click **Browse** and select **All Systems**.
12. On the **Membership Rules** page, define these settings:
    a. Enable **Use incremental updates for this collection**.
    b. Click **Add Rule**, **Query Rule**.
    c. Name the rule **SUM SRV Manual** and click **Edit Query Statement**.
    d. Select the **Criteria** tab.
    e. Click the **yellow icon** to build the criteria, and then click **Select**.
    f. Select **System Resource** as the **Attribute class**.
    g. Select **System Group Name** as the **Attribute**.
    h. Click **OK** to return to the Criterion Properties dialog box.
    i. Click **Operator** and select **is equal to**, in **Value**, type **CORP\SUM_SRV_Manual**. (You also can click Value and select the group name from a list of groups.)
    j. Click **OK** three times to return to the Memberships Rules page.
13. Click **Next** twice, and then click **Close**.
14. Finish the wizard using the defaults. You should now have all the needed collections to support the software update feature in ConfigMgr.

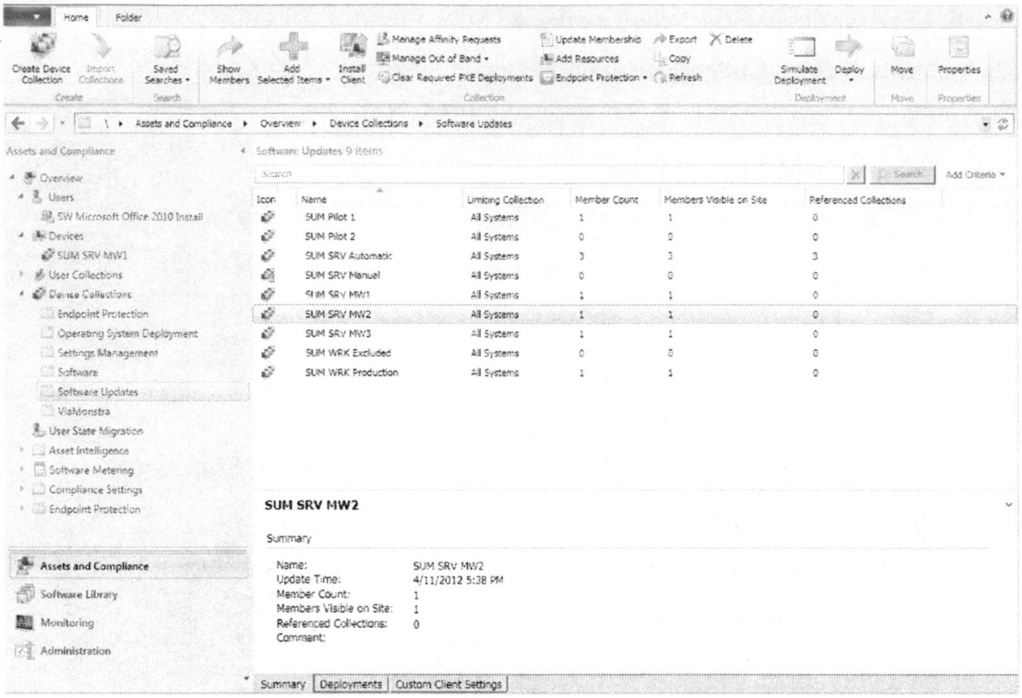

The needed software updates collections.

Automate Adding Queries to Device Collections Using PowerShell

This example shows you how to automate the process of adding a dynamic query to a device collection:

1. Open **PowerShell** as **Administrator**.
2. Navigate to the folder containing the scripts.
3. Type **. .\CM12_Function_Library.ps1** and press **Enter**.
4. Create a device collection:
    a. Type **Set-CMCollectionQueryRule -SiteServer Localhost -SiteCode PS1 -Query 'select * from SMS_R_System where SMS_R_System.SystemGroupName = "CORP\\SUM_MW1"' -QueryName " SUM MW1 " -QueryType Device -CollectionName "SUM SRV MW1"**.
    b. Press **Enter**.

Automate Creating Include Rules Using PowerShell

In this example, you create an Include rule for the SUM SRV MW1 collection in the SUM Server Automatic collection. (This is just a sample, and these steps are not required for any of the other guides in this book.)

1. Open **PowerShell** as **Administrator**.

2. Navigate to the folder containing the script.
3. Type **.\CM12_Function_Library.ps1** and press **Enter**.
4. Type **Set-CMCollectionIncludeRule -SiteCode PS1 -SiteServer localhost -CollectionName "SUM SRV Automatic" -IncludeCollectionName "SUM SRV MW1"**; then press **Enter**.

Maintenance Windows

Maintenance windows define when software can be installed on any given computer. Maintenance window also control when a computer reboot can occur. Maintenance windows should be defined based on Active Directory group membership. When a deployment occurs, it is evaluated against each maintenance window on the client. A device will apply maintenance windows from all the collections of which it is a member. Maintenance windows are cumulative which requires some planning. In ViaMonstra, you will create maintenance windows only in the Software Updates collection hierarchy.

Maintenance Window	Active Directory group
Sunday 01:00 – 04:00	SUM_MW1
Monday 01:00 – 04:00	SUM_MW2
Saturday 10:00 – 01:00	SUM_MW3

Create Maintenance Windows

1. Log on to **CM01** as **Administrator** and open the **ConfigMgr console**.
2. Navigate to the **Assets and Compliance** workspace and select the **Software Update** folder.
3. Select the **SUM SRV MW1** collection and click **Properties** on the ribbon.
4. Select the **Maintenance Windows** tab, click the **yellow icon**, and create a new maintenance window with these settings:
    a. Name: **MW1 - Sunday 01:00 - 04:00**
    b. Start: **1:00 AM**
    c. End: **4:00 AM**
    d. Recurrence pattern: **Weekly, Sunday**

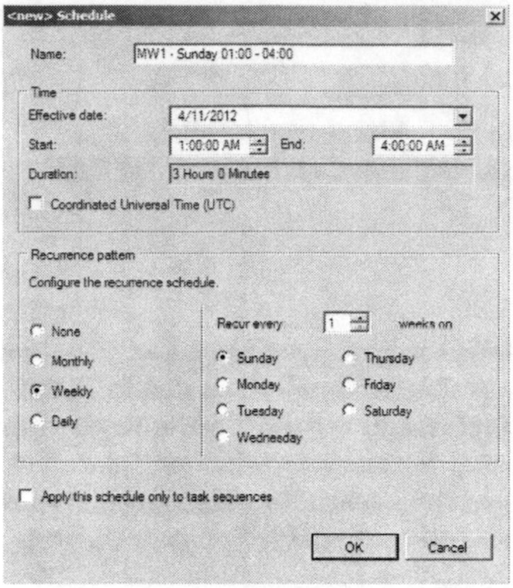

Creating a maintenance window.

5. Click **OK** twice and close the collection properties.
6. Select **SUM SRV MW2** and open the collection properties.
7. Select the **Maintenance Windows** tab, click the **yellow icon**, and create a new maintenance window with these settings:
    a. Name: **MW2 - Monday 01:00 - 04:00**
    b. Start: **1:00 AM**
    c. End: **4:00 AM**
    d. Recurrence pattern: **Weekly, Monday**
8. Click **OK** twice and close the collection properties.
9. Select **SUM SRV MW3** and open the collection properties.
10. Select the **Maintenance Windows** tab, click the **yellow icon**, and create a new maintenance window with these settings:
    a. Name: **MW3 - Saturday 10:00 - 01:00**
    b. Start: **10:00 PM**
    c. End: **1:00 AM**
    d. Recurrence pattern: **Weekly, Saturday**
11. Click **OK** twice and close the collection properties.

Real World Note: You should only configure maintenance windows on a very limited number of collections. A computer will inherit maintenance windows from all the collections of which it is a member. If the computer is a member of ten different collections that all has a different maintenance window, you end up with a computer for which the effective maintenance window might be 20 hours a day.

Software Updates Procedures

Now when we have the collection design in place, it's time to plan the procedures for when software updates must be deployed. At ViaMonstra, you will deploy software updates in several stages with enough time to validate whether the updates are installed successfully and do not break any business applications or services.

Workstation Software Updates Procedures

1. Approved updates are deployed to computers in workstation pilot group 1. Updates in this group are installed with a deadline as soon as possible.
2. Approved updates are deployed to computers in workstation pilot group 2. Updates in this group have a two-day deadline.
3. After updates are successfully installed in pilot group 2, they can be deployed to all workstations in production. Updates in this group have a one-week deadline. This gives users one week to download and install the updates according to their own business schedules before the updates are applied.

Deployment Group	Updates Released Day x from Release	Deadline Day x from Release
Pilot group 1	Day 2	One day
Pilot group 2	Day 4	Two days
Workstation production	Day 7	Seven days

No computers will be automatically restarted during the update process.

VPN and Remote Locations

All VPN and other remote clients must download and install updates marked as extremely critical and critical, like other workstations in production.

Server Software Update Procedures

1. Approved updates are deployed to computers in workstation pilot group 1. Updates in this group will be installed no later than two days from release.
2. Approved updates are deployed to computers in Server Manual with a purpose of available and no deadline.
3. Approved updates are deployed to computers in Server Automatic with a deadline not ignoring maintenance windows.

Deployment Group	Updates Released Day x from Release	Deadline Day x from Release
Pilot group 1	Day 2	One day
Server Manual	Day 7	No deadline
Server Automatic	Day 7	According to defined maintenance windows

The Software Update Compliance Plan

The Official Microsoft Severity Rating System issues a bulletin for any product vulnerability that could, in Microsoft's judgment, result in multiple systems being affected, no matter how unlikely or limited the impact. The following list describes the different severity ratings:

- **Critical.** A vulnerability whose exploitation could allow the propagation of an Internet worm without user action.
- **Important.** A vulnerability whose exploitation could result in the compromise of the confidentiality, integrity, or availability of users' data, or of the integrity or availability of processing resources.
- **Moderate.** Exploitability is mitigated to a significant degree by factors such as default configuration, auditing, or difficulty of exploitation.
- **Low.** A vulnerability whose exploitation is extremely difficult, or whose impact is minimal.

Note: Ensure that you are familiar with the Microsoft security bulletins and that you subscribe to the monthly newsletter. For more information, visit http://www.microsoft.com/technet/security/bulletin/rating.mspx.

ViaMonstra Severity Rating System

At ViaMonstra, the severity rating system is based loosely upon the Official Microsoft Severity Rating System. As a rule of thumb, Microsoft Critical and Important ratings both become Critical in ViaMonstra's ratings. Similarly, ViaMonstra treats both Microsoft Moderate and Low as

Moderate. ViaMonstra also has introduced an "Extremely Critical" rating, which corresponds to what is often referred to as "Zero-Day Exploit."

Microsoft Rating	**ViaMonstra Rating**
N/A	Extremely Critical ("Zero-Day Exploit")
Critical	Critical
Important	
Moderate	Moderate
Low	

Planning for Compliance

A very important part of planning for software updates is planning for the acceptable compliance level. Without a defined SLA, you never know when management is satisfied and when you have to start working harder to track down the non-compliant devices. Any compliance plan should contain the various severities and multiple achievable success criteria.

Workstation Compliance Success Criteria

ViaMonstra Severity	**Success Criterion Week 1**	**Success Criterion Week 2**	**Success Criterion Week 3**
Extremely critical	100%	100%	100%
Critical	50%	80%	95%
Moderate	50%	75%	90%

Server Compliance Success Criteria

ViaMonstra Severity	**Success Criterion Week 1**	**Success Criterion Week 3**	**Success Criterion Week 5**
Extremely critical	100%	100%	100%
Critical	50%	80%	100%
Moderate	50%	75%	100%

Software Update Components

Update Packages

A software update package is like any other package in ConfigMgr except that it only contains the software update binary files. Deployment packages and deployments are only related in the sense that the update must be present in one available software update package. ViaMonstra has decided to create two update packages per year. The update packages are stored in the same source location as all the other packages using this folder structure:

Software Updates. Top-level share

Software Updates\2012-1. Contains the approved updates for the first half of the year

Software Updates\2012-2. Contains the approved updates for the second half of the year

Software Update Templates

Software update deployments can be controlled by the use of templates. In ViaMonstra, you will have one template for each unique deployment scenario. Unlike previous versions of ConfigMgr, this version allows you to create a new template only when you create a deployment. These are the templates you will create:

- **Pilot 1.** All computers that participate in the first test deployment. This template will require that updates are installed and applied automatically. This deployment will offer full interaction with the end user.
- **Pilot 2.** All computers that participate in the second deployment. All deployments to this collection will be a 100-percent match to the production collection.
- **Workstation Production.** All workstations that are not part of the WRK Excluded collection.
- **Server Automatic.** All servers where an installation and restart will be performed automatically.
- **Server Manual.** All servers where an installation and restart will be performed manually.

Update Groups

An update group is a group of selected software updates that can be deployed to clients and used to track compliance. You can create update groups automatically using the Automatic Update Rule feature or by manually selecting the updates. Within a single update group, you can have zero or multiple deployments. In ViaMonstra, you will create a monthly update group containing all the deployments for that month.

Manually Create Update Groups

Although update groups can be created automatically, there are several scenarios in which you want to manually create an update group. For instance, you might want to create an update group with all required updates and use that update as the foundation for a software update compliance report. Manually creating update groups makes perfectly sense when the update group is created for an ad-hoc task.

1. Log on to the **CM01** server as **Administrator** and open the **ConfigMgr console**.
2. Select the **Software Library** workspace, and click **Software Updates, All Software Updates**.
3. Place the cursor in the **Search** column and click **Add Criteria** on the ribbon. Select the following criteria and click **Add**. Notice the extra lines with the criteria.
   a. **Expired**
   b. **Superseded**
   c. **Required**
4. Select **Expired** from the list of criteria.
5. Click the link **is less than or equal to**; then select **is greater than or equal to** and type **1**.
6. Change the value in **And Superseded** from **Yes** to **No.**
7. Change the value in **And Expired** from **Yes** to **No.**
8. Click **Search**, and you should get a list with all required updates.

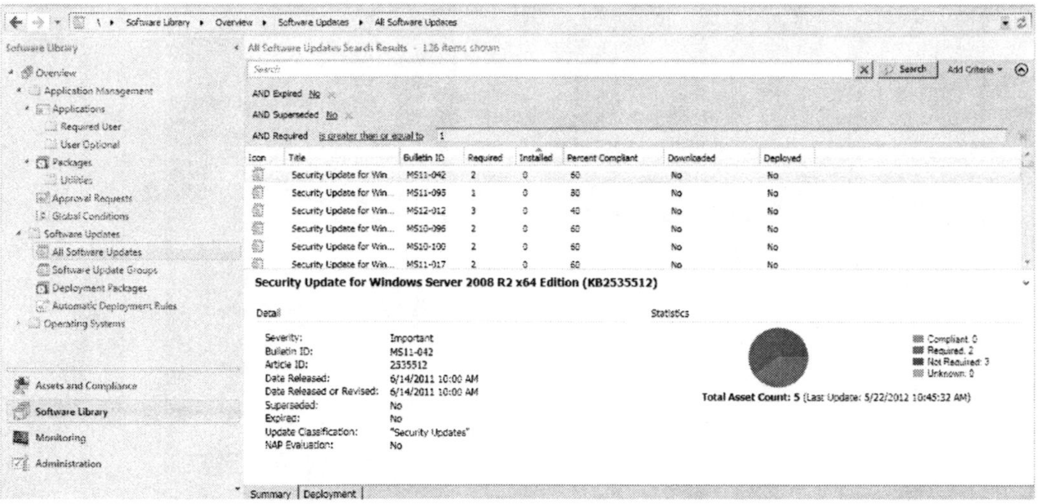

Searching for all required updates.

9. Click **Save Current Search** on the ribbon and save the search as **All Required Updates**.
10. Click **Saved Searches** on the ribbon and select **Manage Searches for Current Node**.

11. Select **All Required Updates** and click **OK**.

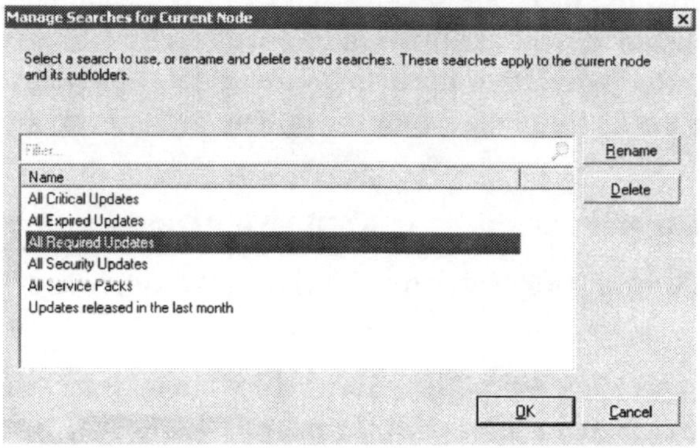

Working with saved searches.

12. Press **Ctrl+A** to select all updates; then right-click and select **Create Software Update Group**.
13. In **Name**, type **All Required Updates** and click **Create**.
14. Select **Software Update Groups** and notice the group. The compliance data are not updated. To update the data, click **Run Summarization** on the ribbon. Select the **All Required updates** update groups and click **Refresh**.

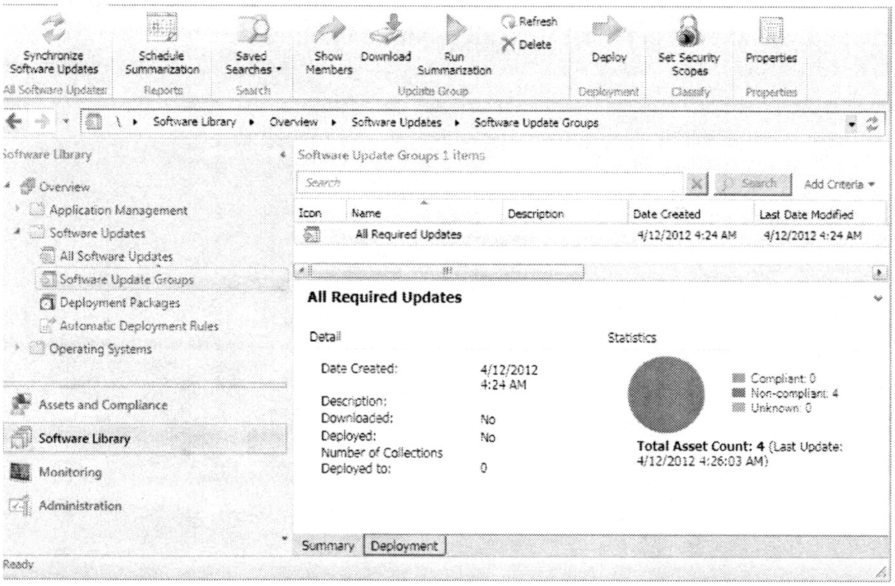

The software update group.

Automatic Deployment Rules

Automatic Deployment Rules is a very powerful feature that allows you to fully automate the software update deployment process. The rule contains information about run time, what updates to download, where to store the updates, and whether the deployment will be automatically enabled. In ViaMonstra, you will create an update group for each month with these settings:

- All security and critical updates
- All Windows updates except Windows Server Itanium
- Place all updates in a new update group
- Create the first deployment to the SUM Pilot 1 collection
- Ensure that the deployment is disabled

Create the Patch Tuesday Automatic Deployment Rule

1. Log on to the **CM01** server as **Administrator** and open the **ConfigMgr console.**
2. Select the **Software Library** workspace, click **Software Updates**, **Automatic Deployment Rules**, and then click **Create Automatic Deployment Rule** on the ribbon.
3. On the **General** page, configure these settings and click **Next**:
    a. Name: **Patch Tuesday**
    b. Description: **Create new software update group every second Tuesday**
    c. Collection: **SUM Pilot 1**
    d. Select **Create a new Software Update Group**
    e. Enable the deployment after this rule is run: **Disable**

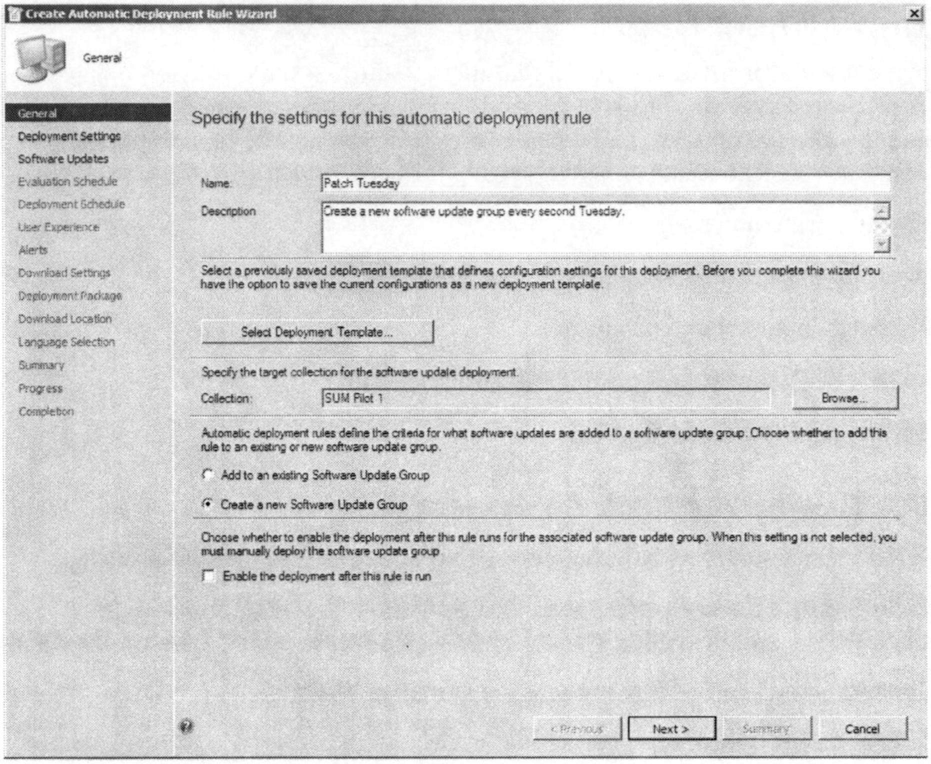

Creating the Patch Tuesday automatic deployment rule.

4. On the **Deployment Settings** page, keep the default settings and click **Next**.
5. On the **Software Updates** page, configure these settings and click **Next**:
    a. Date Released or Revised: **Last 1 month**
    b. Product: **Office 2010, Windows 7, Windows Server 2008 R2**
    c. Title: **-Itanium**
    d. Update classification: **Critical Updates**, **Security Updates**

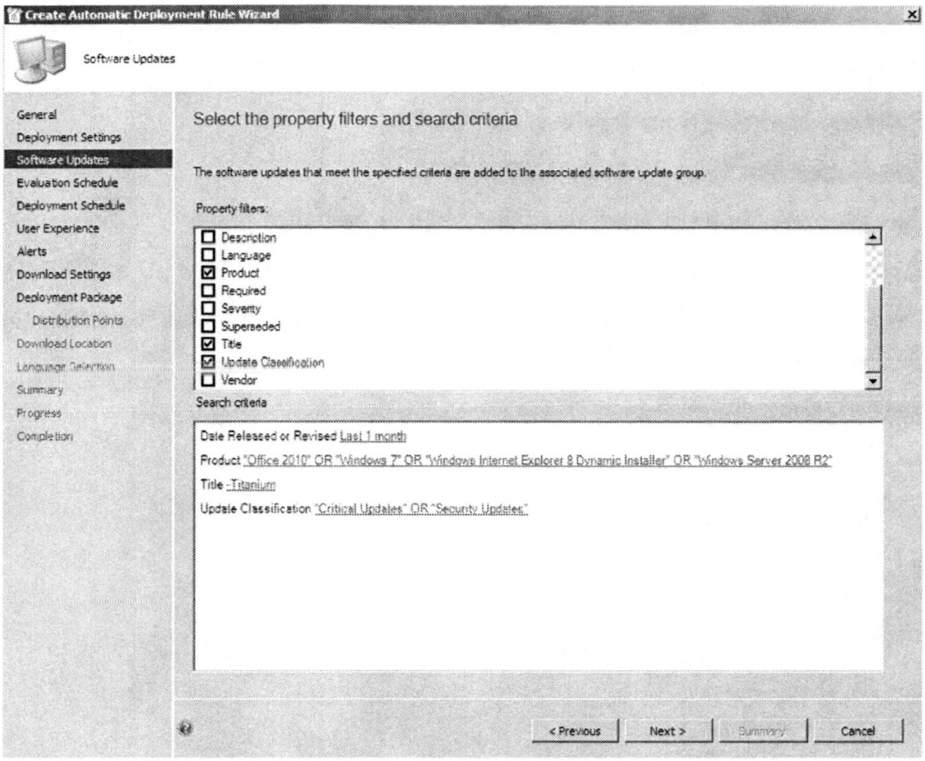

Defining the software updates in the automatic deployment rule.

6. On the **Evaluation Schedule** page, configure this setting and click **Next**:

   Click **Customize** and configure the rule to run **Second Tuesday** every month at **10:00 PM**.

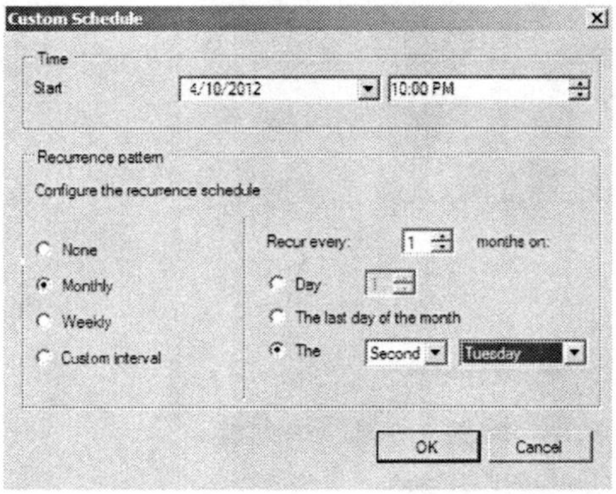

Configuring the automatic deployment rule schedule.

7. Click **OK** to close the Custom Schedule dialog box.

8. On the **Deployment Schedule** page, configure these settings and click **Next**:
   a. Time based on: **Client local time**
   b. Software available time: **As Soon As Possible.**
   c. Installation deadline: **As Soon As Possible.**
9. On the **User Experience** page, configure these settings and click **Next**;
   a. User visual experience: **Display in Software Center and show all notifications**
   b. Device restart behavior: Enable **Suppress the system restart on the following devices** for **Servers** and **Workstations**.

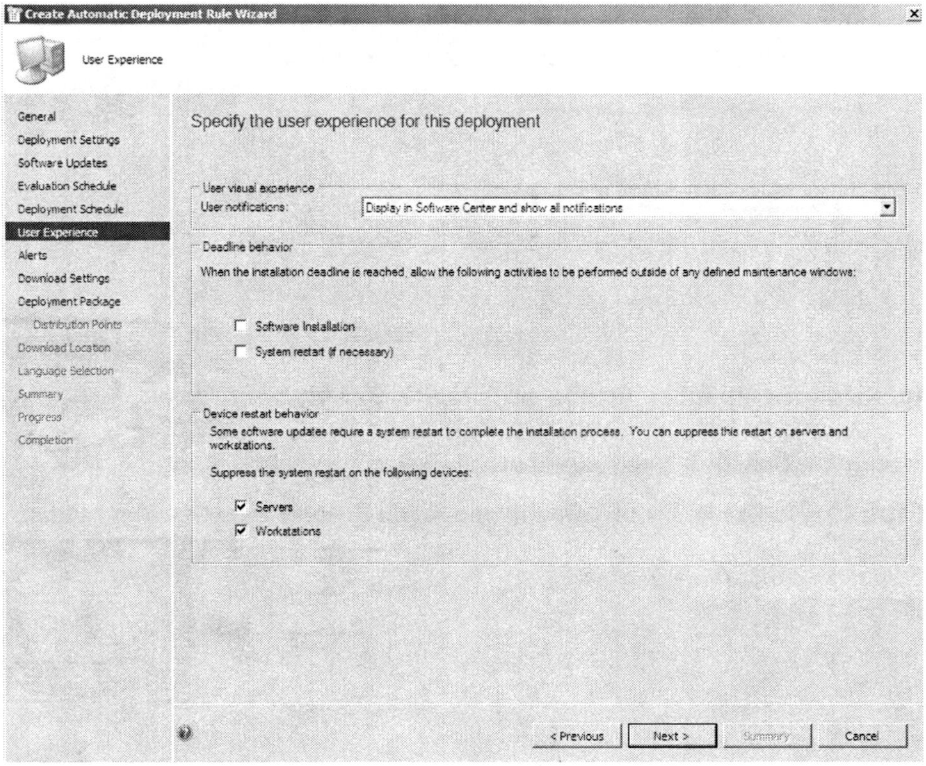

Configuring the user experience.

10. On the **Alerts** page, configure these settings and click **Next**:
    a. Generate an alert when the following conditions are met: **Enable**
    b. Client compliance is below the following percent: **95**
    c. Offset from the deadline: **21 Days**

11. On the **Download Settings** page, configure these settings and click **Next**:

a. Deployment options for client within a slow or unreliable network boundary: Enable **Download software update from distribution point and install**.

b. When software updates are not available on any preferred distribution points. Client can download and install software updates from a fallback source location for content: Enable **Download and install software updates from the fallback content source location**.

12. On the **Deployment Package** page, configure these settings and click **Next**;

a. Name: **2012-1**

b. Description: **2012-1**

c. Package Sources**: \\CM01\Sources$\Updates\2012-1** (Note that you must create the folder manually.)

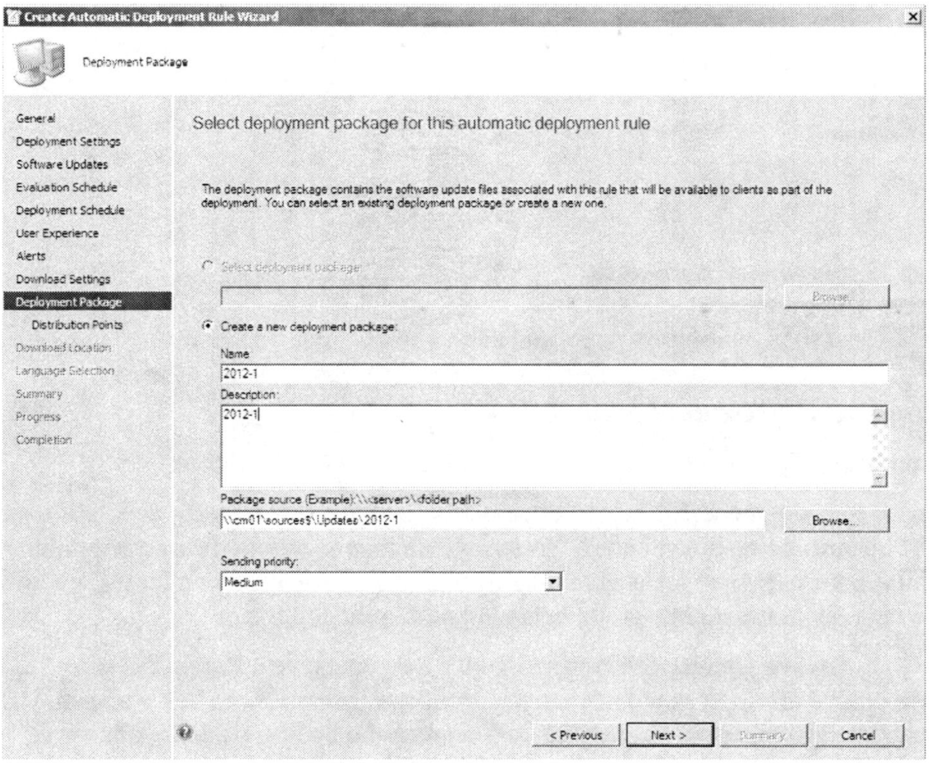

Creating the deployment package.

13. On the **Distribution Points** page, configure this setting and click **Next**:

Click **Add, Distribution Point Group**; then select the **All Content** distribution point group and click **OK**.

14. On the **Download Location** page, configure this setting and click **Next**:

    Download software update from the Internet: **Enabled**.

15. On the **Language Selection** page, configure this setting and click **Next**:

    Ensure **English** is the only selected language.

16. On the **Summary** page, configure this setting and click **Next**:

    Click **Save As Template**. Type **Pilot 1** in the template **Name** field and click **Save**.

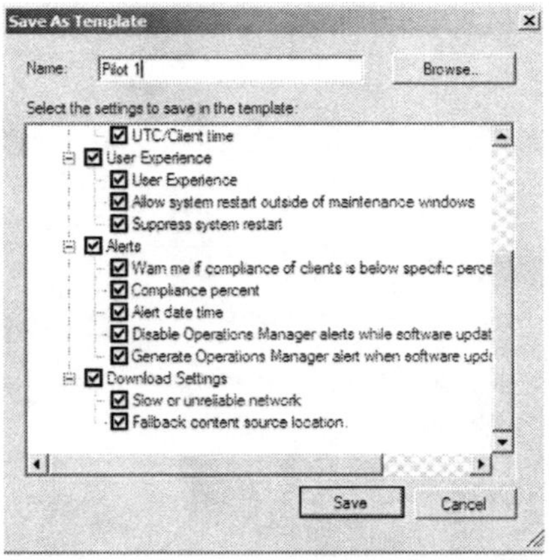

Creating the deployment template.

17. Click **Next,** read the **Completion** page, and click **Close**.

Force the Automatic Deployment Rule to Run

1. Select **Automatic Deployment Rules** and click **Run Now** on the ribbon.
2. Click **Yes** to start the process. The process can easily take a few minutes depending on the number of updates being downloaded. You use CMTrace to monitor the activity along with the number of selected updates in the ruleengine.log. After a few minutes, you will see in the new computer update group being created in the log file.
3. Navigate to **Software Update Groups** and verify that you have a **Patch Tuesday date+time** update group. If you don't see the group yet, press **F5** or click **Refresh**. Right-click the update group, select **Properties**, and rename the update group to **Year + Number of Month + Name of Month**, e.g. **2012 06 June**.

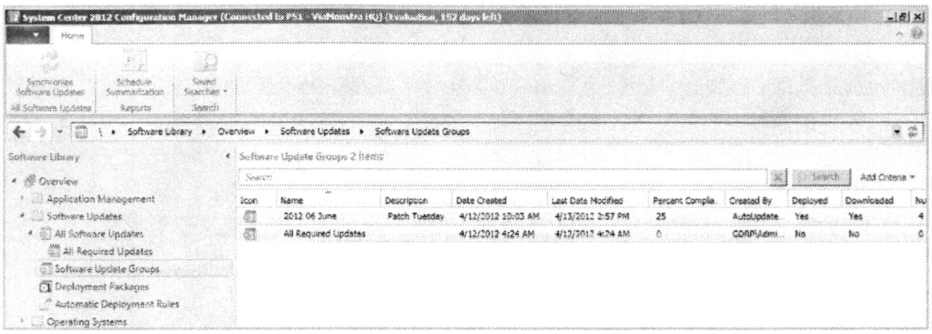

Renaming the automatically created update group.

4. Right-click the update group and select **Show Members**. When you navigate down the different updates in the group, notice that the compliance data are updated.

Deployments

The deployment is a child object to an update group. Like any other deployment, it contains information about the installation purpose (required or available), time and day of the deployment, user experience, and so forth. The automatic deployment rule creates only the first deployment target at the pilot collection. The remaining deployments must be created manually. It's absolutely not a time-consuming process when you have the deployment templates created. The following guides take you through the creation of the first deployment in each of the environments. As part of the deployment process, we also create the deployment template.

Enable the Pilot Deployment

1. Navigate to the new **Software Update Group**, select the **Deployment** tab, right-click the automatically created deployment, and click **Properties**.
2. Rename the deployment *Year + Number of Month + Name of Month* Pilot 1, e.g. **2012 06 June Pilot 1**, and click **OK**.

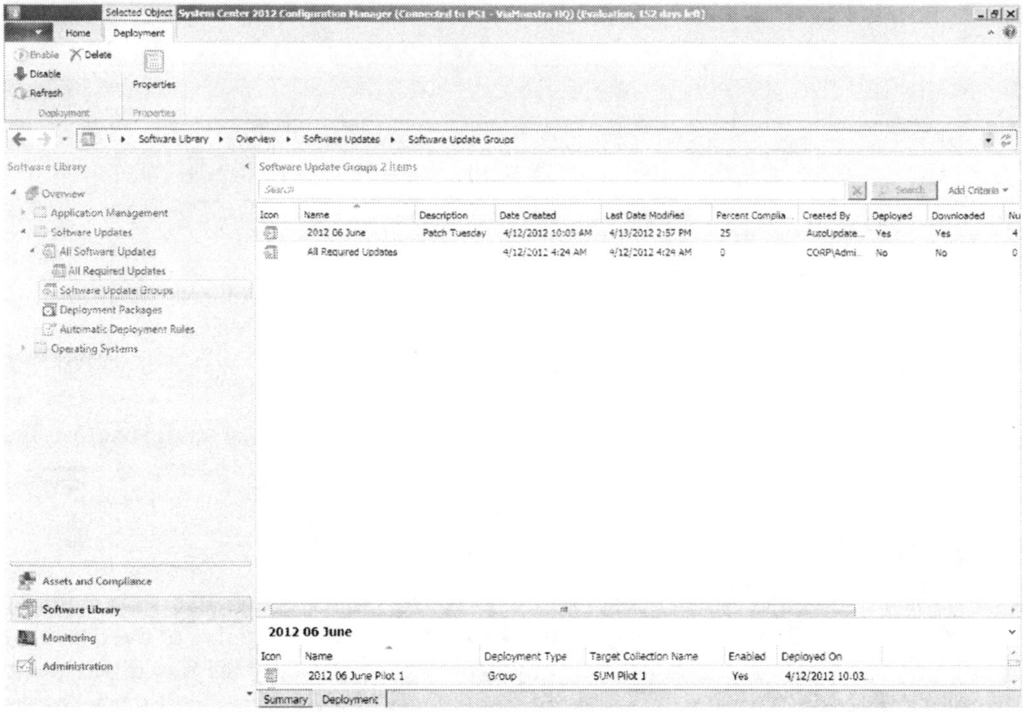

Renaming the automatically created deployment.

3. Right-click the deployment and click **Enable**. This enables the first deployment with an as soon as possible deadline. The client downloads the machine policy and starts installing within two hours. The two hours is a non-configurable offset that ensures you don't get 4,000 clients hammering the distribution point at the exact same time.

Create the Workstation Production Deployment

You create the workstation production deployment with these settings:

- Limited user experience where only the restart notification is displayed.
- Suppress restart.

Complete the following steps:

1. Navigate to the new **Software Update Group**, and click **Deploy** on the ribbon.
2. On the **General** page, configure these settings and click **Next**:
    a. Name: WRK *Year* + *Number of Month* + *Name of Month* Production, e.g. **WRK 2012 06 June Production**
    b. Description: **All workstations that are not excluded**
    c. Collection: **SUM WRK Production**

3. On the **Deployment Settings** page, configure these settings and click **Next**:
    a. Type of deployment: **Required**
    b. Detail level: **Normal**
4. On the **Deployment Scheduling** page, configure these settings and click **Next**:
    a. Software available time: **As soon as possible**
    b. Installation deadline: **7 days from today**
5. On the **User Experience** page, configure these settings and click **Next**;
    a. User notifications: **Display in Software Center and show only notifications for computer restarts**
    b. Suppress the system restart on the following devices: **Workstations**

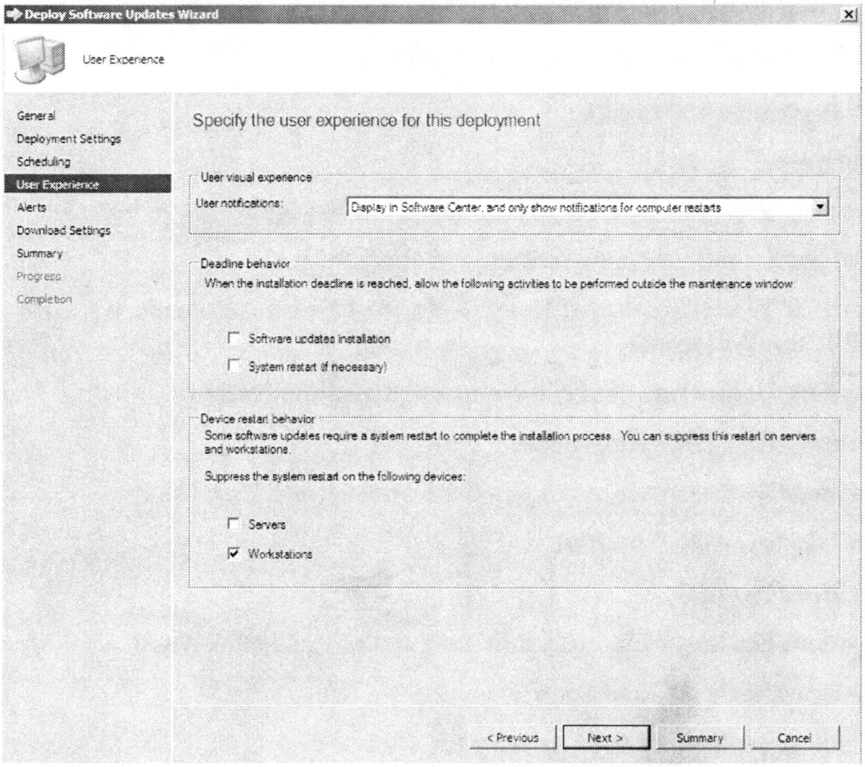

Configuring the user experience for workstations.

6. On the **Alerts** page, configure these settings and **click Next;**
    a. Generate an alert when the following conditions are met: **Enable**
    b. Client compliance is below the following percent: **95**
    c. Offset from the deadline: **21 Days**

7. On the **Download Settings** page, configure these settings and click **Next**:
    a. Deployment options for client within a slow or unreliable network boundary: Enable **Download software update from distribution point and install**.
    b. When software updates are not available on any preferred distribution points. Client can download and install software updates from a fallback source location for content: Enable **Download and install software updates from the fallback content source location.**
8. On the **Summary** page, click **Save As Template**, type **Workstation Production** as the name, and click **Save.**
9. Click **Next** and then **Close**.

Create the Automatic Server Deployment

You create the Server Automatic deployment with these settings:

- Full user experience where all notifications are displayed.
- Install as soon as possible and restart.

Complete the following steps:

1. Navigate to the new **Software Update Group**, and click **Deploy** on the ribbon
2. On the **General** page, configure these settings and click **Next**:
    a. Name: SRV *Year* + *Number of Month* + *Name of Month* Automatic, e.g. **SRV 2012 06 June Automatic**
    b. Description: **All servers that can be updated automatically**
    c. Collection: **SUM SRV Automatic**
3. On the **Deployment Settings** page, configure these settings and click **Next**:
    a. Type of deployment: **Required**
    b. Detail level: **Normal**
4. On the **Deployment Settings** page, configure these settings and click **Next**:
    a. Software available time: **As soon as possible**
    b. Installation deadline: **As soon as possible**
5. On the **User Experience** page, configure this setting and click **Next**:

    User notifications: **Display in Software Center and show all notifications**

6. On the **Alerts** page, configure these settings and click **Next**.:
   a. Generate an alert when the following conditions are met: **Enable**
   b. Client compliance is below the following percent: **95**
   c. Offset from the deadline: **21 Days**
7. On the **Download Settings** page, configure these settings and click **Next**:
   a. Deployment options for client within a slow or unreliable network boundary: Enable **Download software update from distribution point and install.**
   b. When software updates are not available on any preferred distribution points. Client can download and install software updates from a fallback source location for content: Enable **Download and install software updates from the fallback content source location**.
8. On the **Summary** page, click **Save As Template**, type **Server Automatic** as the name, and click **Save**.
9. Click **Next** and then **Close**.

Create the Manual Server Deployment

You create the Server Manual deployment with these settings:

- Full user experience where all notifications are displayed.
- Updates are only made available but never installed automatically.

Complete the following steps:

1. Navigate to the new **Software Update Group**, and click **Deploy** on the ribbon
2. On the **General** page, configure these settings and click **Next**:
   a. Name: SRV *Year + Number of Month + Name of Month* Manual, e.g. **SRV 2012 06 June Manual**
   b. Description: **All servers that can updated automatically**
   c. Collection: **SUM SRV Manual**
3. On the **Deployment Settings** page, configure these settings and click **Next**:
   a. Type of deployment: **Available**
   b. Detail level: **Normal**
4. On the **Deployment Settings** page, configure this setting and click **Next**:

   Software available time: **As soon as possible**
5. On the **User Experience** page, configure this setting and click **Next**:

   User notifications: **Display in Software Center and show all notifications**

6. On the **Alerts** page, click **Next.**
7. On the **Download Settings** page, configure these settings and click **Next**:
    a. Deployment options for client within a slow or unreliable network boundary: Enable **Download software update from distribution point and install.**
    b. When software updates are not available on any preferred distribution points. Client can download and install software updates from a fallback source location for content: Enable **Download and install software updates from the fallback content source location.**
8. On the **Summary** page, click **Save As Template**, type **Server Manual** as the name, and click **Save.**
9. Click **Next** and then **Close.**

How and When Updates Are Downloaded to the Client

Clients only download required software updates, regardless of the number of updates in the software update package. If a deployment purpose is required, then updates start downloading when the client reads the machine policy. Updates remain in cache and are applied according to the deadline in the deployment. If a deployment purpose is available, then updates are downloaded when the client initiates the installation.

Monitor the Deployments

1. Log on to **PC001**, open the **Control Panel**, select the **System and Security** category, and then open **Configuration Manager Properties**.
2. On the **Actions** tab, select **Software Updates Deployment Evaluation Cycle** and click **Run Now**. It might take a few minutes for the client to perform the evaluation cycle.

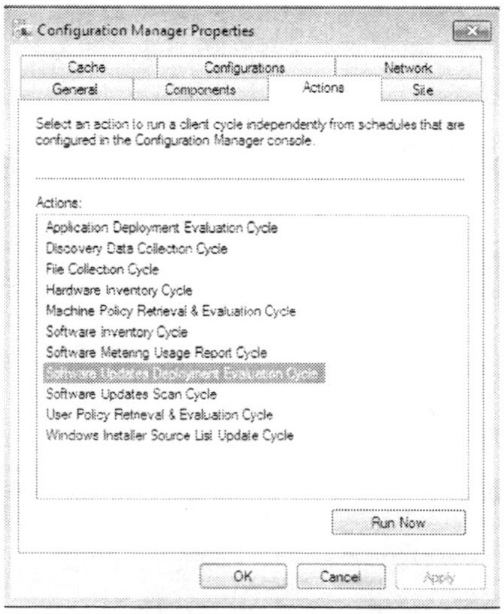

Initiating the software update evaluation cycle.

3. From the **Start** menu, select **All Programs**, **Microsoft System Center 2012**, **Configuration Manager**, **Software Center**.

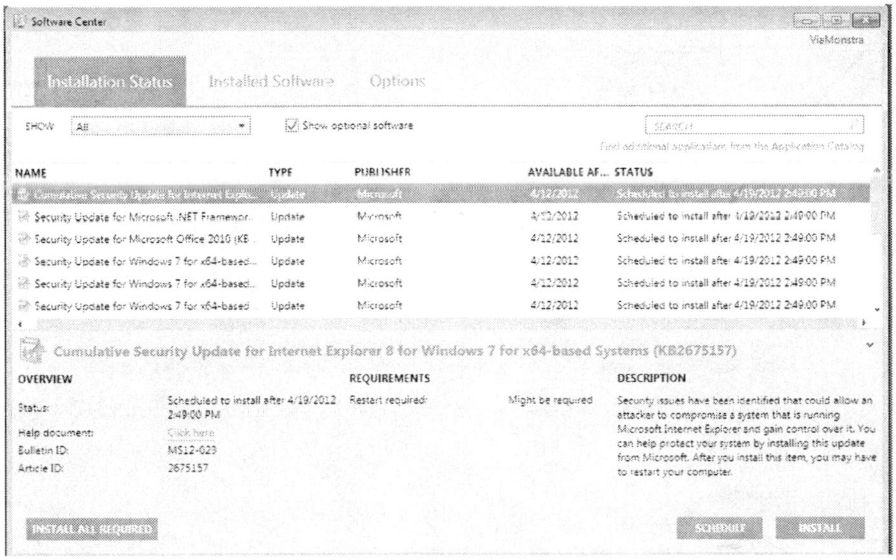

Monitoring the deployment from the Software Center.

4. Click **INSTALL ALL REQUIRED** and click **OK**.
5. Click **Restart** after all the updates are installed.
6. Log on to **CM01** as **Administrator** and open the **ConfigMgr console**.
7. Navigate to the **Monitoring** workspace, and select **Deployments**.
8. Type **2012 06 June** in the search field. You should see the four deployments.
9. Select the deployment target for the **SUM Pilot 1 Deployment** collection and click **View Status** in the dashboard.
10. Depending on your maintenance windows, you should be able to see the deployment states as either **Compliant** or **In Progress**. If the status is **Unknown**, click **Run Summarization and Refresh**.

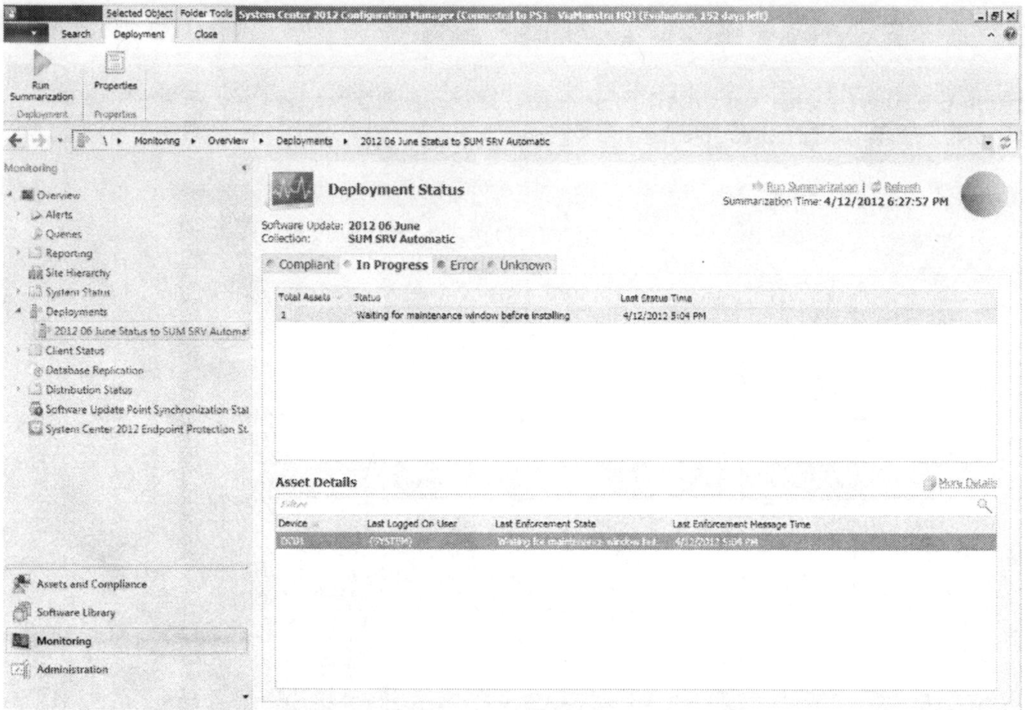

Monitoring the server automatic deployment.

11. In the **In Progress** tab, select **DC01** and click **More Details**.

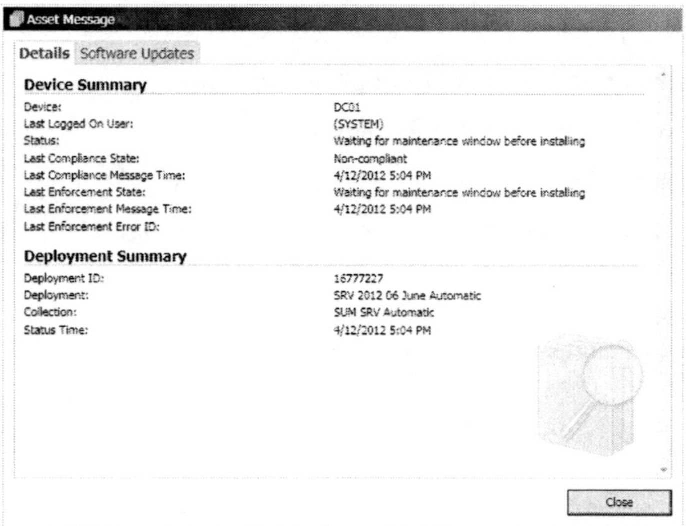

Detailed deployment summary

12. Select the **Software Updates** tab and see the number of updates that will be installed during the next maintenance window.
13. Close the **Asset Message** window.

Monitor the Deployments Using Reports

1. Open **Internet Explorer** and go to **http://CM01/Reports/Pages/Folder.aspx**.
2. Navigate to **ConfigMgr_PS1/ Software Updates - C Deployment States**, and run the report **States 1 - Enforcement states for a deployment**.
3. In **Deployment**, select the **SRV 2012 06 Automatic** deployment and click **View Report**.

House Cleaning and Deleting Expired Updates

As time goes by, updates will be superseded or expired by Microsoft. Expired updates are not requested by any client, but they remain in the update packages and in the source folders. Over time this can result in several gigabytes of data just filling up your discs. ConfigMgr has a non-configurable maintenance task that automatically removes expired updates from distribution points. The process, however, does not remove updates that are still part of a deployment. For that reason, you should incorporate a process to remove expired updates from active deployments.

After the updates are removed from the deployments, you also should remove them from the software update source folder. Microsoft has published a script that you use in this section to perform that process of deleting expired updates that are no longer part of any active deployment. Jason Gither, the author of the script, graciously allowed me to add the script to the sample files of this book.

Find and Remove Expired Updates from Deployments

1. Log on to the **CM01** server as **Administrator** and open the **ConfigMgr console**.
2. Select the **Software Library** workspace, and click **Software Updates**, **All Software Updates**.
3. Place the cursor in the **Search** column and click **Add Criteria** on the ribbon.
4. Select **Expired** from the list of criteria. Notice the extra line with the criteria.
5. Click **Search**. You should get a list with all expired updates.
6. Click **Save Current Search** on the ribbon and save the search as **All Expired updates**.
7. Click **Saved Searches** on the ribbon and select **Manage Searches for Current Node**.
8. Select **All Expired Updates** and click **OK**.

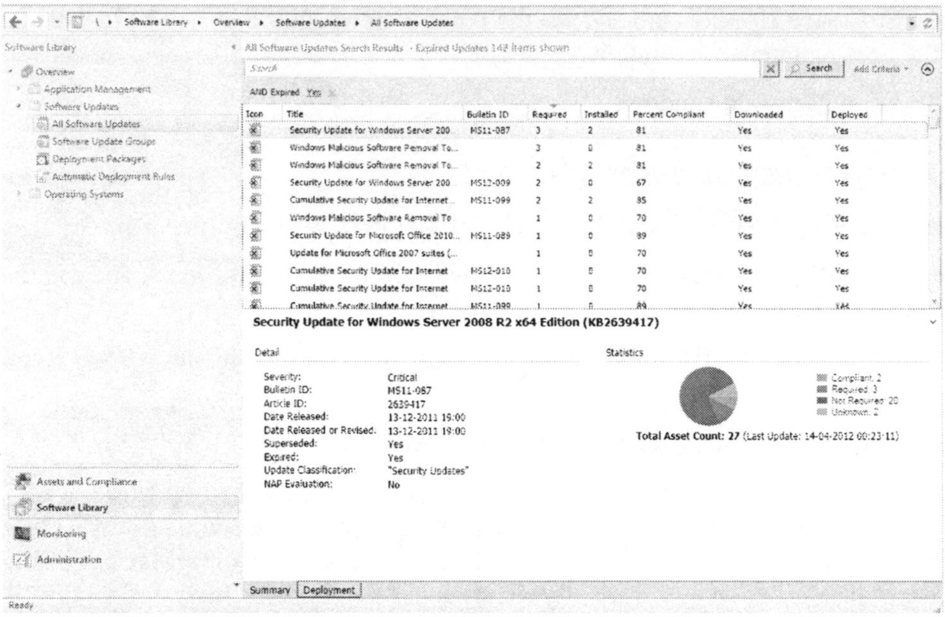

Finding all expired updates.

9. Press **Ctrl+A** to select all the updates, and then click **Edit Membership** on the **Home** tab in the ribbon.

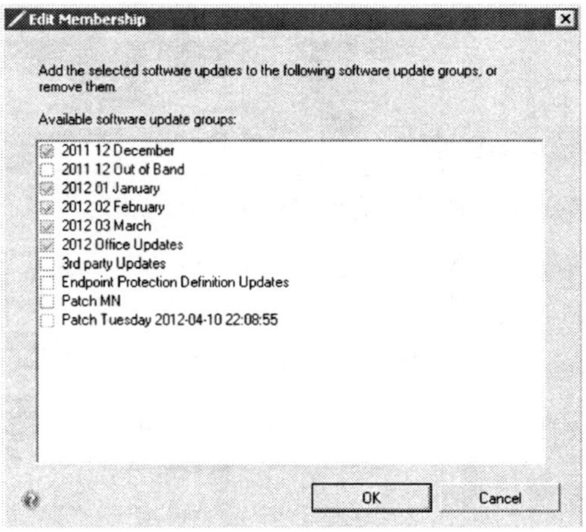

Removing updates from deployments.

10. Remove the updates by unchecking each of the update groups. Note that the illustration above is not taken from the ViaMonstra installation.

11. Click **OK** to return to the ConfigMgr console.

Remove Expired Updates from the Source Folder

1. Log on to **CM01** as **Administrator**.
2. Copy the **RemoveExpired.vbs** script from the book sample files to **D:\Sources\Updates** on **CM01**.
3. Open a command prompt as **Administrator** and navigate to **D:\Sources\Updates**.
4. Run **cscript.exe RemoveExpired.vbs**.

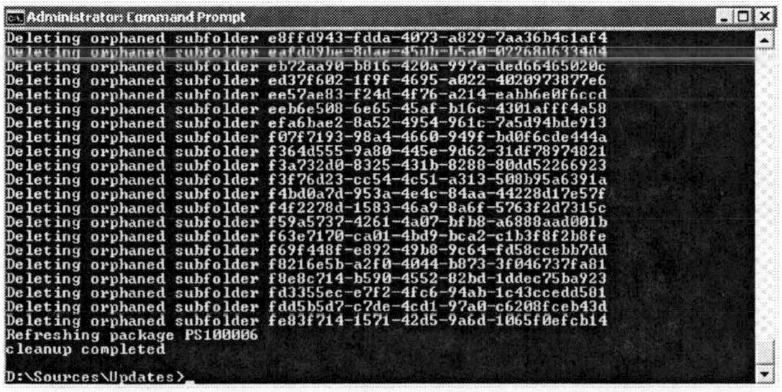

Removing expired updates from the source folders.

The following screenshots are taken before and after running the script on a site server with four months of updates. Almost 4 GB of data were removed.

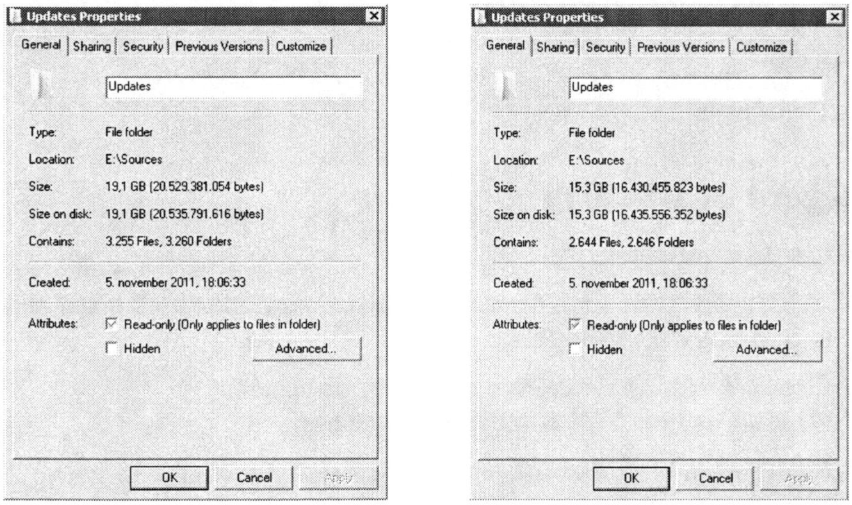

Before running the script on the left and after on the right.

Deploy Custom Software Updates

Any software update policy should contain more than just a focus on Windows updates. Out of the box, there is no real good way to deploy third-party updates with ConfigMgr. What most organizations do is integrate either Microsoft System Center Updates Publisher (SCUP) or a third-party solution like Secunia CSI or Solarwinds Patch Manager.

System Center Updates Publisher (SCUP)

SCUP 2011 is a free updates publishing and authoring application. You can benefit from this application by downloading free catalogs from vendors Like Adobe, HP, and Dell, or by subscribing to the SCUPdates catalog from VMware (a service that is not free). Furthermore, you can author your own updates and publish those to WSUS. The benefit of using SCUP vs. application deployment in ConfigMgr is the detection methods. As with any Microsoft update, your updates will be installed only if the computer requires the update.

SCUP 2011 can be downloaded from http://tinyurl.com/7llvmvy.

SCUP Requirements

- Supported Operating Systems
- Windows Vista, Windows 7, Windows Server 2008, Windows Server 2008 R2
- Update WSUS-KB2530390-x64.exe
- Windows Server Update Services (WSUS) 3.0 SP2
- .NET Framework 4.0
- Trusted Signing Certificate

Install and Configure SCUP 2011

1. Log on to **CM01** as **Administrator**.
2. Download **WSUS-KB2530678-x64.exe** from **http://tinyurl.com/wsusupdatex64** and save the update in **D:\Setup\SCUP\Update**.
3. Open a command prompt with administrative privileges, navigate to **D:\Setup\SCUP\Update** and run **WSUS-KB2530678-x64.exe**.
4. Download **SCUP 2011** from **http://tinyurl.com/7jfd8kk** and save the file in **D:\Setup\SCUP**.
5. Open a command prompt with administrative privileges, navigate to **D:\Setup\SCUP**, and run **SystemCenterUpdatesPublisher.msi**.

6. Click **Next** to start the installation.

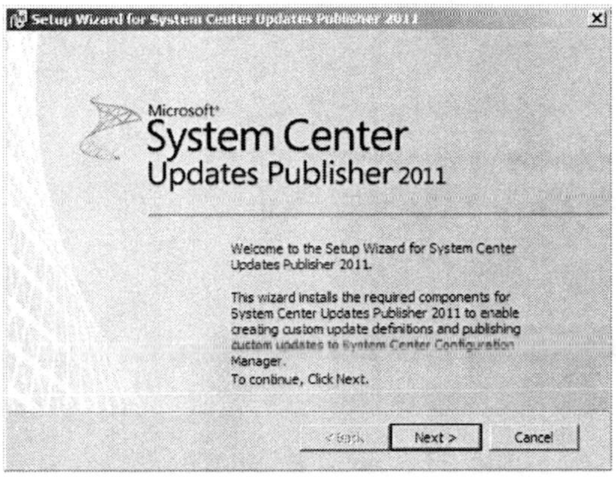

Installing SCUP 2011.

7. Click **Next**.
8. Accept the license terms and click **Next**.
9. Modify the installation location to **D:\Program Files (x86)\System Center Updates Publisher 2011**, and finish the wizard using the default settings.

Configure SCUP

You'll need to configure SCUP before you can use the application to publish updates. The configuration integrates SCUP with WSUS, creates the needed WSUS certificate, and integrates with ConfigMgr.

1. From the **Start** menu, right-click **System Center Custom Publisher** and select **Run as administrator**.
2. Click the top menu above the ribbon, and to the left of the **Home** tab, select **Options**.

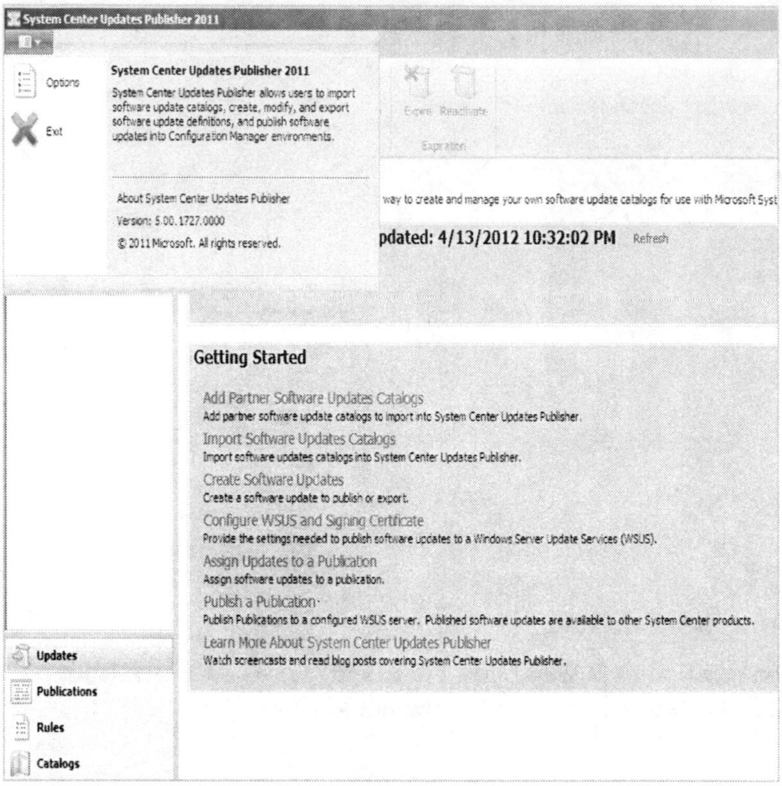

Configuring the SCUP options.

3. Select **Enable publishing to an update server** and click **Test Connection**.

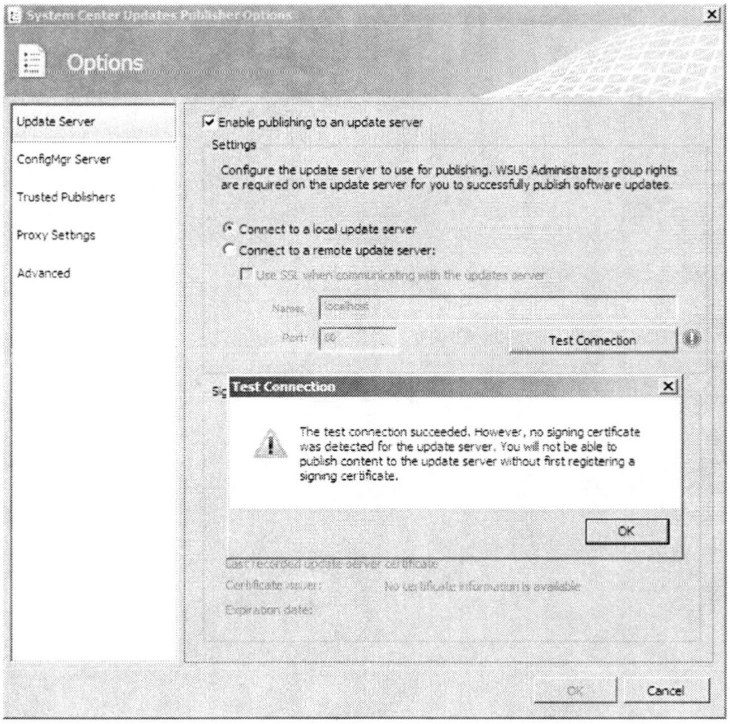

Configuring SCUP as a publishing server.

4. Read the Information about the signing certificate and click **OK**.
5. In **Signing Certificate**, click **Create** and then **OK**.

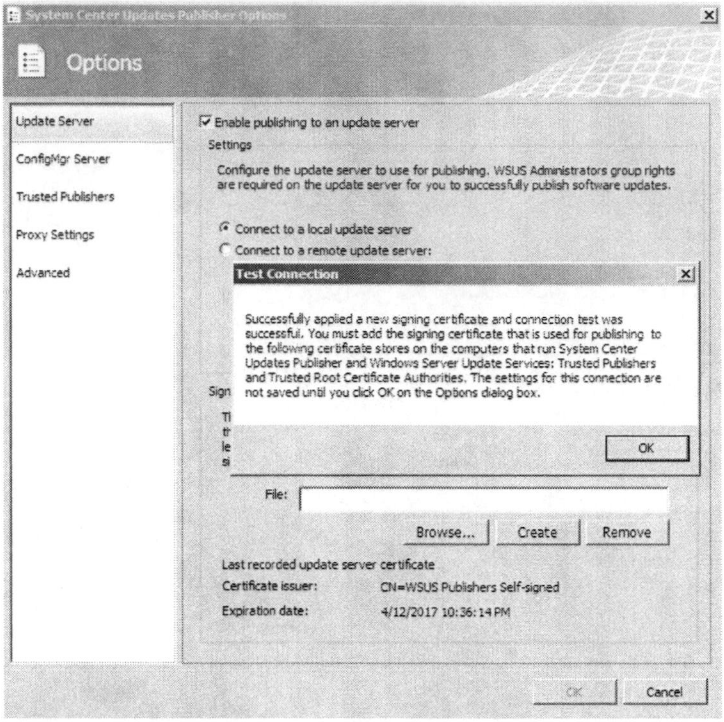

Creating the signing certificate.

6. Select **ConfigMgr Server** in the navigation pane.
7. Enable **Configuration Manager integration**.
8. Click **Test Connection** and click **OK**.
9. In **Requested client count threshold**, type **5**. This value specifies how many clients in ConfigMgr must request the update before SCUP downloads the binaries and changes the update status from automatic to full. Only updates that are deployed with full content can be installed on a client.
10. In **Package source size threshold (MB)**, type **20**. This value specifies that maximum file size of the update. You can still deploy updates beyond the size, but SCUP will not automatically convert the update into a full content update.
11. Click **OK** to save the changes.

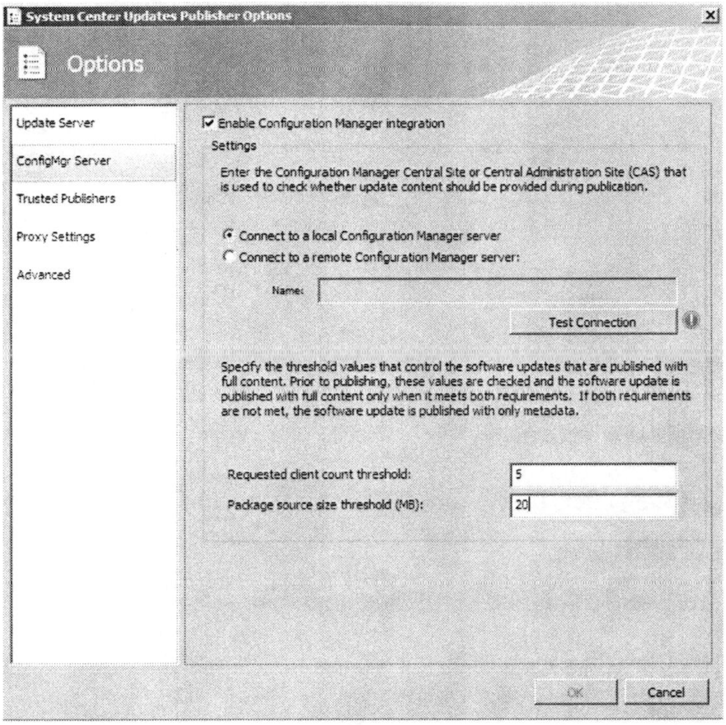

Configuring ConfigMgr integration.

Prepare the Certificate

The certificate must be deployed the local Trusted Root Certification Authorities and Trusted Publisher certificate stores. There are several ways to do that. I often prefer creating a package in ConfigMgr because I don't always have access to Active Directory and the Group Policy Management Console (GPMC). The certificate must be installed on the ConfigMgr server and all clients.

1. Log on to **CM01** as **Administrator**.
2. From the **Start** menu, click **Run** and enter **MMC**.
3. Press **Ctrl+M** and click **Add** to open the Add/Remove snap-in. Select **Certificates** and click **Add**.
4. Select **Computer account** and click **Next**.

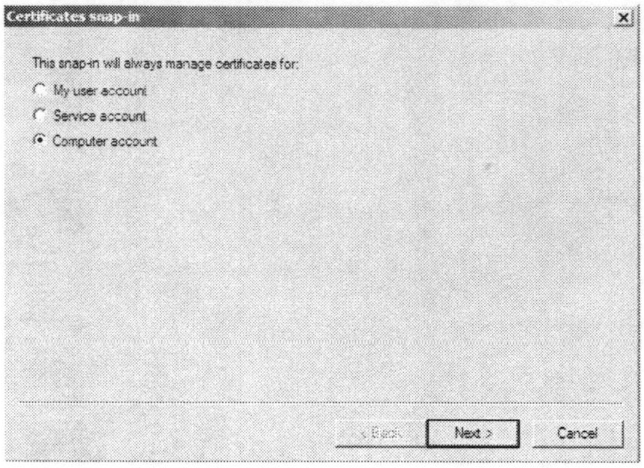

Opening the computer certificate store.

5. Select **Local Computer**, and then click **Finish** and **OK**.
6. Select **Certificates\WSUS\Certificates**.
7. Right-click the **WSUS Publisher Self-signed** certificate, and then select **All Tasks**, **Export**.

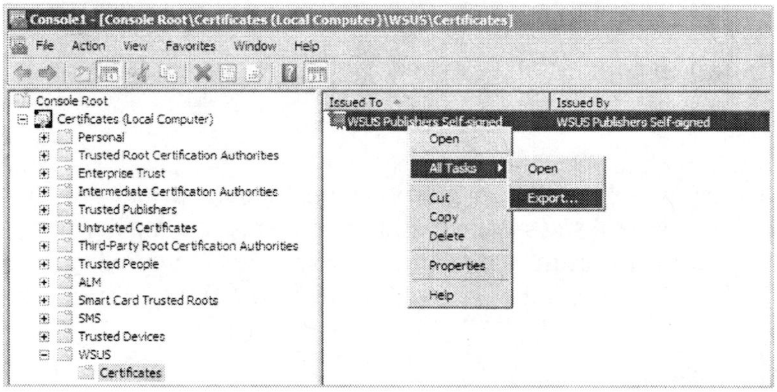

Exporting the WSUS self-signed certificate.

8. In the **Certificate Export Wizard**, click **Next**.
9. Make sure **No, do not export the private key** is selected and click **Next**.
10. Click **Next**.
11. Save the certificate as **scup2011.cer** in **D:\Sources\Software\SCUP Certificate**. Note that you need to create the folder first.
12. Click **Next**, **Finish**, and **OK** to close the wizard.

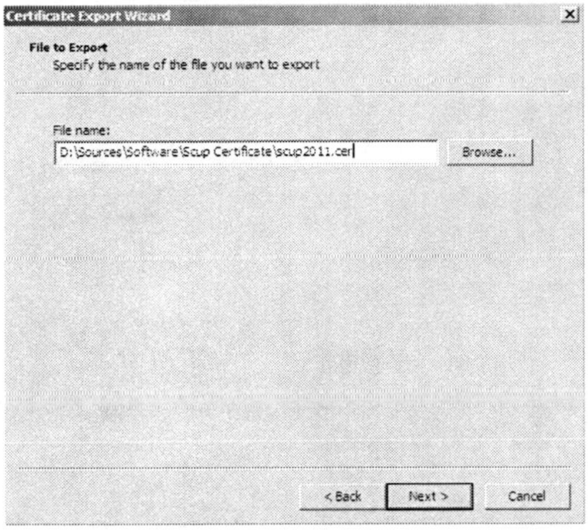

Exporting the certificate.

Create a Package and Deployment

The next step in the process is to deploy the certificate to all client computers. The installation is a simple command line and as such a good candidate for a package and not an application. You can install the certificate in the local certificate store by running the certutil.exe command. Certutil is found in C:\Windows\System32 on the Windows 7 clients.

1. Open the **ConfigMgr console** and navigate to the **Software Library** workspace.
2. Select **Application Management**, **Packages**, **Utilities**, and then click **Create Package** on the ribbon.
3. On the **Package** page, type these settings and click **Next**:
    a. Name: **SCUP 2011 Certificate**
    b. Description: **Install the WSUS publishing certificate into trusted publisher and trusted root certificate stores**
    c. Manufacturer: **ViaMonstra**
    d. Version: **1.0**
    e. This packages contains source files: **Enable**
    f. Source folder: **\\CM01\Sources$\Software\SCUP Certificate**

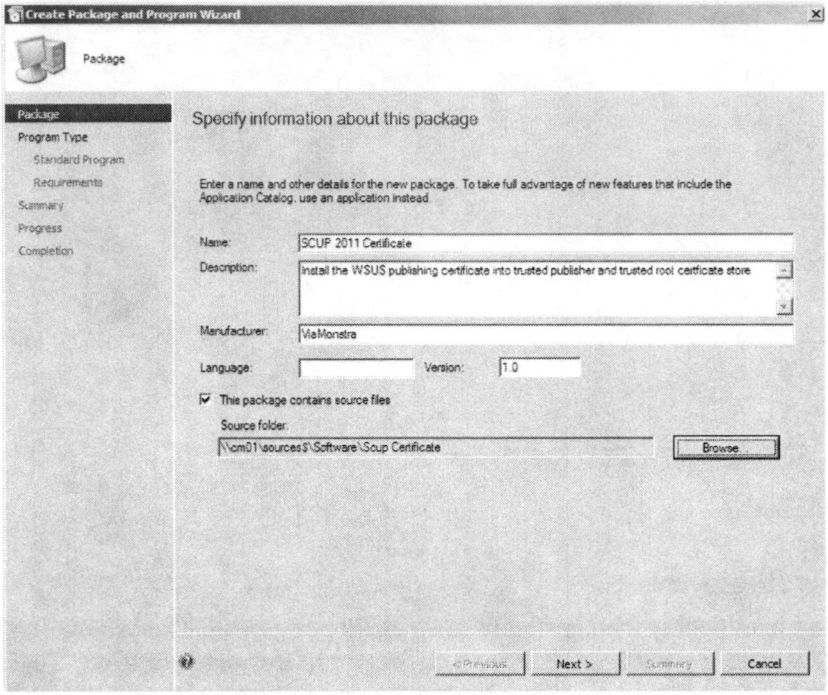

Creating the WSUS certificate package.

4. On the **Program Type** page, select **Standard program** settings and click **Next**.
5. On the **Standard Program** page, configure these settings and click **Next**:
    a. Name: **Import WSUS certificate into Root**
    b. Command line: **certutil.exe -addstore Root scup2011.cer**
    c. Program can run: **Whether or not a user is logged on**
6. On the **Requirements** page, click **Next**.
7. On the **Summary** page, read the summary, click **Next** to start creating the package, and then click **Close**.
8. Select the **SCUP 2011 Certificate** package and click **Create Program** on the ribbon.
9. On the **Program Type** page, select **Standard program** settings and click **Next**.
10. On the **Standard Program** page, configure these settings and click **Next**:
    a. Name: **Import WSUS certificate into Trusted**
    b. Command line: **certutil.exe -addstore TrustedPublisher scup2011.cer**
    c. Program can run: **Whether or not a user is logged on**

11. On the **Requirements** page, configure these settings and click **Next**:
    a. Run another program first: **Enable**
    b. Package: Click **Browse**, select **ViaMonstra SCUP 2011 Certificate 1.0**, and click **OK**.
    c. Program: **Import WSUS certificate into Root**
12. On the **Summary** page, read the summary, click **Next** to start creating the package and **Close**.
13. Click **Finish**.
14. Select the **SCUP 2011 Certificate** package and click **Distribute Content** on the ribbon.
15. On the **General** page, click **Next**.
16. On the **Content Destination** page, select **Add, Distribution Point Group**.
17. Select the **All Content** distribution point group, click **OK**, and then click **Next**.
18. On the **Summary** page, read the summary and click **Next** to start the distribution.
19. Click **Close**.
20. Select the **SCUP 2011 Certificate** package and click **Deploy** on the ribbon.
21. On the **General** page, configure these settings and click **Next**:
    a. Software: Click **Browse** and select **Import WSUS certificate into Trusted**.
    b. Collection: Click **Browse** and select the **All Desktop and Server Clients** collection.
22. On the **Content** page, verify that the content is distributed to all distribution points and click **Next**.
23. On the **Deployment Settings** page, verify that purpose is **Required** and click **Next**.
24. On the **Scheduling** page, click **New** and then click **Assign immediately after this event**. Verify that **As soon as possible** is selected as the event, click **OK** and **Next**.
25. On the **User Experience** page, click **Software installation** to allow the program to run outside a maintenance window (the second check box on the page) and then click **Next**.
26. On the **Distribution Points** page, enable **Allow clients to use a fallback source location for content** and click **Next**.
27. On the **Summary** page, read the summary and click **Next** to start the deployment.
28. Click **Close**.

Import Custom Updates

The easiest way to get started with SCUP is by importing existing update catalogs. The free catalogs aren't that rich and often require additional testing. For those organizations that have Adobe Reader and Adobe Flash installed, I recommend starting with the Adobe catalog.

1. Open **System Center Updates Publisher** from the **Start** menu.
2. Navigate to the **Catalogs** workspace and click **Add Catalogs** on the ribbon.
3. Select all the **Adobe Systems** catalogs and click **Add**.

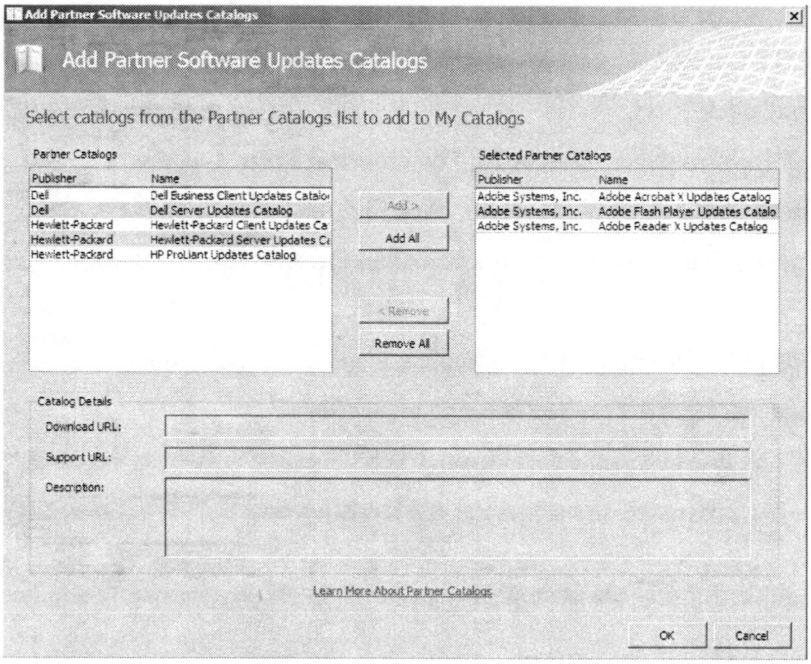

Adding the Adobe updates.

4. Click **OK** and navigate to the **Updates** workspace.
5. Click **Import** on the ribbon, select all catalogs, and click **Next** twice.
6. When prompted, select **Always accept content from "Adobe Systems, Incorporated"**, and click **Accept**. Click **Close** to finish the import.

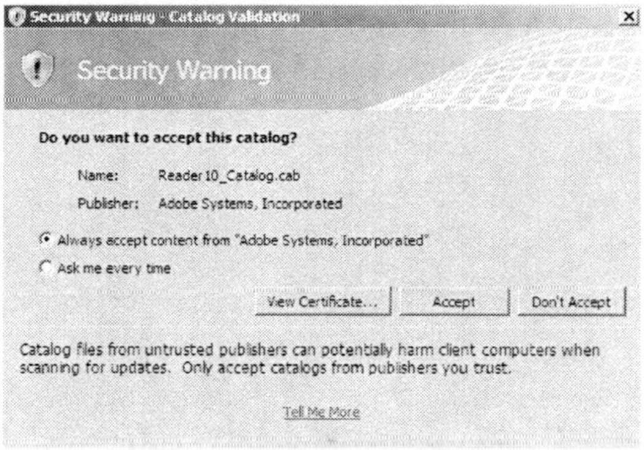

Accepting content from Adobe.

Publish Updates

Before you can start deploying custom updates through ConfigMgr 2012, you first have to publish them from SCUP into WSUS. When publishing updates, you have three options for each update. You can publish them as *metadata*, *full content*, or *automatic*.

- **Metadata.** When published as metadata, updates can be used only to track compliance. Metadata is not enough to install the update.
- **Full content.** Full content tells SCUP to download all the binaries needed for the update and publish them along with metadata to WSUS.
- **Automatic.** This option chooses either metadata or full content depending on the ConfigMgr integration that you have configured. SCUP 2011 performs a WMI query against ConfigMgr 2012 for all updates marked as automatic. If the update is required by more than the a specific number of hosts and the update binary size is less than the valued specified, then updates are published with full content; otherwise, updates are published with metadata only.

Publications

A publication is a list of updates that you have selected to work with. Usually you create a publication list and add the updates you to want to publish. By doing that, it is easier to find and manage the published updates. ViaMonstra has decided to create a new publication list every month using the same naming standard as that used for update groups.

Real World Note: Make sure the certificates have been deployed to **CM01** before publishing custom updates.

Publish Custom Updates

1. Open **System Center Updates Publisher** from the **Start** menu.
2. Navigate to **Adobe Systems, Inc\Adobe Flash Player**. Select the latest Flash Player versions (both the 32-bit and x64-bit plugins) and click **Assign** on the ribbon.

3. Select **Full Content** as the publication type. Select **Assign software updates to a new publication**, name the new publication **2012 06 June**, and click **OK**.

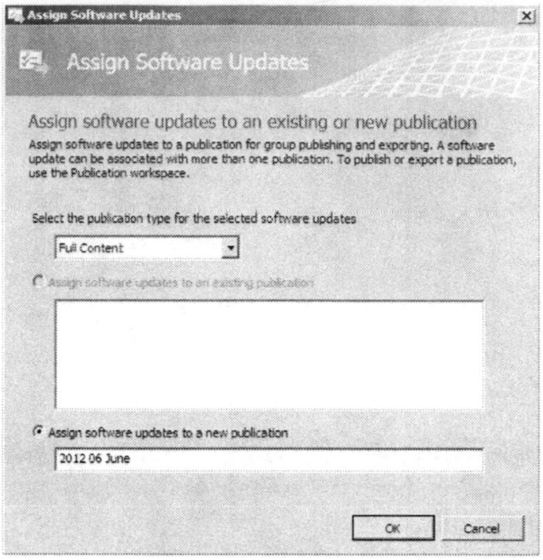

Creating the publication.

4. Navigate to **Adobe Systems, Inc\Adobe Reader**. Select the latest Reader version, click **Assign** on the ribbon and assign the update with **Full Content** to the **2012 06 June** publication.
5. Navigate to the **Publications** workspace and select **2012 06 June**. You should see all updates in the publication. Click **Publish** on the ribbon.
6. On the **Publish Options** page, click **Next**.
7. On the **Summary** page, read the summary and click **Next** to start publishing the updates.
8. On the **Confirmation** page, click **Close**.
9. Open the **ConfigMgr console** and navigate to the **Software Library** workspace.
10. Select **Software Updates, All Software Updates**, and then click **Synchronize Software Updates** on the ribbon. Click **Yes** in the dialog box and start the synchronization process.
11. Even though the in-console monitoring has improved a lot, it's still valuable to use the log files as they give you much more detailed real-time information. Open **D:\Program Files\Microsoft Configuration Manager\Logs\wsyncmgr.log** and monitor the process.

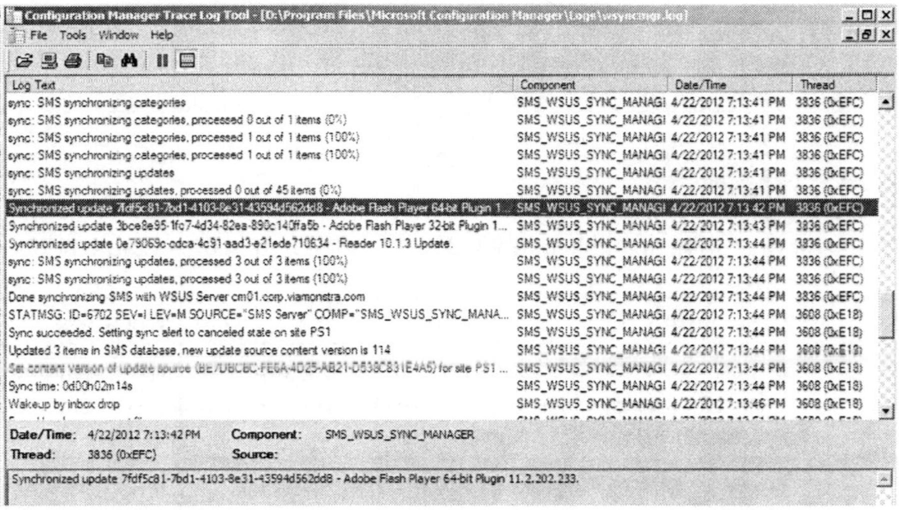

Monitoring the wsyncmgr.log file.

12. Open the **ConfigMgr console**, navigate to the **Software Library** workspace, and select **All Software Updates**.
13. Place the cursor in **Search** and click **Add Criteria** on the ribbon.
14. From the list of criteria, select **Vendor**.
15. Notice that **Adobe Systems, Inc** is selected in the Search Criteria (not really magic, the list is sorted alphabetically). Click **Search**.
16. Select all the **Adobe Systems** updates and click **Create Software Update Group** on the ribbon.
17. Type **CU 2012 06 June** as the name in Description **type Contain all custom updates published in June 2012** and click **Create**.

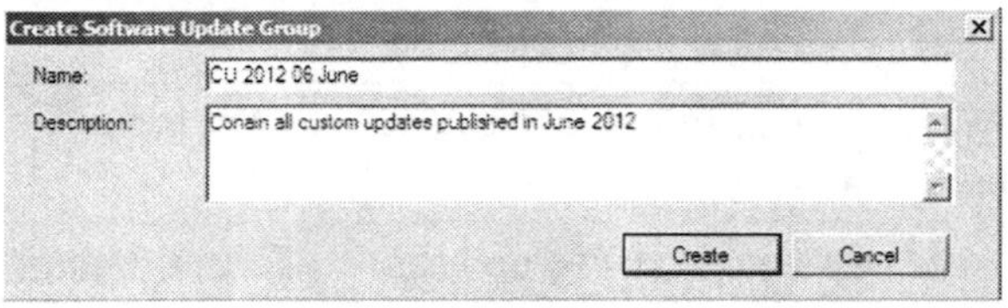

Creating a custom software update group.

The rest of the deployment process is similar to deploying Windows updates. ConfigMgr client does not treat third-party updates any differently than normal Windows updates. Having said that, in ViaMonstra, I prefer to create separate software update groups for the third-party updates and not mix them with our "normal" Microsoft Patch Tuesday updates.

Real World Note: Always manage the entire live cycle from the SCUP console. That includes expiring and deleting updates. When you expire and update from SCUP, the metadata are automatically synchronized to WSUS and ConfigMgr.

Useful Log Files

You can use the log files in the following table to track activity related to your software updates.

Log File	Description	Location
WCM.log	Records information about the SUP configuration, subscribed categories, classifications, and languages on the SUP server.	Server default
wsyncmgr.log	Records information about the synchronization process.	Server default
wctrl.log	Records information about the configuration, database connectivity, and health of the WSUS server.	Server default
scup.log	Records information about downloading and synchronizing custom updates to WSUS.	%temp% on the computer with the SCUP console installed
patchdownloader.log	Records information about downloading software updates from the update source to the specified source location for the Update package.	Client default on the computer from which the download was initiated
ruleengine.log	Records information about processing the automatic update rules.	Server default
windowsupdate.log	Default Windows Update agent log file. Records activity about scanning and installing updates.	C:\windows
WUAHandler.log	Records information about searching for updates	Client default
UpdatesDeployment.log	Records information about deployment, evaluations, and enforcements on the client.	Client default
UpdatesHandler,log	Records information about compliance scanning, and the download and installation of updates on the client.	Client default
UpdateStore.log	Records information about the compliance of updates that are scanned as part of the compliance scanning.	Client default

SoftwareDistribution.log	Records information about the software updates that are synchronized from the update source to the WSUS database	WSUS server %program files%\Update Services\Logfiles

Chapter 9 Endpoint Protection

Malware protection has over the years become more and more important. With ConfigMgr 2012, managing malware in a client environment has never been easier. The System Center Endpoint Protection feature is completely integrated with ConfigMgr without the need to install an additional reporting server or new database. Configuring and managing the solution can be divided into three major areas:

- Configuring the site system role and definition update settings
- Configuring the client settings and malware policies
- Configuring alerts and monitor the environment

Your first step before configuring your solution, however, is preparing for it by creating the proper collections. That is where I'll start.

Preparing for Endpoint Protection

Like with any other feature, it is important that your antimalware solution has a collection design that allows you to ease the administrative work while keeping complete control of the feature. When designing collections, it's important that you allow for a pilot group, applying different malware policies and excluding computers from being controlled by Endpoint Protection.

Endpoint Protection Collections

This section guides you through creating the needed Endpoint Protection collections. With those collections, you can create an Endpoint Protection solution in which you can run a pilot and allow for different malware templates.

- **EP Pilot 1.** Contains all computers that participate in the pilot test.
- **EP WRK Production.** All workstations in production that will have the Endpoint Protection client installed.
- **EP WRK Excluded.** Workstations that for any reason must be excluded from installing the Endpoint Protection client.
- **EP SRV ConfigMgr.** All System Center 2012 ConfigMgr servers.
- **EP SRV Domain Controllers**. All Windows domain controllers.
- **EP All Client**. Will include all EP collections and be used as target collection for the Endpoint Protection definitions deployments.

Create the Endpoint Protection Collections

1. Log on to **CM01** as **Administrator** and open the **ConfigMgr console**.
2. Navigate to the **Assets and Compliance** workspace, and select the **Endpoint Protection** folder.
3. Click **Create Device Collection** on the ribbon.
4. On the **General** page, define these settings and click **Next**:
    a. Name: **EP Pilot 1**
    b. Comment: **All computers that are part of the SCEP pilot**
    c. Limiting Collection: Click **Browse** and select **All Systems**.
5. On the **Membership Rules** page, define these settings and click **Next**:
    a. Enable **Use incremental updates for this collection**.
    b. Click **Add Rule, Direct Rule**.
6. On the **Welcome** page, click **Next**.
7. On the **Search Resources** page, type **PC001** in **Value** and click **Next**.
8. On the **Select Resources** page, select **PC001** and click **Next**.

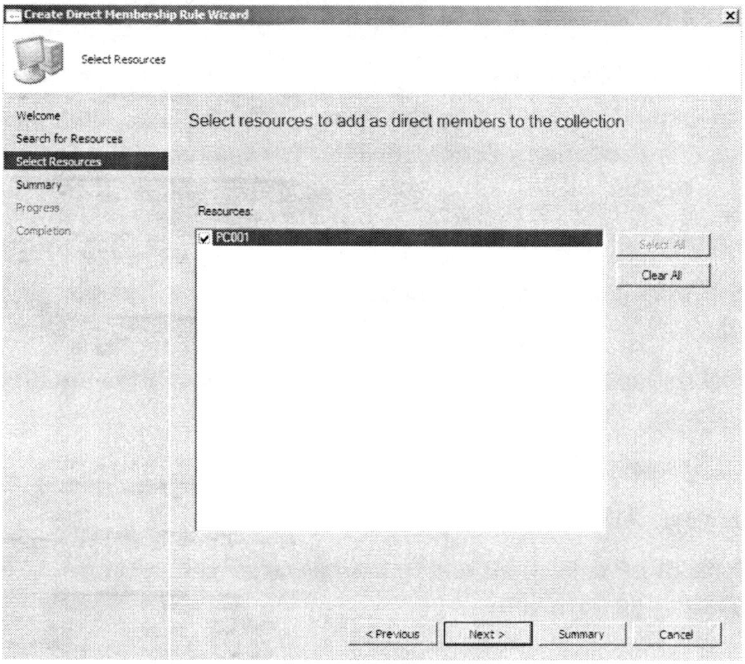

Creating a direct membership rule.

9. On the **Summary** page, read the summary and click **Next**.

10. On the **Completion** page, click **Close**.
11. On the **Membership Rules** page, verify that you have a direct rule and click **Next**.
12. On the **Summary** page, read the summary and click **Next**.
13. On the **Completion** page, click **Close**.

Create the Workstation Collections

1. Click **Create Device Collection** on the ribbon.
2. On the **General** page, define these settings and click **Next**:
   a. Name: **EP WRK Excluded**
   b. Comment: **All workstation computers that are excluded from Endpoint Protection**
   c. Limiting Collection: Click **Browse** and select **All Systems**.
3. On the **Membership Rules** page, click **Next** and **OK** in the warning dialog box.
4. On the **Summary** page, read the summary and click **Next**.
5. On the **Completion** page, click **Close**
6. Click **Create Device Collection** on the ribbon.
7. On the **General** page, define these settings and click **Next**:
   a. Name: **EP WRK Production**
   b. Comment: **All workstations in production that will have the Endpoint Protection client installed**
   c. Limiting Collection: Click **Browse** and select **All Systems**.
8. On the **Membership Rules** page, define these settings and click **Next**:
   a. Enable **Use incremental updates for this collection**.
   b. Click **Add Rule, Query Rule**.
   c. Name the rule **EP WRK Production** and click **Edit Query Statement**.
9. Select the **Criteria** tab.
10. Click the **yellow icon** to build the criteria and click **Select**.
11. Select **System Resource** as the **Attribute class**.
12. Select **Operating System Name and Version** as the **Attribute**.
13. Click **OK** to return to the Criterion Properties window.
14. Click **Operator** and select **is like** in **Value** type **%Workstation%**.
15. Click **OK** three times and return to the **Memberships Rules** page.

16. Click **Add Rule**, **Exclude Collections**.
17. Click the **Endpoint Protection** folder, select **EP WRK Excluded** and click **OK**.

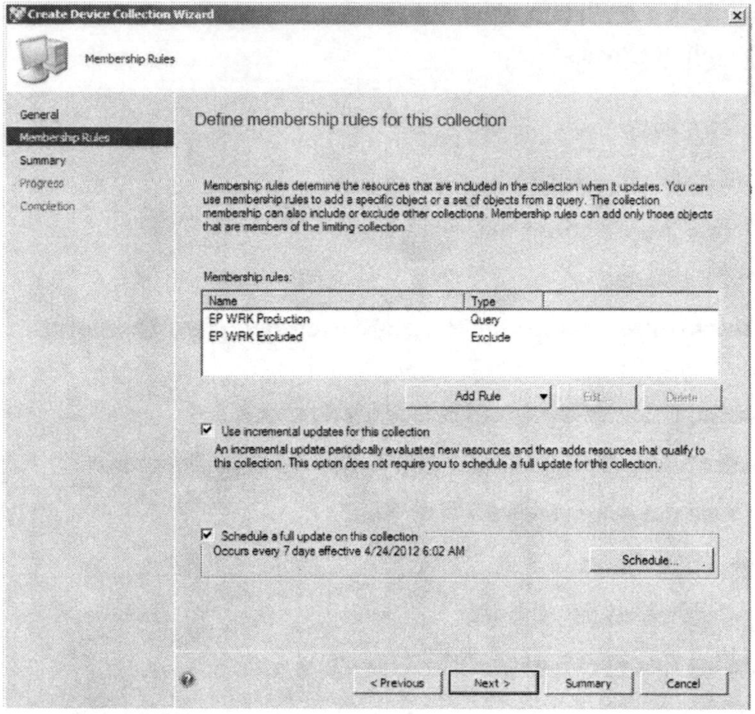

Creating the EP Workstations collection.

18. Finish the Create Device Collection Wizard using the default settings.

Automate Creating Exclude Rules in Collections Using PowerShell

In this example, you create an Exclude rule for the EP WRK Excluded collection in the EP WRK Production collection. (This is just a sample command and is not required for any of the guides in this book.)

1. Open **PowerShell** as **Administrator**.
2. Navigate to the folder containing the script.
3. Type **. .\CM12_Function_Library.ps1** and press **Enter**.
4. Type **Set-CMCollectionExcludeRule -SiteCode PS1 -SiteServer localhost -CollectionName "EP WRK Production" -ExcludeCollectionName "EP WRK Excluded"**; then click **Enter**.

Create the Server Collections

1. Click **Create Device Collection** on the ribbon.
2. On the **General** page, define these settings and click **Next**:
    a. Name: **EP SRV Domain Controllers**
    b. Comment: **All Domain Controllers**
    c. Limiting Collection: Click **Browse** and select **All Systems**.
3. On the **Membership Rules** page, define these settings and click **Next**:
    a. Enable **Use incremental updates for this collection**.
    b. Click **Add Rule, Query Rule**.
    c. Name the rule **EP SRV Domain Controllers** and click **Edit Query Statement**.
    d. Select the **Criteria** tab.
    e. Click the **yellow icon** to build the criteria and click **Select**.
    f. Select **Server Feature** as the **Attribute class.**
    g. Select **Name** as the **Attribute**.
    h. Click **OK** to return to the **Criterion Properties** window.
    i. Click **Operator** and select **is equal to**; in **Value**, type **Active Directory Domain Services.** (You also can click Value and select the group name from a list of applications.)
    j. Click **OK** three times to return to the Memberships Rules page.
4. Finish the wizard using the default settings.
5. Click **Create Device Collection** on the ribbon.
6. On the **General** page, define these settings and click **Next**:
    a. Name: **EP SRV ConfigMgr**
    b. Comment: **All System Center 2012 ConfigMgr servers**
    c. Limiting Collection: Click **Browse** and select **All Systems**.
7. On the **Membership Rules** page, define these settings and click **Next**:
    a. Enable **Use incremental updates for this collection**.
    b. Click **Add Rule, Query Rule**.
    c. Name the rule **EP SRV ConfigMgr** and click **Edit Query Statement**.
    d. Select the **Criteria** tab.
    e. Click the **yellow icon** to build the criteria and click **Select**.

f. Select **Add/Remove Programs(64)** as the **Attribute class**.

g. Select **Display Name** as the **Attribute**.

h. Click **OK** to return to the Criterion Properties dialog box.

i. Click **Operator** and select **is like**; in **Value**, type **Microsoft System Center 2012 Configuration Manager%**. Click **OK** three times to return to the Memberships Rules page.

8. Finish the wizard using the default settings.

Create the EP All Client Collection

1. Click **Create Device Collection** on the ribbon.
2. On the **General** page, define these settings and click **Next**:
   a. Name: **EP All Clients**
   b. Comment: **All clients with SCEP installed**
   c. Limiting Collection: Click **Browse** and select **All Systems**.
3. On the **Membership Rules** page, define these settings and click **Next**:
   a. Enable **Use incremental updates for this collection**.
   b. Click **Add Rule**, **Include Collection Rule**.
   c. Navigate to the **Endpoint Protection** folder and select all EP collections except **EP WRK Excluded** and click **OK**.

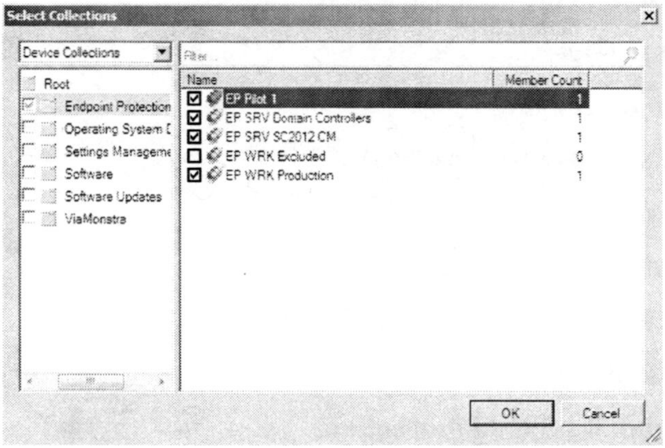

Create the EP All client collection

4. Finish the wizard using the default settings.

Configuring the Site System Role and Definition Update Settings

Install the Endpoint Protection Site System Role

1. Log on to **CM01** as administrator and open the **ConfigMgr console**.
2. Navigate to the **Administration** workspace and select **Site Configuration**, **Servers and Site System Roles**.
3. Click **CM01** and click **Add Site System Roles** on the ribbon.
4. Click **Next**.
5. On the **Site System Role Selection** page, select **Endpoint Protection Point**, accept the warning dialog, and click **Next**.
6. On the **Site System Role Selection** page, read and accept the license terms and then click **Next**.
7. On the **Site System Microsoft Active Protection Service** page, select **Advanced membership** and click **Next**.
8. On the **Summary** page, read the summary and click **Next** to enable the site system role.
9. On the **Completion** page, click **Close**.
10. Open the **EPSetup.log** file on the site server and monitor the EP installation.

Real World Note: A System Center Endpoint Protection client is installed automatically on the site server when you enable the site system role. The client is not a full protected client and is assigned a special malware policy called Reporting Server Default Policy. This policy does not enable real-time protection.

Configure Automatic Deployment of Definitions

One way to keep definition files up to date is by creating an automatic deployment rule using the software update feature:

1. Navigate to the **Software Library** workspace and select **Software Updates**, **Automatic Deployment Rules**.
2. Click **Create Automatic Deployment Rule** on the ribbon.
3. On the **General** page, configure these settings and click **Next**:
   a. Name: **Endpoint Protection Definitions**
   b. Collection: **EP All clients**

c. Enable: **Add to an existing Software Update Group**

d. Enable: **Enable the deployment after this rule is run**

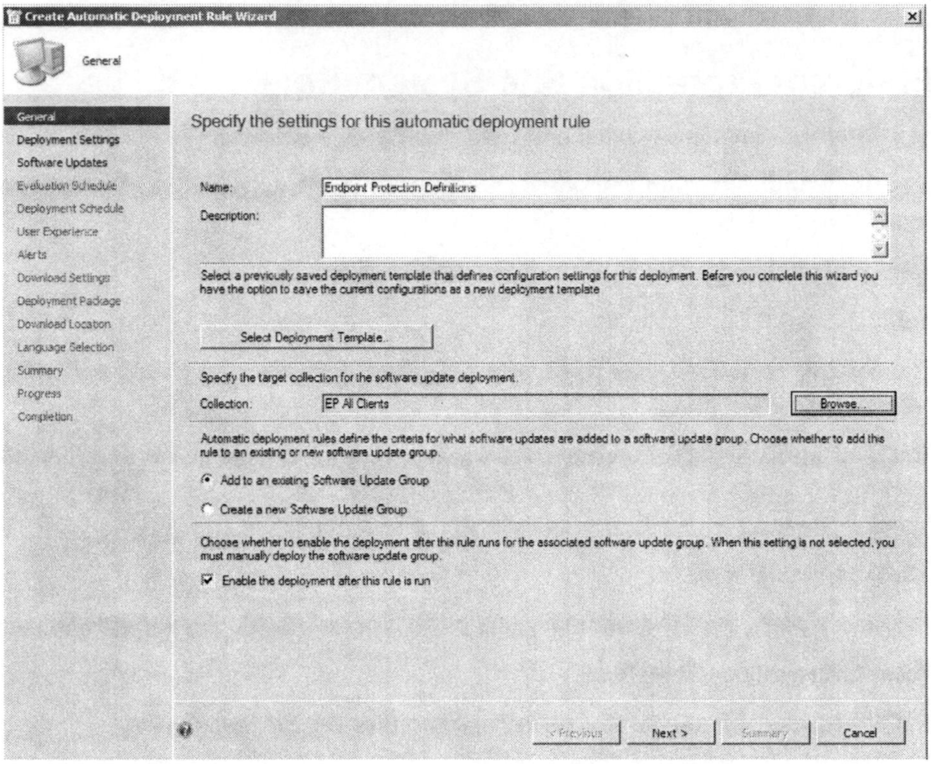

Creating an automatic deployment rule.

4. On the **Deployment** page, select **Minimal State message detail level** and click **Next**.
5. On the **Software Updates** page, select these settings and click **Next**:

   a. Date Released or Revised: **Last 1 month**

   b. Product: **Forefront Endpoint Protection 2010**

   c. Update classification: **Definition Updates**

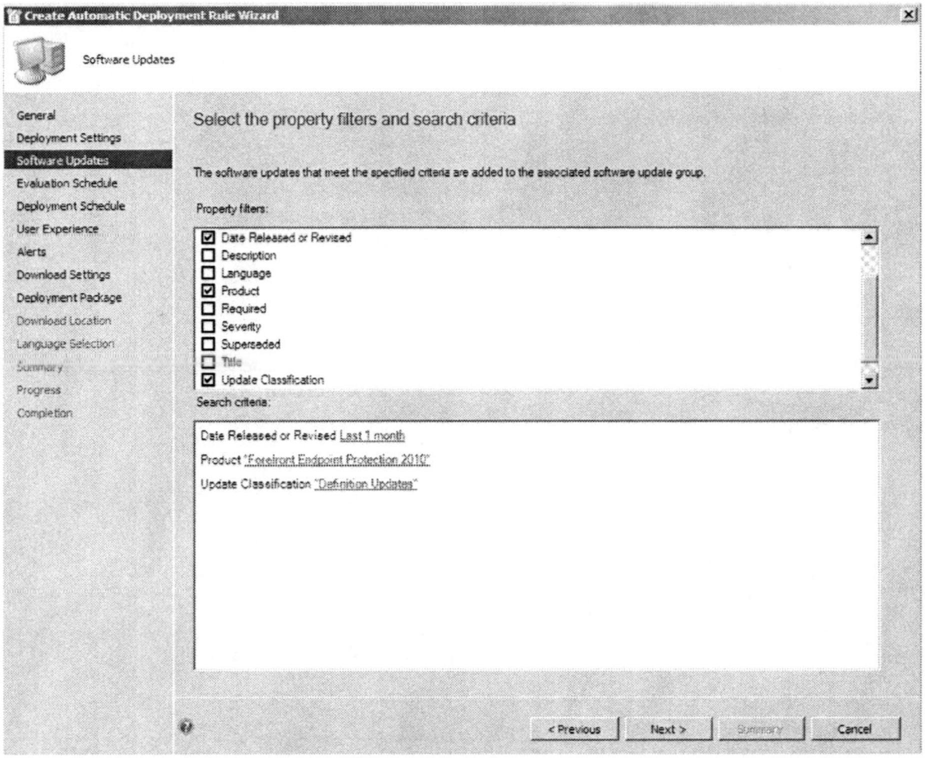

Filtering the definition updates.

6. On the **Evaluation Schedule** page click **Customize**, configure the rule to run every **8 hours** and click **Next**.
7. On the **Deployment Schedule** page, configure these settings and click **Next**:
    a. Software available time: **As soon as possible**
    b. Installation deadline: **As soon as possible**
8. On the **User Experience** page, configure these settings and click **Next**:
    a. User notifications: **Hide in Software Center and all notifications**
    b. Deadline behavior: Enable **Software Installation**.
    c. Device Restart Behavior: Enable **Servers and Workstations**.

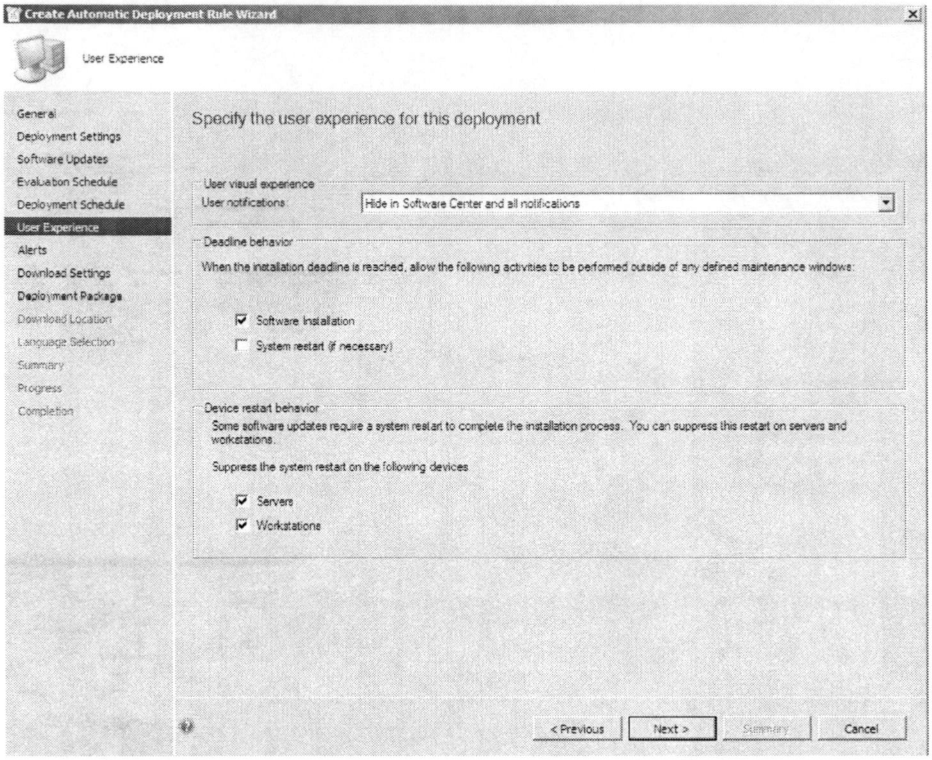

Hiding update activity for the user.

9. On the **Alerts** page, click **Next**.
10. On the **Download Settings** page, configure these settings and click **Next**:
    a. Deployment options for clients within a slow or unreliable network: **Download software updates from distribution point and install**
    b. Deployment options for when updates are not available on any preferred distribution points: **Download software updates from distribution point and install**
11. On the **Deployment Package** page, create a new deployment package with these settings and click **Next**:
    a. Name: **EP Definition Updates**
    b. Description: **EP Definition Updates**
    c. Package Sources: **\\CM01\Sources$\Updates\Definitions** (You need to create the Definitions folder manually.)
12. On the **Distribution Points** page, click **Add**, **Distribution Point Group**, **All Content** and then click **Next**.

13. On the **Download Location** page, ensure **Download software updates from the Internet** is selected and click **Next**.
14. On the **Language Selection** page, ensure **English** is the only selected language and click **Next**.
15. On the **Summary** page, click **Save As Template**. Type **EP Updates** in the template name, and then click **Save** and **Next**.
16. On the **Completion** page, click **Close**.
17. Select the **Endpoint Protection Definitions** automatic deployment rule and click **Run Now** on the ribbon. You can monitor the process by reading the **ruleengine.log** on the site server.
18. Click **Yes** to start the process.

Configuring Client Settings and Malware Policies

You control the SCEP client installation through Client Settings. This allows you to create a custom set of settings and deploy to a group of pilot computers. Endpoint Protection automatically removes existing antimalware client software on the computer prior to installing the new SCEP client. This works for some but not all antimalware clients. The only way for you to make sure that it will work in your environment is to test, test, and test. The following clients will be removed:

- Symantec AntiVirus Corporate Edition version 10
- Symantec Endpoint Protection version 11
- Symantec Endpoint Protection Small Business Edition version 12
- McAfee VirusScan Enterprise version 8
- Trend Micro OfficeScan
- Microsoft Forefront Codename Stirling Beta 2
- Microsoft Forefront Codename Stirling Beta 3
- Microsoft Forefront Client Security v1
- Microsoft Security Essentials v1
- Microsoft Security Essentials 2010
- Microsoft Forefront Endpoint Protection 2010
- Microsoft Security Center Online v1

> **Note:** If any of the preceding clients are not automatically removed, make sure that you remove the password from the client.

After the client is installed, you can control the antimalware policies by editing the default client antimalware policy or creating one or more custom policies. A client can only apply a single policy, and in the event of a conflict, the policy order value determines which one is applied. The one with the lowest value will take precedence over any higher value policies.

Installing and Managing EP Clients

Install the Client on the EP Pilot Collection

1. Log on to **CM01** as **Administrator** and open the **ConfigMgr console**.
2. Navigate to the **Administration** workspace.
3. Select **Client Settings** and click **Create Custom Client Device Settings** on the ribbon.
4. In **Name**, type **Endpoint Protection**.
5. From the list of custom settings, select **Endpoint Protection** and configure these settings:
    a. Manage Endpoint Protection on client computers: **True**
    b. Install Endpoint Protection client on client computers: **True**
    c. Automatically remove any previously installed antimalware software before Endpoint Protection is installed: **True**
    d. Suppress any required computer restarts after the Endpoint Protection client is installed: **True**
    e. Disable alternate sources: **True**

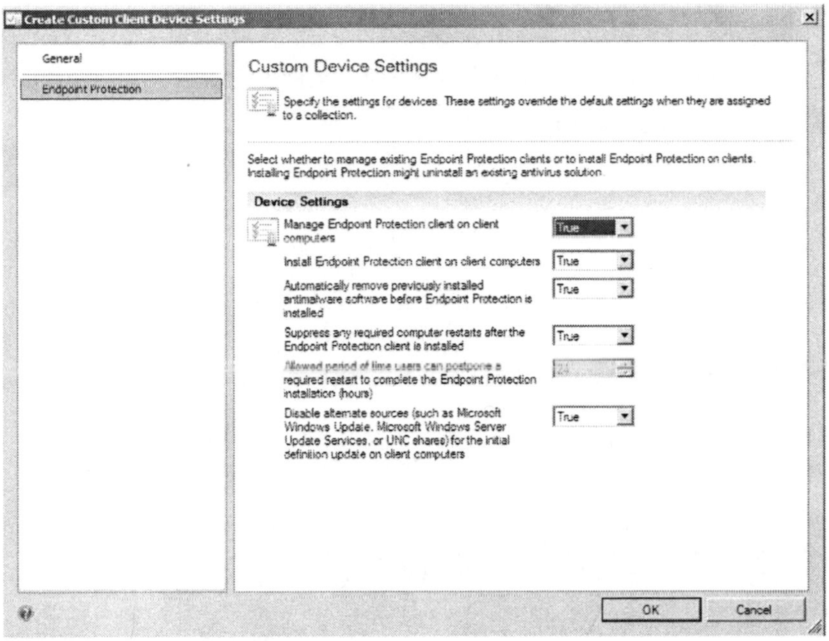

Configuring SCEP client properties.

6. Click **OK** to close the custom settings.
7. From the list of available client settings, select **Endpoint Protection** and click **Deploy** on the ribbon.
8. Navigate to the **Endpoint Protection** folder, select **EP Pilot 1** and click **OK**.
9. The installation starts as soon as the machine policy is updated.
10. You can monitor the installation in the **Deployments** section of the **Monitoring** workspace, or from the **EndpointProtectionAgent.log** file on the client.

Real World Note: To install the client manually, use SCEPInstall.exe /s /q /policy "full path to policy".

Verify the SCEP Client

Installing the client will take place as soon as the machine policy has been updated. The client will be installed from a local source using this command line:

C:\Windows\ccmsetup\SCEPInstall.exe" /s /q /NoSigsUpdateAtInitialExp /policy "C:\Windows\CCM\EPAMPolicy.xml"

After the client is installed, it connects to the ConfigMgr infrastructure and starts updating the SCEP engine and definitions.

View the Local SCEP Agent

1. Log on to **PC001** as **Administrator** and click **Show hidden icons** in the notification area.
2. Right-click the **SCEP** icon and select **Open**.

Opening the local SCEP settings.

The interface has four tabs, from which the client can read information about the protection status and, depending on the malware policy, also modify the settings.

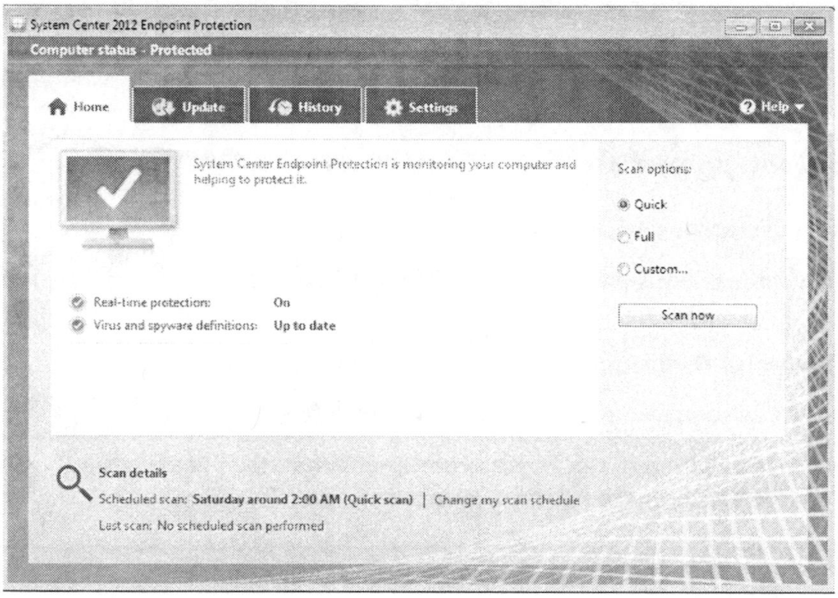

The SCEP client interface.

3. To view the applied malware policy, click the drop-down arrow next to **Help** and select **About System Center Endpoint Protection**.

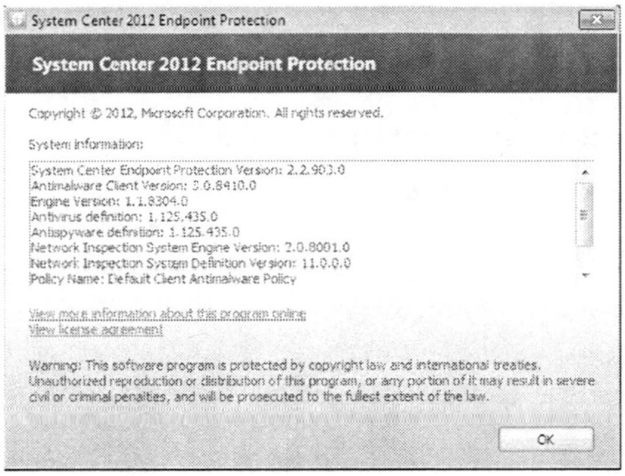

The SCEP system information.

4. Click **OK** to close the system information.

Edit the Default Antimalware Policy

An Antimalware policy is used to control how clients are protected against different types of malware. Malware means "**malicious software**," which is software or a piece of code designed to steal sensitive data or in any other way gain access to your computer. When creating an antimalware policy, you can control things like when to run a scan, excluding files and processes from the scan, enabling real-time protection, and much more. In ViaMonstra, the malware policy must include these settings:

- A daily quickly scan
- A weekly full scan every Friday morning 09:00
- Scan email
- Scan USB devices
- Enable real-time protection
- Configure Windows updates as the second download sources

Complete these steps:

1. Log on to **CM01** as **Administrator** and open the **ConfigMgr console**.
2. Navigate to the **Assets and Compliance** workspace, expand **Endpoint Protection**, and then select **Antimalware Policies**.
3. Select the **Default Client Malware Policy** and click **Properties** on the ribbon.
4. Click **Scheduled scans** and configure these settings:
    a. Run a schedule scan on client computers: **True**
    b. Scan type: **Full Scan**

c. Scan day: **Friday**

d. Scan time: **9 AM**

e. Check for the latest definition updates before running a scan: **True**

f. Run a daily quick scan on client computers: **True**

g. Daily quick scan schedule time: 12 PM

h. Check for the latest definitions before scanning: **True**

i. Limit CPU usage during scans to (%): **30**

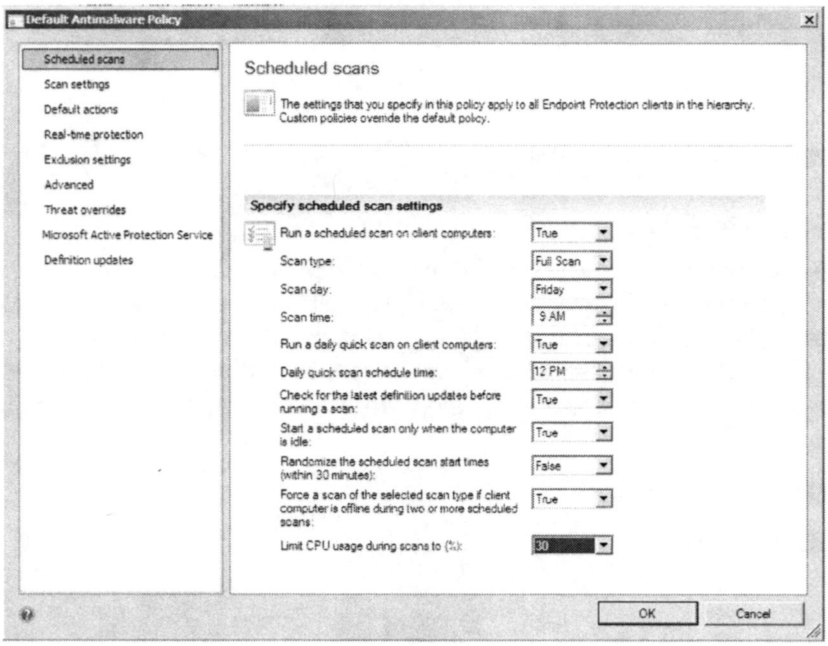

Modifying the default antimalware scheduled scan settings.

5. Click **Scan settings** and configure these settings:

   a. Scan email and email attachments: **True**

   b. Scan removable storage devices such as USB drives: **True**

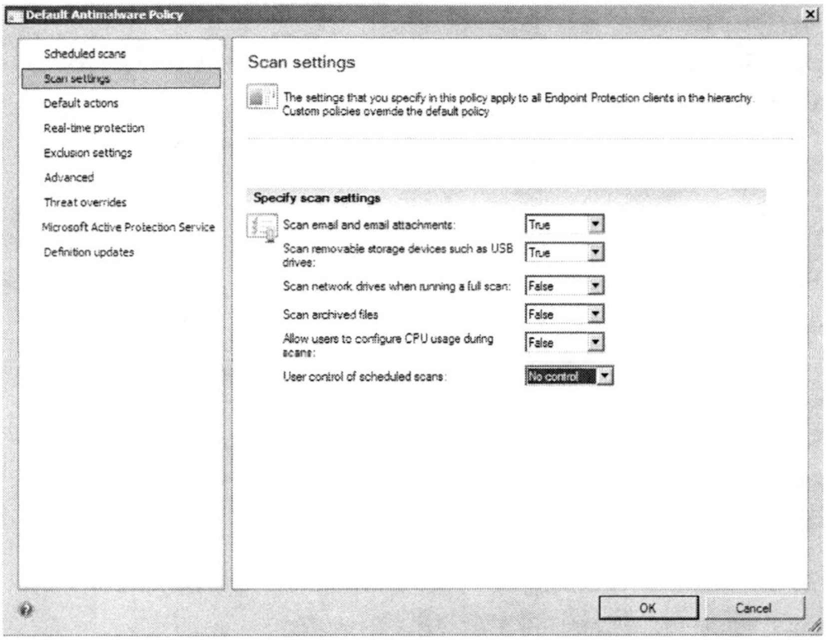

Configuring the default antimalware scan settings.

6. Click **Advanced** and configure this setting:

   Show notifications messages to users on client computer: **True**

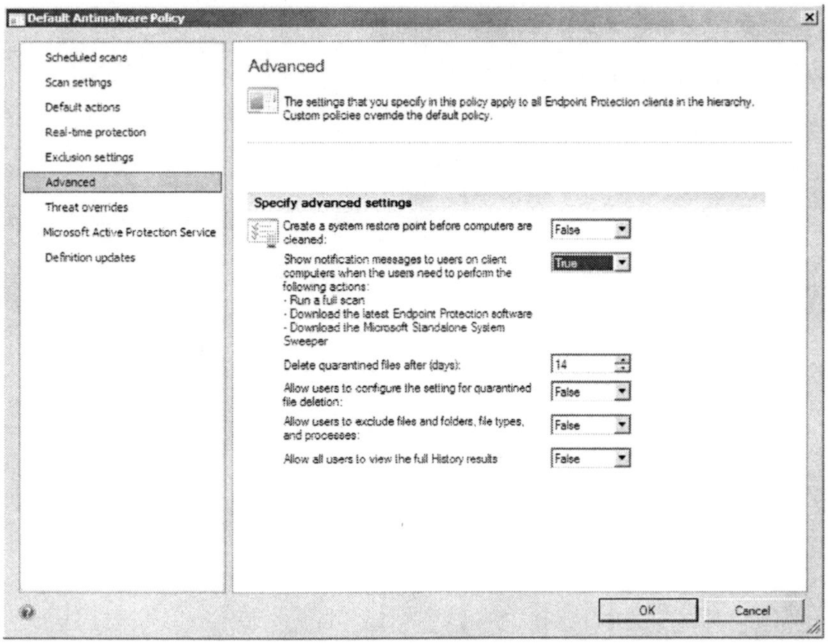

Configuring the default antimalware advanced settings.

7. Click **Definition updates** and configure this setting:

   Click **Set Source**, configure **Updates distributed from Microsoft Update** to be second in the list, and then click **OK**.

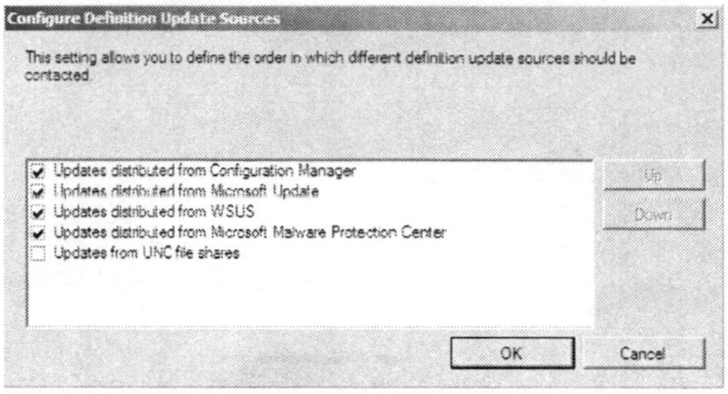

Configuring the definition update sources.

8. Click **OK**.

Create an Antimalware Policy for ConfigMgr 2012 Servers

1. Navigate to the **Assets and Compliance** workspace and select **Endpoint Protection**.
2. Select **Antimalware Policies** and click **Import** on the ribbon.
3. Scroll down the list of XML files, select **SCEP12_Default_CfgMgr2012.xml** and click **Open**.
4. Select **Real-time protection** and configure this setting:

   Enable real-time protection: **False**

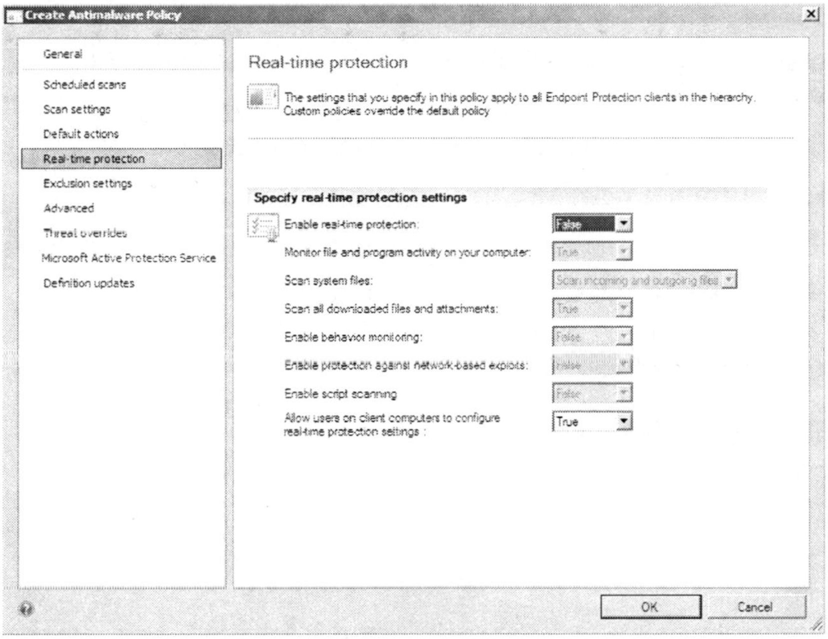

Disabling real-time protection on site servers.

5. Click **OK**.
6. Click **Import** on the ribbon.
7. Scroll down the list of XML files, select **FEP_Default_SQL2008.xml**, and click **Open**.
8. Click **OK** to close the policy without making any changes.
9. Select both of the two new antimalware policies (**Endpoint Protection SQL 2008** and **Endpoint Protection Configuration Manager 2012**) and click **Merge** on the ribbon.
10. Type **Configuration Manager 2012** as the **New Policy Name**, and configure the **Endpoint Protection Configuration Manager 2012** as the **Base Policy**.

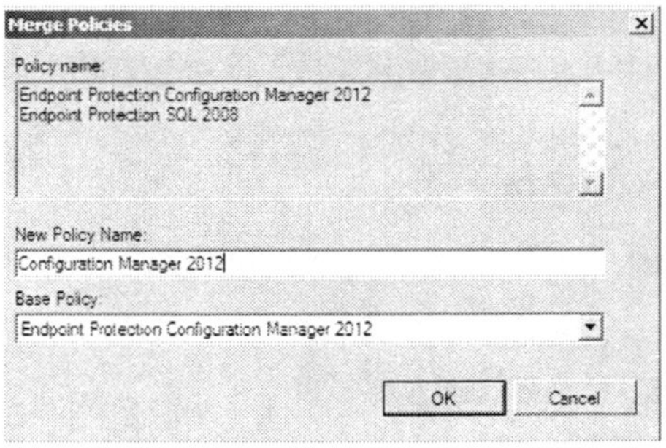

Merging antimalware policies.

11. Click **OK**.

Deploy Endpoint Protection

When the pilot phase is over, it's time to deploy the Endpoint Protection client to all other computers in the environment:

1. Log on to **CM01** as **Administrator** and open the **ConfigMgr console**.
2. Navigate to the **Administration** workspace.
3. Click **Client Settings,** select the **Endpoint Protection** and click **Deploy** on the ribbon.
4. Select **Endpoint Protection**, **EP All Clients** and click **OK**.

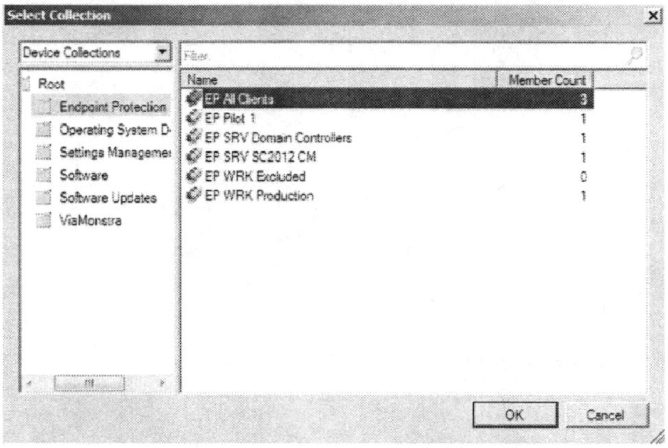

Deploying Endpoint Protection to all EP clients.

Deploy the ConfigMgr 2012 Antimalware Policy

1. Navigate to the **Assets and Compliance** workspace.
2. Navigate to **Endpoint Protection**, **Antimalware Policies**.
3. Select the **Configuration Manager 2012** policy and click **Deploy** on the ribbon.
4. Select the **EP SRV ConfigMgr** collection from the **Endpoint Protection** folder and click **OK**.
5. On the **Configuration Manager 2012** server, open the **Endpoint 2012** client from the notification area.
6. Click **Help**, **About System Center Endpoint Protection.**

   You should be able to see the current policy name.

Configuring Alerts and Monitor Malware Activity

Endpoint Protection is at present the only feature in ConfigMgr where you can configure email alert settings. As part of the planning process, you must plan for when you receive alerts and how you will react to those.

Configure Collection Alerts

Alerts are used to control when email notifications are being sent and whether collections are visible on the Endpoint Protection dashboard. It's not uncommon to have different alert settings for different workstations and servers.

1. Navigate to the **Assets and Compliance** workspace, and select **Device Collections** and the **Endpoint Protection** folder.
2. Right-click the **EP All Clients** collection and open the collection properties.
3. Select the **Alerts** tab, and enable **View this collection** on the **Endpoint Protection** dashboard.
4. Click **Add** and enable all the malware alerts. Click **OK** to close the dialog box.
5. Select the different conditions and notice the definitions.

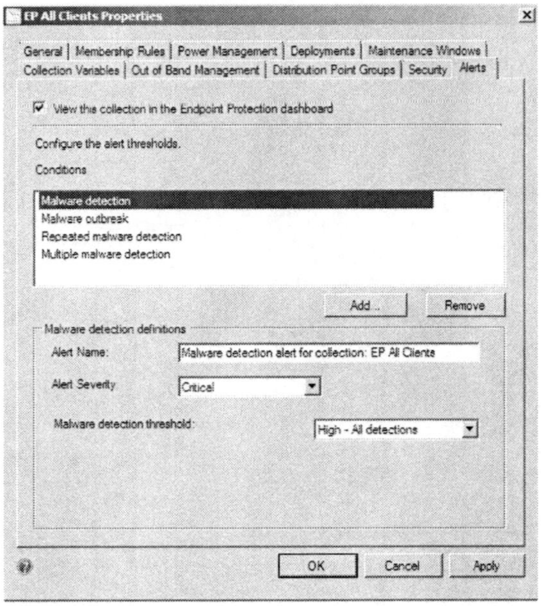

Configuring Endpoint Protection alerts.

6. Click **OK** and close the collection properties.

Configure Email Settings

1. Navigate to the **Administration** workspace, and select **Site Configuration, Sites**.
2. From the ribbon, select **Settings, Configure Site Components, Email Notification.**
3. Select **Enable email notification** and configure these settings:
   a. Enable email notification for Endpoint Protection alerts: **True**

   b. FQDN or IP Address of the SMTP server: **EX01.corp.viamonstra.com**
   c. SMTP Connection Account: **None (anonymous access)**.
   d. Sender address for email alerts: **administrator@corp.viamonstra.com**

4. Click **Test SMTP Server**, type **administrator@ corp.viamonstra.com** as the recipient, and click **Send test email**.

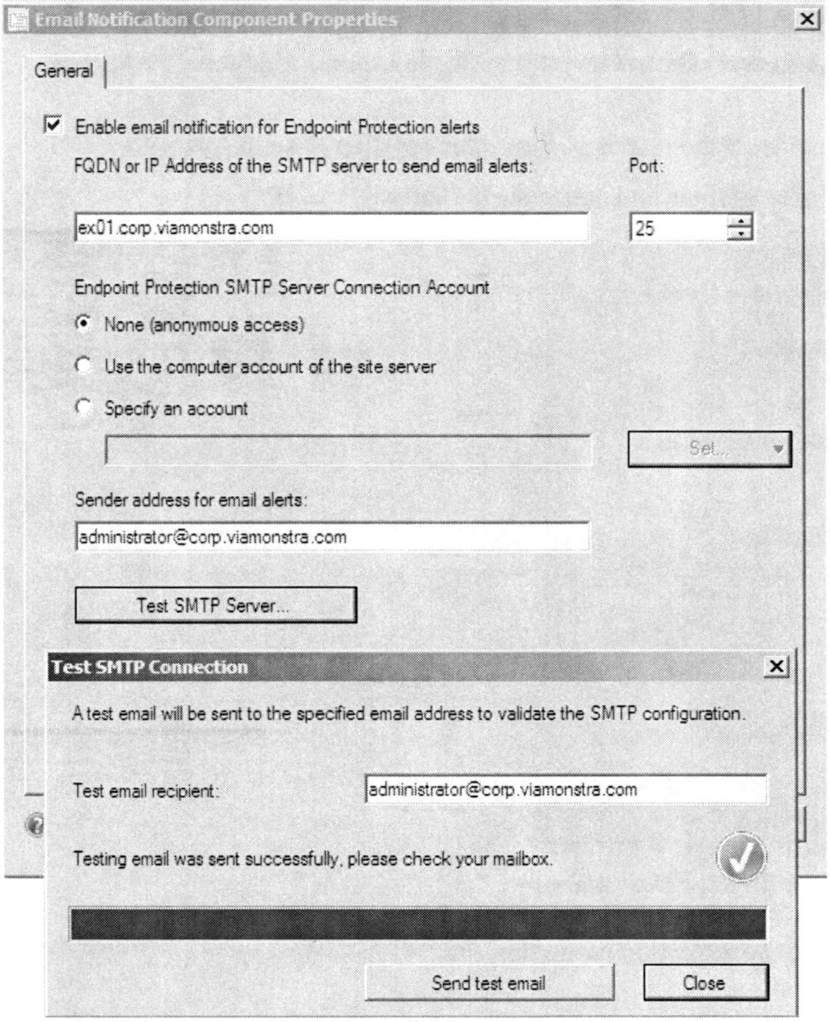

Configuring email notifications.

5. Click **Close** and **OK**.

Real World Note: Configuring email notification requires knowledge about the SMTP server and the ports used by the mail server. There is no guarantee the specific settings in the book can be used in your environment.

Configure Email Subscriptions

1. Navigate to the **Monitoring** workspace, and select **Alerts**, **Subscriptions**.
2. Click **Create Subscription** on the ribbon, configure these settings, and click **OK**:
    a. Name: **Malware alerts**
    b. Email address: **administrator@corp.viamonstra.com**
    c. Email language: **English**
    d. Alert: Enable **all alerts**.

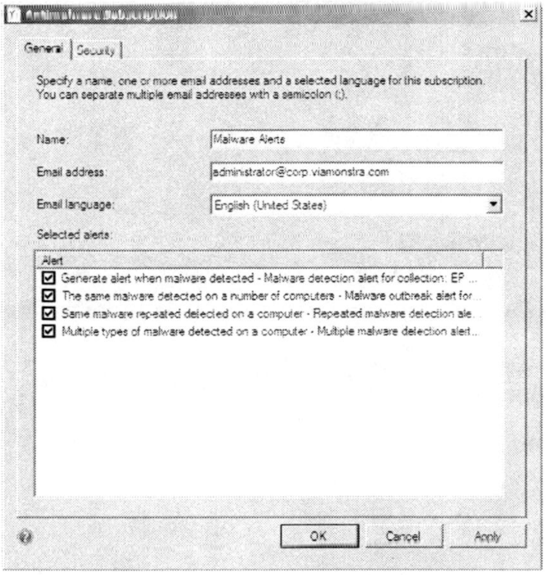

Creating new a malware email subscription.

3. Click **OK**.

Monitor Malware Activity

Monitoring malware activity is a daily task that you can perform either from within the ConfigMgr console using the Endpoint Protection dashboard or by reading one the Endpoint Protection reports. To create activity, you can download a safe malware from http://www.eicar.org/85-0-Download.html. The malware is completely harmless and can be used to test the antimalware client.

1. Log on to **PC001** as **administrator** and open **Internet Explorer**.
2. Type **http://www.eicar.org/85-0-Download.html** and download the **eicar_com.zip** file to the desktop. You should receive an Endpoint Protection alert the very second you choose to download the file.

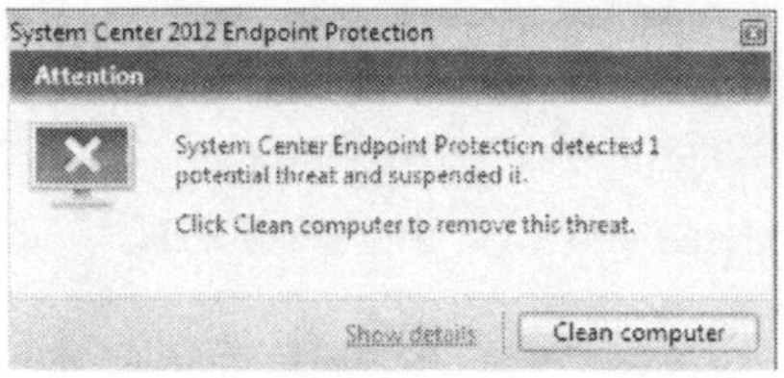

Generating malware activity.

It will take a little time until Endpoint Protection cleans the computer. After it is cleaned, the following dialog box is shown.

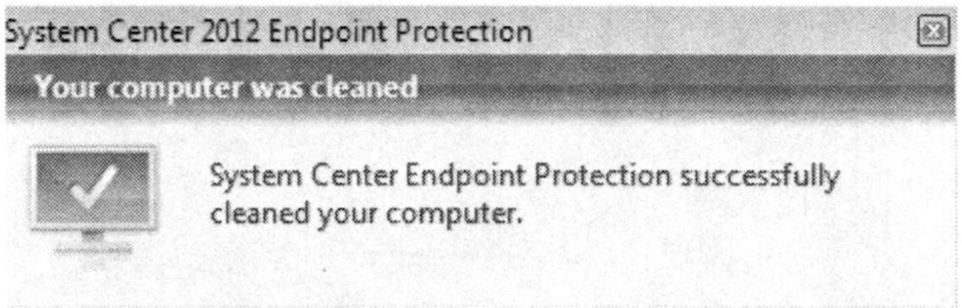

Malware successfully removed from the computer.

3. It's safe to download the other files from the web page and generate some more malware activity.
4. Click **Show hidden icons** in the notification area.
5. Right-click the **SCEP** icon and select **Open**.
6. Select the **History** tab and click **View details**.

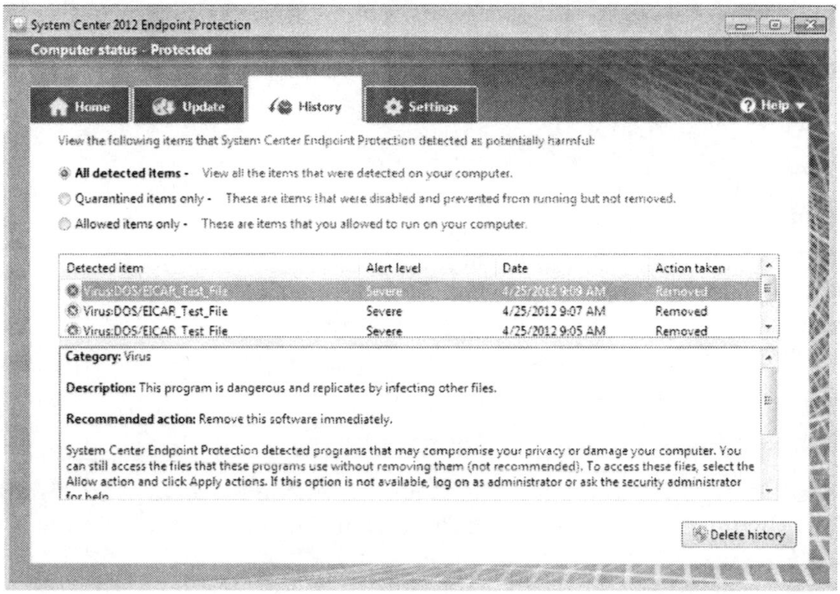

Viewing malware activity on the client.

View Malware in the ConfigMgr Console

1. Navigate to the **Monitoring** workspace, and select **System Center 2012 Endpoint Protection**.

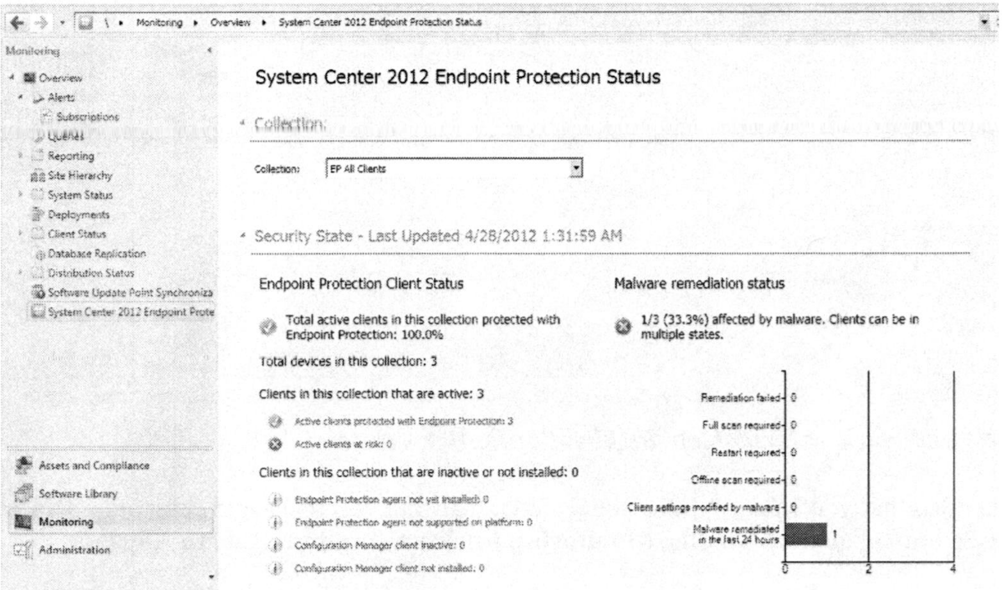

The Endpoint Protection dashboard.

2. Notice the Malware remediation status in the right column. Click the **Malware remediated in the last 24 hours** chart.

   The click creates a query-based node containing all devices for which malware has been remediated within the last 24 hours.

3. Select the **Malware Detail** tab and notice the information about the malware.

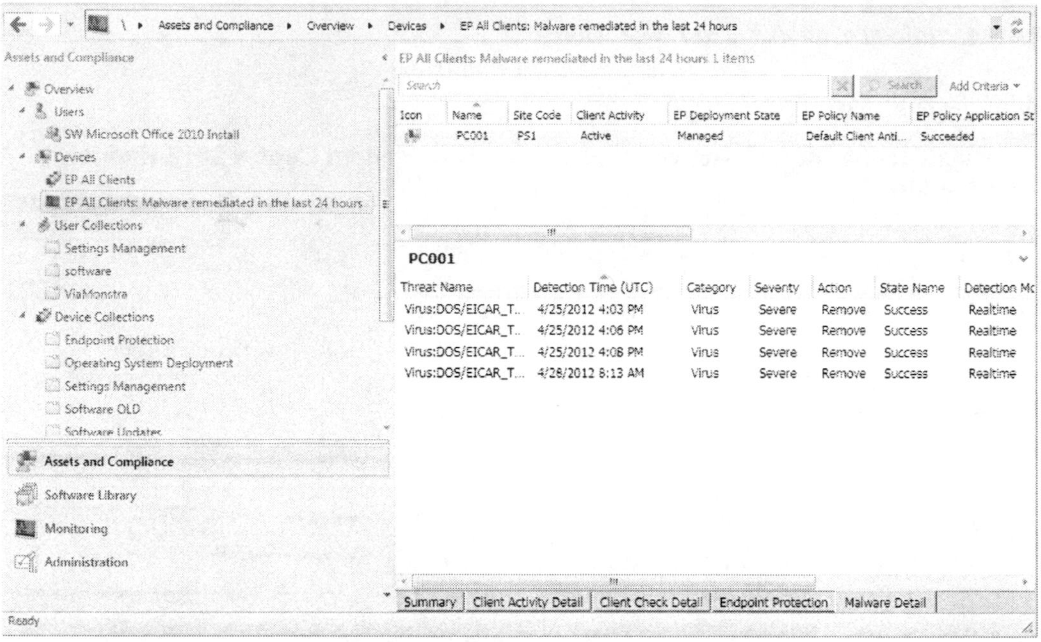

Viewing malware information in the ConfigMgr console.

4. Provided that you have configured the alerts, malware outbreaks and detections also will create critical alerts. Select the **Monitoring workspace** and navigate to **Alerts**.

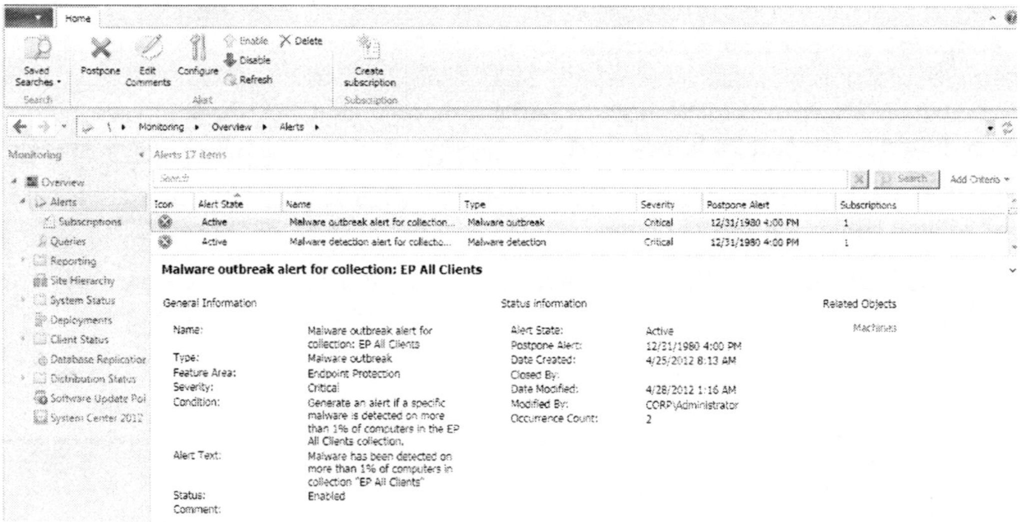

Malware detection alert.

If you configured email support, then alerts also trigger an email message.

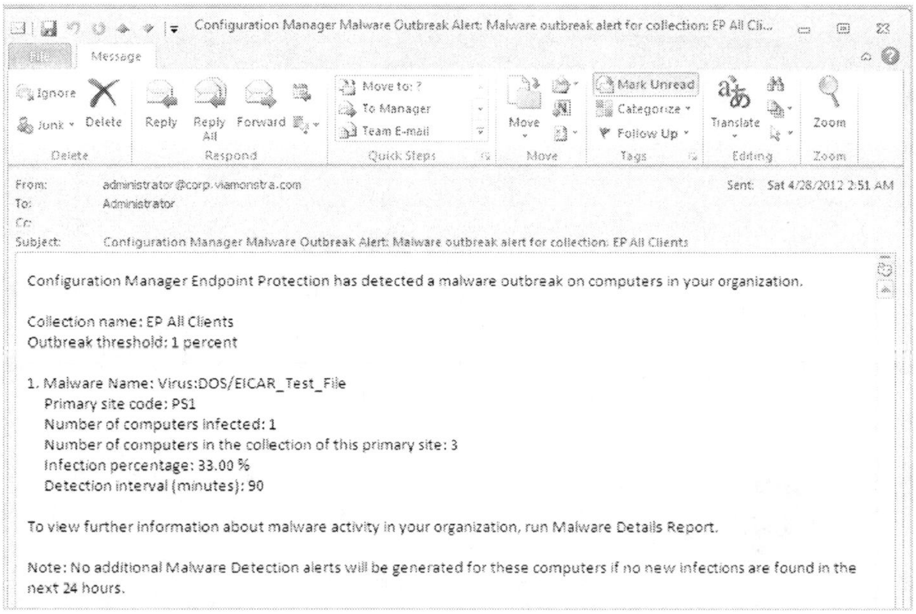

SCEP email notification.

View Malware Information Using Reports

1. Open **Internet Explorer** and open **http://cm01/reports**.
2. Select the **ConfigMgr_PS1** folder and the **Endpoint Protection** subfolder.
3. Select the **Dashboard** report; then from the collection list, select **EP All Clients** and click **View Report**. The Dashboard report is like a cockpit providing you with the high-level overview. If you want to dig a bit deeper, all you need to do is click one of the chart objects. That action will launch one of the hidden Endpoint Protection reports with detailed information.

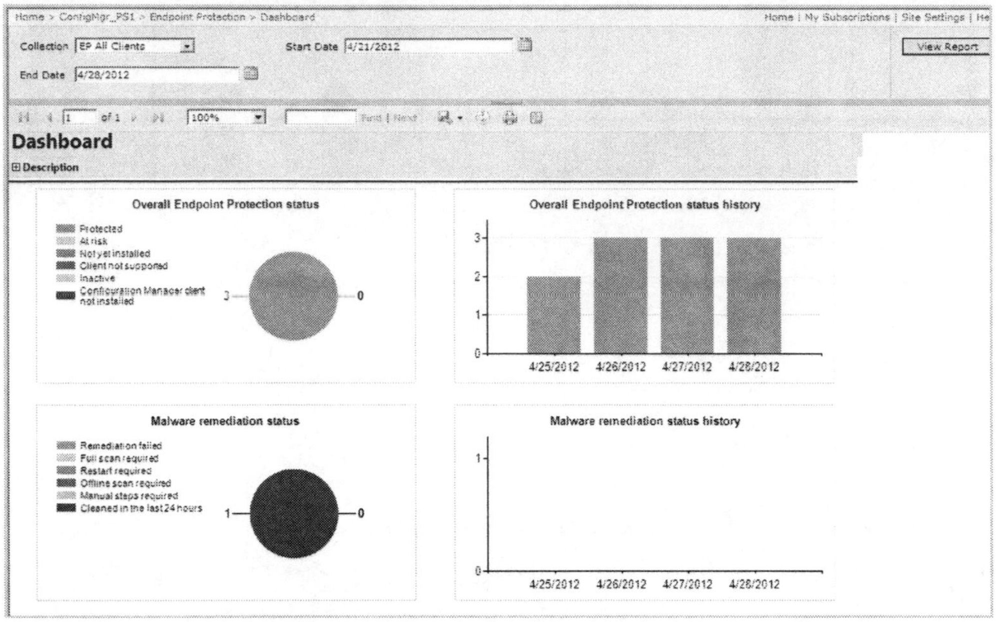

The Endpoint Protection dashboard.

4. Click the **Malware remediation status** chart.

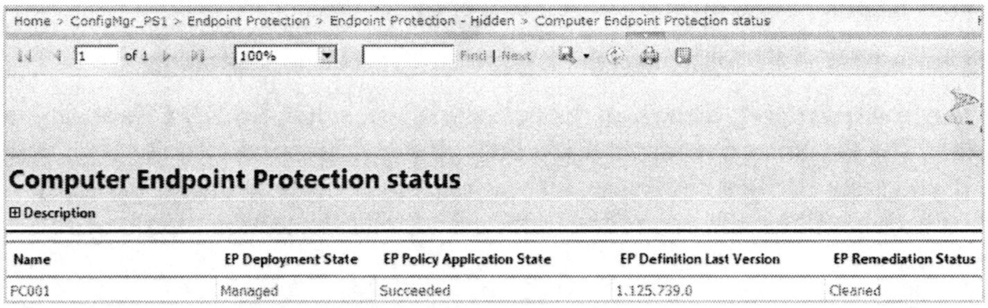

Malware remediation report.

Note: To view the hidden Endpoint Protection reports, open the report manager in Internet Explorer. Navigate to the Endpoint Protection folder and click Details View. You will see a folder called Endpoint Protection - Hidden. Click the folder, and you will see a list of the hidden reports. If you want to unhide the folder or any of the reports, all you need to do is open the properties for the object and deselect "Hide in tile view."

Chapter 10 Operating System Deployment

Operating system (OS) deployment is one of the most commonly used features in ConfigMgr. If you are familiar with ConfigMgr 2007, you will quickly discover that the OS deployment features haven't changed that much. One of the nice new features, however, is the ability to service your operating system images offline from within the ConfigMgr console.

After reading this chapter, you will be able to configure support for OS deployment, deploy your images, and manage your drivers in your environment.

Planning for Operating System Deployment

Before you deploy any operating system, you need to plan what kind deployment scenarios you must support and whether you have the needed infrastructure to support those demands. The infrastructure planning mostly includes creating user accounts, configuring site system roles, and integrating Microsoft Deployment Toolkit (MDT).

Configuring the Required Infrastructure

Configure the Network Access Account

Before you are able to use the OS deployment features, you need to configure the Network Access Account (CM_NA) that you created in Chapter 3. The Network Access Account is used to establish a connection from WinPE to a distribution point and download the image.

1. In the **Administration** workspace, navigate to **Site Configurations, Sites**.
2. Select the **PS1 – ViaMonstra HQ** site and select **Settings**, **Configure Site Components**, **Software Distribution**.
3. Select the **Network Access Account** tab.
4. Select **Specify the account that accesses network locations**, and then select **Set**, **New Account**.
5. Click **Browse** and search for **CM_NA**; then click **OK**.
6. Supply the password (**Password01**) twice and click **OK**.

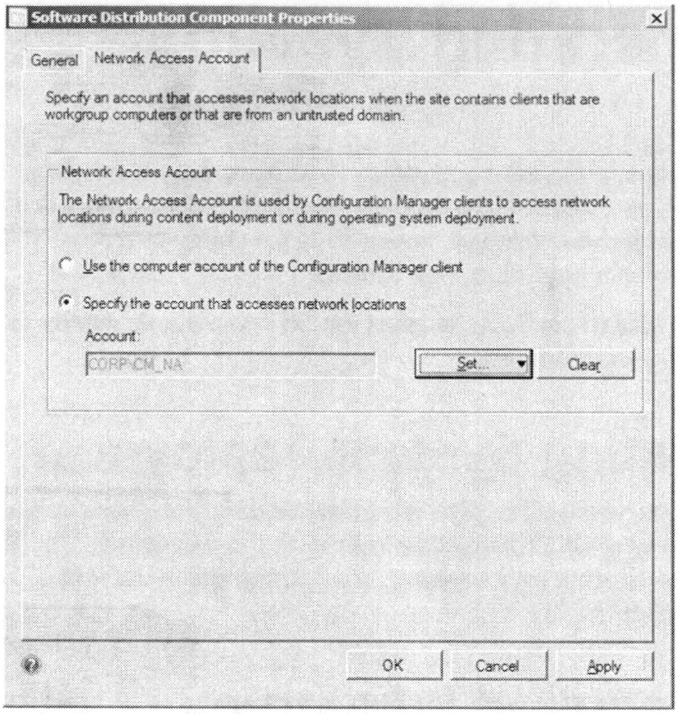

Configuring the Network Access Account.

7. Click **OK**.

Install and Configure WDS

Windows Deployment Services, or WDS, is only one of the different methods that you can use to start the image installation process. Many prefer WDS because an installation can be initiated by simply pressing F12 on keyboard. You can install and configure WDS manually prior to configuring the PXE feature on the distribution point role. If WDS is not installed, ConfigMgr automatically installs it when you enable the PXE role on a distribution point. For ViaMonstra, I like to have control and for that reason have installed WDS, as described in Appendix A.

Configure a PXE-Enabled Distribution Point

1. In the **Administration** workspace, select **Distribution Points**.
2. Double-click the **CM01** distribution point role.
3. Select the **PXE** tab.
4. Select the **Enable PXE support for clients** check box, and click **Yes** in dialog box.

5. Configure the following settings:
   - Allow this distribution point to respond to incoming PXE requests: **Enabled**
   - Enable unknown computer support: **Enabled**, and click **OK** after reading the warning about enabling unknown computer support.
   - Require a password when computers use PXE: **Enabled**, and supply a secret password.
   - User device affinity: **Allow user device affinity with automatic approval**.

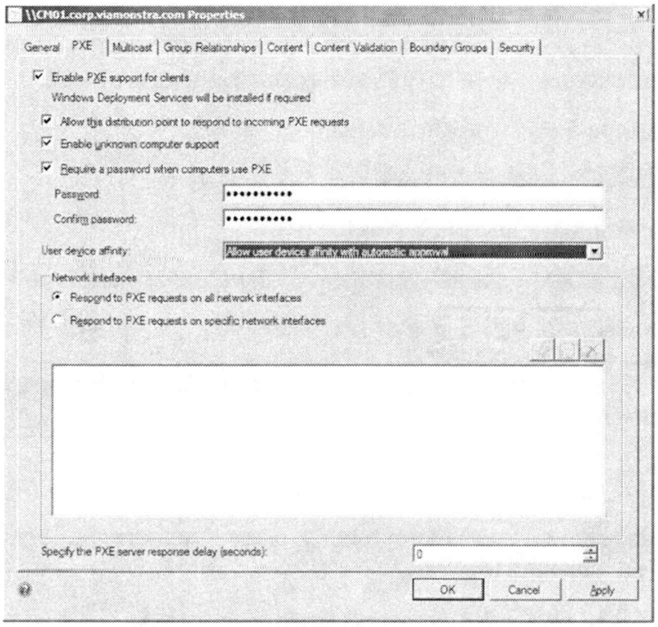

Enabling and configuring PXE support.

6. Click **OK**.

Install and Configure MDT 2012

Your next step in configuring an OS deployment is to install Microsoft Deployment Toolkit (MDT) 2012. MDT 2012 is not a requirement for OS deployment in ConfigMgr, but is used frequently to ease the process of building boot images and because of the massive number of cool scripts that ships with the product. It allows you to create a smooth Zero Touch deployment experience.

1. On **CM01**, log on as **CORP\Administrator**.
2. Download the **Microsoft Deployment Toolkit 2012** from **http://tinyurl.com/6rrjacy**, and save the file in **D:\Setup\MDT 2012**.

3. Open a command prompt with administrative rights and navigate to **D:\Setup\MDT 2012**.
4. Start the installation by running **MicrosoftDeploymentToolkit2012_x64.msi**.
5. Go through the installation and accept all the default settings.
6. From the **Start** menu, select **All Programs**, **Microsoft Deployment Toolkit, Deployment Workbench**, and then start **Microsoft Deployment Toolkit**.
7. Using the **Deployment Workbench**, right-click **Deployment Shares** and select **New Deployment Share**.
8. On the **Path** page, configure the **Deployment share path** to **D:\MDTProduction** and click **Next.**
9. On the **Share** page, configure the share name to **MDTProduction**$ and click **Next**.
10. On the **Descriptive Name** page, type **MDT** and click **Next**.
11. On the **Options** page, keep the defaults and click **Next**.
12. On the **Summary** page, read the summary and click **Next**.
13. On the **Confirmation** page, click **Finish** to start the creation of the Deployment Workbench.

> **Note:** Notice the View Script button on the Confirmation page. You can use it to find the needed PowerShell script used to create the deployment share.

Create the Logs$ Share

With MDT, you are able to create extra logging of your deployment process. To store the log files, you need to create a share where MDT can store the log files.

1. Using **Windows Explorer**, create the **D:\Logs** folder and share it as **Logs$**.
2. Allow the **Everyone** group **Change** permissions (Sharing Permissions).

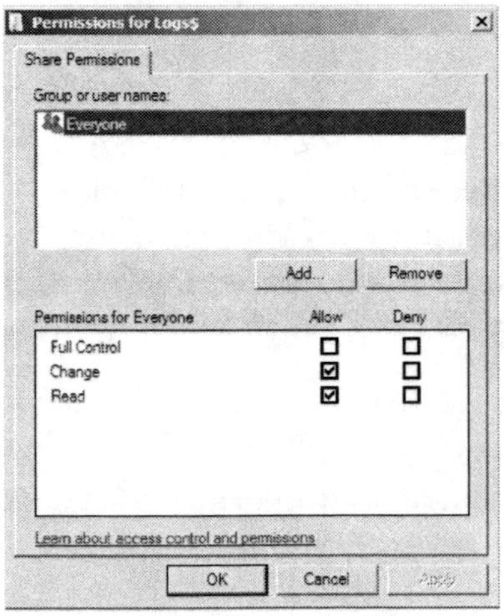

Everyone must have change share permissions.

3. Allow the **CM_NA** user account **Modify** permissions (NTFS Permissions).

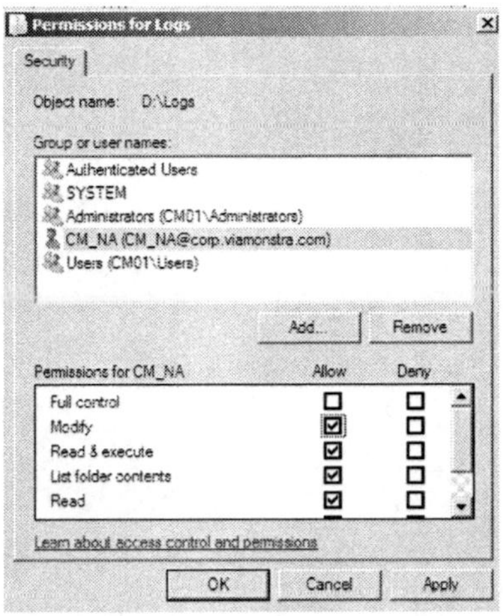

The Network Access Account must have modify permissions.

Configure ConfigMgr 2012 Integration

MDT integrates with the ConfigMgr Console. The integration gives you extra deployment options, like enhanced task sequences and boot images with scripting support.

1. Close the **ConfigMgr console** before continuing. The reason for this is that the integration adds console extensions that are applied when you start the ConfigMgr console.
2. From the **Start** menu, run the **Microsoft Deployment Toolkit;** then select **Configure ConfigMgr Integration** and configure the following settings:
    a. Site Server Name: **CM01.corp.viamonstra.com**
    b. Site code: **PS1**

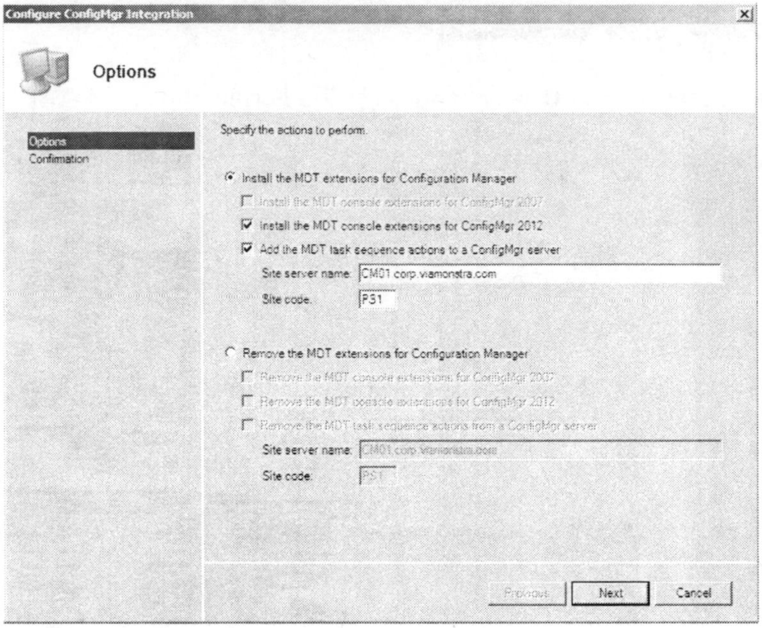

Integrating MDT 2012 with ConfigMgr 2012.

3. Click **Next**, and then click **Finish** to configure the integration.

Boot Images

Boot images are essential to the OS deployment process. It's the boot image that will be used to establish the contact between the computer and the network. A boot image contains a version of Windows PE, the needed NIC and storage drivers, and any logic that you find needed to start the deployment process (scripts, tools, and so forth). To begin, create two custom boot images.

Create Custom Boot Images

The MDT integration gives you the option to create boot images using MDT.

1. Using **Windows Explorer**, create these folders: **D:\Sources\OSD\MDTboot\x64** and **D:\Sources\OSD\MDTboot\x86**.
2. Open the **ConfigMgr console**.
3. In the **Software Library** workspace, select **Operating Systems**, **Boot Images**.
4. Select **Create Boot Image using MDT** from the ribbon.
5. On the **Package Source** page, specify the package source folder: **\\CM01\Sources$\OSD\MDTBoot\x64** and click **Next**.

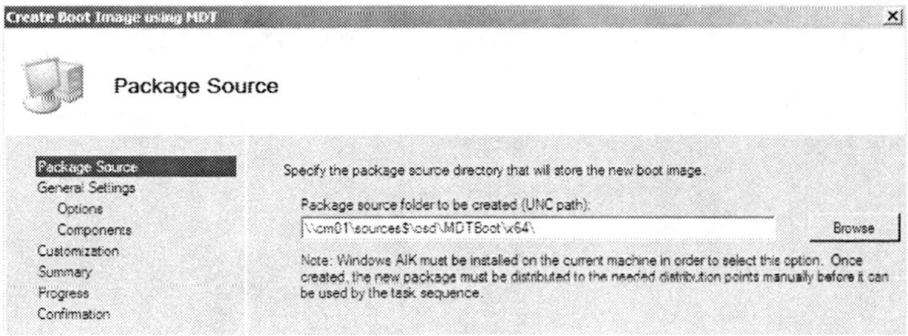

Specifying the package source for the x64 boot image.

6. On the **General Settings** page, configure these settings and click **Next**:
    a. Name: **MDTBoot Image x64**
    b. Version: **1.0**
    c. Comments: **Custom MDT Boot image**
7. On the **Options** page, configure these settings and click **Next**:
    a. Platform: **x64**
    b. Scratch space: **512MB**
8. On the **Components** page, leave the default settings and click **Next.**
9. On the **Customization** page, leave the default settings and click **Next.**
10. On the **Summary** page, read the summary and click **Next**.
11. Repeat steps 4–10 and create a custom **x86** boot image.

Distribute the MDT Boot Images

To be able to use the MDT boot image, you need to deploy it to the distribution points:

1. In the **Software Library** workspace, select **Operating Systems**, **Boot Images**.
2. Select the **MDTBoot Image x64**.
3. Open the **Properties**.
4. Select the **Data Source** tab, enable **Deploy this boot image from the PXE service point**, and click **OK**.

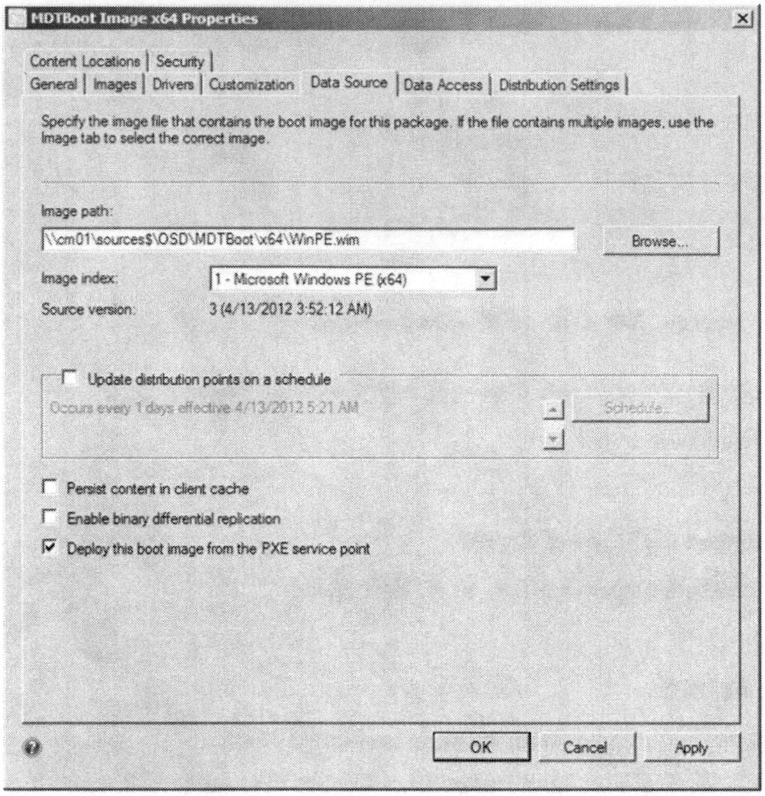

Enabling PXE support on the boot image.

5. Repeat steps 1-4 for the **MDTBoot Image x86** boot image.
6. Click **OK**.
7. Select both custom boot images and click **Distribute Content** on the ribbon.
8. On the **General** page, click **Next**.
9. On the **Content Destination** page, click **Add, Distribution Point Group**. Select the **All Content** group, and click **OK** and then **Next**.
10. On the **Summary** page, click **Next**.
11. On the **Completion** page, click **Close**.

Configure State Migration Point

When using OS deployment in your environment, you might want to preserve local data on your workstations and laptops. To be able to preserve the local data, you need to configure the state migration point. You can use the state migration point to store the user state data that are gathered during the OS deployment process by the User State Migration Toolkit. Data stored on the state migration point is encrypted, and to preserve disk space, you can configure how many days the data will stored on the server.

1. Browse to the **Administration** workspace and select **Site Configuration, Servers and Site System Roles**.
2. Select the **\\CM01.corp.viamonstra.com** server and click **Add Site System Roles** on the ribbon.
3. On the **General** page, click **Next**.
4. On the **System Role Selection** page, click **State migration point** and click **Next**.
5. On the **State Migration Point** page, click the **yellow icon**.
6. Configure these settings, and then click **OK**:
   a. Folder details and in Storage : **D:\StateMigration\Storage1**
   b. Maximum clients: **500**
   c. Maximum free space: **20 GB**

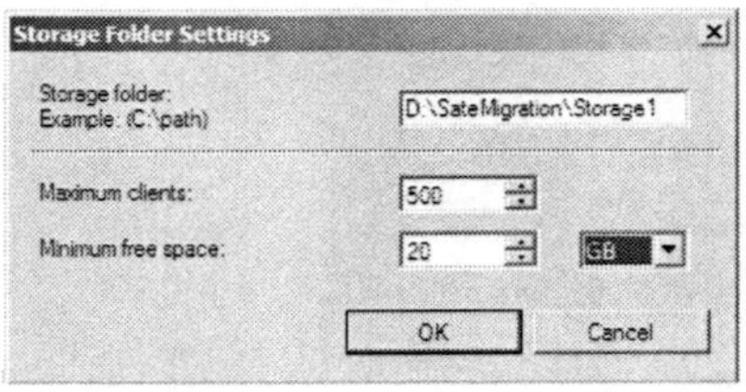

Configuring the storage folder.

7. In the **Deletion policy** section, configure **Delete after** to **7 days**. It is not wise to delete the data immediately, so choose a value that suites your needs. Before refreshing numerous workstations to Windows 7, monitor the disk space to ensure that the user data can be kept for the configured amount of time.

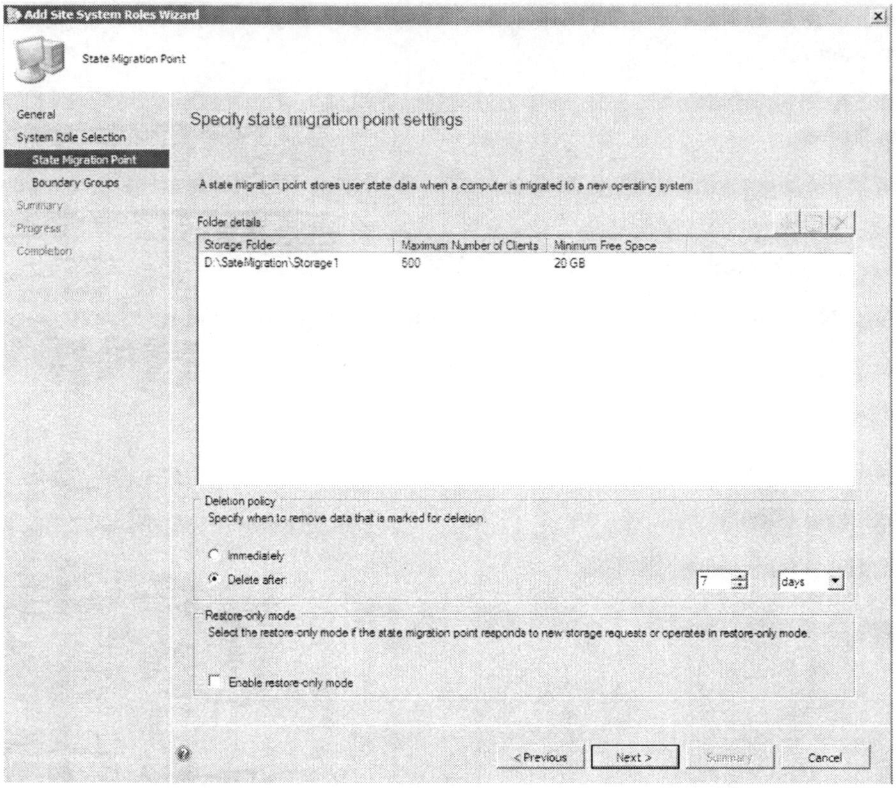

Configuring the storage folder and deletion policy.

8. On the **Configure the Boundary Groups** page, ensure that **CL HQ** is added and click **Next**.
9. On the **Summary** page, read the summary and click **Next**.
10. On the **Completion** page, click **Close**.

Real World Note: If you have a large environment, you can create as many storage folders as your disk size permits. When sizing your state migration point, look at the number of OS deployments that need to be done, how long the user state needs to be stored, and the average size of the user state.

Add an Operating System Install Source

Before you are able to create your custom Windows image, you need to add the source content of the operating system that you want to deploy. ViaMonstra wants to create and deploy a custom and fully patched Windows 7 image, so add the Windows 7 source to Configuration Manager. In order to follow the following steps, you need the Windows 7 Enterprise SP1 x64 source files copied to **D:\sources\OSD\Windows7Source**.

1. Browse to the **Software Library** workspace and select **Operating Systems, Operating System Installers**.
2. Click **Add Operating System Installer** on the ribbon.
3. On the **Data Source** page, type **\\CM01\Sources$\OSD\Windows7Source** in **Path**, and then click **Next**. (This folder must be manually created before you can add the image.)
4. On the **General** page, configure these settings and click **Next**:
   a. Name: **Windows 7 SP1 x64 Enterprise**
   b. Version: **1.0**
   c. Comment: **Windows 7 installation source**

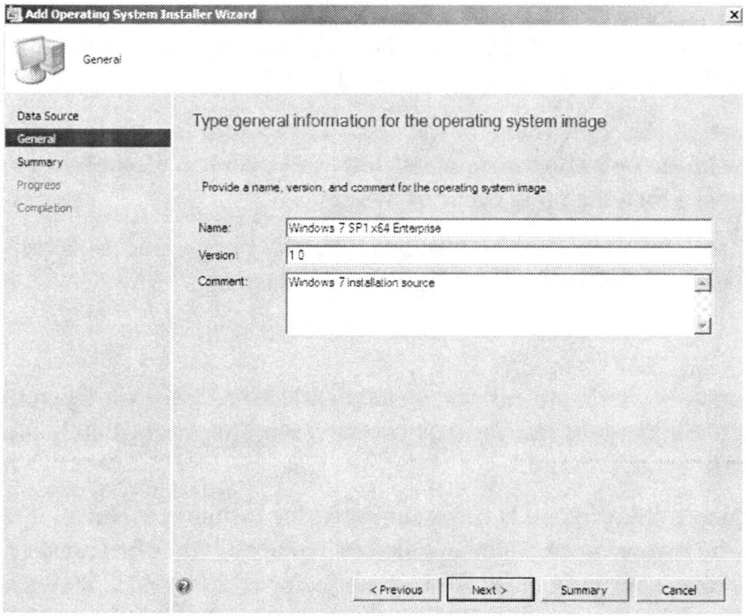

Adding metadata to the operating system installer package.

5. On the **Summary** page, read the summary and click **Next**.
6. On the **Completion** page, click **Close**.
7. Distribute the operating system install package to all distribution points. Select the **Windows 7 SP1 x64 Enterprise** operating system install package and click **Distribute Content** on the ribbon.
8. On the **General** page, click **Next**.
9. On the **Content Destination** page, click **Add, Distribution Point Group**. Select the **All Content** group, and then click **OK** and **Next**.
10. On the **Summary** page, click **Next**.

11. On the **Completion** page, click **Close**.

Creating a Custom WIM Image

Now you are set to create a custom Windows 7 SP1 image. Depending on the SLAs for deployment time, you can choose for different kind of images: thin, thick, and hybrid. There is no absolute right or wrong; but before deciding on a strategy, you need to know the differences between the three image types.

Types of Images

Thin Images

Thin images are images that do not contain any applications. The applications are installed separately after the installation of the image is finished.

A big advantage of thin images is that the deployment of the operating system is very fast, since the image is small and contains only the operating system and software updates. The management of thin images is less time consuming than the other types of images.

A disadvantage of thin images is that software must be installed after the image process is finished either automatically, via the Software Center or from the Application Catalog.

Thick Images

Thick images contain all the commonly used applications, usually called the Common Operating Environment. An advantage of a thick image is that the user can start working immediately after the deployment process is finished.

A big disadvantage is that managing a thick image is more complex; for instance, when an update for an application that resides in the images needs to be updated or replaced, you often need to recreate the image. This can be a time-consuming task. One scenario for which a thick image is a disadvantage is a developer image where the end user (the developer) is reinstalling the operating system once a week and the image deployment time must be kept at a minimum.

Hybrid Images

Hybrid images are the best of both thin and thick images. This type of image allows you to add, for instance, Microsoft Office 2010 to your image. The rest of the applications can be installed during the operating system deployment process or via the Software Center or Application Catalog.

The offline servicing feature within Configuration Manager 2012 allows you also to update the Microsoft Office 2010 application without needing to recreate the operating system image.

Creating the Custom Windows 7 Image

For ViaMonstra, I have decided to go for a hybrid Windows 7 SP1 image with Microsoft Office 2010 that is fully patched with the latest approved software updates.

Before you can deploy a custom image, you first need to create the reference image. You can install the reference OS by hand, make changes to it, and capture the reference OS. You also can automate the build and capture of the Windows 7 installation, the customizations, and the installation of Microsoft Office 2010. This way you know that you always have the same golden version of your Windows 7 operating system. To be able to automate the build and capture process, you need to create a build and capture task sequence.

Real World Note: Always use a virtual machine to create a reference image of an operating system. By using a virtual machine, you add only a limited number of drivers during the process.

Create a New Microsoft Office 2010 Application

Before creating the build and capture task sequence, you have to create a new Microsoft Office 2010 application. The application you created in Chapter 7 has two deployment types which are not supported when installing the application through a task sequence. The easiest way to create a new application is simply to copy the existing application created in Chapter 7 and modify it.

1. On **CM01**, using the **ConfigMgr console**, navigate to the **Software Library** workplace. Expand **Application Management**, expand **Applications**, and select the **Required User** folder.
2. Right-click the **Microsoft Office 2010** application and select **Copy**.
3. Right-click the new **Microsoft Office 2010-copy** application and select **Properties**
4. In the **General** tab, change the name to **Microsoft Office 2010 OSD**.
5. In the **Deployment Types** tab, delete the **Microsoft Office 2010 x32 MSI** deployment type. Then select the **Microsoft Office 2010 x64 MSI** deployment type and click **Edit**.
6. In the **User Experience** tab, change the **Logon Requirement** to **Whether or not a user is logged on** and click **OK** twice.
7. Distribute the new application to all distribution points. Select the **Microsoft Office 2010 OSD** application and click **Distribute Content** on the ribbon.
8. On the **General** page, click **Next**.
9. On the **Content Destination** page, click **Add, Distribution Point Group**. Select the **All Content** group, and then click **OK** and **Next**.

Create the Build and Capture Task Sequence

1. On **CM01**, using **Windows Explorer**, create the **D:\Sources\OSD\Windows7** folder and grant the **CORP\CM_NA** account **modify** permissions to it (NTFS Permissions).
2. In the **Software Library**, select **Operating Systems, Task Sequences**.
3. Click **Create Task Sequence** on the ribbon.
4. On the **Create New Task Sequence** page, select **Build and Capture a reference operating system image** and click **Next**.

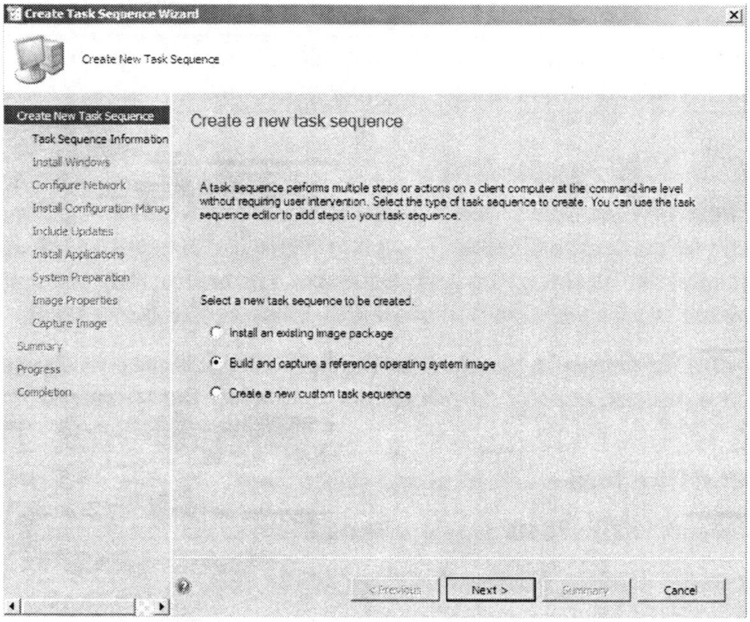

Creating the build and capture task sequence.

5. On the **Task Sequence Information** page, configure these settings and click **Next**:
   a. Name: **Build and Capture Windows 7 Enterprise x64**
   b. Boot image: **MDTBoot Image x64**
6. On the **Install Windows** page, configure these settings and click **Next**:
   a. Image Package: Click **Browse** and select **Windows 7 SP1 x64 Enterprise**
   b. Product key: <leave empty>
   c. Always use the same administrator password: **Password01**

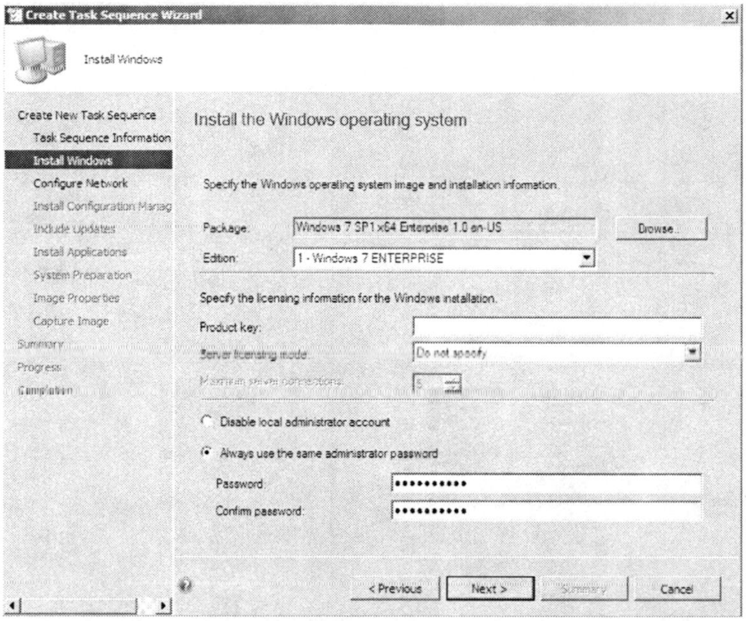

Specifying the OS install files.

7. On the **Configure Network** page, configure this setting and click **Next**:

   Join a Workgroup: **CM2012Install**

8. On the **Install Configuration Manager** page, click **Browse**, select the **Configuration Manager Client Package**, and click **Next**.
9. On the **Include Updates** page, select **All Software Updates** and click **Next**.
10. On the **Install Applications** page, configure these settings and click **Next**:
    a. Click the **yellow icon** and select the **Microsoft Office 2010 OSD** application.
    b. Enable **If an application installation fails, continue installing other applications in the list**.

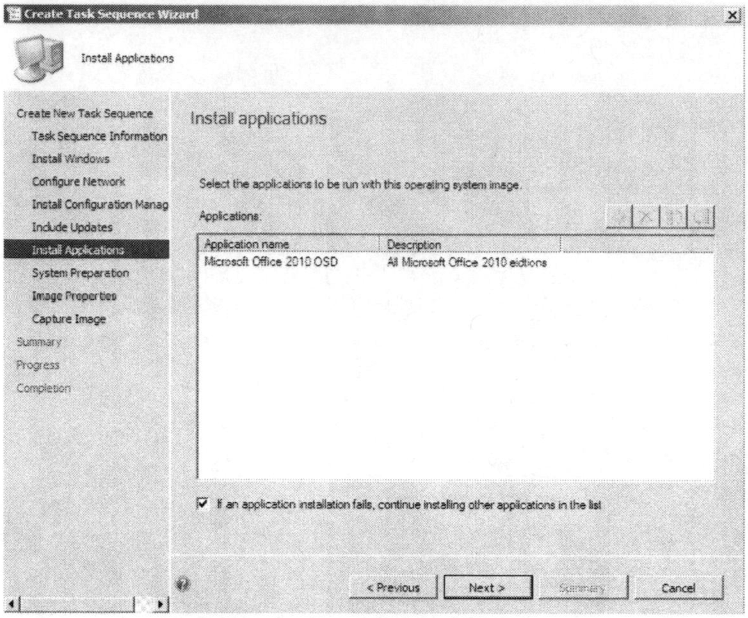

Adding a single application in the task sequence.

11. On the **System Preparation** page, click **Next**.
12. On the **Image Properties** page, configure these settings and click **Next**:
    a. Creator: **ViaMonstra Administrator**
    b. Version: **1.0**
    c. Comments: **Fully patched Windows 7 SP1 and Microsoft Office 2010 SP2 image created 28/04/2012.**
13. On the **Capture Image** page, configure these settings and click **Next**:
    a. Path: **\\CM01\Sources$\OSD\Windows7\Win7SP1_x64_Ent_v1.wim**
    b. Account: **CORP\CM_NA** (with password)
14. On the **Summary** page, read the summary and click **Next**.
15. On the **Completion** page, click **Close**.

Deploy the Build and Capture Task Sequence

Now that the build and capture task sequence is created, you need to deploy the task sequence:

1. Navigate to the **Software Library**, and select **Operating Systems**, **Task Sequences**.
2. Select the **Build and Capture Windows 7 Enterprise x64** task sequence and click **Deploy** on the ribbon.

3. On the **General** page, in **Collection**, click **Browse**; then select the **All Unknown Computers** collection and click **Next**. You also can choose to import a known computer to an existing collection and specify that.
4. On the **Deployment Settings** page, configure these settings and click **Next**:
    a. Action: **Install**
    b. Purpose: **Available**
    c. Make available to boot media and PXE: **Enabled**

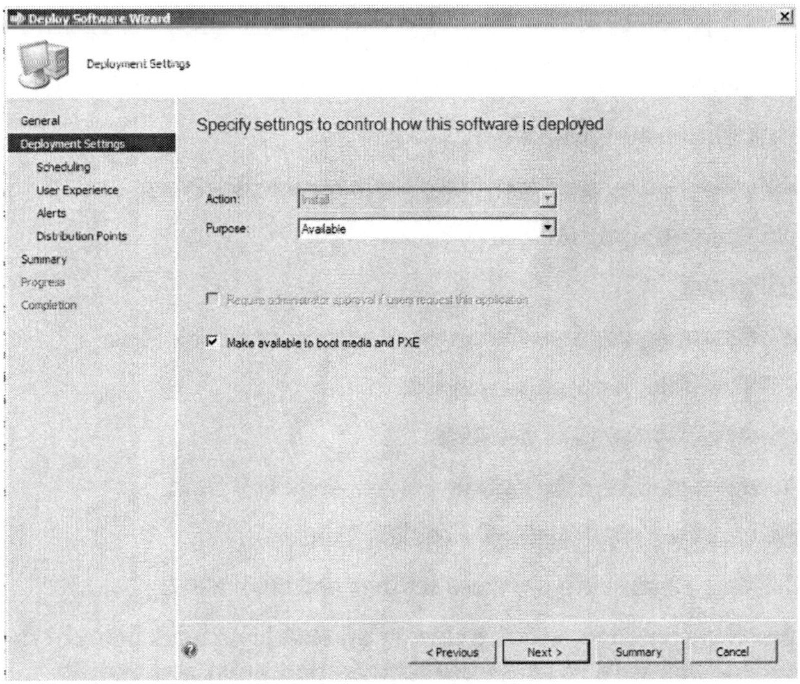

Configuring the deployment as available.

5. On the **Scheduling** page, leave the default and click **Next**.
6. On the **User Experience** page, leave the default and click **Next**.
7. On the **Alerts** page, click **Next**.
8. On the **Distribution Points** page, leave the defaults and click **Next**.
9. On the **Summary** page, read the summary and click **Next**.
10. On the **Completion** page, click **Close**.

Deploy Updates to the All Unknown Device Collection

In the next section, you start the deployment of the build and capture task sequence; but, in order for the reference image to install the software updates, you need to deploy them to the All Unknown Computers collection:

1. On **CM01**, using the **ConfigMgr console**, navigate to the **Software Library** workplace. Expand **Software Updates**, and select **Software Update Groups**.
2. Right-click the **2012 06 June** software update group and select **Deploy**.
3. On the **General** page, configure these settings and click **Next**:
    a. Name: **2012 06 June OSD**
    b. Description: **Updates for OSD**
    c. Collection: **All Unknown Computers**
4. On the **Deployment Settings** page, configure these settings and click **Next**:
    a. Type of deployment: **Required**
    b. Detail level: **Normal**
5. On the **Deployment Scheduling** page, configure these settings and click **Next**:
    a. Software available time: **As soon as possible**
    b. Installation deadline: **As soon as possible**
6. On the **User Experience** page, accept the default settings and click **Next**.
7. On the **Alerts** page, accept the default settings and click **Next**.
8. On the **Download Settings** page, configure these settings and click **Next**:
    a. Deployment options for client within a slow or unreliable network boundary: Enable **Download software update from distribution point and install**.
    b. When software updates are not available on any preferred distribution points, the client can download and install software updates from a fallback source location for content: Enable **Download and install software updates from the fallback content source location**.
9. On the **Summary** page, click **Save As Template**, type **OSD Updates** as the name, and click **Save**.
10. Click **Next**, and then click **Close**.

Start the Deployment

The next logical step in the process is to start the deployment. For ViaMonstra, you use Hyper-V to create a new virtual machine for the purpose:

1. Launch the **Hyper-V Manager** on the host computer.
2. From the **Action** pane, click **New**, **Virtual Machine**.
3. On the **Specify Name and Location** page, configure a name (I used the name BuildAndCapture) and location for the new machine, and then click **Next**.

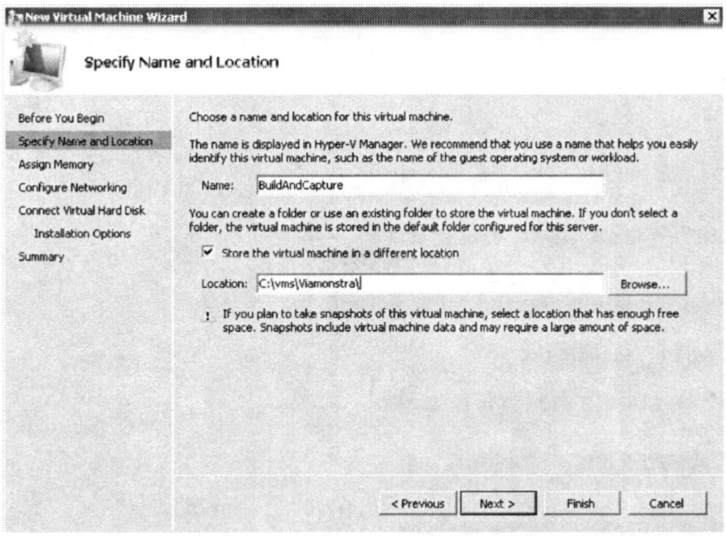

Creating a new virtual machine.

4. On the **Assign Memory** page, assign **1024 MB** and click **Next.**
5. On the **Configure Networking** page, configure the same network as the site server and click **Next**.
6. On the **Connect Virtual Hard Disk** page, leave the defaults and click **Next**.
7. On the **Installation Options** page, select **Install an operating system from a network-based installation server** and click **Next**.

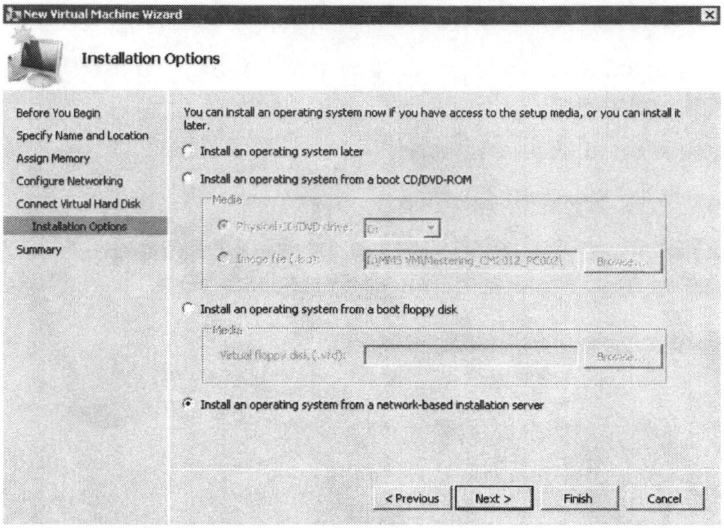

Configuring the virtual machine to boot from PXE.

8. On the **Summary** page, read the summary and click **Finish**.
9. Start the new **BuildAndCapture** machine.
10. When prompted, press **F12** to initiate the PXE process.

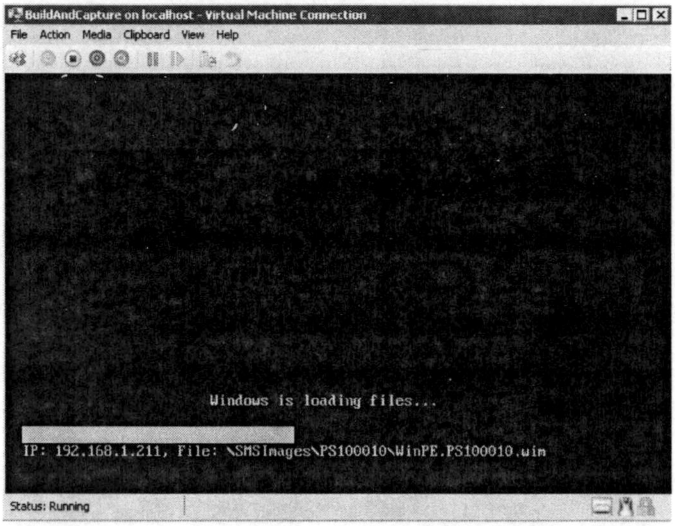

Downloading the boot image using PXE.

11. Type the PXE password and click **Next**.
12. Select the **Build and Capture Windows 7 Enterprise x64** task sequence and click **Next**.

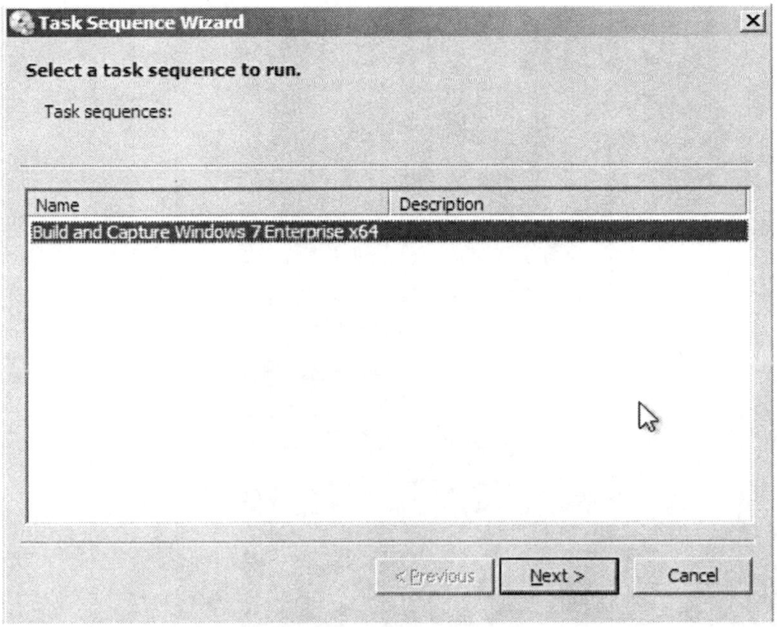

Starting the Build and Capture task sequence

The operating system will be installed and captured to the configured location. After this step is complete, you are able to proceed with the OS image deployment, which is covered in the next section.

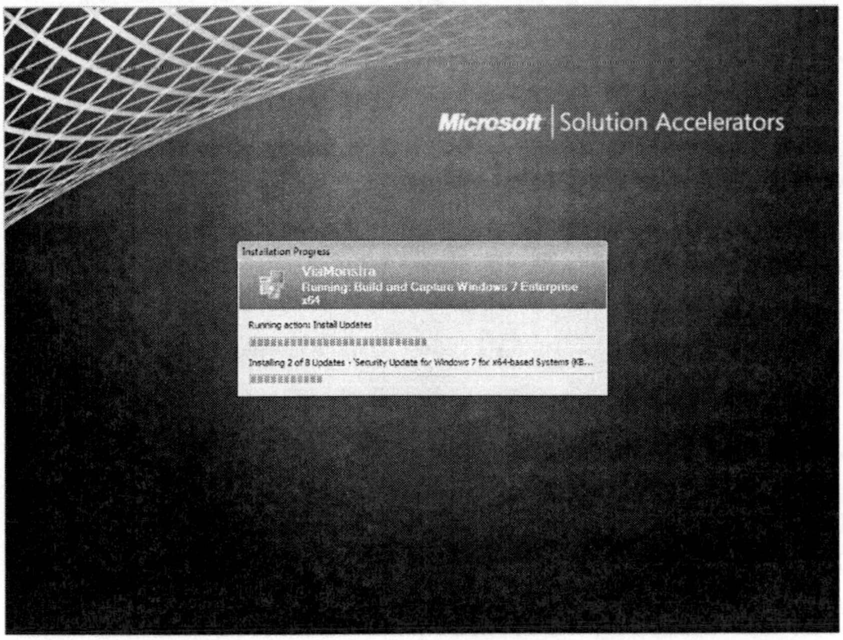

The reference image being deployed, currently installing updates.

Creating the Windows 7 WIM Image.

Deploying the Custom Windows 7 Image

Now that you have a custom Windows 7 image, you can add this operating system image to ConfigMgr and start deploying the image to your workstations.

Adding a Custom Windows 7 Operating System Image

After creating a fresh custom Windows 7 operating system image, you need to add the image to ConfigMgr and distribute it to all of your distribution points:

1. Navigate to the **Software library** workspace, and select **Operating System**, **Operating System Images**; then click **Add Operating System Image** on the ribbon.
2. On the **Data Source** page, click **Browse** and select **\\CM01\Sources$\OSD\Windows7\Win7SP1_x64__Ent_v1.wim.**
3. On the **General** page, configure these settings and click **Next**:
    a. Name: **Windows 7 Enterprise x64**
    b. Version: **1.0**
    c. Comments: **Standard ViaMonstra corp image**

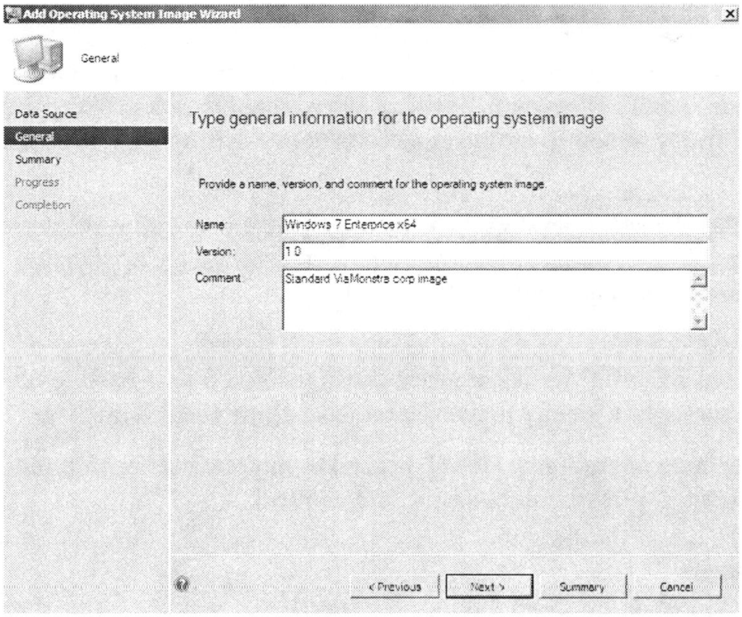

Adding a custom image.

4. In the **Summary** page, read the summary and click **Next**.
5. On the **Completion** page, click **Close**.
6. Select the **Windows 7 Enterprise x64** image and click **Distribute Content** on the ribbon.
7. On the **General** page, click **Next**.
8. On the **Content Destination** page, click **Add, Distribution Point Group**. Select the **All Content** group, and click **OK** and then **Next**.
9. On the **Summary** page, click **Next**.
10. On the **Completion** page, click **Close**.

Creating a Deploy Task Sequence

To be able to deploy the custom Windows 7 image, you need to create a task sequence. The task sequence is the engine that takes care of the unattended installation of the Windows 7 image. The task sequence wizard in ConfigMgr assists you in creating a basic bare metal deployment task sequence. However, if you also want to support other deployment scenarios, you will find it easier to work with the enhanced task sequences. During the very first task sequence, you are asked to create several packages. The OSD packages below are not all required but can be very useful in your deployments. Likewise, you can reuse all these packages in other task sequences.

OSD Packages

- **MDT Toolkit package** (contains the needed MDT scripts). The scripts can be used throughout the task sequence and assist you in creating more complex tasks. Without the toolkit package, you will find yourself spending numerous hours writing what is already written by Microsoft.
- **Settings package** (contains the MDT settings). The settings package contains rules used in the deployment process. A rule can be anything, such as controlling the application being installed, the OU used, language settings, et.al..
- **Configuration Manager client package**. One requirement for installing an image with ConfigMgr is that you have a ConfigMgr client agent package. You do not have to create a new ConfigMgr client package; it's okay to use the one that ships with ConfigMgr.
- **USMT package** (for user state migrations). USMT is used to migrate user profile settings like Internet Explorer favorites, pictures, documents, and so forth.

Create a MDT Task Sequence

1. Navigate to the **Software Library** workspace, and select **Operating Systems**, **Task Sequences**.
2. Click **Create MDT Task Sequence** on the ribbon.
3. On the **Choose Template** page, select **Client Task Sequence** and click **Next**.

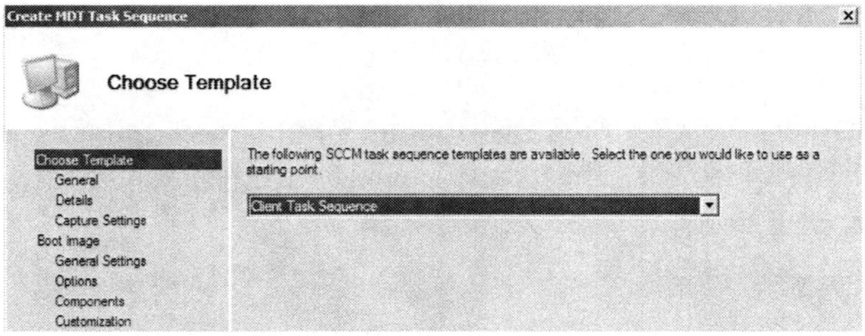

Selecting the client task sequence template.

4. On the **General** page, configure these settings and click **Next**:
   a. Task sequence name: **Windows 7 Enterprise Eng x64**
   b. Task sequence comments: **ViaMonstra corp image**
5. On the **Details** page, configure these settings and click **Next**:
   a. Join Workgroup or Domain
      i. Join a domain: **corp.viamonstra.com**
      ii. Account: **CORP\CM_JD**

iii. Password: **Password01**

b. Windows Settings

i. User name: **ViaMonstra**

ii. Organization name: **ViaMonstra**

iii. Product key: supply product key or leave blank if you are using a KMS.

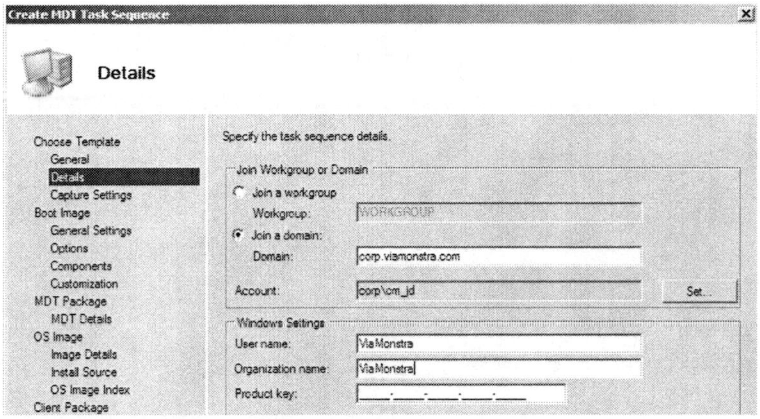

Configuring the domain information.

6. On the **Capture Settings** page, configure this setting and click **Next**:

   This task sequence will never be used to capture an image: **Enabled**

7. On the **Boot Image** page, configure this setting and click **Next**:

   In **Specify an existing boot image package**, click **Browse**, select the **MDTBoot Image x86 1.0 en-US** package, and click **OK**.

8. On the **MDT Package** page configure this setting and click **Next**:

   Select **Create a new Microsoft Deployment Toolkit Files Package**, and type **\\CM01\Sources$\OSD\Toolkit** in **Package source folder to be created (UNC path)**.

9. On the **MDT Details** page, configure these settings and click **Next**:

   a. Name: **Deployment Toolkit package**

   b. Version: **2012**

   c. Language: **US**

   d. Manufacturer: **Microsoft**

10. On the **OS Image** page, configure this setting and click **Next**:

Select **Specify an existing OS image**, click **Browse**, select the **Windows 7 Enterprise x64** image, and click **OK**.

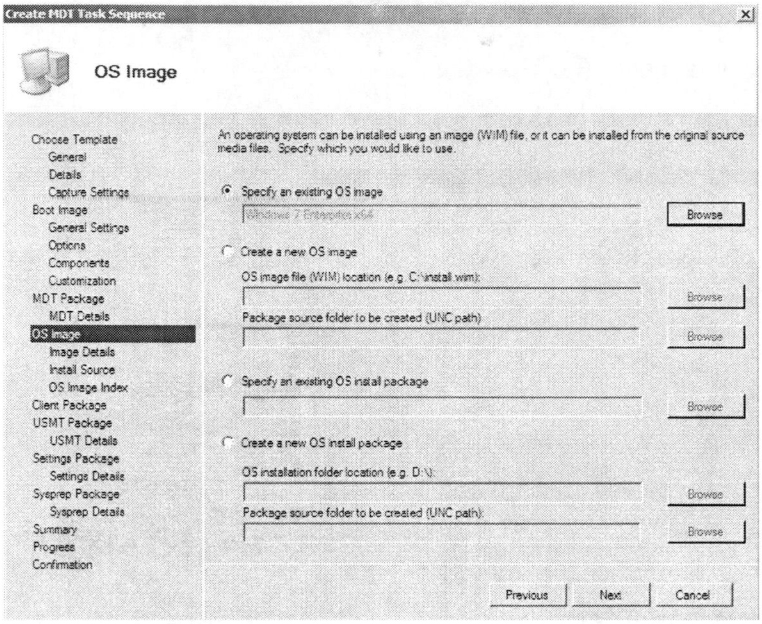

Selecting the operating system image file.

11. On the **Client Package** page, configure this setting and click **Next**:

    Select **Specify a ConfigMgr client package**, click **Browse**, select the **Microsoft Corporation Configuration Manager Client Package**, and click **OK**.

12. On the **USMT Package** page, configure these settings and click **Next**:

    a. Select **Create a new USMT Package** with the default settings.

    b. In **Package source folder to be created (UNC Path),** type **\\CM01\Sources$\OSD\USMT 4.0**.

13. On the **USMT Details** page, configure these settings and click **Next**:

    a. Name: **User State Migration Toolkit**

    b. Version: **4.0**

    c. Language: **US**

    d. Manufacturer: **Microsoft**

14. On the **Settings Package** page, configure this setting and click **Next**:

    Click **Create a new settings package**; in **Package source folder to be created (UNC Path)**, type **\\CM01\Sources$\OSD\Win7Settings**.

15. On the **Settings Details** page, configure these settings and click **Next**:
    a. Name: **Windows 7 Deploy Settings**
    b. Version: **2012**
    c. Language: **US**
    d. Manufacturer: **Microsoft**
16. On the **Sysprep Package** page, select **No Sysprep package is required** and click **Next**.
17. On the **Summary** page, read the summary and click **Next** to start creating the task sequence and the packages.

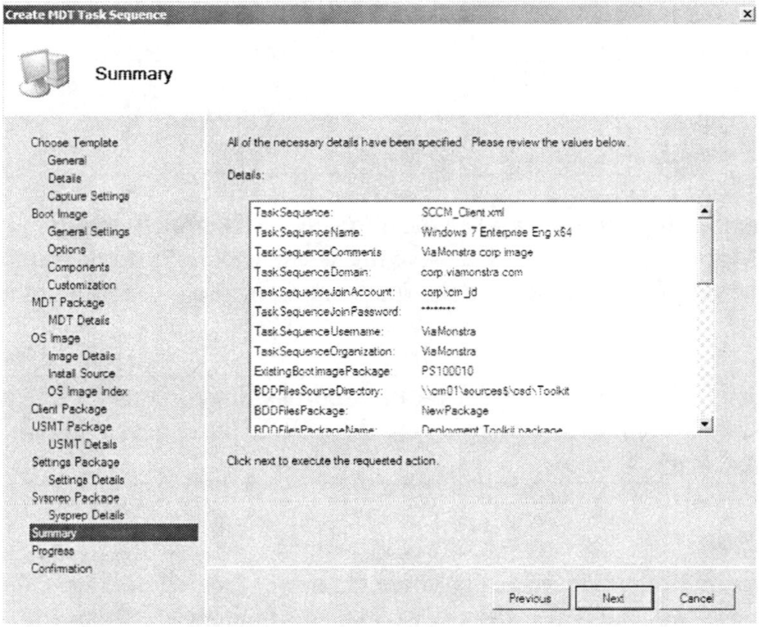

Summary of all settings and packages for the MDT task sequence.

18. On the **Confirmation** page, click **Finish**.

Edit the Rules (Settings Package)

After finishing the creation of the MDT task sequence, you need to change some rules in the CustomSettings.ini file within your settings package. The settings package is customizable; you are able to change the Unattend.xml and CustomSettings.ini files. In CustomSettings.ini, you are able to edit the existing rules and add new rules.

1. Use **Windows Explorer** to open **\\CM01\Sources$\OSD\Win7Settings**, and open **CustomSettings.ini** using **Notepad**.

2. Edit the **CustomSettings.ini** file so it reflects the settings file in the example below. You also can find the CustomSettings.ini file along with the other files and scripts used in this book.

```
[Settings]
Priority=Default
Properties= OSDMigrateConfigFiles,OSDMigrateMode

[Default]
SLShare=\\CM01\logs$
DoCapture=NO
ComputerBackupLocation=NONE
BDEInstallSuppress=YES
MachineObjectOU=ou=workstations,dc=corp,dc=viamonstra,dc=com
OSDMigrateMode=Advanced
OSDMigrateAdditionalCaptureOptions=/ue:*\* /ui:CORP\*
OSDMigrateConfigFiles=Miguser.xml,Migapp.xml
```

3. After editing the **CustomSettings.ini** file, update the **Windows 7 Deploy Settings** package in the **ConfigMgr console**. Even if you have not yet distributed the content for this package, you still need to update it because the first version is already stored in the content library.

Real World Note: For in-depth information about MDT custom settings, I recommend that you acquire *Deployment Fundamentals* – Volume 3, written by the three OSD "über geeks" Johan Arwidmark, Mikael Nyström, and Chris Nackers.

Distribute the MDT Packages

After editing the CustomSettings.ini file, you need to distribute the newly created packages. You can do this via the packages themselves, but it is easier to distribute the content via the newly created task sequence. This way you are certain that all the content referenced by the task sequence is distributed to the distribution points. The approach also checks whether the related boot image and Windows 7 image are distributed.

1. Navigate to the **Software Library** workspace, select **Operating Systems, Task Sequences**. You should see the newly created task sequence **Windows 7 Enterprise x64**. If not, refresh the console view.
2. Select the **Windows 7 Enterprise x64** task sequence and click **Distribute Content** on the ribbon.
3. On the **General** page, click **Next**.
4. On the **Content** page, verify that all packages and images referenced by the packages are listed, and then click **Next**.

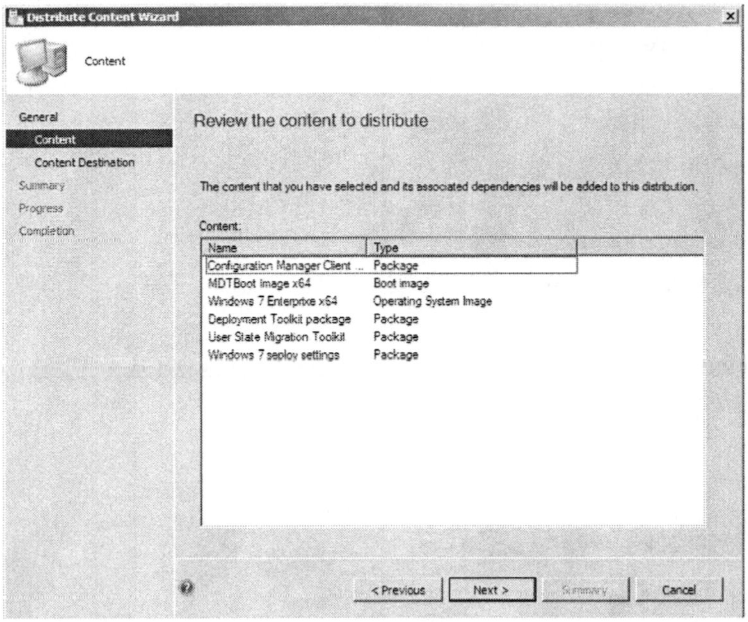

An easy way to ensure that all packages referenced by the task sequence are distributed.

5. On the **Content Destination** page, click **Add, Distribution Point Group**; then select **All Content** and click **OK** and **Next**.
6. On the **Summary** page, read the summary and click **Next**.
7. On the **Completion** page, click **Close**.

Applications in the OS Deployment Process

There are several ways to deploy applications as part of the OS deployment process. Applications can be deployed in five different phases of the process. In which phase you plan to deploy the application, depends on factors like:

- The importance of deployment speed
- The number of applications you want to deploy
- Whether you want to deploy applications before a user is assigned as primary user for a device
- Whether you want to deploy applications before the user is logged on

The operating environment consists of five layers, and each one represents another way or method of installing applications on your Windows 7 operating system.

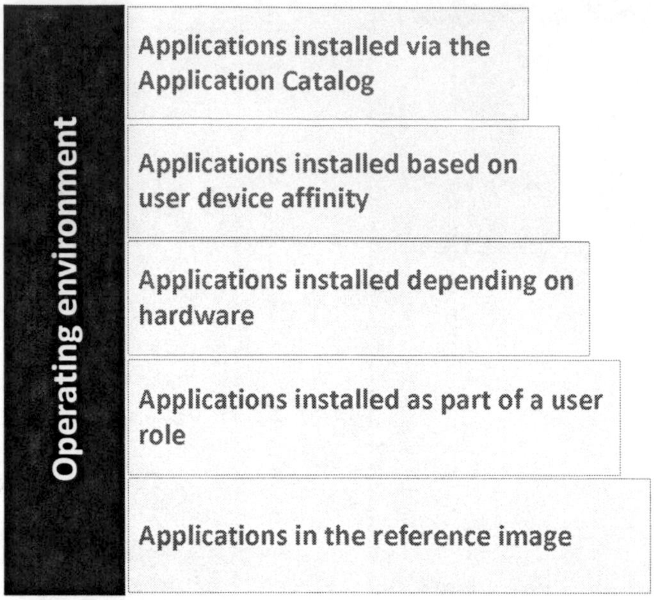

Application layers of the operating environment.

Applications in the Reference Image

The reference image includes Windows 7 SP1 and Microsoft Office 2010 SP1, with all the approved software updates in place. After the reference image is created, you are able to service the image by incorporating approved software updates offline.

Applications Installed as Part of a User Role

Depending on group membership, user role applications can be installed via a ConfigMgr task sequence when the user next logs on, or via the Software Center / Application Catalog from which the users can install or request software that is available for them.

Applications Installed Depending on Hardware

With a task sequence, you are able to install applications for different hardware types. For instance, you can specify what software in installed depending on the type of hardware.

In the task sequence, you are allowed to add conditions to a task. A condition can be a WMI query which checks what kind of hardware you are using, or a task sequence variable. Depending on the condition, a task will run or not. As an example, you can use the task sequence variable **IsLaptop** to install certain applications only on laptops.

1. In the **Software Library** workspace, select **Operating Systems**, **Task Sequences**.
2. Select the **Windows 7 Enterprise x64** task sequence you created earlier and click **Edit** on ribbon.

3. Go to the **State Restore** phase of the task sequence, select the **Install Application** task, and select **Options.**

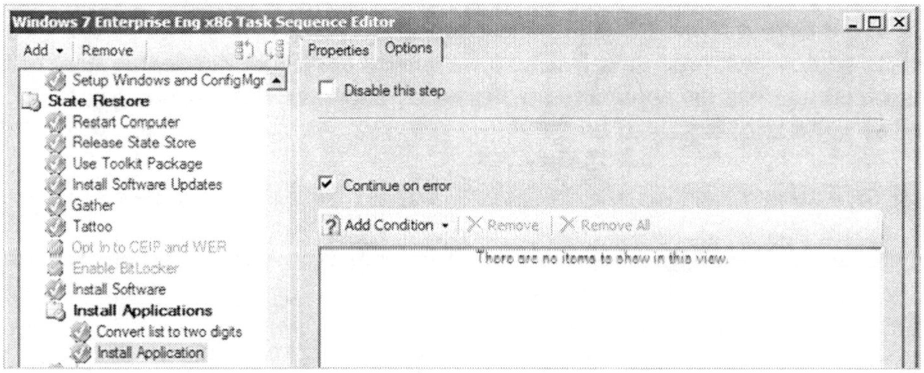

Selecting the Install Application task.

4. Click **Add Condition**, and select **If Statement**.
5. Click **Add Condition**, and select **Task Sequence Variable**.
6. Use the following values:
    a. Variable: **IsLaptop**
    b. Condition: **Equals**
    c. Value: **True**

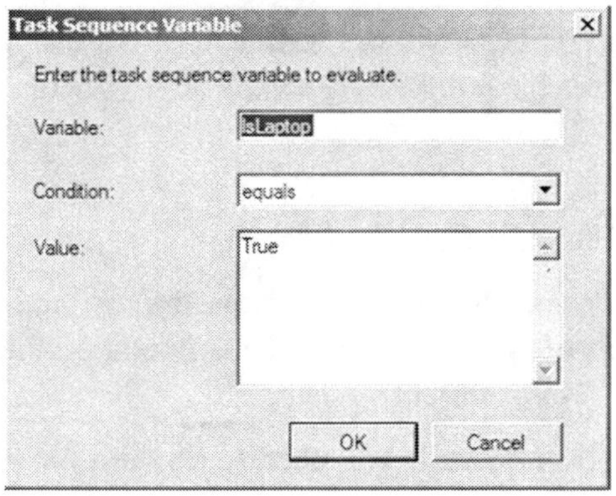

Setting the task sequence variable.

7. Select **OK** twice to submit the values and close the task sequence.

Instead of configuring the IF statement on one task, you also can create a group and set the statement there. This statement is then valid for all tasks in the group.

Applications Installed Based on User Device Affinity

In Chapter 6, you learned how to configure user device affinity; this feature also can be integrated with the OS deployment process. This means that the applications that are normally deployed to the user can be deployed as part of the OS deployment process. This way a user can work immediately after the deployment process is finished. Be sure to configure the deployment of the applications as **required** and that the application is **deployed automatically according to schedule whether or not a user is logged on**.

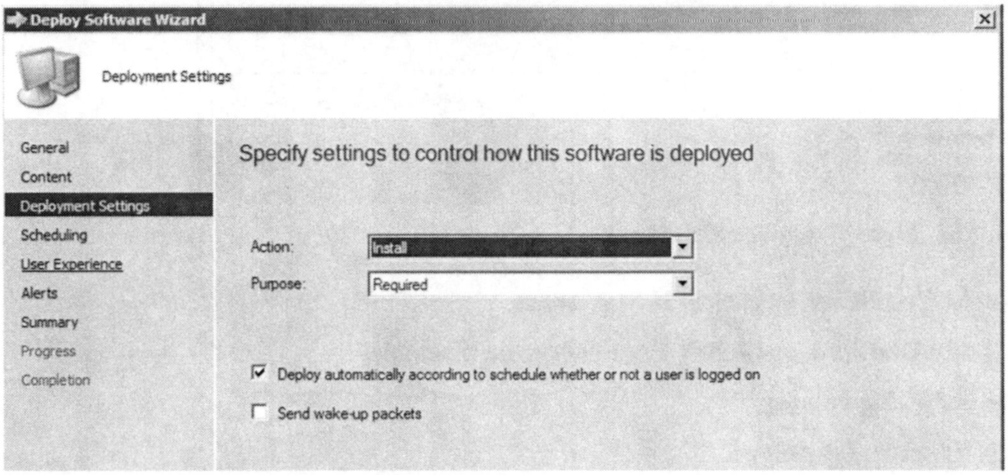

Configuring the application deployment.

Applications Installed via the Application Catalog

In Chapter 6, you learned how to configure applications and deploy those to the Application Catalog. Applications deployed to the Application Catalog are not part of the OS deployment process but still worth mentioning in this model.

Integrating Endpoint Protection

When deploying a new operating system without an Endpoint Protection solution, the machine may be vulnerable to possible viruses or other unwanted software. A safe solution is embedding the Endpoint Protection solution in your OS deployment environment.

To install the Endpoint Protection client while installing Windows 7, you need to do the following:

1. In the **Software Library** workspace, select **Operating Systems, Task Sequences**.
2. Right-click **Windows 7 Enterprise Eng x64** and select **Edit**.
3. Go to the **Install Applications** group and select **Add**, **General**, **Run Command line**.
4. Configure the task with the following settings:
    a. Name: **SCEP Install**

b. Command line: **SCEPInstall.exe /s /q /policy "ep_defaultpolicy.xml"**

c. Package: **Configuration Manager Client Package**

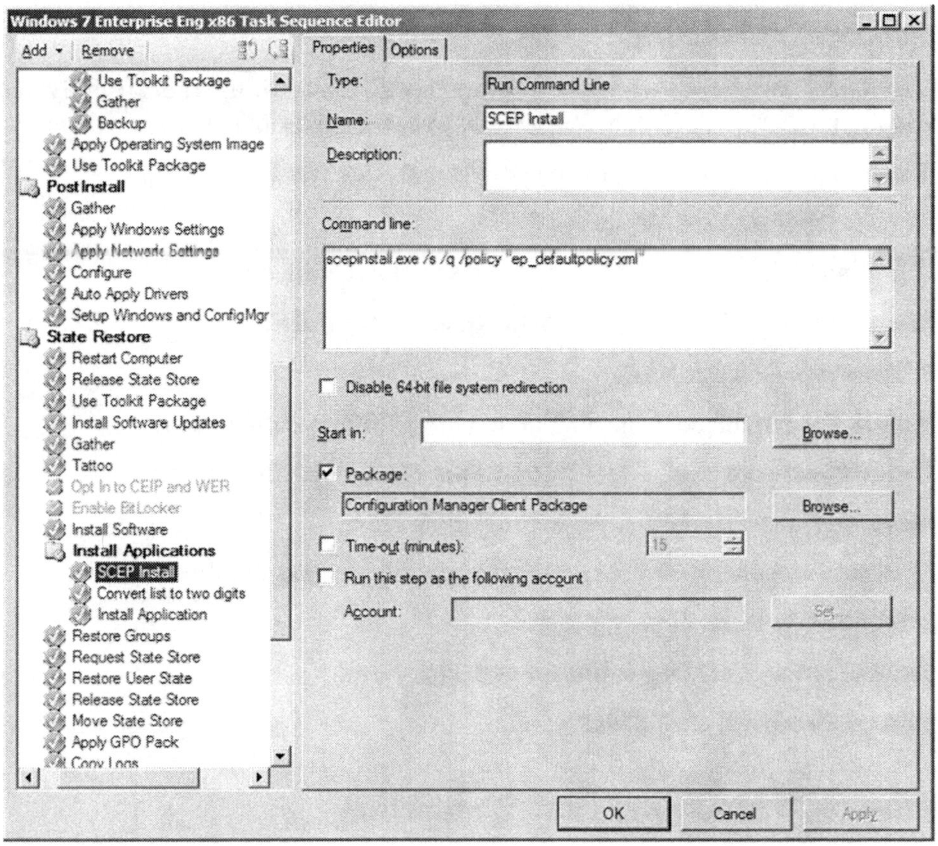

The SCEP install task.

5. Select **OK** to save the settings of the task sequence.

Real World Note: The file ep_defaultpolicy.xml is part of the standard Configuration Manager Client Package. If you want a custom file, you can install the client manually by using **SCEPInstall.exe /s /q /policy "full path to policy"**.

Refreshing Windows XP to Windows 7

After preparing the ViaMonstra environment for deploying a new custom Windows 7 image, it is time to migrate the Windows XP workstations to Windows 7. Before you are able to do that, you need to deploy the task sequence to a collection with your old Windows XP workstations.

> **Real World Note:** Never deploy any OS task sequence to members of the All System collection. Always use one or more specific collections for the Windows XP migrations.

Create a Custom Collection

1. In the **Asset and Compliance** workspace, select **Device Collection, Operating System Deployment**, and then click **Create Device Collection** on the ribbon.
2. On the **General** page, enter the following details and click **Next**:
    a. Name: **OSD Refresh Windows 7**
    b. Limiting Collection: Click **Browse** and select **All Systems**.
3. On the **Membership Rules** page, click **Add Rule, Direct Rule**.
4. On the **Welcome** page, click **Next**.
5. On the **Search for Resources** page, in **Value**, type **PC002** and click **Next**.
6. On the **Select Resources** page, select **PC002** from the list and click **Next**.
7. On the **Summary** page, read the summary and click **Next**.
8. On the **Completion** page, click **Close** and return to the Membership Rules page.
9. On the **Membership Rules** page, click **Next**.
10. On the **Summary** page, read the summary and click **Next**.
11. On the **Completion** page, click **Close**

Deploy the Refresh Machine Task Sequence

1. Navigate to the **Software Library** workspace and select **Operating Systems, Task Sequences, Windows 7 Enterprise x64**; then click **Deploy** on the ribbon.
2. On the **General** page, click **Browse** and select the just created collection **OSD Refresh Windows 7** collection in the **Operating System Deployment** folder; then click **Next**.
3. On the **Deployment Settings** page, ensure the **Purpose** is **Required** and click **Next**. You also can configure the deployment to be Available; by doing that, you not forcing the upgrade.
4. On the **Scheduling** page, click **New** in **Assignment Schedule**, click the **Schedule** button, and configure the assignment schedule to one week from now. Click **OK** twice and then **Next**.
5. On the **User Experience** page, configure these settings and click **Next**:

    Notification settings

        Allow users to run the program independently of assignments: **Enable**

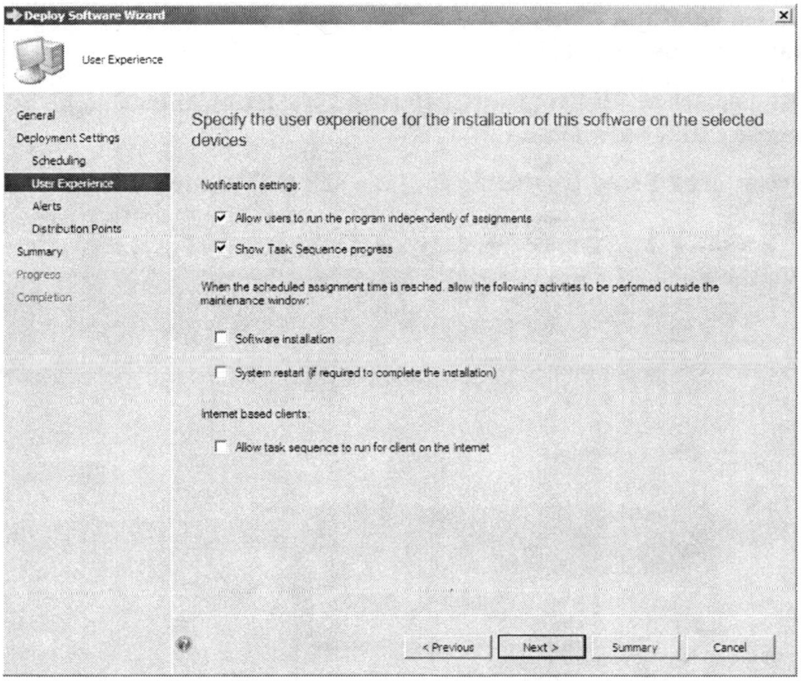

Allowing the end user to run the deployment prior to deadline.

6. On the **Alerts** page, configure these settings and click **Next**:
    a. Create a deployment alert when the threshold is lower than the following: **Enable**
    b. Percent success: **95**.
    c. After: **8 days from now**.
    d. Create a deployment alert when the threshold is higher than the following: **Enable**
    e. Percent failure: **1**.
7. On the **Distribution Points** page, click **Next**.
8. On the **Summary** page, read the summary and click **Next**.
9. On the **Completion** page, click **Close**.

Run the Refresh Task Sequence

1. Log on to **PC002** as **JAP** and perform a few changes on the desktop, like changing the wallpaper, create some shortcuts, and so forth.
2. **Log off** the computer to save the profile.
3. Log back on to **PC002** as **JAP**, open the **Control Panel**, and navigate to the **Configuration Manager** icon in the **Performance and Maintenance** category.

4. Select the **Actions** tab in **Configuration Manager Properties**, select **Machine Policy Retrieval & Evaluation Cycle**, and click **Run Now**.
5. Open the **Start** menu, and select **All Programs**, **Microsoft System Center 2012**, **Configuration Manager**, **Software Center**.
6. In the **Software Center**, click **Show Operating System**, select **Windows 7 Enterprise x64**, and click **Install**.

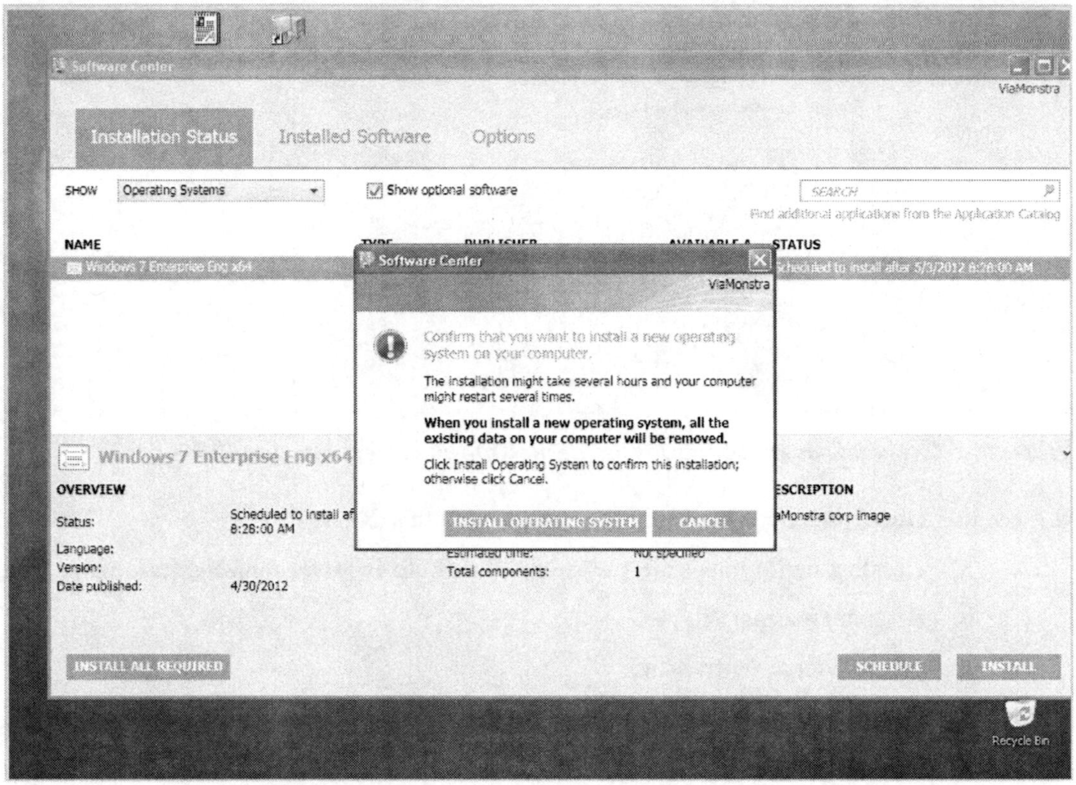

Starting the refresh of Windows XP to Windows 7.

7. After you select **INSTALL OPERATING SYSTEM**, the task sequence starts and prepares the installation of Windows 7.

After the deployment is finished, notice that the documents on the desktop were preserved during the update to Windows 7. The User State Migration Toolkit and the earlier configured state migration point took care of this.

Bare Metal Deployment

When a new workstation comes out of the box, you want to be sure that it receives the corporate Windows 7 image without too much administrative effort. ConfigMgr supports bare metal deployment by enabling you to add a resource record for a new machine manually or by using the Unknown Computer support. You can use the existing MDT task sequence to perform a bare metal deployment or create a new task sequence. For the fun of it, create a new ConfigMgr task sequence so that you can compare the MDT task sequence with a native ConfigMgr task sequence. You will not use this task sequence in the other guides.

Create a Configuration Manager Deploy Task Sequence

1. In the **Software Library** workspace, select **Operating Systems, Task Sequences.**
2. Click **Create Task Sequence** on the ribbon.
3. On the **Create New Task Sequence** page, select **Install an existing image package** and click **Next.**
4. On the **Task Sequence Information** page, configure these settings and click **Next**:
    a. Task sequence name: **Windows 7 x64 Enterprise Bare Metal**
    b. Boot image: Click **Browse** and select the **MDTBoot Image x86 1.0 en-US.**

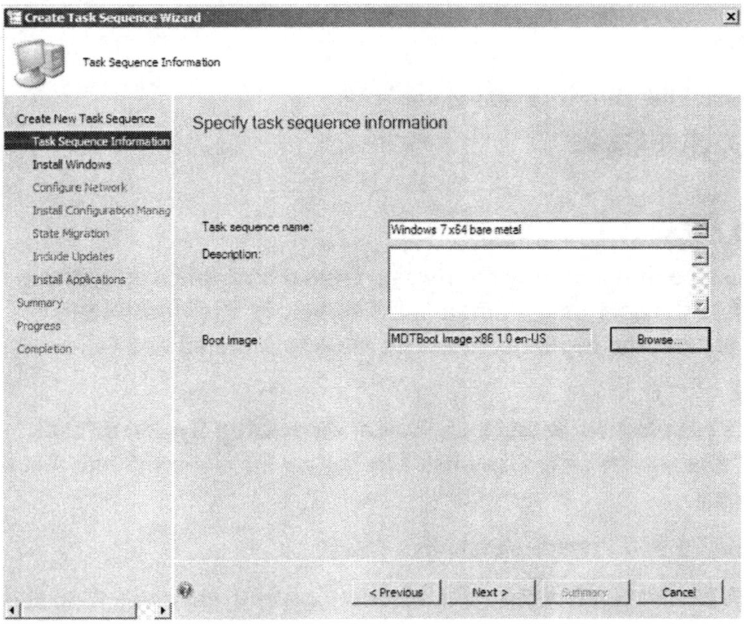

Creating the bare metal task sequence.

5. On the **Install Windows** page, configure these settings and click **Next**:
   a. Image package: Click **Browse** and select the **Windows 7 x64 Enterprise** image.
   b. Always use the same administrator password: **Enable** and assign **Password01** as the password.
6. On the **Configure Network** page, configure these settings and click **Next**:
   a. Join a domain: **corp.viamonstra.com**
   b. Domain OU: **LDAP://OU=workstations,DC=corp,DC=viamonstra,DC=com**
   c. Account: **CORP\CM_JD** with **Password01** as password
7. On the **Install Configuration Manager** page, click **Browse**, select the **Configuration Manager Client Package**, and click **Next**.
8. On the **State Migration** page, configure these settings and click **Next**:
   a. Capture user settings: **Disabled**
   b. Capture network settings: **Disabled**
   c. Capture Windows settings: **Disabled.**
9. On the **Include Updates** page, select **All software updates** and click **Next.**
10. On the **Install Application** page, click **New** and select the applications that you want to install. Enable **If an application installation fails, continue installing other applications** and click **Next**.
11. On the **Summary** page, read the summary and click **Next**.
12. On the **Completion** page, click **Close**.

Deploy a Client Using PXE

The image deployment process can be initiated in several ways, from a bootable media like a DVD, CD, USB or by downloading the boot image thru a WDS server. In ViaMonstra our preferred method is PXE due to the fact the deployment media often is outdated and has a tendency to disappear.

1. Navigate to the **Software Library** workspace, and select **Operating Systems, Task Sequences, Windows 7 Enterprise x64**; then click **Deploy** on the ribbon. (Note that this is the MDT task sequence.)
2. On the **General** page, configure this setting and click **Next**:

   Collection: Click **Browse**, select the **All Unknown computers** collection, and click **OK**.

3. On the **Deployment Settings** page, configure these settings and click **Next**:
    a. Purpose: **Available**
    b. Make available to boot media and PXE: **Enabled**.

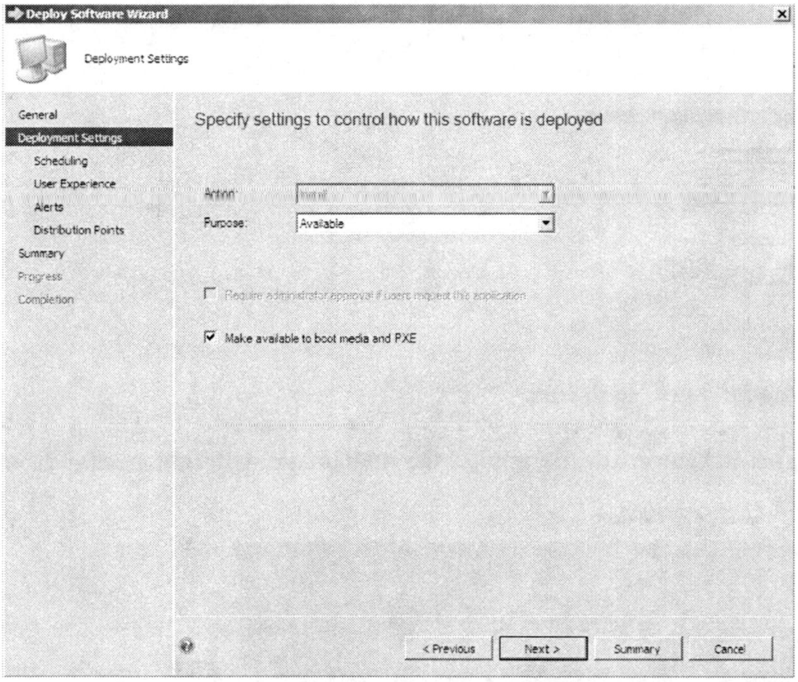

Creating an available deployment task sequence.

4. On the **Scheduling** page, keep the default settings and click **Next**.
5. On the **User Experience** page, keep the default settings and click **Next**.
6. On the **Alerts** page, configure the threshold for a failed deployment failure to **1%** and click **Next**.
7. On the **Distribution Points** page, keep the default settings and click **Next**.
8. On the **Summary** page, read the summary and click **Next**.
9. On the **Completion** page, click **Close**.

Deploy the Bare Metal Client

Before you can start deploying the client, you need to create a new virtual machine named PC003 as described earlier in this chapter:

1. Create a new virtual machine named **PC003** and start it.
2. Start the PXE deployment process by pressing **F12** during the **PC003** virtual machine startup.

3. In the **Welcome to the Task Sequence** wizard, type **Password01** and click **Next**.
4. Select the **Windows 7 Enterprise Eng x64** task sequence and click **Next**.

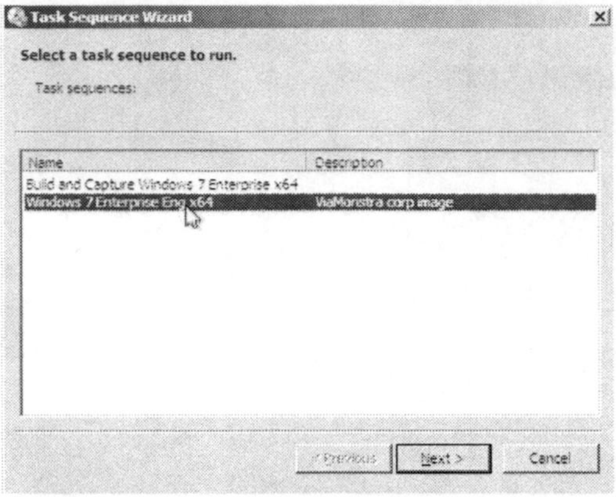

Selecting the bare metal task sequence.

The installation begins and automatically applies the new image with information from the task sequence.

The Use Toolkit Package step being processed.

Import Computer Information

Another way of deploying bare metal computers is to import information about the new computers into ConfigMgr. You can do this with the following procedure:

1. In the **Assets and Compliance** workspace, select **Device Collections** and the **Operating System Deployment** folder.
2. Click **Create Device Collection** on the ribbon.
3. On the **General** page, configure these settings and click **Next**:

   a. Name: **OSD Bare Metal**
   b. Comment: **Computers added to this collection will be able to start a bare metal deployment.**
   c. Limiting Collection: **All Systems**

4. Finish the wizard using the default settings.
5. In the **Assets and Compliance** workspace, select **Devices**.
6. Click **Import Computer Information** on the ribbon.
7. On the **Select Source** page, select **Import single computer** and click **Next**
8. On the **Single Computer** page, configure these settings and click **Next**:
   a. Computer name: **PC004**
   b. MAC Address: 00:00:00:00:00:00 (Type the actual MAC address.)

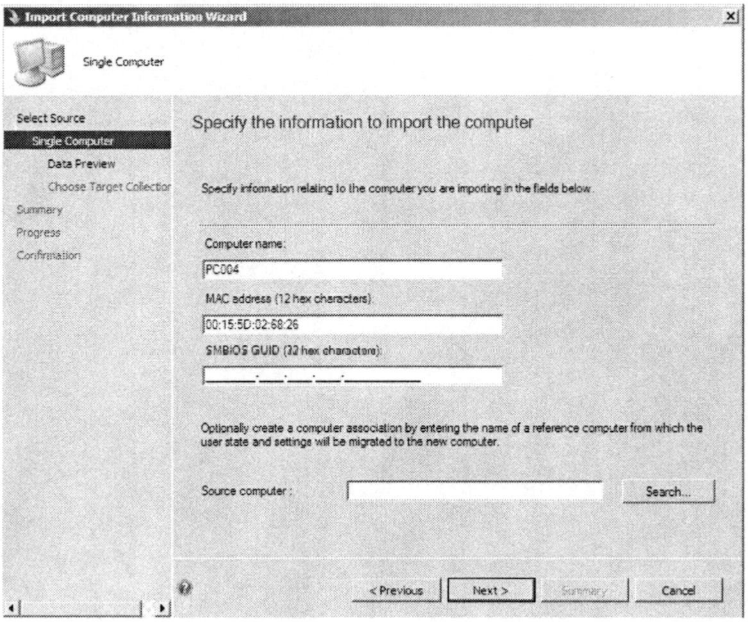

Importing a computer.

9. On the **Data Preview** page, confirm the information and click **Next**.
10. On the **Choose Target Collection** page, configure this setting and click **Next**:

    Add computers to the following collection: Click **Browse** and select the **OSD Bare Metal** collection in the **Operating System Deployment** folder.

11. On the **Summary** page, read the summary and click **Next**.
12. On the **Completion** page, click **Close**.

Automate Importing Computers Using PowerShell

In this example, you import a new computer object into the OSD Bare Metal collection:

1. Open **PowerShell** as **Administrator**.
2. Navigate to the folder containing the script.
3. Type **. .\CM12_Function_Library.ps1** and press **Enter**.
4. Type **Create-CMAccount -MACAddress 00:15:5D:C2:A3:20 -SiteServer localhost -SiteCode PS1 -AccountName PC004 -CollectionName "OSD Bare Metal"**; then press **Enter**.

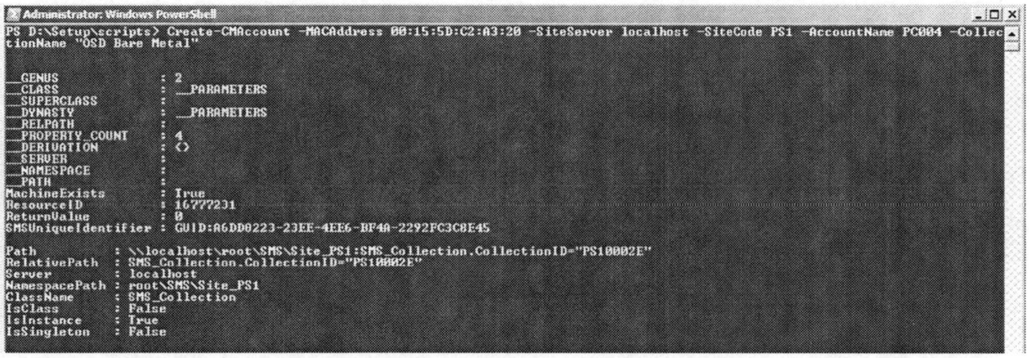

Importing computers using PowerShell.

Device Driver Handling

When deploying operating systems to different kinds of machines, you need to add the device drivers to ConfigMgr. You can add the drivers in several ways. To keep your device drivers structured, I recommend that you create a unique driver category per hardware model. In a later stage, you will see the advantage of creating these categories. The first step after downloading the drivers is importing them to the driver store in ConfigMgr.

ViaMonstra acquired a new Lenovo W510 laptop, and the drivers need to be integrated within the deployment process.

Import Drivers

1. On **CM01**, use **Windows Explorer** to create the following folder(s):

   D:\Sources\OSD\Drivers\Windows7\x64\Lenovo\W510

2. On **CM01**, navigate to the **Software Library** workspace, and select **Operating Systems**.
3. Right-click **Drivers** and click **Folder, Create Folder**.
4. Name the folder **Windows 7 x64**.

5. Right-click the **Windows 7 x64** folder and click **Folder, Create Folder**. Name the folder **Lenovo W510**.
6. Right-click the root of the **Drivers** node and select **Import driver**.
7. On the **Locate Driver** page, configure this setting and click **Next**:

   In **Source folder**, type the source location of your extracted device drivers.

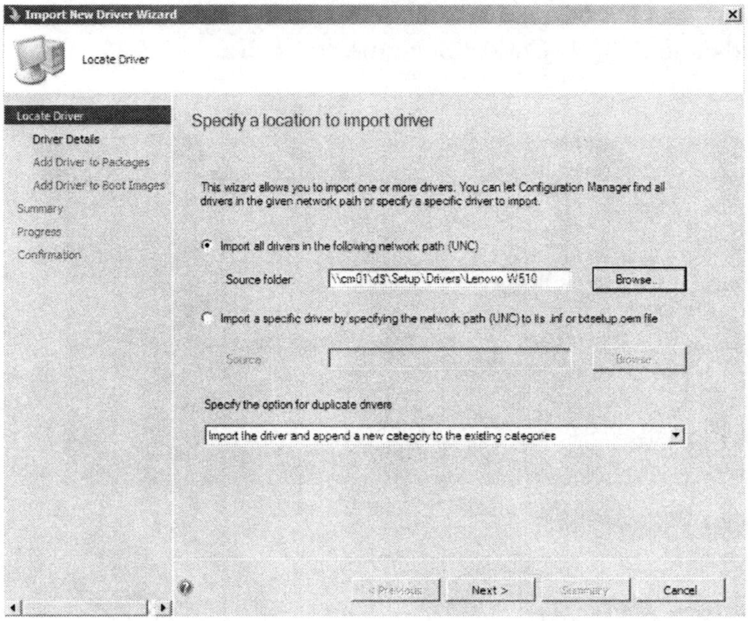

Specifying the source driver source location.

8. On the **Driver details** page, configure this setting and click **Next**:

   Click **Categories**, click **Create**, and create a category called **Windows 7 x64 Lenovo W510**; then click **OK** twice.

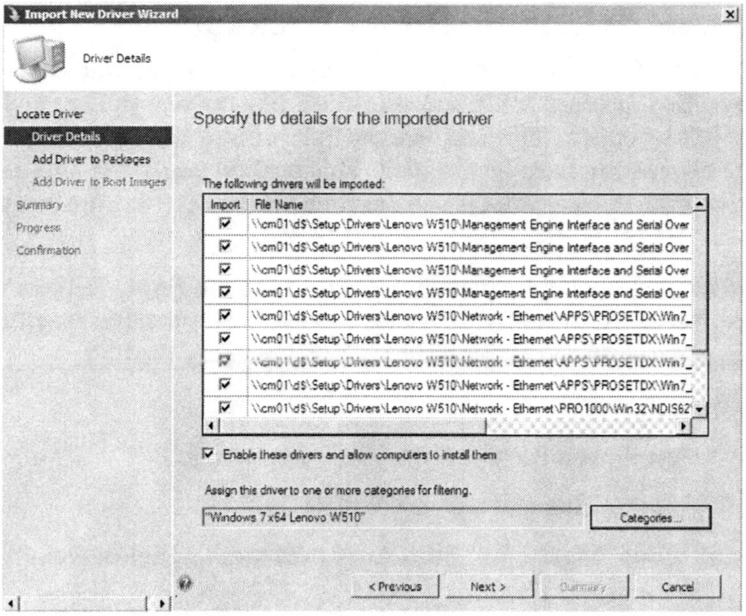

Assigning a unique category per model.

9. On the **Add Driver to Packages** page, configure these settings and click **Next**:

   Click **New Package**. Create a new package with these settings and click **OK**.

   i. Name: **Windows 7 x64 Lenovo W510**

   ii. Path: **\\CM01\sources$\OSD\Drivers\Windows7\x64\Lenovo\W510**

10. On the **Add Driver to Boot Images** page, leave the defaults and click **Next**.

11. On the **Summary** page, read the summary and click **Next**.

12. On the **Completion** page, click **Close**.

13. After the drivers are imported, you will find them in the **Drivers** root and not the folder you created. Select all the drivers with the category **Windows 7 x64 Lenovo W510**, click **Move** on the ribbon, and move them to the **Windows 7 x64\ Lenovo W510** folder.

Deploy the Driver Package

You now need to deploy the new driver package to the distribution points within your environment:

1. Select **Drivers Packages**. You should see the newly created **Windows 7 Lenovo x64 W510** driver package. (You also can move the package to an appropriate folder.)

2. Select the driver package and click **Distribute Content** on the ribbon.

3. Distribute the package to your distribution point groups.

Modify the Task Sequence to Include Driver Packages

When deploying device drivers as part of the operating system deployment process, you are able to do that in several different ways. The standard MDT task sequence, like the one you created earlier, comes with an Auto Apply Drivers task. This task lets the PnP process within WinPE determine which drivers from the driver store must be installed. This method works but also can determine the wrong driver for a specific device, even if you configure the task to use the created category.

A better way of implementing drivers in your deployment process is to use the Apply Driver Package task in the task sequence. You need to configure the task to run only when the specific hardware needs that driver package. You can do this by adding a WMI query to the task.

The following steps show you how to configure the task:

1. In the **Software Library**, select **Operating Systems**, **Task Sequences**.
2. Right-click **Windows 7 Enterprise Eng x64** and select **Edit**.
3. Navigate to the **Post Install** group. Right-click **Auto Apply drivers** and select **Delete**.
4. Click **Yes** to delete the step.
5. From the menu, select **Add**, **Drivers**, **Apply Driver Package**.
6. In **Name**, type **Apply Driver Package Lenovo W510**.
7. For **Driver Package**, click **Browse** and select the **Windows 7 x64 Lenovo W510** driver package.

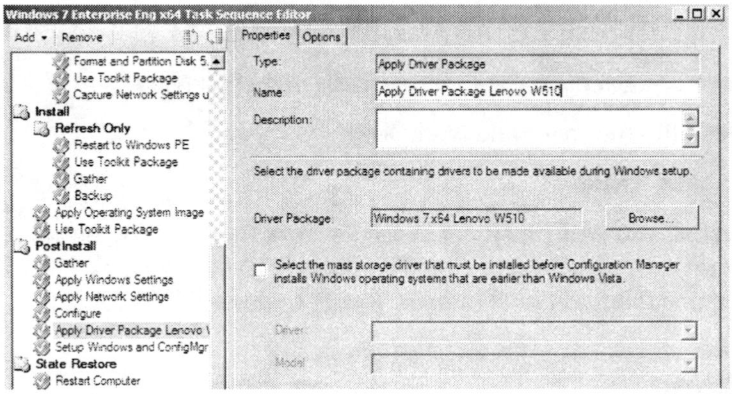

Applying a driver package.

8. Select the **Options** tab, click **Add Condition** and select **Query WMI**.
9. In **WQL Query**, type the following:

   SELECT * FROM Win32_ComputerSystem WHERE Model LIKE "%431929G%"

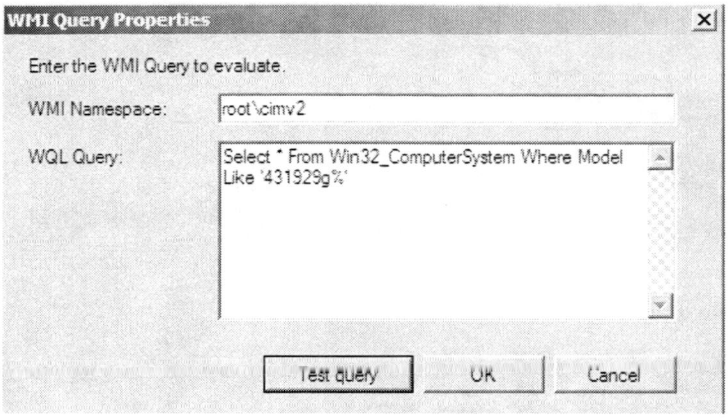

Configuring the task sequence with the WMI query.

10. Click **OK** to close and save the task sequence.

Note: You can get the model number in many ways. One is opening a command prompt and typing **wmic computersystem get model** on the target computer.

Maintaining a WIM Image

After creating a custom WIM image, you definitely need to have a strategy for how often you want to update the reference image. ConfigMgr allows you deploy software updates to the WIM image directly from the console. To keep your deployment process quick and the golden image safe from security breaches, you should service your WIM image offline at least four times a year with security updates. Waiting longer extends the deployment process because the approved software updates will have to be installed during this process.

1. In the **Software Library** workspace, select **Operating Systems**, **Operating System Images**.
2. Click **Schedule Updates** on the ribbon.
3. On the **Choose Updates** page, select the updates you want to inject into the image and click **Next**.

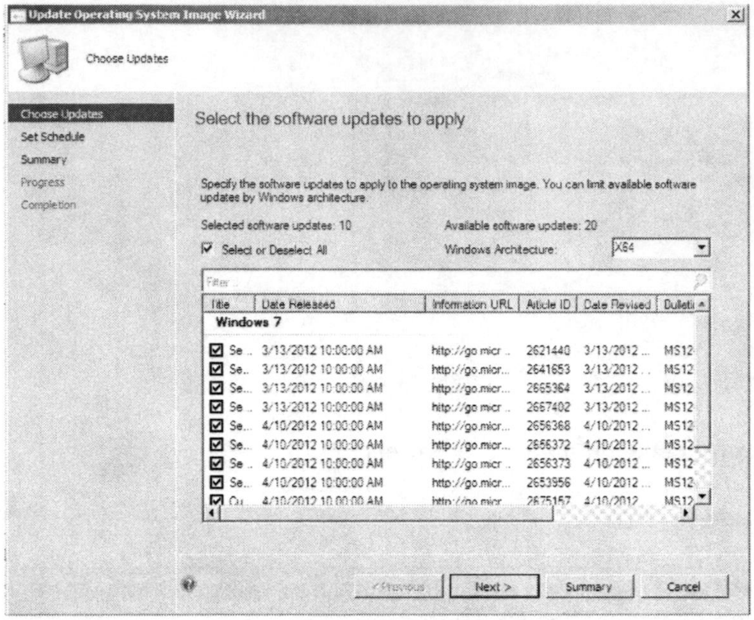

Selecting the updates that need to be injected.

4. On the **Set Schedule** page, configure a schedule or select **As soon as possible** and click **Next**.
5. In the **Update Operating System Image** window, select the top three updates and click **Next.**
6. On the **Summary** page, read the summary and click **Next**.
7. On the **Completion** page, click **Close**.

Useful Log Files

You can use the log files in the following table to track the OS deployment activity.

Log File	Description	Location
OSDImageproperties.log	This log file records activity about maintaining the boot images.	Server
OfflineServicingMgr.log	When you service your WIM images offline, this log file tells you everything about the offline servicing process and helps you to troubleshoot the process.	Server

Log File	**Description**	**Location**
Smspxe.log	This log file provides information about the PXE role on the Configuration Manager distribution point.	Server
Drivercatalog.log	When importing or updating drivers in the driver catalog, this file can be used for troubleshooting.	Server
Smsts.log	While deploying an operating system, the task sequence logs the result of every task in this log file. You can find the log file in several locations: • On WINPE: x:\windows\temp\smstslog\smsts.log • <CCM Install Dir>\Logs • %Temp%\SMSTSLOG • <largest fixed partition> _SMSTaskSequence • %Windir%\System32\Ccm\Logs • %Windir%\SysWOW64\Ccm\Logs • <largest fixed partition> \SMSTSLOG	Client
setupact.log	This Windows Installation log file is useful for troubleshooting installation failures.	Client C:\Windows\panther

Chapter 11 Compliance Settings

The ConfigMgr 2012 compliance settings feature is an updated version of ConfigMgr 2007's Desired Configuration Management. The compliance settings feature allows you to run a check on your clients against a set of rules. Those rules are called configuration items (CIs) that are grouped together in a configuration baseline. You can easily create your own CIs and baselines, or you can download preconfigured configuration packs from http://tinyurl.com/c7rlc34.

There is a wealth of different configuration packs ranging from Microsoft best practice for securing your environment to regulations configuration packs from organizations like SOX.

Configuration Items

A CI is a rule containing one or more checks that are evaluated by the client. A CI contains a setting type and a set of compliance rules. In the setting type, you define what setting you want to check and the compliance rules determine what happens if the client reports noncompliance. For some of the settings, you are able to remediate the settings automatically. You can create different CIs for your mobile and "normal" Windows devices.

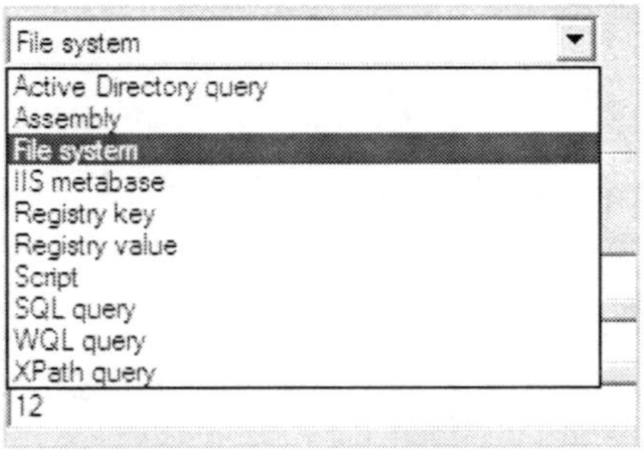

A list of the available setting types in a CI.

Note: Auto-remediate only works for these setting types: Script, Registry and WMI.

Baselines

A baseline is a collection of CIs that you deploy to a user or device collection. The baseline can be deployed as "monitor only," or you can enable remediation. If you enable remediation, then all CIs configured for automatic remediation automatically remediate the compliance setting from noncompliant to compliant.

Creating CIs and Baselines

In ViaMonstra, you won't allow servers to run the automatic ConfigMgr client remediation, but you still want the client to upload client health information. To achieve that, you can either use the command line notifyonly=true when installing the client, or modify this registry value HKLM\Software\Microsoft\CCM\Ccmeval\NotifyOnly from False to True.

Create a Device CI

1. In the **Assets and Compliance** workspace of the **ConfigMgr console**, select **Compliance Settings, Configuration Items.**
2. Right-click **Configuration Items**, and select **Folder, Create Folder.**
3. Type **Server Compliance** as the folder name and click **OK.**
4. Select the **Server Compliance** folder and click **Create Configuration Item** on the ribbon.
5. On the **General** page, configure these settings and click **Next**:
    a. Name: **Disable automatic client remediation**
    b. Categories: Click **Categories**, select **Servers**, and click **OK.**
6. On the **Supported Platforms** page, click **Next.**
7. On the **Settings** page, click **New** and configure these values:
    a. Name: **Disable automatic client remediation**
    b. Setting type: **Registry value**
    c. Data type: **String**
    d. Hive: Click **Browse** and complete the following settings:
        i. Navigate to **HKLM\SOFTWARE\Microsoft\CCM\CcmEval** and select the **NotifyOnly** key.
        ii. Select **The registry value must exist on the client device.**
        iii. Select **The registry value must satisfy the following rule if present** and set it for **Equals TRUE.**
        iv. Click **OK.**

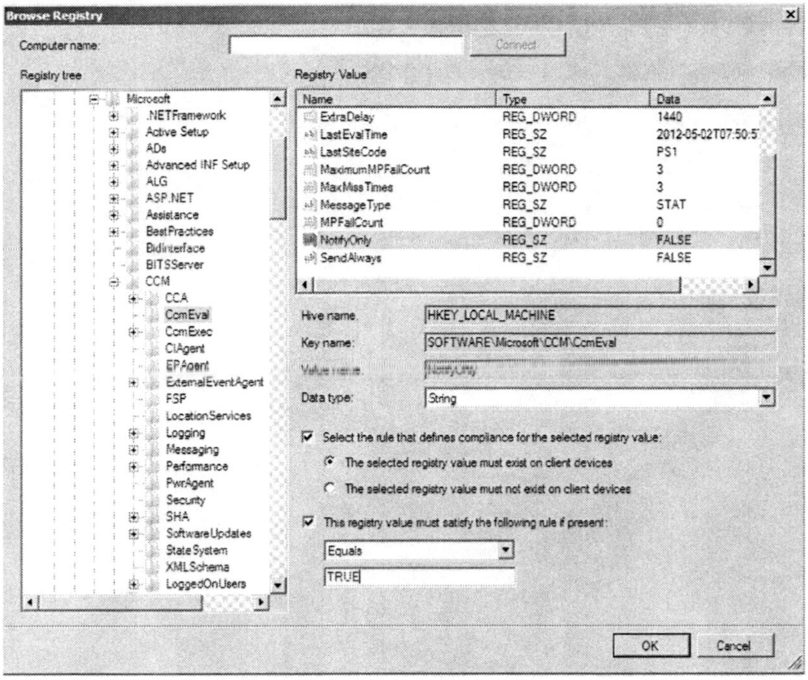

Selecting the registry key.

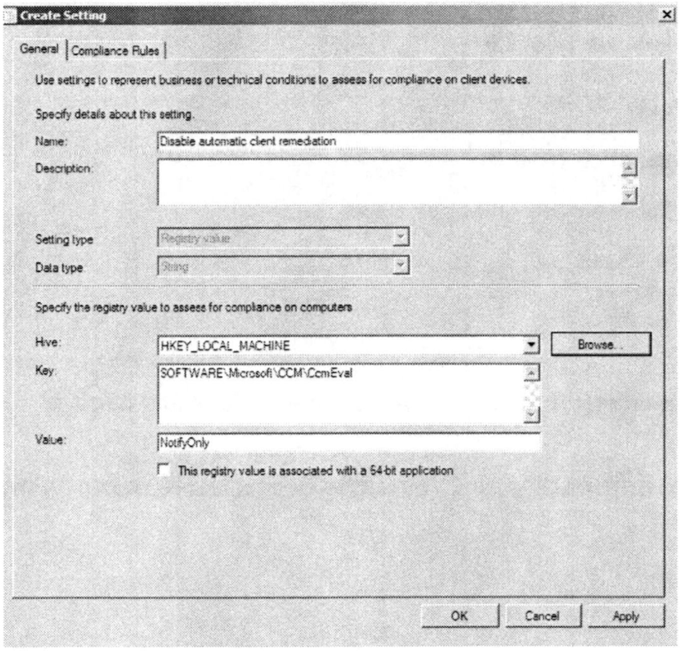

The final registry settings.

8. Select the **Compliance Rules** tab.

9. Select **NotifyOnly Equals TRUE** and click **Edit**.
10. Enable **Remediate noncompliant Rules when supported** and click **OK** twice.

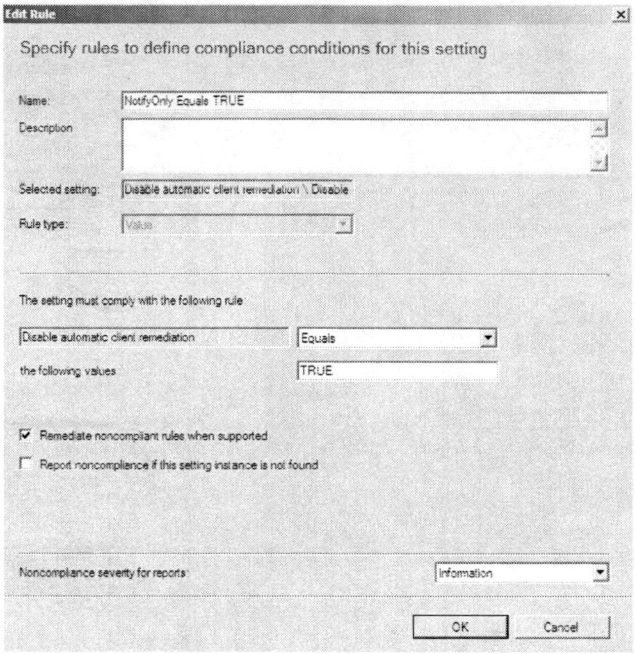

Enabling automatic remediation on the CI.

11. On the **Settings** page, click **Next**.
12. On the **Compliance Rules** page, click **Next**.
13. On the **Summary** page, read the summary and click **Next**.
14. On the **Completion** page, click **Close**.

Create a Device Baseline

1. Right-click **Configuration Baselines**; then select **Folder**, **New Folder** and name it **Server Compliance**.
2. Select the **Server Compliance** folder and click **Create Configuration Baseline** on the ribbon.

3. Configure a baseline with these settings and click **OK**:

    a. Name: **Server Compliance**

    b. Configuration data: Click **Add**, **Configuration Items**. Select **Disable automatic client remediation**, and then click **Add** and **OK**.

    c. Click **Categories**, select **Server**, and click **OK**.

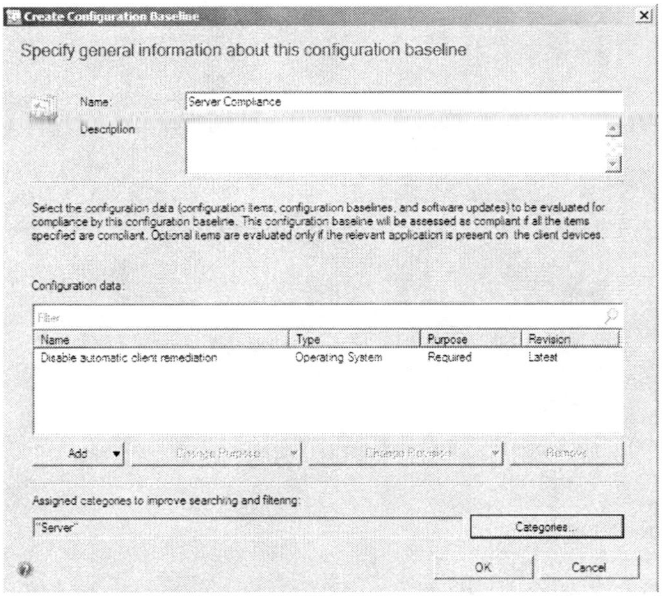

Creating the baseline.

Deploy the Baseline

1. Back in the **ConfigMgr console**, select the newly create **Server Compliance** baseline and click **Deploy** on the ribbon.

2. Configure these settings and click **OK**:

    a. Remediate noncompliant rules when supported: **Enabled**

    b. Allow remediation outside the maintenance window: **Enabled**

    c. Generate an alert: **Enabled** and configured for **90%**

3. Click **Browse** and from **Device Collections** select, **\ViaMonstra\VM All Servers** collection.

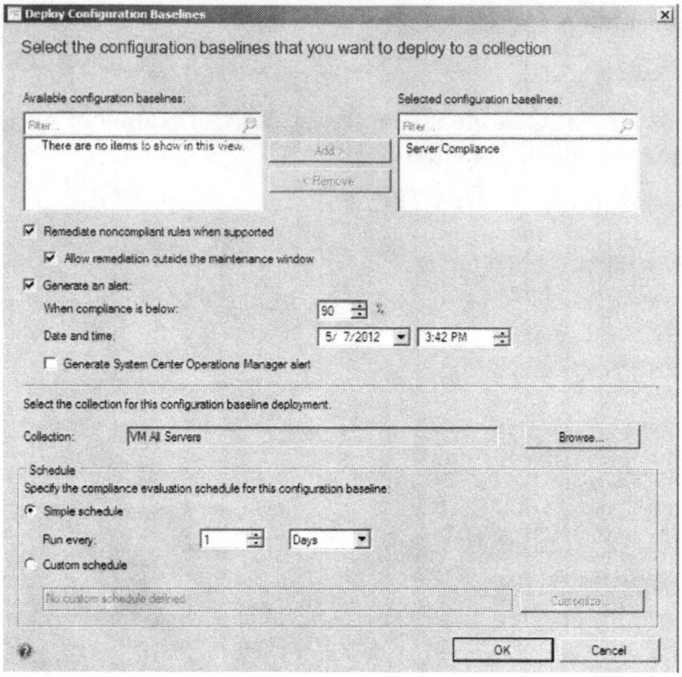

Deploying a baseline.

4. Click **OK** to finish the deployment.

Create a User CI

1. In the **Assets and Compliance** workspace, select **Compliance Settings**, **Configuration Items**.
2. Right-click **Configuration Items**, and select **Folder, Create Folder**.
3. Type **Desktop Compliance** as the folder name and click **OK**.
4. Select the **Desktop Compliance** folder and click **Create Configuration Item** on the ribbon.
5. On the **General** page, configure these settings and click **Next**:
   a. Name: **IE Proxy Enabled**
   b. Categories: Click **Browse**, select **Client**, and click **OK**.
6. On the **Supported Platforms** page, leave all operating systems selected and click **Next.**
7. On the **Settings** page, click **New** and configure these settings:
   a. Name: **IE Proxy Enabled**
   b. Setting type: **Registry value**

c. Data type: **String**

d. Click **Browse** and complete the following settings:

   i. Navigate to **HKEY_CURRENT_USER\Software\Microsoft\Windows\CurrentVersion\Internet Settings** and select the **ProxyEnable** key.

   ii. Select **This registry value must satisfy the following rule if present** and set it for **Equals 0**.

   iii. Click **OK**.

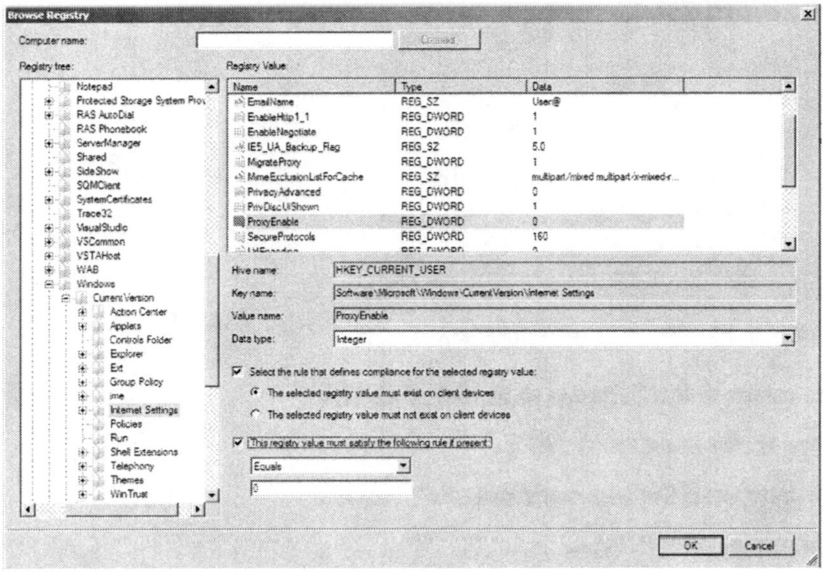

Using a reference machine to create the CI.

8. Select the **Compliance Rules** tab.
9. Select **ProxyEnable Equals 0**, click **Edit**, and configure this setting:

   Remediate noncompliant rules when support: **Enabled**

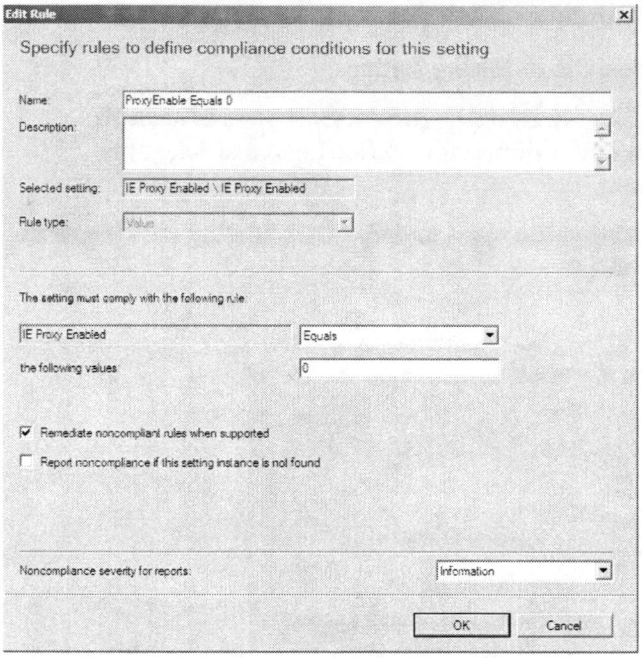

Configuring the user CI to auto-remediate.

10. Click **OK** twice to return to the **Settings** page and click **Next**.
11. On the **Compliance Rules** page, click **Next**.
12. On the **Summary** page, read the summary and click **Next**.
13. On the **Completion** page, click **Close**.

Create the User Baseline

1. In the **Assets and Compliance** workspace, select **Compliance Settings**, **Configuration Baselines**.
2. Right-click **Configuration Baselines**, and select **Folder**, **Create Folder**.
3. Type **Desktop Compliance** as the folder name and click **OK**.
4. Select the **Desktop Compliance** folder and click **Create Configuration Baseline** on the ribbon.
5. In the **Name** box, type **Client Policy**.
6. Click the **Add** button and select **Configuration Items.**
7. Select the **IE Proxy Enabled** CI, click **Add**, and click **OK**.
8. Click **Add**, **Software Updates**.

9. In the **Add Software Updates** dialog box, navigate to **Service Packs\Microsoft \Windows 7**, and select **Windows 7 Service Pack 1 for x64-based Systems**.

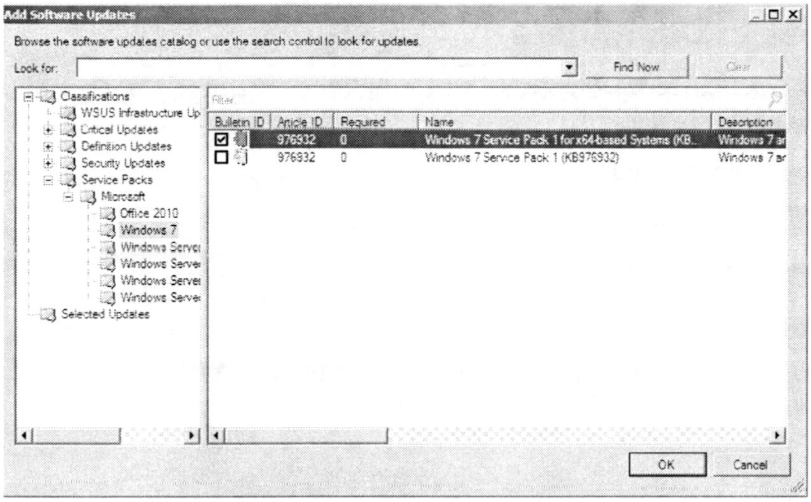

Adding a required update to the baseline

10. Click **Categories**, select **Client**, and click **OK**.

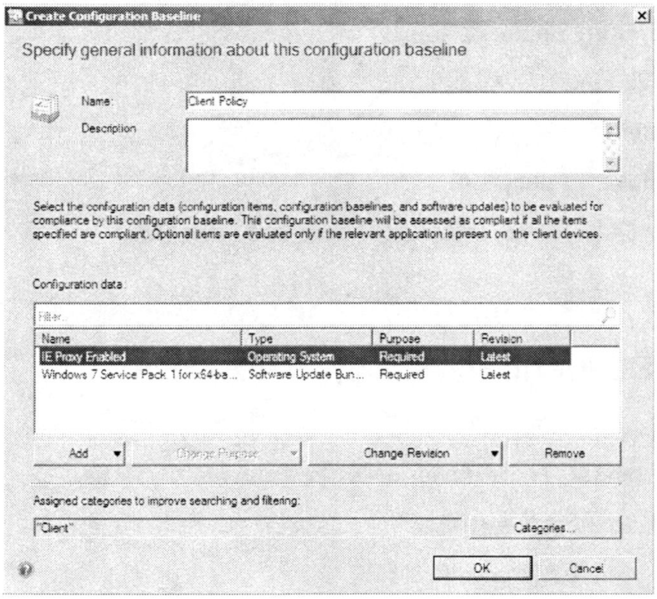

A baseline with a mix of user and computer settings.

11. Click **OK**.

Deploying Configuration Baselines

Deploy the Baseline to Computers

1. In the **Assets and Compliance** workspace, select **Compliance Settings, Configuration Baselines, Desktop Compliance**.
2. Select **Client Policy** and click **Deploy** on the ribbon.
3. Configure these settings and click **OK**:
   a. Generate an alert: **Enabled**
   b. When compliance is below: **90 percent**
   c. Collections: From **Device Collections**, select **ViaMonstra\VM All Workstations** and click **OK**.
4. Click **OK**.

Deploy the Baseline to Users

1. In the **Assets and Compliance** workspace, select **Compliance Settings, Configuration Baselines, Desktop Compliance**.
2. Select **Client Policy** and click **Deploy** on the ribbon.
3. Configure these settings and click **OK**:
   a. Generate an alert: **Enabled**
   b. When compliance is below: **90 percent**
   c. Collections: From **User Collections**, select **All Users** and click **OK**.
4. Click **OK**.

Generate a Noncompliant Scenario

1. Log on to **PC001** as **CORP\Administrator**.
2. Open **Internet Explorer**, and from the **Tools** menu, open the **Internet Options**.
3. Select the **Connections** tab and click **LAN settings**.
4. Enable **Use a proxy server for your LAN** and click **OK**.

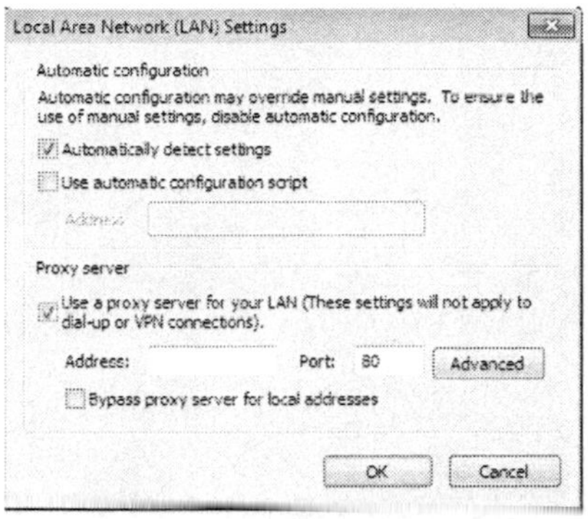

Configuring IE to use a non-valid proxy server.

5. Click **OK** to close the Internet Options.

Verify Baselines

1. Log on to **PC001** as **CORP\Administrator**.
2. Open the **Control Panel**, select the **System and Security** category, and open the **Configuration Manager** properties.
3. Select the **Actions** tab, highlight **Machine Policy Retrieval & Evaluation Cycle**, and click **Run Now**.
4. Click **OK** in the information dialog and select the **Configurations** tab.

   If the machine policy has been applied correctly, you will be able to see the Client Policy. Notice that the Compliance state is Unknown, that's because the baseline has not yet been evaluated.

5. Select the **Client Policy** and click **Evaluate**.

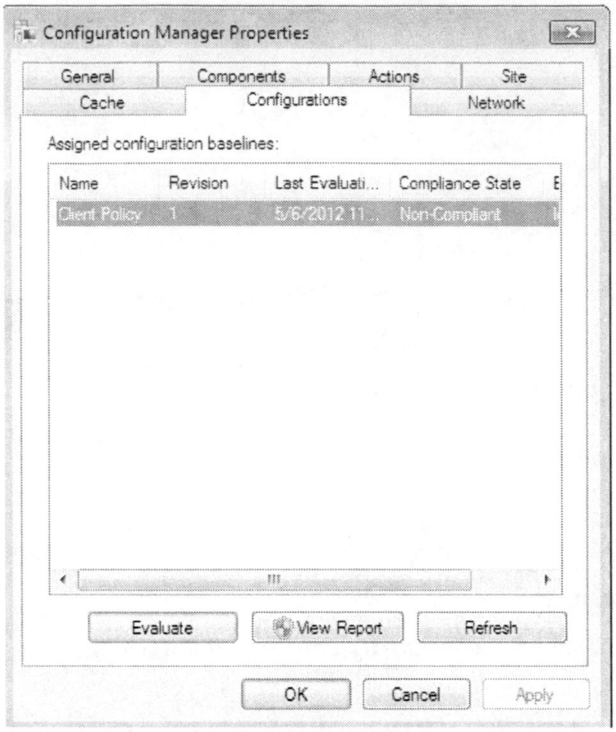

Manually running a compliance evaluation.

6. Click the **View Report** button.
7. From **Summary**, click the **IE Proxy Enabled** link, which takes you to the rule.

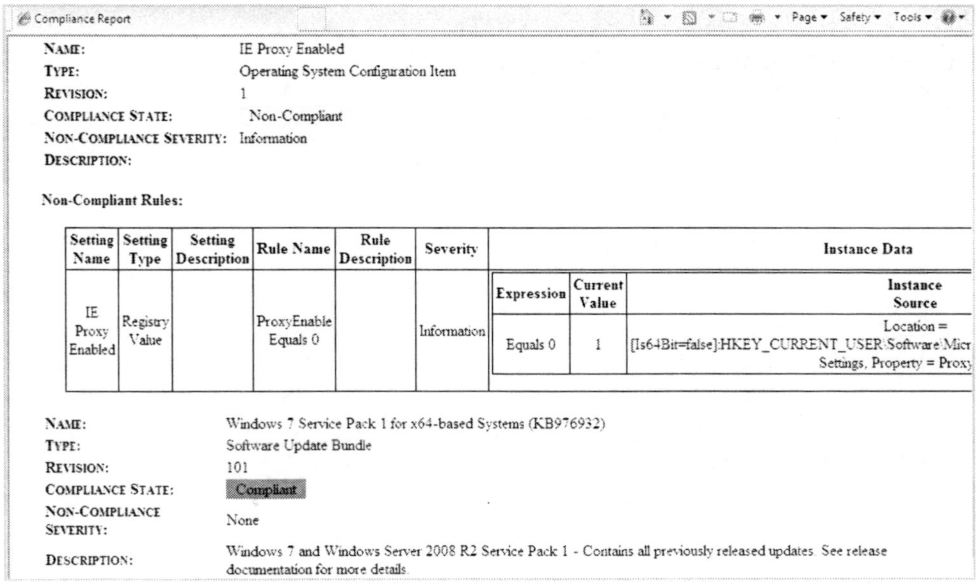

The compliance report. Notice that the rule is listed as Non-Compliant.

8. Close the report.

Verify Baselines Using Reporting

1. Log on to **CM01** as **CORP\Administrator** and open the **ConfigMgr console**.
2. In the **Monitoring** workspace, select **Deployments**.
3. In **Search**, type **Client Policy** and press **Enter**. You most likely do not have any compliance information yet.
4. Select both Client Policy deployments, click **Run Summarization** on the ribbon and click **OK** in the information dialog.
5. Select **Reporting\Reports**.
6. In the search box, type **summary compliance**.
7. From the list of reports, select **Summary compliance by Configuration baseline** and then click **Run** on the ribbon.
8. Click the **Client Policy** baseline link to open the sub report. Notice that the report lists both CIs and a unique compliance level for each CI.
9. Scroll the report to the right until you can see the **Non-Compliant** column.

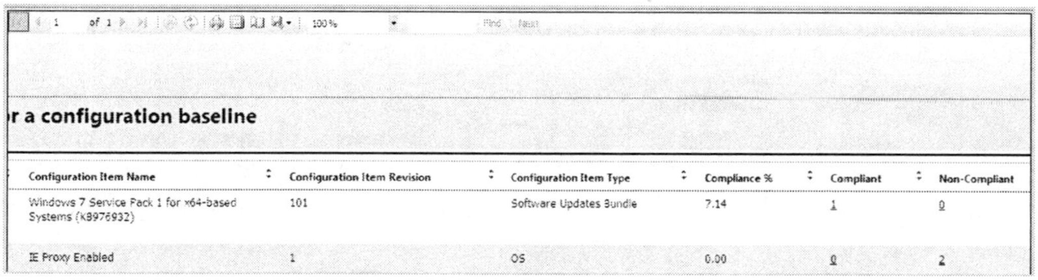

Viewing compliance data.

10. In the **IE Proxy Enabled** row, click the **Non-Compliant** link (2). This opens another sub-report showing all the users that are noncompliant

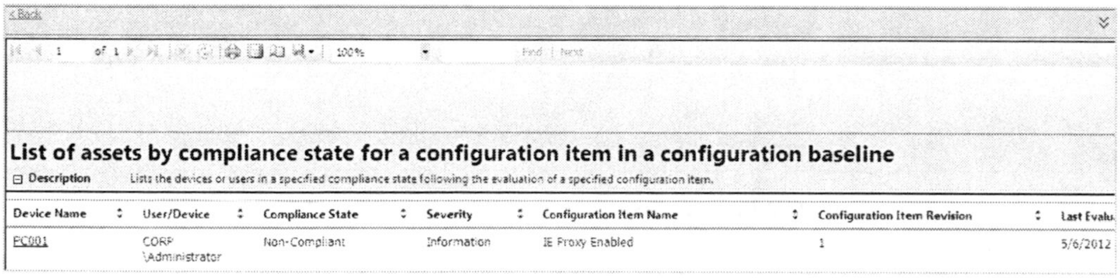

Showing a list of noncompliant users.

11. Close the reports.

Create a Collection with Noncompliant Objects

1. In the **Assets and Compliance** workspace, select **Compliance Settings**, **Configuration Baselines**, **Desktop Compliance**.
2. Select **Client Policy** and click **Deployments**.
3. Select the **All Users** deployment and click **Create New Collection**, **Non-compliant** from the ribbon.

Creating a dynamic collection containing noncompliant users.

4. On the **General** page, configure this setting and click **Next**:

Name: Add a **SM** prefix to the default name. That way you have a unique prefix for the compliance settings collections.

5. On the **Membership Rules** page, configure this setting and click **Next**:

   Use incremental updates for this collection: **Enabled**

6. On the **Summary** page, read the summary and click **Next**.
7. On the **Completion** page, click **Close**.
8. Select **User Collections**, right-click the new **SM Client Policy_All Users_Noncompliant** collection and select **Move**.
9. In the **Move Selected Items** dialog box, select **Settings Management** and click **OK**.

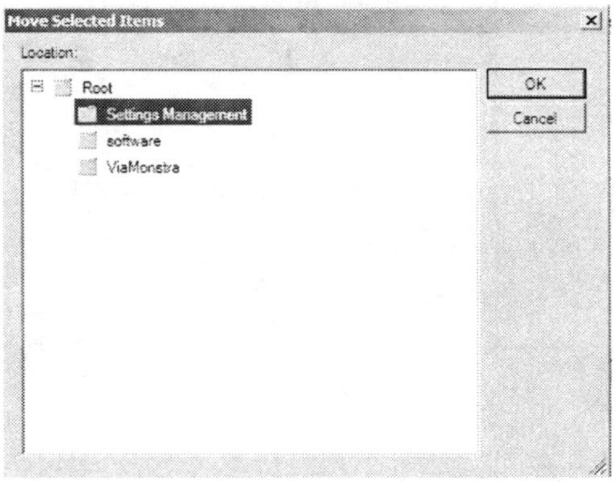

Moving a collection.

10. From the **User Collection**, **Settings Management** folder, select **SM Client Policy_All_Users_Noncompliant** and click **Show Members** on the ribbon.

Configure Remediation for an Existing Deployment

1. In the **Assets and Compliance** workspace, select **Compliance Settings**, **Configuration Baselines**, **Desktop** Compliance.
2. Select the **Client Policy**, click **Deployments**, and open the properties for the **All Users** deployment.
3. Configure these settings and click **OK**:
   a. Remediate noncompliant rules when supported: **Enabled**
   b. Allow remediation outside of the maintenance window: **Enabled**

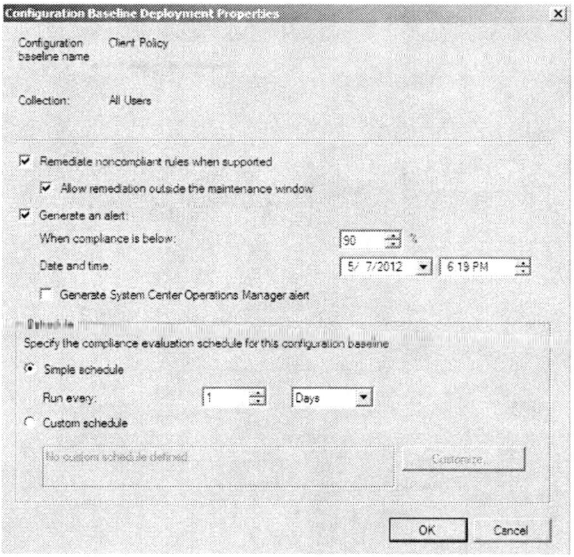

Enabling remediation on an existing deployment.

Remediate a Noncompliant User

1. Log on to **PC001** as **CORP\Administrator**.
2. Perform a **Machine policy refresh** and a **User policy refresh** from the **Configuration Manager** client agent in the **Control Panel**.
3. Select the **Configuration** tab and click **Evaluate**. The Compliance State should change from **Non-Compliant** to **Compliant**.
4. Click **View Report** and notice that the user is now compliant. The computer has been compliant all along.

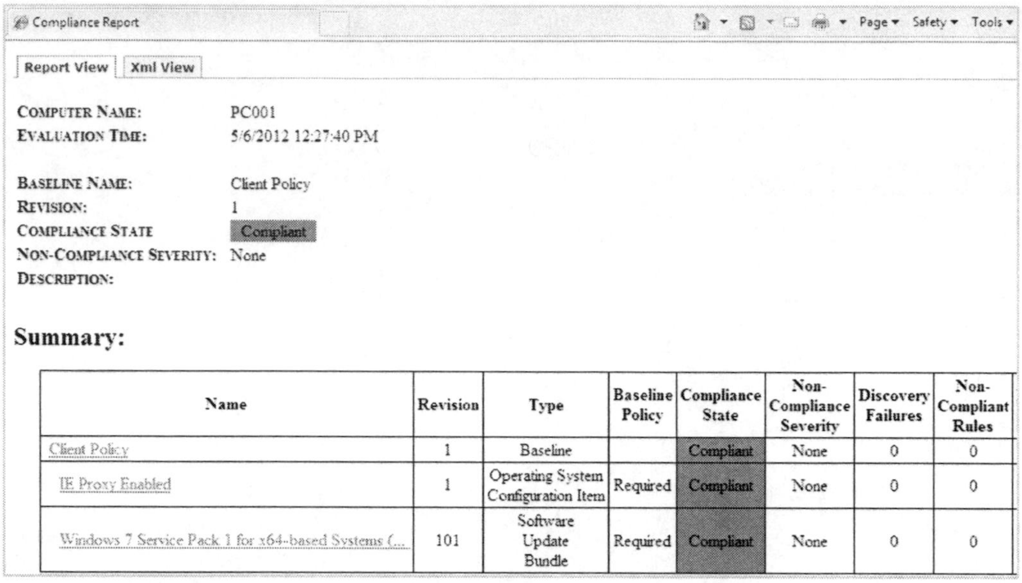

User is now compliant.

5. Open **Internet Explorer**, and from the **Tools** menu, open the **Internet Options**.
6. Select the **Connections** tab and click **LAN settings**.
7. Notice the setting in **Use a proxy server for your LAN** and click **OK**.

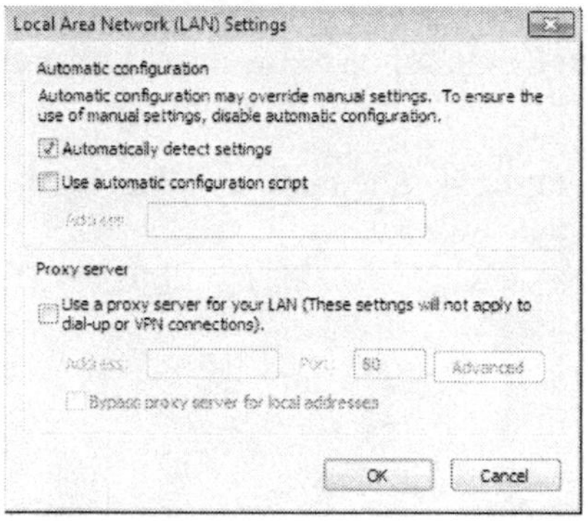

IE proxy settings after remediation.

8. Click **OK** to close the Internet Options.

Useful Log Files

The log files in the following table contain useful compliance settings activity information.

Log File	Description
Statemessage.log	Contains the state messages send by CI ID and baseline ID
Ciagent.log	Conatins details about the CIs in the baselines
Cistatestore.log	Contains details about the CI versions cached
PolicyAgent.log	Requests policies by using the Data Transfer service (to look for new Inventory classes to report)
PolicyAgentProvider.log	Records policy changes
PolicyEvaluator.log	Records new policy settings
Dcmagent.log	Contains details about dcmagent jobs
Dcmreporting.log	Contains details about the baselines evaluated

Chapter 12 Planning for Backup and Recovery

As with any application, you need to plan for backup and also test the restore process at least once. Unlike previous versions, ConfigMgr 2012 relies on SQL Server only when restoring the site. This gives you the opportunity to select whether you want to run backups internally from the ConfigMgr console, or you want to configure backup only from SQL Server. For ViaMonstra, I have decided to configure backup from within the ConfigMgr console.

The Backup

To create a complete backup of your ConfigMgr site, you can configure the Backup ConfigMgr Site Server maintenance task. The site maintenance task automatically includes a backup of:

- The ConfigMgr SQL database
- The needed folders on the primary site server
- The needed registry keys on the primary site server.

Configure Backup

In ViaMonstra, you need a daily backup of ConfigMgr. Configuring the backup should be one of the first things you do, which is why we did it in Chapter 4.

1. Navigate to the **Administration** workspace, and select **Site Configuration**, **Sites**.
2. Select the site and click **Settings**, **Site Maintenance** from the ribbon.
3. Select the **Backup Site Server** task; then click **Edit** and enable the task.
4. Click **Set Paths**, type the path for the backup folder, and click **OK**.
5. Select **Enable alerts** for backup task failures and click **OK**.

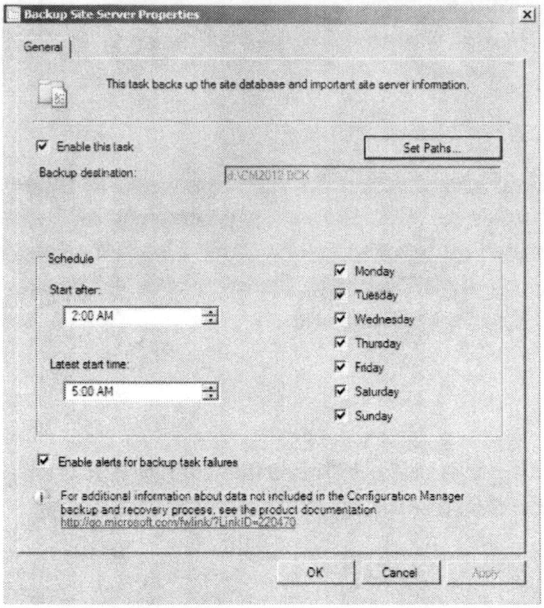

Configuring a daily backup.

What Happens When a Backup Runs?

When ConfigMgr starts a backup, the SMS_SITE_BACKUP service starts and performs a backup based on the information that is stored in the backup control file, located in:

D:\Program files\Microsoft Configuration Manager\Inboxes\smsbkup.box\smsbkup.ctl

The backup process automatically creates a folder and stores the backup files in that folder. ConfigMgr automatically overwrites the backup files each time it performs a backup.

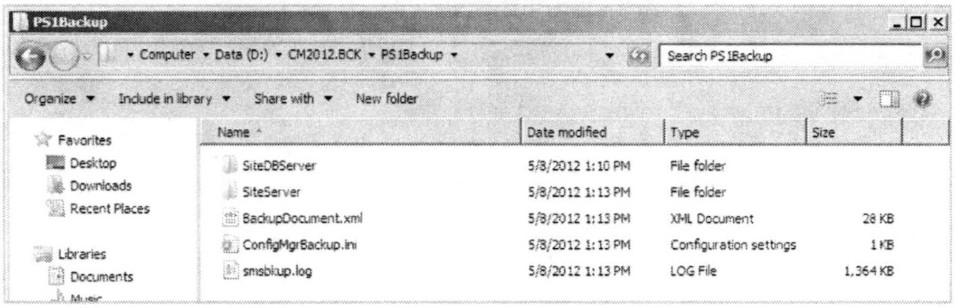

The files and folders created by the backup process.

> **Real World Note:** It's highly recommended to store the backup files on another server or archive the Backup Snapshot to another server. You can automate the process by writing the needed commands and saving them to a file called AfterBackup.bat in:
>
> D:\Program files\Microsoft Configuration Manager\inboxes\smsbkup.box
>
> ConfigMgr automatically processes whichever command it finds in that specific file.

Manually Start Backup

If necessary, you can start the backup process manually:

1. Log on to the site server as **Administrator**.
2. From the **Start** menu, open a command prompt as **Administrator**.
3. Type **Net Start SMS_Site_Backup** and press **Enter** to start the backup process.

Back Up the Secondary Site and Remote Site Systems

There are no recovery options for secondary sites or remote site system roles. In order to restore a secondary site or remote site role, you have to reinstall the server and the role(s) or site. The most time-consuming task in this process is redistributing the content to the content library. Appendix E walks you through how you can prestage content on remote distribution points and thus save a lot of network bandwidth and replication time.

What Is Not Included in the Backup

ViaMonstra uses several non-core ConfigMgr services to support its ConfigMgr environment. Those services along with some additional ones are not part of the site maintenance backup process and must be included in the overall backup plans:

- Microsoft Deployment Toolkit (MDT)
- Site system roles
- The content library
- SQL Server Reporting Services and custom reports
- WSUS database
- System Center Updates Publisher (SCUP)

What Happens When a Site or Site System Fails

ConfigMgr is a system made up of a site server and multiple site system roles. Some of the site system roles provide fault tolerance by allowing multiple instances of the same role. Other roles, including the site server, do not offer multiple instances of the same role.

The Site Server Is Down

If the site server is down, you will not be able to perform any site administration. Remote site system roles and clients will still work to some extent. However, in most cases, deployments will not run, and clients will be limited to working with cached information and inventory.

Fault tolerance options: **None**

SQL Server Database

If the SQL Server is down, life's not good. You will not be able to perform any site administration, and clients will be able to work only with cached information. Although you can install SQL in a cluster, I usually recommend spending the money on better hardware, including more and faster disks, and ensuring that you have tested a full recovery in production.

Move the Site Database

You need to run a site reset on order to move the site database to another SQL Server. Prior to running the site reset you need to copy the database to the new SQL server.

Fault tolerance options: **Install SQL Server in a cluster**.

SMS Provider

If the SMS provider is down, no administrators will be able to connect to the database and perform any administration of the site. You can install two instances of the SMS provider for fault tolerance. In that event, the console will automatically perform a failover after five unsuccessful attempts. For performance reasons, it's recommended that you install the SMS provider on the database, the primary site server, and lastly on any other server. You can add another provider by running a site reset and selecting **Modify SMS provider information**.

Fault tolerance options: **Install two providers**.

Management Point

The management point is the primary contact between the client and the site server. If the management point fails, clients will not be able to upload or download any inventory data or new policies. Unlike previous versions, ConfigMgr 2012 enables clients to download a list of management points automatically. In the event that one is not responding, the client automatically selects another management point from the list.

Fault tolerance options: **Install 10 management points**.

Distribution Point

The distribution point is needed anytime a client requires access to a package. After a distribution point is selected for a package, the client retries that distribution point for 8 hours and then performs a different source location request. If the package is not available at the primary distribution point, the client uses a remote distribution point (if one is configured). You can configure the distribution point as a fallback source in the properties for the site system role, as we did previously for the distribution point in the datacenter.

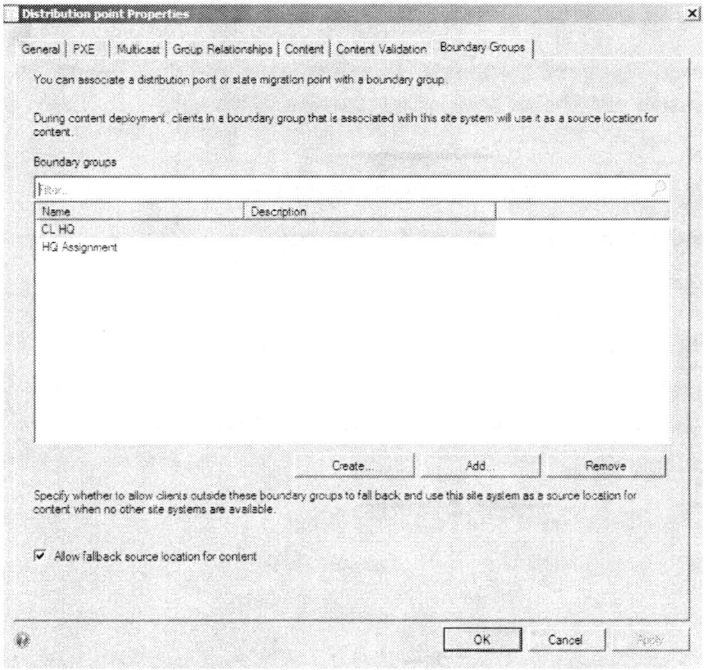

Distribution point configured as a fallback source.

Fault tolerance options: **Install multiple distribution points**.

Software Update Point

The software update is initiated by the client when it performs an online scan of software updates. If a software update point isn't present, the client won't be able to scan for compliance and, as a result, will not see updates as required.

Fault tolerance options: **Install a Windows NLB with multiple WSUS servers**.

Recovering ConfigMgr

ConfigMgr offers a few recover options. In order to select the correct option, you need to know what you want to restore:

- If data is lost or the server fails, you have to perform a site restore.
- If you experience problems with ConfigMgr services or components, you should try a site reset. A site reset does not restore any data, but performs a reinstall of all the components, including services.

Perform a Site Restore

In order to recover a ConfigMgr site server, you need a server with same name and disk layout. It doesn't have to be the same operating system version as long as the name and domain membership are the same.

1. Install the operating system with same name and domain membership.
2. Install all needed ConfigMgr prerequisites, as explained in Appendix A.
3. Install and configure **SQL Server**.
4. On the site server, open a command prompt with administrative privileges.
5. Start the ConfigMgr installation and select the **Recover Site** option. You will be given several recovery options; select **Recover this site server using an existing backup**.
6. On the **Before You Begin** page, click **Next**.
7. On the **Getting Started** page, select **Recover a site** and click **Next**.

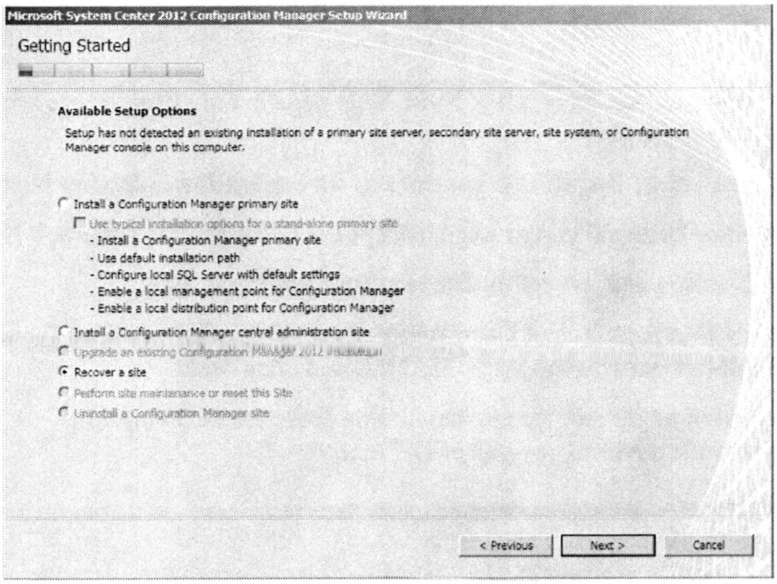

Starting the recovery process.

8. On the **Site Server and Database Recovery Options** page, configure these settings and click **Next**:
   a. Recover this site server using an existing backup: Click **Browse** and navigate to **D:\CM2012.BCK\PS1Backup**.
   b. Recover the site database using the backup set at the following location: Click **Browse** and navigate to **D:\CM2012.BCK\PS1Backup**.

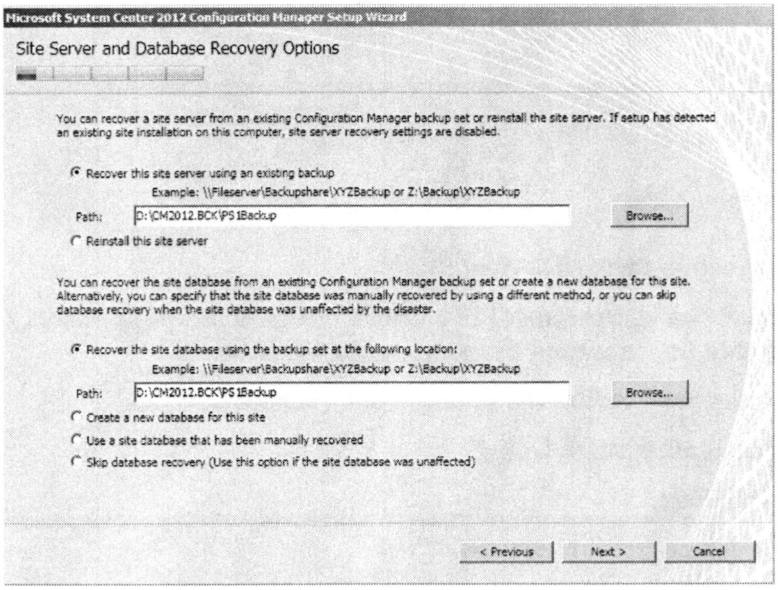

Selecting the backup files.

9. On the **Site Recovery Information** page, click **Next**. This page is only used if you are storing a CAS or a primary child site.
10. On the **Product Key** page, select **Install this product as an evaluation** and click **Next**.
11. On the **Microsoft Software License Terms** page, accept the license terms and click **Next**.
12. On the **Prerequisites License** page, accept all license terms and click **Next**.
13. On the **Updated Prerequisite** page, select **Use previously downloaded updates from the following location**; then type **D:\Setup\CM2012DL** and click **Next**.
14. On the **Site and Installation** page, modify the installation folder to **D:\Program Files\Microsoft Configuration Manager**, and click **Next**.

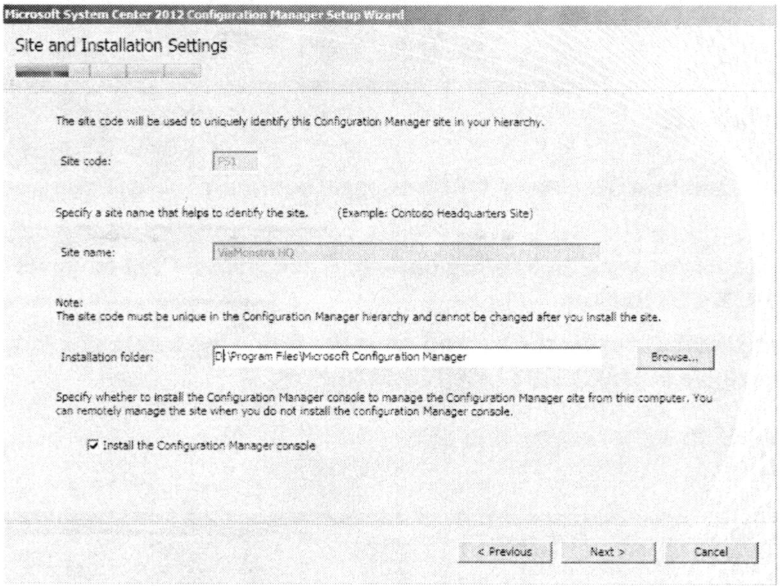

Specifying the installation folder.

15. On the **Database Information** page, click **Next**.
16. On the **Customer Experience Improvement Program Configuration** page, enable **Join the Customer Experience Improvement Program,** and click **Next**.
17. On the **Settings Summary** page, review the summary and click **Next**.
18. On the **Prerequisites** page, click **Begin Install.**
19. On the **Install** page, click **Next**.

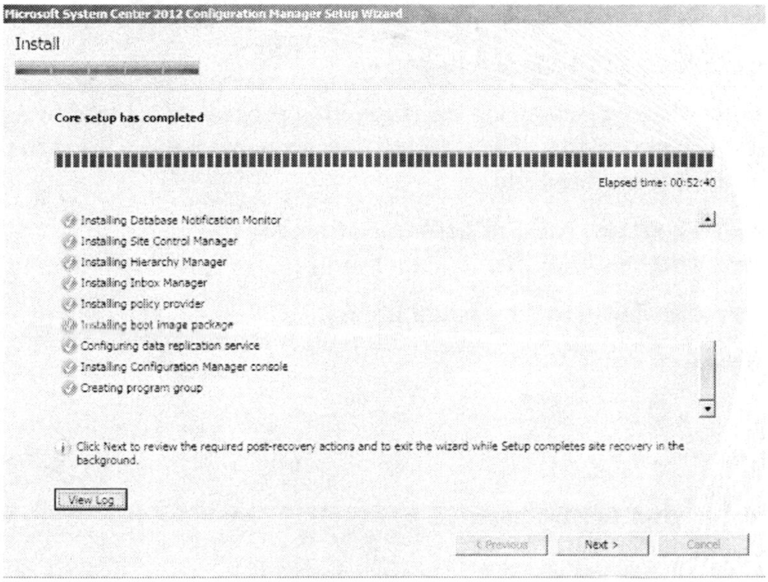

The restore is finished.

20. On the **Finished** page, make a note of all the post recovery tasks and click **Close**.

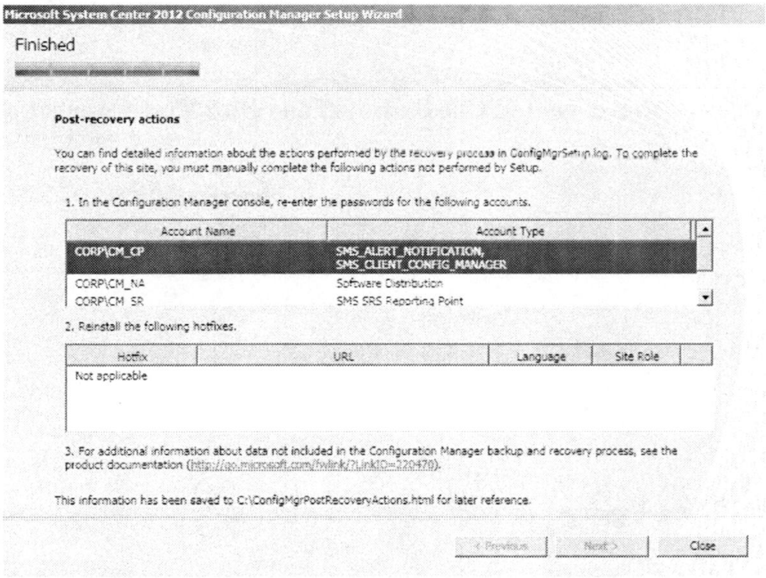

Information about post-recovery tasks.

Post-Recovery Tasks

Once the site is recovered there are still a few tasks left to do:

1. All ConfigMgr user passwords are reset during the recovering process. You need to reset the passwords in the ConfigMgr console. The effected user accounts will be listed in the C:\ConfigMgrPostRecoveryActions.html file.
2. Reinstall previously applied hotfixes. A list of hotfixes is found in the C:\ConfigMgrPostRecoveryActions.html file.
3. Ensure that all content is redistributed to the content library.
4. Restore the WSUS database.
5. Restore custom reports.
6. Reinstall MDT 2012.
7. Reinstall SCUP 2011 and recover the database.

Reset the ConfigMgr User Passwords

1. In the **Administration** workspace, select **Security**, **Accounts**.
2. Select the **CORP\CM_CP** account and click **Properties** on the ribbon.
3. Click **Set**.
4. Type the password twice.
5. Click **Verify**, and in **Network share**, type **\\PC001\admin$** and click **Test Connection**.

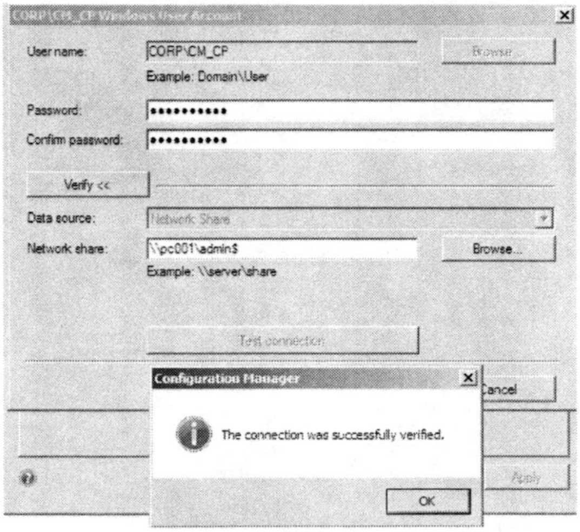

Verifying the account.

6. Click **OK** three times to close the account properties.

7. Repeat the steps for the remaining accounts. If you want to verify the new password, create a connection to **\\DC01\SYSVOL.**

Perform a Site Reset

A site reset reinstalls site components, reset permissions, and restore registry keys.

1. From the **Start** menu, open **All Programs**, **Microsoft System Center 2012**, **Configuration Manager**.
2. Start **Configuration Manager Setup**.
3. On the **Before You Begin** page, click **Next**.
4. On the **Available Setup Options** page, click **Perform site maintenance or reset this Site** and click **Next.**
5. On the **Site Maintenance** page, select **Reset site with no configuration changes** and click **Next**.

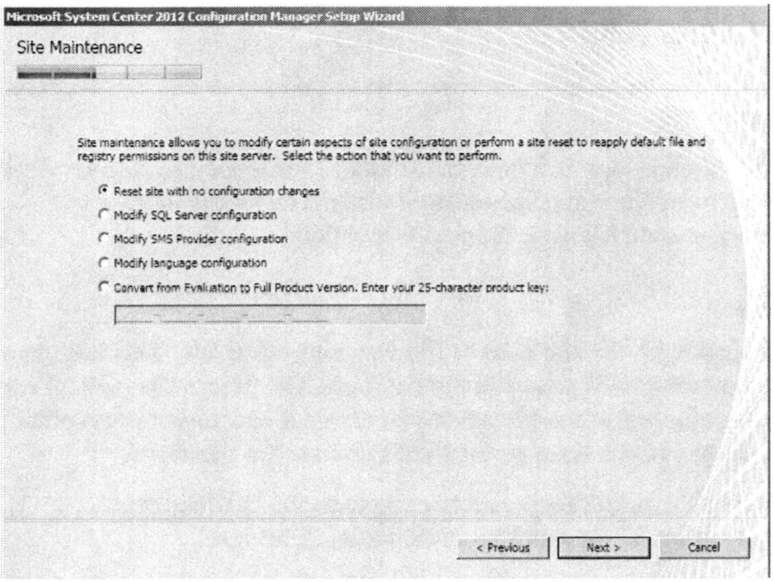

Starting the site reset process.

6. Click **Yes** in the information dialog box.
7. On the **Configuration** page, click **Close**.

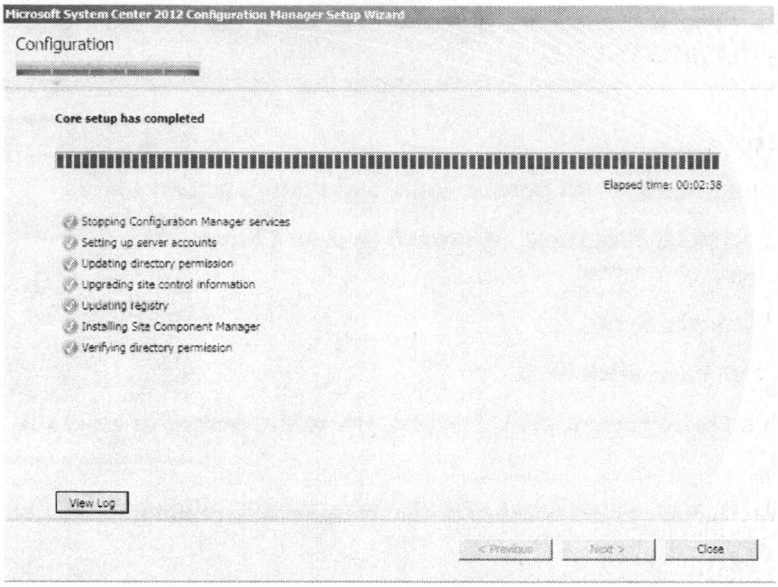

The site reset finished successfully.

The Preinst.exe Tool

The Hierarchy Maintenance tool (preinst.exe) is a built-in tool that can be used to stop services, dump the site control file, and perform other database-related tasks. The tool is located in D:\Program files\Microsoft Configuration Manager\ bin\x64\00000409.

Dump the Site Control File

In previous versions of ConfigMgr/SMS, the site control file was a physical file. This has changed in ConfigMgr 2012, as the site control now is stored in the database. Creating a site control can be useful when you want to see what changes are made when you create a new distribution point. Having this knowledge can assist you if you want to use the SDK to script solutions.

1. Open a command prompt as **Administrator** and navigate to the **D:\Program files\Microsoft Configuration Manager\ bin\x64\00000409 folder**.
2. Run **preinst.exe /dump PS1.** This creates the **sitectrl_PS1.cto** in the root of the drive.
3. Rename the **sitectrl_PS1.cto** file **sitectrl_PS1.old**.
4. Perform the installation of the new distribution point.
5. Run **sitectrl_PS1.cto** again.
6. Compare the two files to see what you need to include in your script.

Other Preinst.exe Command Lines

- **/stopsite** signals ConfigMgr to stop the site component manager service. After the service is restarted, the site component manager performs a site reset.
- **/delsite S01** deletes child site information from the database. This is useful if a secondary site server was not successfully removed.
- **/deljob PS1** deletes all jobs targeted to site PS1.
- **/keyforparent** creates the public key PS2.CT4 in the root of the drive from which the command is run. You must copy the file manually to the hman.box inbox on the primary site server.
- **/keyforchild** creates the public key PS1.CT6 in the root of the drive from which the command is run. You must copy the file manually to the hman.box inbox on the secondary site server.

Note: Preinst.exe has several other command lines. Just run preinst.exe without any command to get a list of available commands.

Chapter 13 A Tribute to the Communities

I have never before in my career as an IT consultant experienced a richer and more dedicated community than the System Center Configuration Manager community. It seems like most ConfigMgr administrators play an active role in the community, contributing custom reports, scripts, deep technical blog posts, videos, and freeware utilities that assist us all in our daily work. In this chapter, I'll document the forums and blogs that I use.

Forums

MyITforum

The mother of all System Management forums in the universe. Especially in the beginning of my SMS voyage, I learned a lot from those guys. At MyITforum, you'll find most of the documents that you need, ranging from blog posts to videos to wikis. I'm a huge admire of the work done by Rod Trent and Ron Crumbaker. You guys have helped more people than you can ever imagine.

http://myitforum.com

Microsoft TechNet

Microsoft TechNet has come a very long way in recent years. I do not know what they feed the technical writers at Microsoft, but they seem to work around the clock, constantly updating the technical articles. Besides the TechNet articles, you also will find the TechNet forums. The forums are monitored by Microsoft, but it is most often community members who are answering everyday questions. From the answers, you will often learn a lot, pick up best practices from industry experts, and generally gain access to a wealth of knowledge.

http://technet.microsoft.com/en-us/ms376608.aspx

http://social.technet.microsoft.com/Forums/en-US/category
/systemcenter2012configurationmanager

System Center Central

System Center Central is more than just a ConfigMgr community. Here you will also find lots of information about all the other System Center products in the family. Besides a very active forum, you will also find interviews, documentation, and very useful articles on how to work with the different System Center products.

http://www.systemcentercentral.com

Windows-Noob

This site was founded in 2006 by Niall Brady (ConfigMgr MVP), who wanted to make step-by-step guides available to the public, that use screenshots to describe the process from start to finish for everything ConfigMgr-related, particularly OSD. The site has plenty of step-by-step guides for System Center 2012 Configuration Manager and has a lively and very active forum full of loyal followers.

http://www.windows-noob.com

Blogs

It's been a while since I dropped my daily newspaper subscription. Instead, I spend the first 10–20 minutes every morning with coffee and a quick look at my RSS feeds.

Official Blogs from Microsoft

- Official ConfigMgr Team Blog: http://blogs.technet.com/b/configmgrteam
- System Center on Technet Edge: http://technet.microsoft.com/en-us/edge/system-center.aspx
- Official System Center Blog: http://blogs.technet.com/b/systemcenter/
- The Configuration Manager Support Team Blog: http://blogs.technet.com/b/configurationmgr
- Michael Niehaus: http://blogs.technet.com/b/mniehaus/
- Recent KB articles for ConfigMgr 2007 and ConfigMgr 2012: http://support.microsoft.com/common/rss.aspx?rssid=12769&in=en-us

Blogs from the Community

- Kent Agerlund: http://blog.coretech.dk/author/kea
- Michael Petersen: http://blog.coretech.dk/author/mip
- Johan Arwidmark: http://www.deploymentresearch.com
- Greg Ramsey: http://gregramsey.wordpress.com
- Kaido Järvemets: http://depsharee.blogspot.com
- Matthew Hudson: http://sms-hints-tricks.blogspot.com
- Peter Daalmans: http://www.systemcenterblog.nl
- Jason Sandys: http://blog.configmgrftw.com
- Chris Nackers: http://www.chrisnackers.com

- Maik Koster: http://myitforum.com/cs2/blogs/maikkoster/rss.aspx
- Garth Jones: http://smsug.ca
- Jakob G. Svendsen: blog.coretech.dk/jgs
- Jörgen Nilsson: http://ccmexec.com
- Raphael Perez: http://wmug.co.uk/blogs/dotraphael
- Rob Marshall: http://wmug.co.uk/blogs/r0b/default.aspx
- Niall C. Brady: http://www.niallbrady.com
- Cliff Hobbs: http://wmug.co.uk/blogs/cliffs_blog/default.aspx
- Ronni Pedersen: http://www.ronnipedersen.com
- Michaël Bertuit: http://systemcenter2012.com/blogs/vnext/default.aspx
- System Center: http://system-center.fr
- Torsten Meringer: http://www.mssccmfaq.de
- Jean-Sébastien Duchêne: http://www.systemcentertouch.fr
- Mikael Nystrom: http://deploymentbunny.com
- John Marcum: http://myitforum.com/cs2/blogs/jmarcum/archive/2012/03/01/160763.aspx
- John Nelson aka Number 2: http://myitforum.com/cs2/blogs/jnelson/archive/2011/09/20/159499.aspx
- Sherry Kissinger: http://myitforum.com/cs2/blogs/skissinger/default.aspx

Community Tools

There are many free community tools that can be very beneficial to use in your ConfigMgr 2012-related projects. The tools in the following section are the ones that I always use. Besides these, you can find a wealth of other tools that are worth taking a closer look at. You can find them via web searches and others in the communities who post to forums or blogs, including those mentioned previously in this chapter.

The Right Click Tools

The famous right click tools are a console extension that allows you to trigger actions on the clients directly from the ConfigMgr console. There are several different right click tools available.

http://tinyurl.com/5zl9cy

The following link will take you to a blog post that explains how you can create your own custom tools:

http://tinyurl.com/7bhffyk

Client Center

The tool is designed for IT Professionals to troubleshoot SMS/SCCM client-related issues. The SCCM Client Center provides a quick and easy overview of client settings, including running services and SCCM settings in a good user-friendly interface.

http://sourceforge.net/projects/smsclictr

Automatic Email Application Approval

By default, application approvals must be done from within the ConfigMgr console. If you have Service Manager 2012, you can use that to implement an approval process.

The solution consists of a website and a web service. None of them have to be installed on the same server. Also there is no requirement to install any the components on the site server.

http://blog.coretech.dk/download/CAA-0.9.0.zip

GUI to Modify Third-Party License Information

ConfigMgr 2007 and 2012 allow you to import license information from a CSV file. The data are shown in the License 15A – General License Reconciliation Report. The problem for many is that it's often a bit too difficult to create the CSV file in the correct format. Highly inspired by the CM2007 AILW utility, Coretech created a new tool that's compliant with both ConfigMgr 2007 and ConfigMgr 2012.

http://blog.coretech.dk/download/CTAILW.zip

Auto Install Warning

One question that is seen again and again in the news forums is "How can I configure a custom message prior to running an application?" This utility—Auto Install Warning—is installed on each client in the hierarchy. The utility allows you to write custom text and add a company logo that will be shown before the actual deployment begins.

http://blog.coretech.dk/jgs/coretech-auto-install-warning-1-0-3-freeware-update/

OSD Frontends

In this book, you have learned how to start OS deployments using the unknown computers collection or by importing a computer object into the ConfigMgr console. As you dig deeper into the OSD feature, you quickly discover a need for automating the process one step further. That automation is often done by adding an OSD frontend from which the end user can initiate the deployment process by selecting a few options like location, keyboard layout, additional applications, operating system, and so forth. The following are several good options:

- windows-noob.com FrontEnd HTA: http://tinyurl.com/bo9gcb3
- Johan Arwidmark's Pretty Good Frontend: http://prettygoodfrontend.codeplex.com
- Maik Koster's MDT Web FrontEnd: http://tinyurl.com/7dqv2sb

RegKeyToMOF

RegKeyToMOF is used to create custom hardware inventory classes based on registry information entries and format them correctly for the Configuration.mof file.

http://myitforum.com/cs2/files/folders/152945/download.aspx

Package Source Changer

As you start migrating from ConfigMgr 2007 to ConfigMgr 2012, one of the requirements is that the package source used for packages must be a UNC and accessible from ConfigMgr 2012. I have seen many site installations in which the package source is either a local source on the site server or a UNC pointing to the site server. In either case, you must somehow update the package source before starting the migration. The package source changer can be used to change the package source in ConfigMgr 2007 before you migrate the packages, or after the packages are migrated to ConfigMgr 2012.

http://blog.coretech.dk/jgs/coretech-package-source-changer-0-3-0-0

User Groups

No matter where you are located, you will most likely be able to find a System Center user group in your area. User groups are community driven and are a great opportunity for you to share your thoughts, ideas, and daily challenges. The easiest way to find a local user group is to "Bing" "System Center User Group".

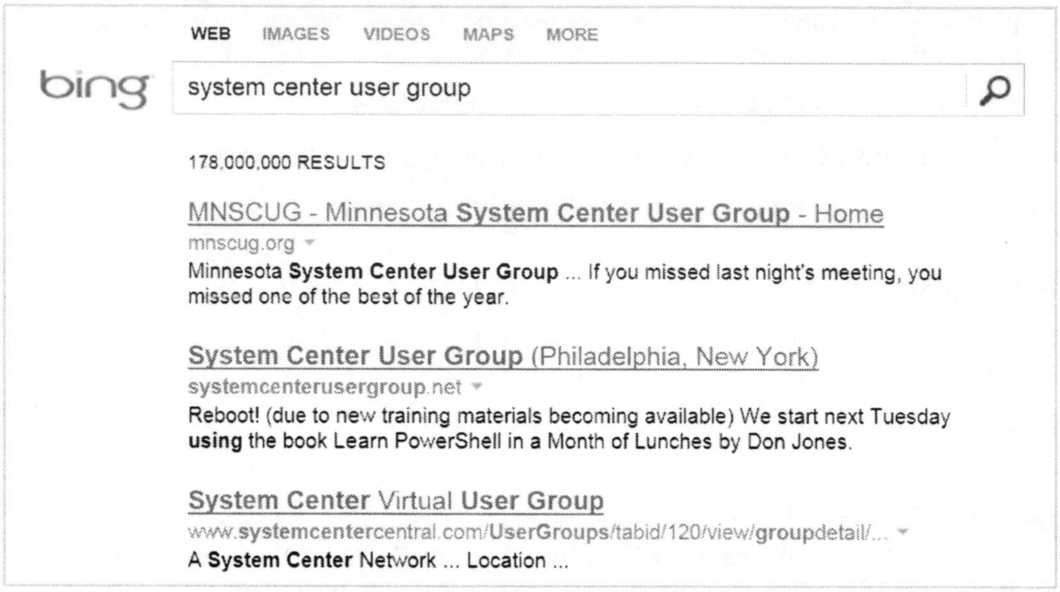

178,000,000 results for "System Center User Group."

Appendix A Using the Hydration Kit to Build the POC Environment

Here are the detailed steps for installing and configuring the hydration kit provided in the book sample files. This kit, along with some post-configuration tasks described in this appendix, allows you to rebuild the same environment that is used for this book in a virtual environment, either Hyper-V or VMware.

Real World Note: As you learned in Chapter 2, you can use virtual machines for the proof-of-concept environment, and if you have a powerful host, you can run them all on the same machine (for lab and test purposes). If you assign the minimum amount of memory, you can complete all steps on a host with 16 GB of RAM, even though 32 GB of RAM is preferred.

If you are thinking about using the same setup in a production environment, you probably want to separate them onto multiple hosts, or even run the servers as physical servers. And you do remember that you should run at least one domain controller on a physical machine, right?

The Base Servers

Using the hydration kit and some post configurations, you will build the following list of servers. The server setups for the New York site will be fully automated. The servers in the Liverpool and Orlando sites will be deployed only with the base operating system since you need to verify things such as network connectivity between the sites before doing the final configuration.

New York Site Servers (192.168.1.0/24)

- DC01, Domain Controller, DNS, and DHCP
- CM01, Member Server (Primary Site Server)

Orlando Site Server (192.168.2.0/24)

CM02, Member Server (Remote Location Distribution Point)

Liverpool Site Server (192.168.3.0/24)

CM03, Member Server (Secondary Site Server)

Real World Note: If you only want a smaller lab and test environment to learn about ConfigMgr 2012, you can start out by deploying only the New York site servers and clients.

The Base Clients

In addition to the servers, you also use a few clients throughout the book guides. Using the hydration kit, you build the following list of clients. The hydration kit clients are assigned to the New York site. I decided not to have any ready-made clients in the Liverpool or Orlando sites, so you will need to deploy new clients to these sites if you choose to use them.

PC001 is used in most chapters as the main ConfigMgr 2012 client. The Windows XP client (PC002) is needed only if you want to do the Windows XP migration guide in Chapter 10.

New York Site Clients (192.168.1.0/24)

- PC001, Windows 7 Enterprise SP1 x64
- PC002, Windows XP SP3 x86

Setting Up the Hydration Environment

Hydration is the concept of using MDT 2012 Lite Touch offline media to do fully automated builds of entire lab, proof-of-concept, or production environments.

How Does the Hydration Work?

The hydration kit that you download is just a folder structure and some scripts. The scripts help you create the MDT 2012 Lite Touch offline media, and the folder structure is there for you to add your own software and licenses when applicable. You also can use trial versions for the lab software, as well. The overview steps are the following:

1. Install MDT 2012 Lite Touch and Windows AIK 2.0.
2. Extract the hydration kit from the sample files.
3. Create an MDT 2012 deployment share using one of the sample scripts.
4. Populate the folder structure with your setup media.
5. Create an MDT 2012 offline media deployment share using one of the sample scripts.
6. Build the MDT 2012 offline media (big ISO) using one of the sample scripts.
7. Create a few virtual machines, boot them on the offline media (ISO), select what servers or clients they should become, and a few hours later you have the base setup.

Prepare the Downloads Folder

In the following steps, you need to have access to the book sample files and also the software media listed in the following guide. The steps are performed on the machine (client or server) that you use to manage Hyper-V or VMware, which if you are using Hyper-V, also can be the Hyper-V host.

1. On the machine (client or server) that you use to manage Hyper-V or VMware, create the **C:\Downloads** folder.
2. Download the following software:
    - MDT 2012
    - Windows AIK 2.0. (named Windows AIK for Windows 7 v3.0 on microsoft.com)
    - Windows Server 2008 R2 Enterprise SP1 (trial or full version)
    - Windows 7 Enterprise SP1 x64 (trial or full version)
    - Windows XP Pro SP3 x86 (trial or full version)

Prepare the Hydration Environment

The machine (client or server) that you use to manage Hyper-V or VMware needs to have PowerShell installed, and I assume that you have downloaded the book sample files.

> **Note:** MDT 2012 requires local administrator rights/permissions. You need to have at least 40 GB of free disk space on C:\ for the hydration kit and at least 200 GB of free space for the volume hosting your virtual machines. Also make sure to run all commands from an elevated PowerShell command window.

1. On the machine (client or server) that you use to manage Hyper-V or VMware, extract **Windows AIK 2.0** (or mount the ISO using an ISO mounting tool like SlySoft Virtual CloneDrive), and install **Windows AIK 2.0** with the default settings.
2. Install **MDT 2012** with the default settings.
3. Copy the **HydrationCM2012Fundamentals** folder from the book sample files to C:\. You should now have a **C:\HydrationCM2012Fundamentals\Source** folder with a few folders and PowerShell scripts.
4. In an elevated (run as Administrator) **PowerShell** command prompt, configure Execution Policy in PowerShell by typing the following command:

    Set-ExecutionPolicy Unrestricted -Force

5. From the PowerShell command prompt, create the **Hydration Deployment Share** by running the following commands (press **Enter** after each command):
    a. **Set-Location C:\HydrationCM2012Fundamentals\Source**
    b. **.\1_CreateHydrationDeployment.ps1**

6. Copy the following folders from **C:\HydrationCM2012Fundamentals\Source \HydrationDS** to **C:\HydrationCM2012Fundamentals\HydrationDS**, replacing any existing files:
   - Applications
   - Control
   - Operating Systems
7. From the **Start** menu, open the **Deployment Workbench**. You will now see a MDT 2012 Deployment Share populated with applications, operating systems, and task sequences.

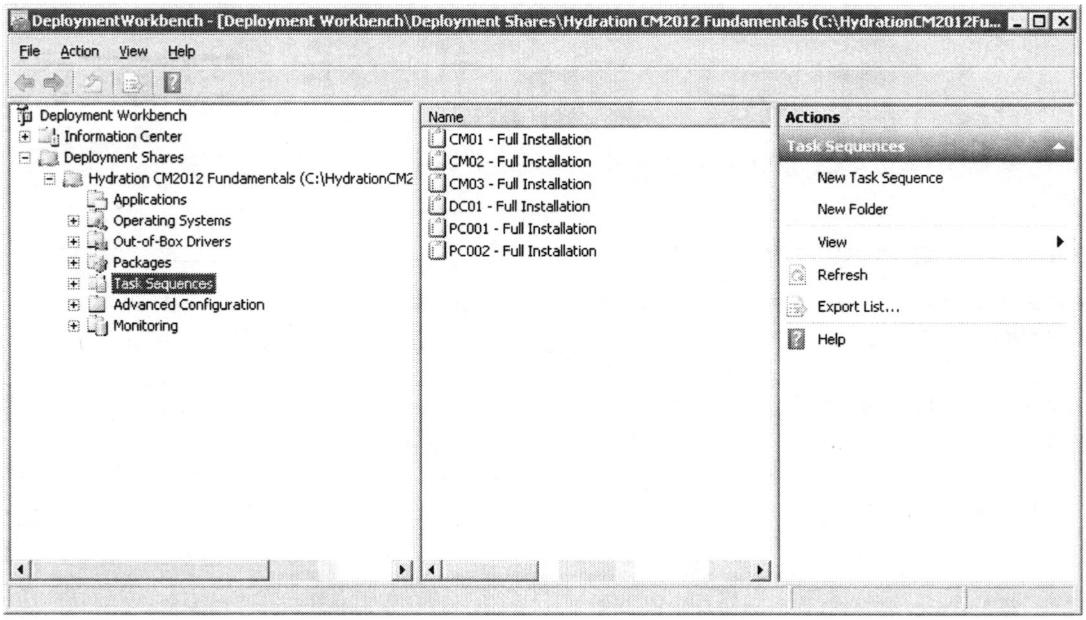

The MDT 2012 Deployment Workbench with the Hydration CM2012 Fundamentals deployment share.

8. Copy the **BGInfo.exe** file from **C:\Program Files\Microsoft Deployment Toolkit\Templates\Distribution\Tools\x86** to **C:\HydrationCM2012Fundamentals\HydrationDS\Applications\Install - BGInfo \Source**.
9. Extract your **Windows Server 2008 R2 Enterprise SP1** installation files (or mount the ISO using an ISO mounting tool like SlySoft Virtual CloneDrive), and copy the **install.wim** file (only) from the **Sources** folder to the **C:\HydrationCM2012Fundamentals\HydrationDS\Operating Systems\Windows Server 2008 R2 SP1 x64** folder.

10. Extract your **Windows 7 Enterprise SP1 x64** installation files (or mount the ISO using an ISO mounting tool like SlySoft Virtual CloneDrive), and copy the **install.wim** file (only) from the **Sources** folder to the **C:\HydrationCM2012Fundamentals\HydrationDS\Operating Systems\Windows 7 Enterprise SP1 x64** folder.
11. Extract your **Windows XP Pro SP3 x86** installation files (or mount the ISO using an ISO mounting tool like SlySoft Virtual CloneDrive), and copy the content to the **C:\HydrationCM2012Fundamentals\HydrationDS\Operating Systems\Windows XP Pro SP3 x86** folder.
12. From the PowerShell command prompt, while still in the **C:\HydrationCM2012Fundamentals\Source** folder, create the Hydration Media Item by running the following command:

    2_CreateHydrationMediaItem.ps1

> **Note:** Do not continue until the 2_CreateHydrationMediaItem.ps1 PowerShell script has completed. After the script has run, you can see a new media item in the Deployment Workbench, Advanced Configuration, Media node. (You may have to press Refresh so see the media item.)

13. Edit the **C:\HydrationCM2012Fundamentals\Source\Media001\Control\CustomSettings_PC002.ini** file, and add the real product key for Windows XP (AAAAA-BBBBB-CCCCC-DDDDD-EEEEE is the place holder).
14. Copy the **C:\HydrationCM2012Fundamentals\Source\Media001\Control** folder to **C:\HydrationCM2012Fundamentals\HydrationISO\Content\Deploy**, replacing any existing files.
15. From the PowerShell command prompt, while still in the **C:\HydrationCM2012Fundamentals\Source** folder, update the Hydration Media Item (and create the ISO) by running the following command:

    3_UpdateHydrationMedia.ps1

> **Note**: The 3_UpdateHydrationMedia.ps1 will take a while to run. A perfect time for a quick break. ☺ You also can update the media item directly from the Deployment Workbench by right-clicking the MEDIA001 media item and selecting Update Media Content.

The Virtual Machines for the New York Site

The following steps assume that you have a dedicated network for the New York site. In my environment, I'm using 192.168.1.0/24 with a default gateway of 192.168.1.254.

Deploy DC01

This is the primary domain controller used in the environment, and it also is running DNS and DHCP.

1. Using **Hyper-V Manager** or **VMware Sphere**, create a virtual machine with the following settings:
    a. Name: **DC01**
    b. Hard drive: **100 GB** (dynamic disk)
    c. Memory: **1 GB** (minimum, recommended is 2 GB)
    d. Network: The virtual network dedicated for the New York site
    e. Image file (ISO): **C:\HydrationCM2012Fundamentals\HydrationISO\HydrationCM2012Fundamentals.iso**
2. Start the **DC01** virtual machine. After booting from the ISO and after WinPE has loaded, select the **DC01** task sequence. Wait until the setup is complete and you see the Hydration Complete message in the final summary.

Configure DC01

After the hydration is completed, you need to configure the Active Directory subnets on DC01:

1. On **DC01**, log on as **Administrator** using a password of **Password01**.
2. Using **Active Directory Sites and Services**, create the following subnets (connect them all with the **HQ** site):
    a. **192.168.1.0/24**
    b. **192.168.2.0/24**
    c. **192.168.3.0/24**
3. After **DC01** is configured, leave it running while installing the other servers and clients.

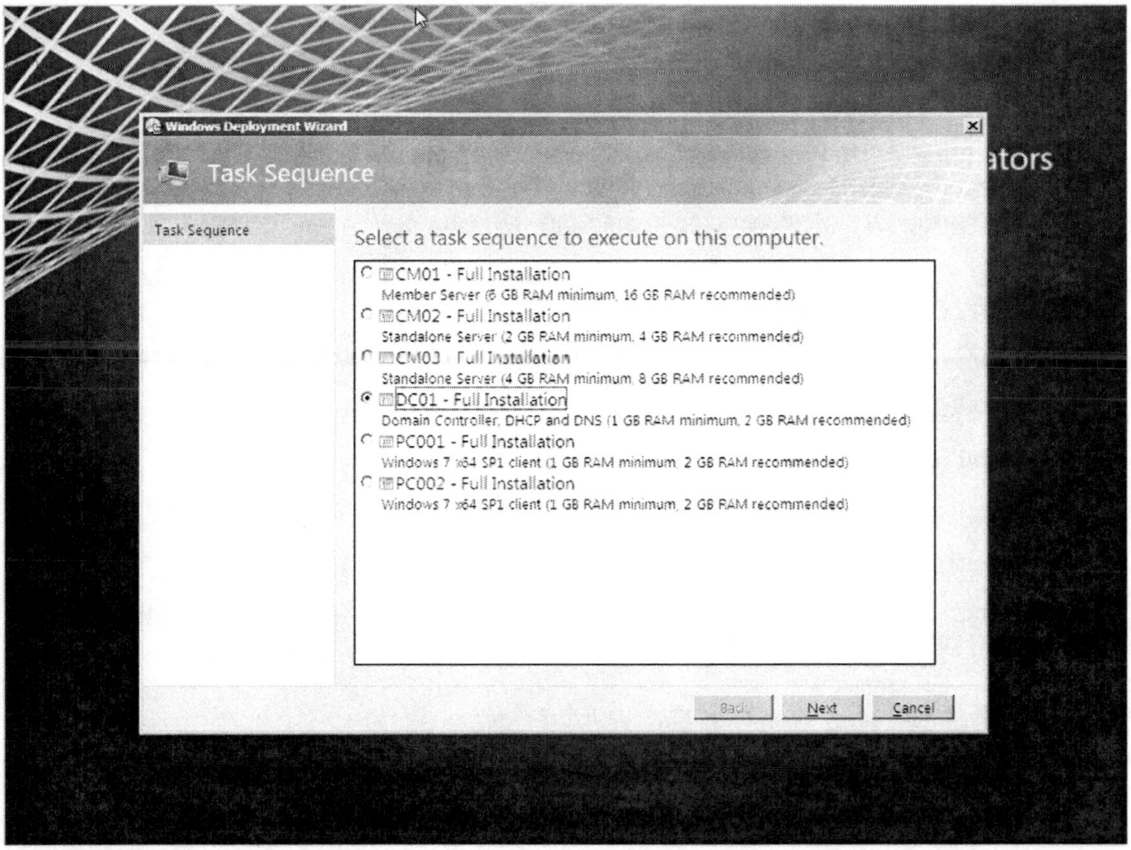

Starting the DC01 virtual machine on the HydrationCM2012Fundamentals.iso.

Deploy CM01

CM01 is the ConfigMgr 2012 primary site server.

1. Using **Hyper-V Manager** or **VMware Sphere**, create a virtual machine with the following settings:
   a. Name: **CM01**
   b. Hard drive #1: **72 GB** (dynamic disk)
   c. Hard drive #2: **650 GB** (dynamic disk)

> **Note:** If using Hyper-V, connect both hard drives to IDE Controller 0 (Location 0 and 1). If using a Hyper-V SCSI disk for hard drive #2, you need to add additional logic to the hydration kit to set the SCSI disk online and rearrange the assigned drive letters.

   d. Memory: **6 GB** (minimum, recommended is 16 GB)

   e. Network: The virtual network dedicated for the New York site
   f. Image file (ISO): **C:\HydrationCM2012Fundamentals\HydrationISO\HydrationCM2012Fundamentals.iso**

2. Start the **CM01** virtual machine. After booting from the ISO and after WinPE has loaded, select the **CM01** task sequence. Wait until the setup is complete and you see the Hydration Complete message in the final summary.

Configuring CM01

After the hydration is completed, you need to complete the following tasks on CM01.

- Install IIS, .BITS and Remote Differential Compression
- Install .NET Framework 3.5.1
- Install .NET Framework 4.0
- Install and Configure WDS

The preceding tasks require that you have downloaded Microsoft .NET Framework 4.0 to the D:\Setup\NET40 folder on CM01.

Install IIS, BITS, and Remote Differential Compression

1. On **CM01,** log in as **CORP\Administrator** using the password **Password01**.
2. Using **Server Manager**, select the **Features** node and click **Add Features** to start the **Add Features Wizard**.
3. On the **Select Features** page of the **Add Features Wizard**:
   a. Select **Background Intelligent Transfer Services (BITS)**. When prompted, click **Add Required Role Services** to add the dependent components, including the **Web Server (IIS)** role.
   b. Select **Remote Differential Compression**, and then click **Next**.
4. On the **Web Server (IIS)** page of the **Add Features Wizard**, click **Next**.
5. On the **Select Role Services** page of the **Add Features Wizard**:
   a. Under **Application Development**, select **ASP.NET** and, when prompted, select **ASP**; then click **Add Required Role Services** to add the dependent components.
   b. Under **Security**, select **Windows Authentication**.
   c. In the **Management Tools** node, under **IIS 6 Management Compatibility**, ensure that both **IIS 6 Metabase Compatibility** (selected by default) and **IIS 6 WMI Compatibility** are selected and then click **Next**.
6. On the **Confirmation** page, click **Install**, and when the installation is completed, click **Close**.

Install .NET Framework 3.5.1

It's recommended to install .NET Framework after IIS has been installed so that the ASP.NET components are registered correctly:

1. Using **Server Manager**, select the **Features** node and click **Add Features** to start the **Add Features Wizard**.
2. On the **Select Features** page, select **.NET Framework 3.51 Features** and complete the following:
    a. Click **Add Required Features**.
    b. Click **Next**.
    c. Click **Install**.
3. Click **Close** to exit the **Add Features Wizard**, and then close **Server Manager**.

Install .NET Framework 4.0 (Manually)

In this appendix, I have added instructions on how to install .NET Framework 4.0 manually or automated via PowerShell. Here is the manual method:

1. Open a command prompt, navigate to **D:\Setup\NET40**, and run **dotNetFx40_Full_x86_x64.exe**.
2. Use the default settings for the installation.

Install.NET Framework 4.0 (Automatically Using PowerShell)

Installing the prerequisites can be automated using the PowerShell script included in this guide. The script is available in the book sample files in the Scripts folder. In this example, you install .NET Framework 4.0, which is located in the D:\Setup\.NET40 folder. The script also adds .NET Framework 3.5.1 if it is not installed already.

1. Open **PowerShell**.
2. Navigate to the folder containing the script, and type the following commands (pressing **Enter** after each command):
    a. **Set-ExecutionPolicy Unrestricted -Force**
    b. **. .\CM12_Function_Library.ps1**

> **Note:** There is a space between the two dots ". ." in the above command. This is needed to install the function library. Also remember to unblock scripts that you download from untrusted sources. Right-click the script, open the properties, and click Unblock.

    c. **Add-Prerequisites -DotNet -File "D:\Setup\NET40\dotNetFx40_Full_x86_x64.exe" -Arguments "/Q /NoRestart"**

Install and Configure WDS (Manually)

In these steps, you install and configure Windows Deployment Services (WDS). You do not add any boot images at this time, but you do prepare the server for it. This configuration assumes that you have added option 60 (PXEClient) on the DHCP Server (DC01).

Like the .NET Framework installation instructions, I have created instructions for both manual and automated installs. First is the manual install:

1. On **CM01**, log on as **Administrator** in the **CORP** domain.
2. Using **Server Manager**, select **Roles**, and then select **Add Roles**.
3. In the **Select Server Roles** list, select **Windows Deployment Services**, and then click **Next**.
4. On the **Overview of Windows Deployment Services** page, click **Next**.
5. On the **Select Role Services** page, accept the default settings and click **Next**.
6. On the **Confirm Installation Selections** page, click **Install**.
7. On the **Installation Results** page, click **Close**.
8. Using **Server Manager**, expand **Roles**, expand **Windows Deployment Services,** and expand **Servers.**
9. Right-click the **CM01.corp.viamonstra.com** server and select **Configure Server**.
10. On the **Before You Begin** page, click **Next**.
11. On the **Remote Installation Folder location** page, in the **Path** text box, type **D:\RemoteInstall**, and then click **Next.**
12. On the **PXE Server Initial Settings** page, select the **Respond to all client computers (known and unknown)** option.

Note: Do not select the Require administrator approval for unknown computers… check box.

13. On the **Operation Complete** page, clear the **Add images to the server now** check box, and click **Finish**.

Install and Configure WDS (Automatically via PowerShell)

1. On **CM01**, log on as **Administrator** in the **CORP** domain.
2. Open **PowerShell**.
3. Navigate to the folder containing the script.
4. Type **. .\CM12_Function_Library.ps1** and press **Enter**.
5. Type **Add-WDS -Folder "D:\RemoteInstall"** and press **Enter**.

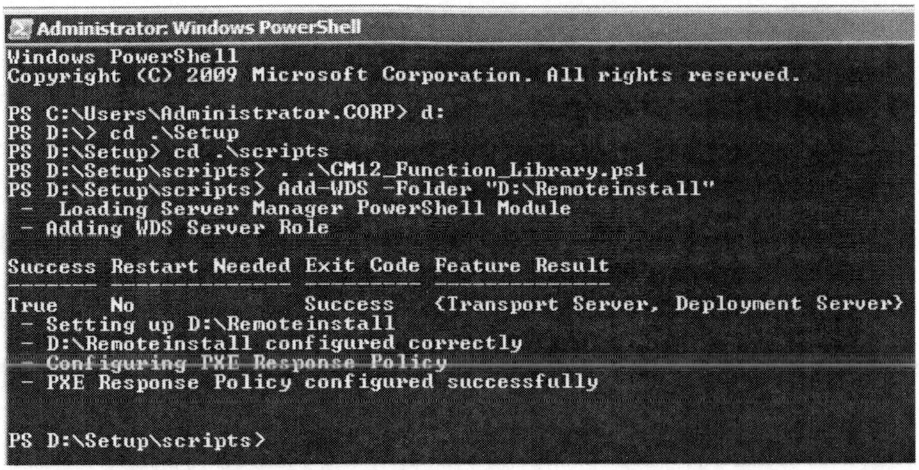

Installing WDS using PowerShell.

Deploy PC001

This is a client running Windows 7 Enterprise SP1 x64 in the corp.viamonstra.com domain.

1. Using **Hyper-V Manager** or **VMware Sphere**, create a virtual machine with the following settings:
    a. Name: **PC001**
    b. Hard drive: **127 GB** (dynamic disk)
    c. Memory: **1 GB** (minimum, recommended is 2 GB)
    d. Network: The virtual network dedicated for the New York site
    e. Image file (ISO): **C:\HydrationCM2012Fundamentals\HydrationISO\HydrationCM2012Fundamentals.iso**
2. Start the **PC001** virtual machine. After booting from the ISO and after WinPE has loaded, select the **PC001** task sequence. Wait until the setup is complete and you see the Hydration Complete message in the final summary.

Deploy PC002

This is a client running Windows XP Pro SP3 x86 in the corp.viamonstra.com domain.

1. Using **Hyper-V Manager** or **VMware Sphere**, create a virtual machine with the following settings:
    a. Name: **PC002**
    b. Hard drive: **127 GB** (dynamic disk)

   c. Memory: **1 GB**
   d. Network: The virtual network dedicated for the New York site. If using Hyper-V, use the Legacy Network Adapter.
   e. Image file (ISO): **C:\HydrationCM2012Fundamentals\HydrationISO \HydrationCM2012Fundamentals.iso**

2. Start the **PC002** virtual machine. After booting from the ISO and after WinPE has loaded, select the **PC002** task sequence. Wait until the setup is complete and you see the Hydration Complete message in the final summary.
3. If using Hyper-V, install the **Hyper-V Integration Services** on **PC002**.

The Virtual Machine for the Orlando Site

The virtual machine for the Orlando site is needed only if you want to learn how ConfigMgr works with a remote distribution point.

The guides in this section assume that you have a dedicated network for the Orlando site. In my environment, I'm using 192.168.2.0/24 with a default gateway of 192.168.2.254. You also need to have routing enabled between the networks.

Real World Note: If you want to run both sites in a virtual environment, you can use a separate Windows Server 2008 R2 virtual machine with Routing and Remote Access enabled, acting as a router. You also can use the free DD-WRT router running as a virtual machine.

Deploy CM02

This is the ConfigMgr 2012 remote distribution point in the Orlando site.

1. Using **Hyper-V Manager** or **VMware Sphere**, create a virtual machine with the following settings:
   a. Name: **CM02**
   b. Hard drive: **300 GB** (dynamic disk)
   c. Memory: **2 GB** (minimum, recommended is 4 GB)
   d. Network: The virtual network dedicated for the Stockholm site
   e. Image file (ISO): **C:\HydrationCM2012Fundamentals\HydrationISO \HydrationCM2012Fundamentals.iso**
2. Start the **CM02** virtual machine. After booting from the ISO and after WinPE has loaded, select the **CM02** task sequence. Wait until the setup is complete and you see the Hydration Complete message in the final summary.

Configure CM02

After thc hydration is complete, you need to join it to the domain:

1. On **CM02**, log on as **Administrator**.
2. Join **CM02** to the **corp.viamonstra.com** domain, and reboot.
3. On **DC01**, move the **CM02** computer account to the **Servers** OU.

The Virtual Machine for the Liverpool Site

The virtual machines for the Liverpool site are needed only if you want to learn how ConfigMgr works with a secondary site.

The guides in this section assume that you have a dedicated network for the Liverpool site. In my environment, I'm using 192.168.3.0/24 with a default gateway of 192.168.3.254. You also need to have routing enabled between the networks.

Real World Note: Again, if you want to run both sites in a virtual environment, you can use a separate Windows Server 2008 R2 virtual machine with Routing and Remote Access enabled, acting as a router. You also can use the free DD-WRT router running as a virtual machine.

Deploy CM03

This is the ConfigMgr 2012 secondary site server in the Liverpool site.

1. Using **Hyper-V Manager** or **VMware Sphere**, create a virtual machine with the following settings:
   a. Name: **CM02**
   b. Hard drive: **300 GB** (dynamic disk)
   c. Memory: **4 GB** (minimum, recommended is 8 GB)
   d. Network: The virtual network dedicated for the Stockholm site
   e. Image file (ISO): **C:\HydrationCM2012Fundamentals\HydrationISO\ HydrationCM2012Fundamentals.iso**
2. Start the **CM03** virtual machine. After booting from the ISO and after WinPE has loaded, select the **CM03** task sequence. Wait until the setup is complete and you see the Hydration Complete message in the final summary.

Configure CM03

After the hydration is complete, you need to join it to the domain:

1. On **CM02**, log on as **Administrator**.
2. Join **CM02** to the **corp.viamonstra.com** domain, and reboot.
3. On **DC01**, move the **CM03** computer account to the **Servers** OU.

Appendix B PowerShell Scripts

In this book, you will find several PowerShell examples. The Cmdlet is a library of useful ConfigMgr-related functions used to create objects like folders, collections, packages, applications, and to install things such as the site system prerequisites. The Cmdlet is developed exclusively for the purpose of this book. The Cmdlet used in the book is **CM12_Function_Library.ps1**.

Getting Started with the Cmdlets

1. Copy the **Cmdlet** to **D:\Setup\Scripts**.
2. From the taskbar, right-click **PowerShell** and select **Run As Administrator**.

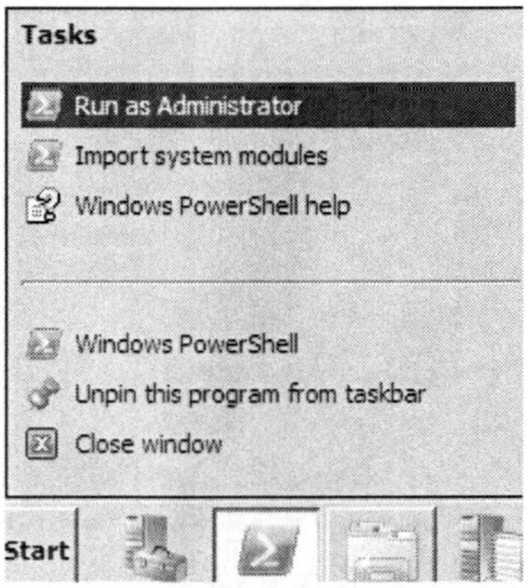

Starting PowerShell as administrator

3. Type **cd d:\setup\scripts** and press **Enter**.
4. To load the library type **. .\CM12_Function_Library.ps1** and press **Enter**. Notice the space between the two dots.

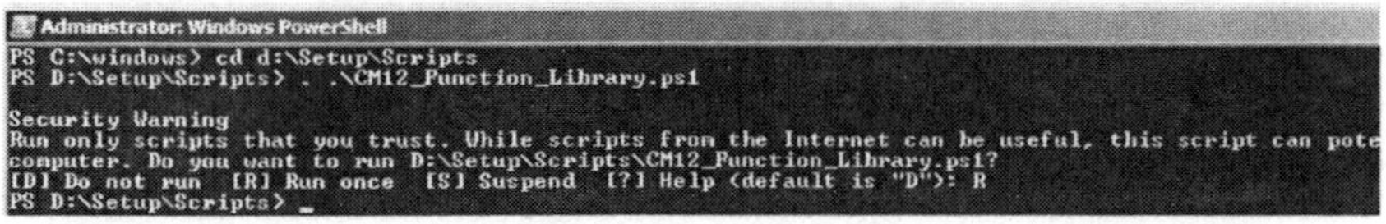

Loading the PowerShell library.

5. To get a list of functions, type **Get-Help .\CM12_Function_Library.ps1** and press **Enter**.

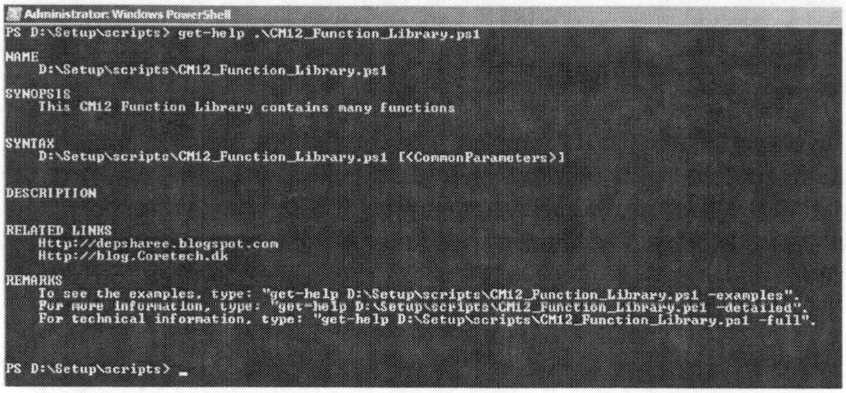

Getting help.

6. To get a list of examples, type **Get-Help CM12_Function_Library.ps1 -Examples** and press **Enter.**

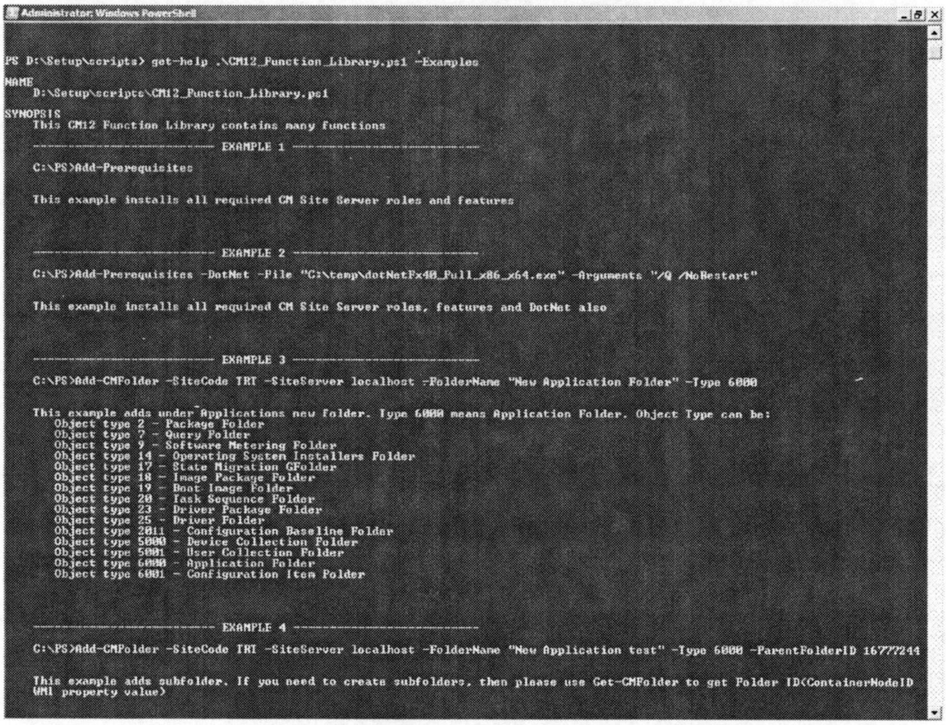

Showing the different PowerShell examples.

Appendix C Changes Made to Active Directory

Here is a list of the Active Directory objects that are created in the various guides throughout the book.

Object Type	Name
OU	Software Groups
OU	Workstations
OU	Servers
OU	Service Accounts
OU	VIM Users
User	CM_CP
User	CM_SR
User	CM_SQ
User	CM_EX
User	CM_NA
User	CM_JD
User	SrvAdmin
User	WrkAdmin
User	JAP (domain user), full name Julie Petersen
User	SAN (domain user), full name Suzanne Angelhart
User	MAC (domain user), full name Mark Carragher
User	MLG (domain user), full name Michael L Gerrad
User	NEP (domain user), full name Nanna E Petersen
User	SMA (domain user), full name Sofie M Andersen
User	WKO (domain user), full name Wally König
User	BOP (domain user), full name Bob Paisly
Group	LocalCorpAdmins
Group	Server Administrators

Object Type	Name
Group	Workstation Administrators
Group	SW_ Office_2010_Install
Group	SW_Office_2010_Uninstall
Group	SW_WinRAR_Install
Group	SW_WinRAR_Uninstall
Group	SW_7-Zip_Install
Group	SW_7-Zip_Uninstall
Group	SUM_Pilot_1
Group	SUM_Pilot_2
Group	SUM_WRK_Excluded
Group	SUM_MW1
Group	SUM_MW2
Group	SUM_MW3
Group	SUM_SRV_Manual

Appendix D Creating the Office 2010 Application

Unlike previous Microsoft Office versions, you don't install Office 2010 using a single MSI file. Instead the install is invoked by running Setup.exe, which will combine a language-neutral core package with one or more language-specific packages. In ViaMonstra, the business language is English, and you will not support any language packages. You will support installing Office 2010 to existing computers while showing the installation progress bar and also supporting a silent installation used in the image process. For ViaMonstra, you use the volume license version of Office 2010 because it offers additional installation options, like administrative setup.

Office setup goes through these phases. As the administrator, you can influence the installation by adding a custom XML file, configuring a MSP file and by adding updates to the Update folder. Some of the settings that you can specify in the XML file can also be added to the MSP file. In the event of conflict settings from the XML file will also take precedence.

1. Run Setup
2. Check prerequisites
3. Read XML data
4. Build the feature tree
5. Create a local installation source on the user's computer
6. Install Office
7. Apply the customization file
8. Apply software updates

Prepare Office 2010 for Deployment

For these steps, you need to have a volume license version of Office 2010. The retail editions do not support administrative installs.

1. The first step in the process is to create the installation point. Create a folder and copy the entire content of the CD/DVD to the folder. In my example, I copied the content from the x64 edition of Office 2010 Professional Plus volume license to **D:\Sources\Software\MS_Office_2010_Pro_X64** on **CM01**. If you want to add additional language support or Office versions, just copy the content to the same folder. When prompted to overwrite existing files, select **No.** (The files that would be overwritten are the common language neutral files.)
2. Start the **OCT** (Office Customization Tool) by running **setup.exe /admin** from **Start, Run**.

3. Select the Office version you want to customize and click **OK**. (This exampleuses Office 2010 Professional Plus x64 for the customization.)

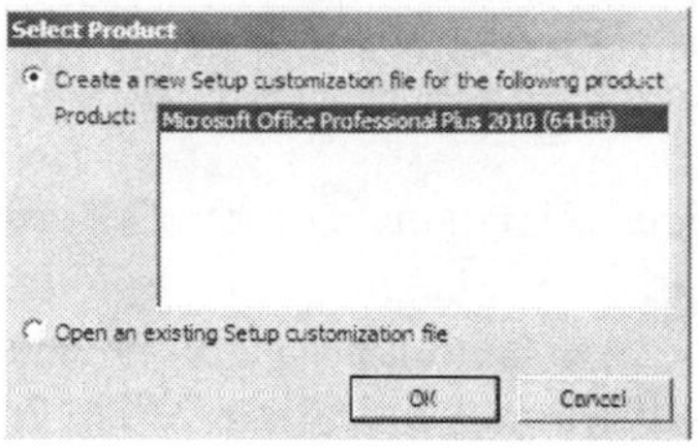

Selecting the Office 2010 version.

4. Select **Install location and organization name** and configure the following setting:

   Organization name: **ViaMonstra**

5. Select **Licensing and User Interface** and complete the following:

   a. Select **Use KMS client key**.

   b. Select **I accept the terms in the license agreement**.

   c. For **Display level**, select:

      i. **Basic** (shows the user a welcome screen, progress bar, error messages but does not require any user input)

      ii. **Suppress modal**

      iii. **No cancel** (prevents user from cancelling the installation)

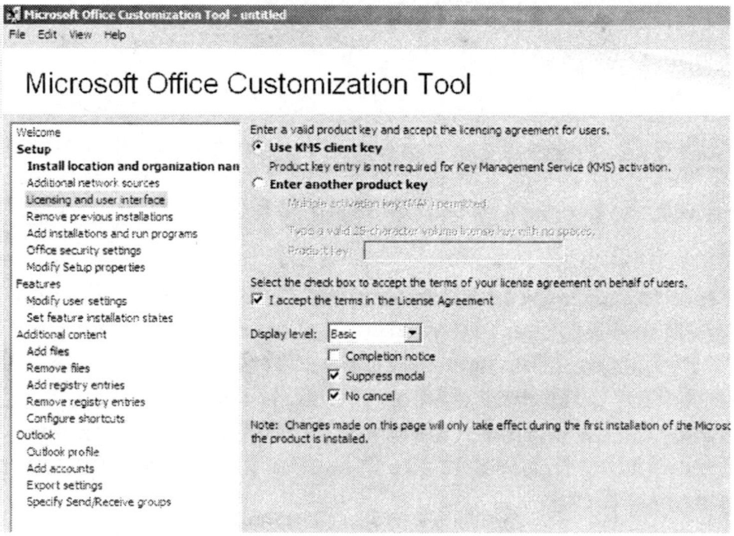

Customizing the Office GUI.

6. Select **Modify Setup properties** and complete the following:

    Click **Add** and type **SETUP_REBOOT** for the property name and **Never** as a value. (This allows ConfigMgr to control the reboot.)

7. Select **File**, **Save** and save the file as **1_VM.MSP** in the **Updates** folder. All patches in the Updates folder are applied automatically (in alphabetic order) during installation. You can place the file in another folder if you are using setup.exe /adminfile.

Add Service Pack Files and Updates

For ViaMonstra, add Microsoft Office Service Pack 1 to the installation by following these steps:

1. On **CM01**, download **Microsoft Office 2010 Service Pack 1** to a folder.
2. Open a command prompt as **Administrator** and navigate to the folder containing the downloaded service pack file.
3. Type **officesuite2010sp1-kb2460049-x64-fullfile-en-us.exe /extract:D:\SP1** and press **Enter**. This command extracts all the files to **D:\SP1**.
4. Copy all the files from **D:\SP1** to **D:\Sources\Software\MS_Office_2010_Pro_X64 \Updates.** All the files added to the Updates folder are applied automatically as the last step in the Office installation.

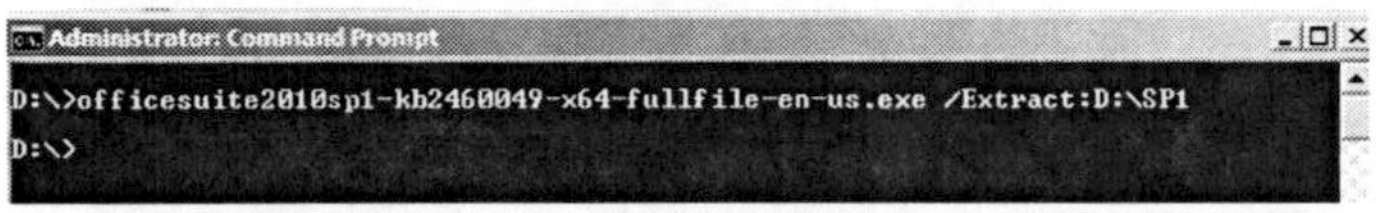

Extracting Microsoft Office 2010 x64 Service Pack 1.

Configure a Silent Install and Uninstall of Microsoft Office

Uninstalling Microsoft Office 2010 and Office applications like Microsoft Visio and Project can be done by running msiexec.exe /x {product code} or by using config.xml. For ViaMonstra, I prefer to use the config.xml file as it provides a bit more control over the process. The following is an example used to perform a silent uninstall of Microsoft Office 2010:

1. Open **Windows Explorer** and navigate to **D:\Sources\Software\MS_Office_2010_Pro_X64\ProPlus.WW**.
2. Open **config.xml**.
3. Remove **<!--** from the line that begins with **<Display level=**, and then remove **-->** from the end of the line.

4. Modify the **Display level** line like this:

   <Display Level="None" CompletionNotice="no" SuppressModal="Yes" AcceptEula="Yes" />

5. Remove **<!--** from the line that begins with **<Logging Type**, and then remove **-->** from the end of the line.

6. Remove **<!--** from the line that begins with **<Setting Id**, and then remove **-->** from the end of the line.

7. Modify the **Setting Id** line like this:

   <Setting Id="SETUP_REBOOT" Value="Never" />

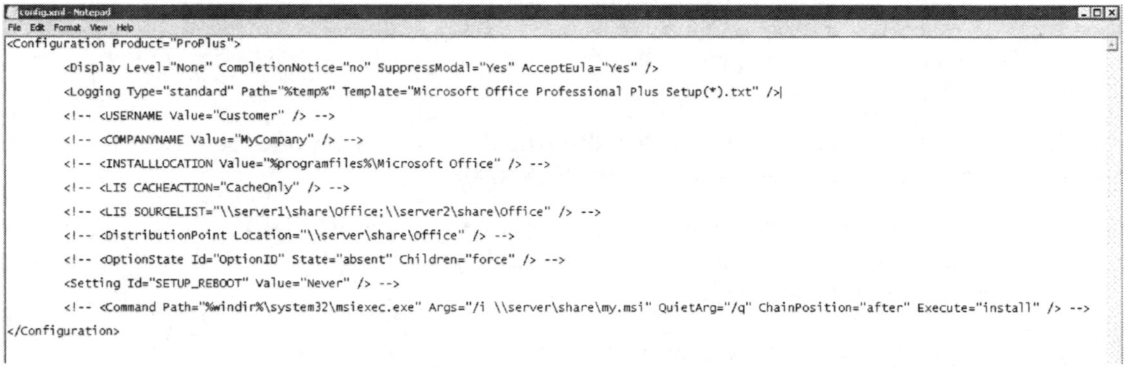


```
<Configuration Product="ProPlus">
        <Display Level="None" CompletionNotice="no" SuppressModal="Yes" AcceptEula="Yes" />
        <Logging Type="standard" Path="%temp%" Template="Microsoft Office Professional Plus Setup(*).txt" />
        <!-- <USERNAME Value="Customer" /> -->
        <!-- <COMPANYNAME Value="MyCompany" /> -->
        <!-- <INSTALLLOCATION Value="%programfiles%\Microsoft Office" /> -->
        <!-- <LIS CACHEACTION="CacheOnly" /> -->
        <!-- <LIS SOURCELIST="\\server1\share\Office;\\server2\share\Office" /> -->
        <!-- <DistributionPoint Location="\\server\share\Office" /> -->
        <!-- <OptionState Id="OptionID" State="absent" Children="force" /> -->
        <Setting Id="SETUP_REBOOT" Value="Never" /> -->
        <!-- <Command Path="%windir%\system32\msiexec.exe" Args="/i \\server\share\my.msi" QuietArg="/q" ChainPosition="after" Execute="install" /> -->
</Configuration>
```

Configuring config·xml to perform a silent uninstall·

8. Save the file. Note that you also can use this file to perform a silent installation of Microsoft Office.

Configure Another Silent Install and Uninstall of Microsoft Office

Repeat the previous steps in this appendix to also create an administrative install and uninstall of the x86 version of Office 2010. Store the Office 2010 x86 installation files in **D:\Sources\Software\MS_Office_2010_Pro_X86** on **CM01**.

Appendix E Prestaging Content on Remote Distribution Points

Prestaging content has long been a feature only available for content that was distributed between site servers. This has changed in ConfigMgr 2012, with which you can now prestage all content. ConfigMgr will create a file with the prestaged content from an existing distribution. For that reason, the content must exist on at least one distribution point before you can create the prestaged content file. In this appendix, the boot images are used as examples.

1. In the **ConfigMgr console,** navigate to the **Software Library** workspace, and select **Operating Systems, Boot Images**.
2. Select the two custom **boot images** and click **Create Prestage Content File** on the ribbon.
3. On the **General** page, click **Browse**, save the file **D:\Setup\boot.pkgx**, and click **Next**.
4. On the **Content** page, click **Next**.
5. On the **Content Locations** page, configure this setting and click **Next**:

   Click **Add**, select **CM01.CORP.VIAMONSTRA.COM**, and click **OK.**

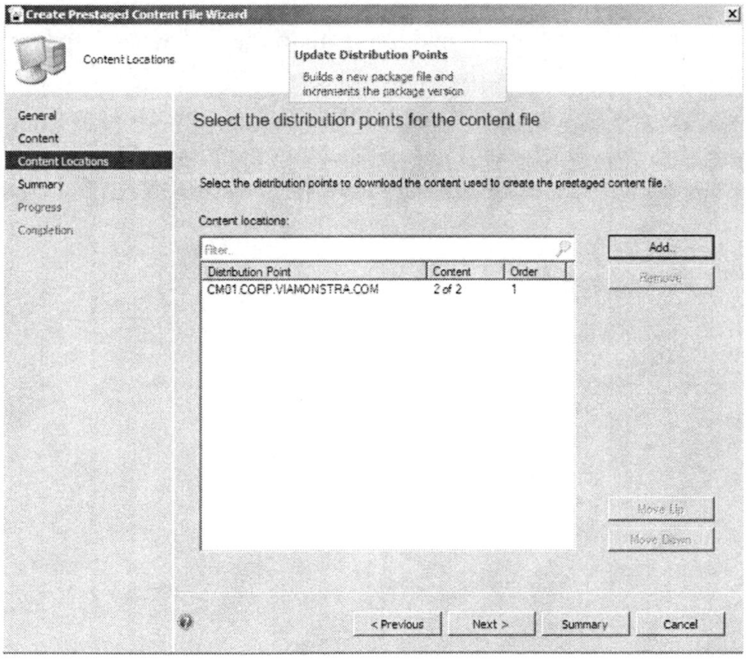

Selecting the source distribution point.

6. On the **Summary** page, read the summary and click **Next**.

7. On the **Completion** page, click **Close**.
8. Copy the **boot.pkgx** file to a remote device for transporting purposes.
9. Log on to the remote distribution point and copy the **boot.pkgx** from the remote device to **D:\SMS_DP$\SMS\Tools**.
10. Open a command prompt as **Administrator** and navigate to **D:\SMS_DP$\SMS\Tools**.
11. Type **ExtractContent.exe /P:D:\SMS_DP$\SMS\Tools\boot.pkgx** and press **Enter**. Notice that you get an error if the content is already present on the remote distribution point. In that case, use the command line /F to force the files to become prestaged.

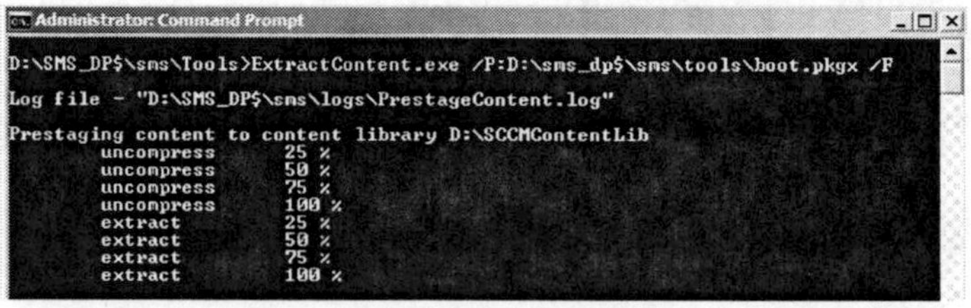

Prestaging packages.

12. Use **CMTrace.exe** to open **D:\SMS_DP$\sms\logs\PrestageContent.log.** From this log file, you are able to monitor the process.
13. Log on to **CM01**, open the **ConfigMgr console** and navigate to the **Software Library** workspace.
14. Select **Operating Systems, Boot Images**, and distribute the content of both boot images to the remote distribution point. ConfigMgr will not redistribute the content because the remote distribution point has uploaded a state message with information about the content being prestaged.

Appendix F Creating a Secondary Site

Due to the many infrastructure changes in ConfigMgr 2012, many companies are never required to install a secondary site server. However, if you do have a remote location with several thousand users, it is a good idea to consider a secondary site. The steps in this appendix take you through the installation and configuration of a secondary site server.

Prerequisites for Installing the Secondary Site Server

Before installing the secondary site server, you need to ensure that these prerequistes are met:

1. Ensure that the user account installing the secondary site is a member of the local administrator group on the secondary site server.
2. Configure SQL Firewall ports.
3. Install Remote Differential Compression (RDC).
4. Install BITS.
5. For site-specific system role requirements, install all the prerequisites as listed in Appendix A.
6. Run the prerequisites checker from ConfigMgr 2012 installation media. (The order in which you first five prerequisites is not important; however, this one must be done last.)

Run the Prerequisites Checker

It's a very good idea to run the prerequisite check before starting the secondary site installation. If you start the installation and the prerequisites are not met, you end up spending hours troubleshooting the failure and determining why it occurred.

1. Log on to the primary site server and open the command prompt as **Administrator**.
2. Navigate to the **ConfigMgr 2012 installation media**.
3. Run this command:

   prereqchk.exe /SEC cm03.corp.viamonstra.com /INSTALLSQLEXPRESS /Ssbport 4022 /Sqlport 1433

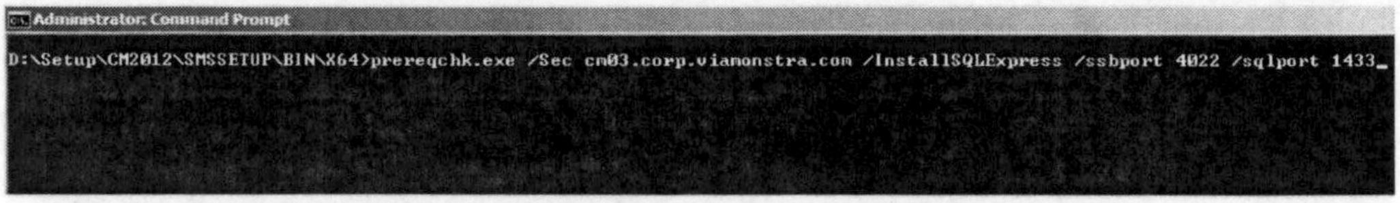

Running the prerequisites check on a secondary site server.

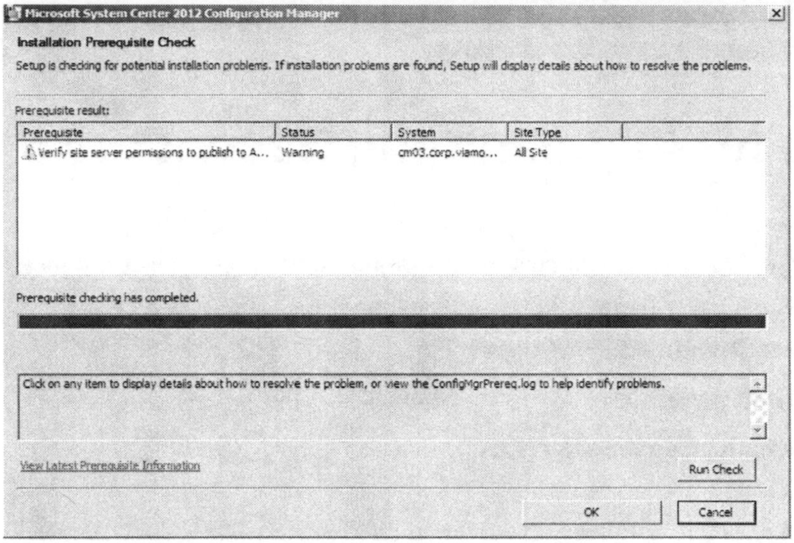

The warning about publishing data is a known issue and can safely be ignored.

4. Click **OK** to close the prerequisites checker.

Install the Secondary Site Server

1. Log on to the primary site server and open the **ConfigMgr console**.
2. Navigate to the **Administration** workspace and select **Site Configuration, Sites**.
3. Click **Create Secondary Site** on the ribbon.
4. On the **Before You Begin** page, click **Next**.
5. On the **General** page, configure these settings and click **Next**:
    a. Site Code: **S01**
    b. Site Server Name: **CM03.corp.viamonstra.com**
    c. Site Name: **Secondary site, Liverpool**
    d. Installation folder: **D:\Program files\Microsoft Configuration Manager**

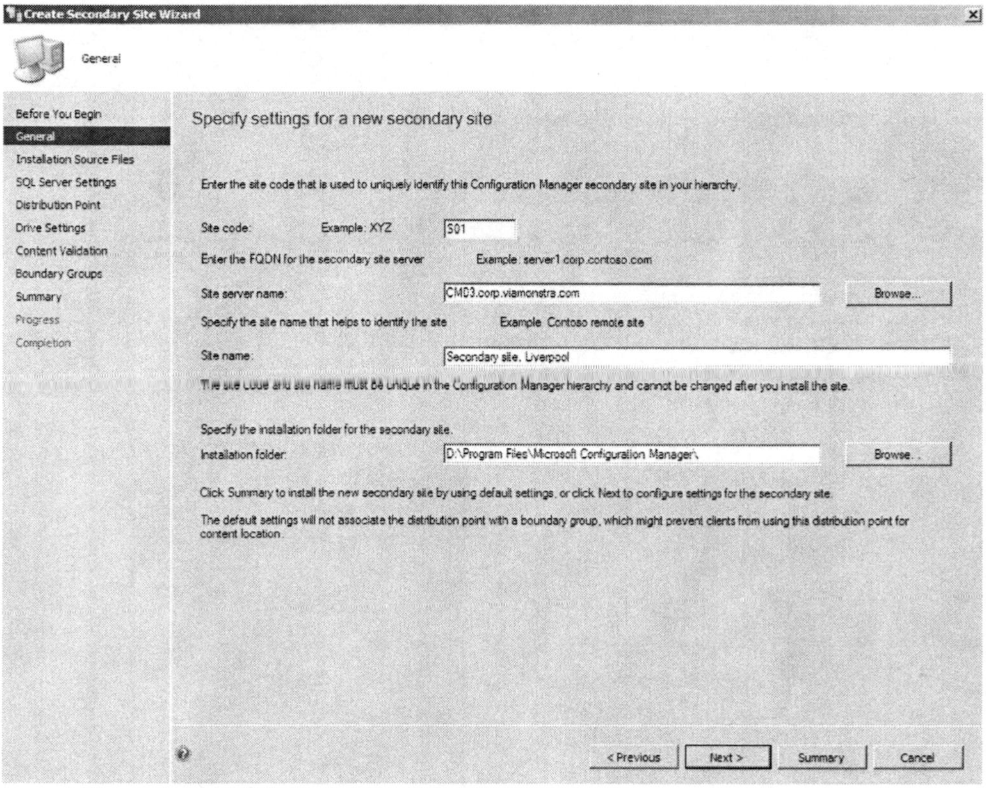

Configuring the site server information.

6. On the **Installation Source Files** page, select **Copy installation source files over the network from the parent site server** and click **Next**.

7. On the **SQL Server Settings** page, keep the default settings and click **Next**. The default settings will install SQL Server Express 2008 R2 SP1.

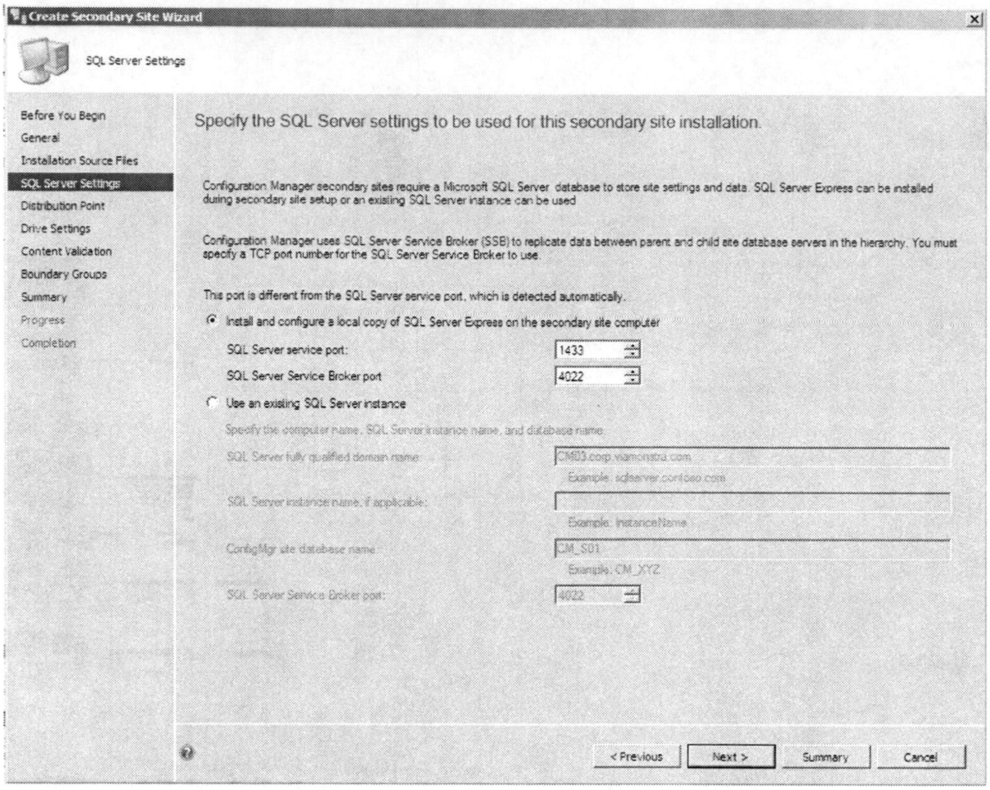

Specifying the local SQL Server.

8. On the **Distribution Point** page, configure this setting and click **Next**:

   Install and configure IIS if required by Configuration Manager: **Enabled**

9. On the **Drive Settings** page, configure these settings and click **Next**.
   a. Drive space reserve (MB): **1024**
   b. Primary content library location: **D**
   c. Primary package share location: **D**

10. On the **Content Validation** page, configure these settings and click **Next**:
    a. Validate content on a schedule: **Enabled**
    b. Schedule: **Daily**

11. On the **Boundary Groups** page, leave the default settings and click **Next**.

12. On the **Summary** page, read the summary and click **Next**.

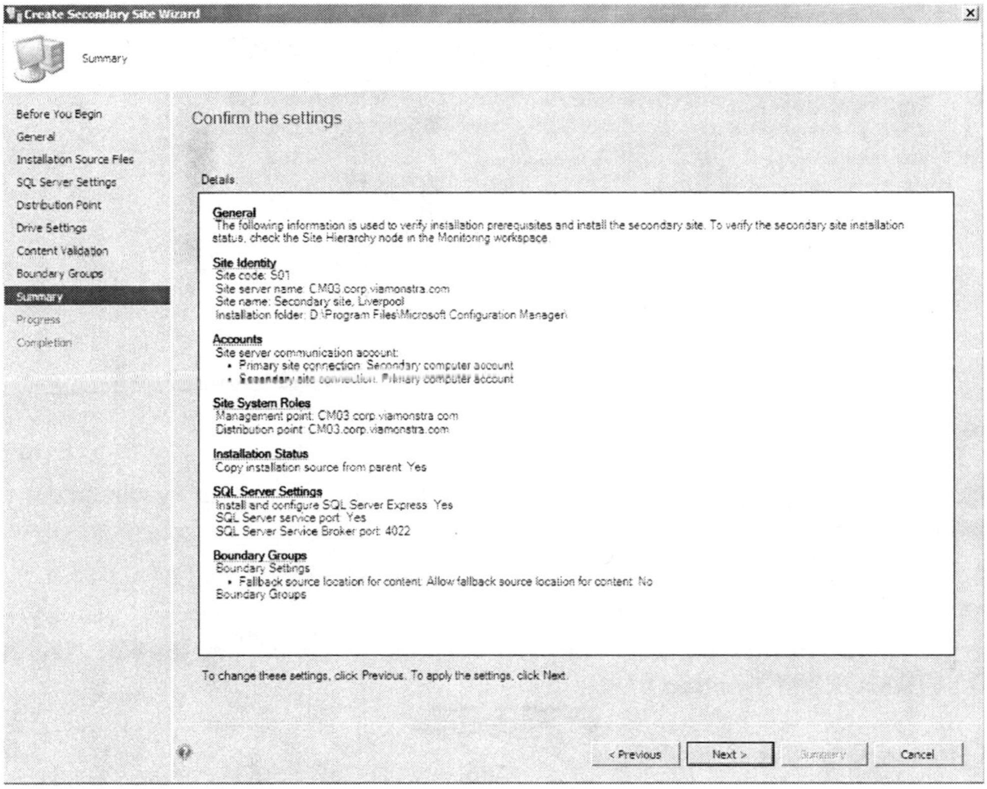

Secondary site server installation summary.

13. On the **Completion** page, click **Close**.

Post-Installation SQL Server Express Configurations

The ConfigMgr installation wizard only installs SQL Server Express version 10.50.2500 which is SQL Server Express 2008 R2 SP1. After the secondary site server installation is done, you should upgrade to SQL Server Express 2008 R2 SP1 CU6.

1. Log on to **CM03** as **CORP\Administrator**.
2. From the **Start** menu, select **Administrative Tools** and open **Services**.
3. Stop these three services:
    a. **SMS Agent host (the Management Point service)**
    b. **SMS Executive**
    c. **SMS Site Component Manager**

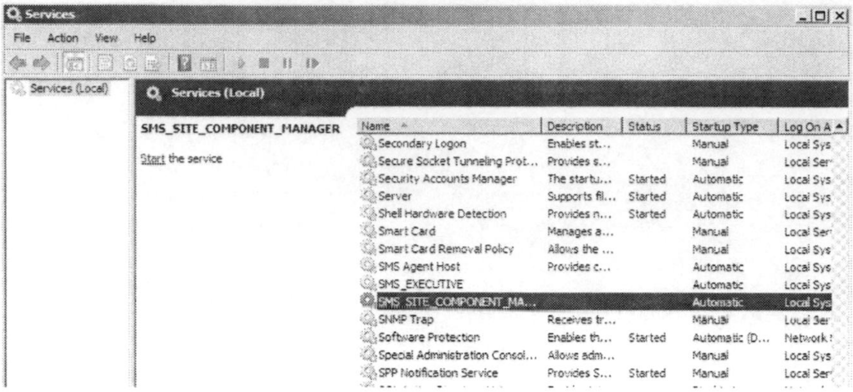

Stopping the main ConfigMgr services.

4. Open a command prompt with administrative permissions, and navigate to the folder containing the **SQL 2008 R2 SP1 CU6** update.
5. Run **SQLServer2008R2-KB2679367-x64.exe /Action=Patch /IAcceptSQLServerLicenseTerms /AllInstances /Quiet**
6. After the upgrade is finished, restart the three ConfigMgr services and the **SQL Server (CONFIGMGRSEC)** service.

Verify the Secondary Site Installation

For me, the easiest way to verify that the installation has started is by looking at the log files. After the installation is done, I monitor the status of the secondary site in the ConfigMgr console:

1. In the **Administration** workspace, select **Site Configuration**, **Sites**.
2. Here you see the status of the secondary site server. After a successful installation (and refresh of the console), the **State** will be listed as **Active**.

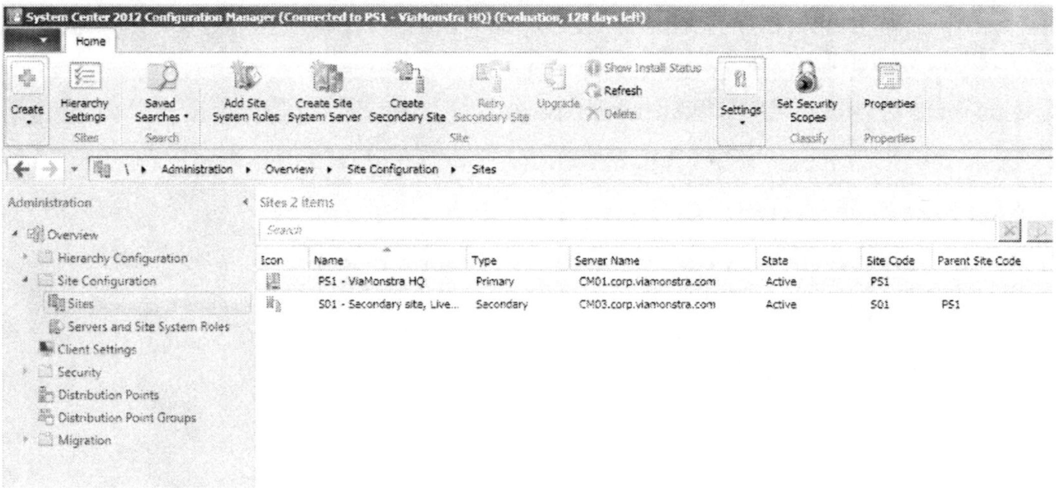

Active Secondary site.

3. Open the **Monitoring** workspace and select **Site Hierarchy**. Here you see a Hierarchy diagram and the overall status of the sites.

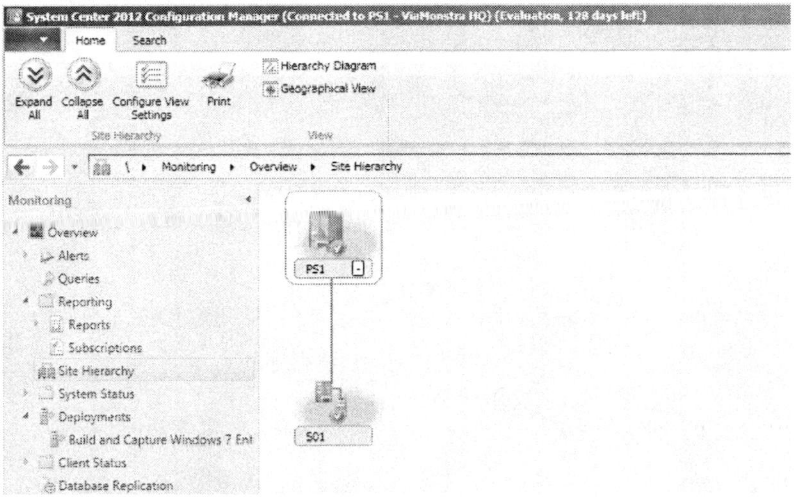

Viewing the hierarchy status.

4. Click **Configure View Settings** on the ribbon and select the **Site Location** tab.
5. Configure these settings and click **OK**:
    a. For site **PS1**, type **New York, United States** in **Location.**
    b. For site **S01**, type **Liverpool, United Kingdom** in **Location.**

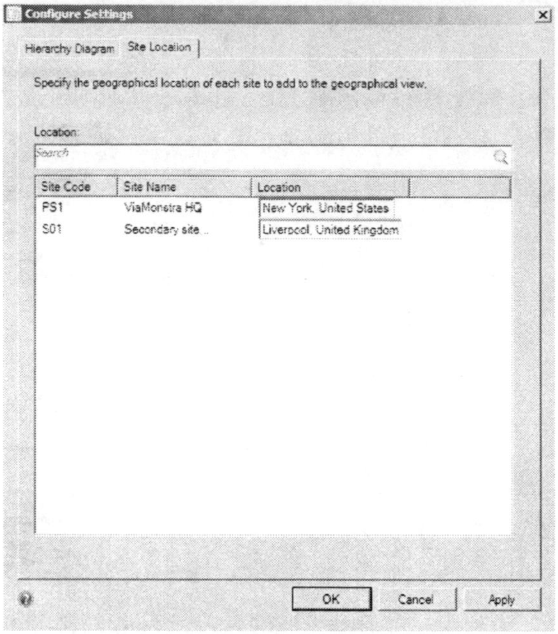

Configuring Bing Map location settings.

6. Back in the site hierarchy settings, click **Geographical View** on the ribbon.

The Bing Map showing the two locations.

7. In the **Monitoring** workspace, select **Database replication**.

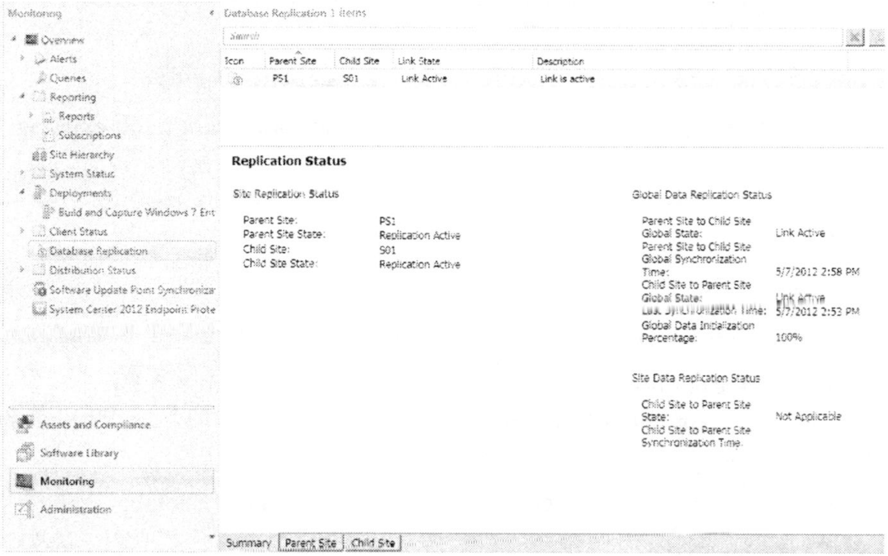

Monitoring database replication.

8. The Summary tab lists the overall replication status. For detailed information, click the **Parent Site** or the **Child Site** tab.

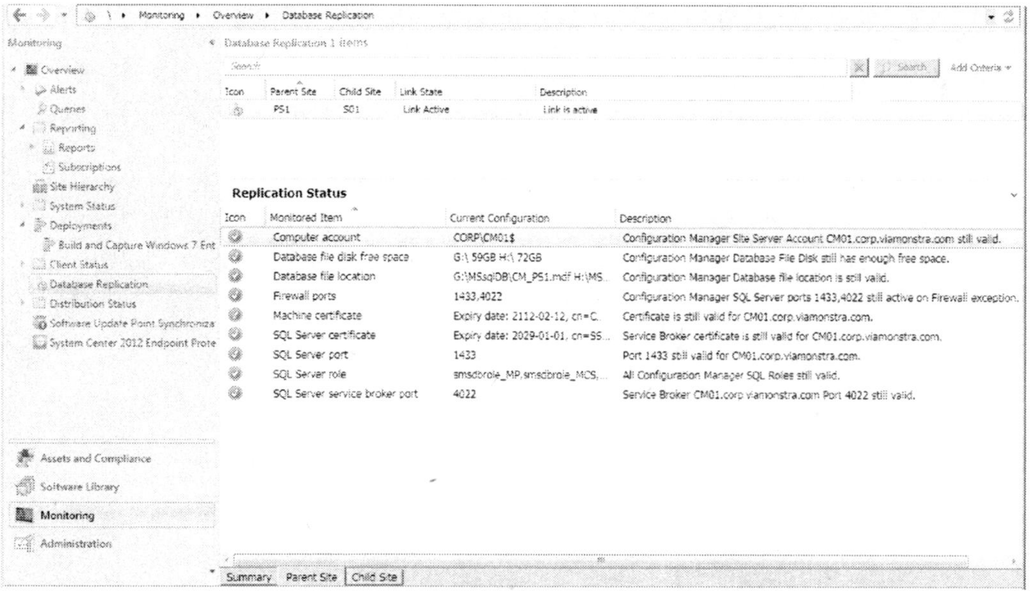

Detailed information about the parent site replication status.

Post-Secondary Site Tasks

After the secondary site is installed, it's time to configure the site which includes the following tasks:

1. Configuring boundaries and boundary groups to service local clients only
2. Creating a new distribution point group or adding the distribution point to an existing distribution point group
3. Installing and configuring additional site system roles

Configure the Secondary Site to Service Local Clients Only

1. In the **Administration** workspace, navigate to **Hierarchy Configuration**, **Boundaries**.
2. Select the IP address range boundary that is used in Liverpool (**192-168.3.1 - 192.168.3.254**) and click **Add Selected Items, Add Selected Items to New Boundary Groups** from the ribbon.
3. On the **General** page, configure these settings and click the **References** tab:
    a. Name: **CL Liverpool**
    b. Description: **Content location boundary group for Liverpool**

4. On the **Reference** tab, configure this setting and click **OK**:

   Click **Add**, and from the list of distribution points, select **\\CM03.corp.viamonstra.com**.

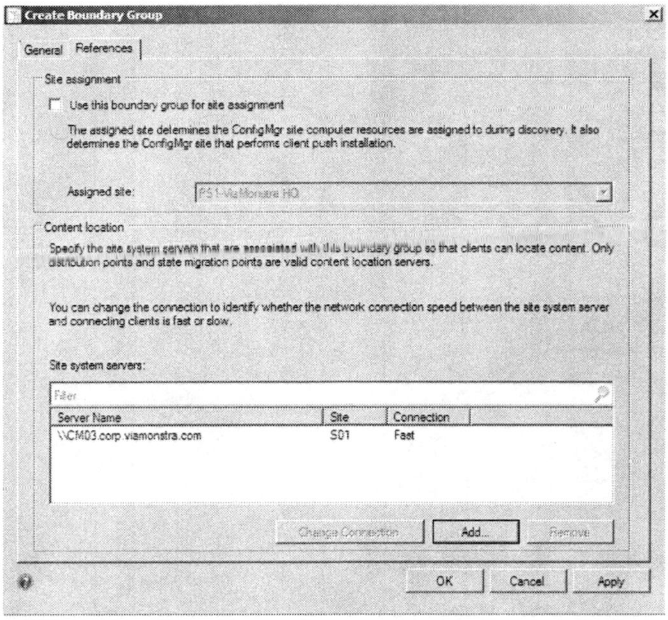

Creating the secondary site boundary group.

5. Still in the **Administration** workspace, navigate to **Site Configuration**, **Servers, Site System Roles**.
6. Select the **\\CM03.corp.viamonstra.com** server and open the **Distribution Point** properties.
7. Select the **Group Relationship** tab, click **Add**, select **All Content**, and click **OK**.
8. Select the **Boundary Groups** tab, remove the checkmark in **Allow fallback source location for content** and click **OK**.

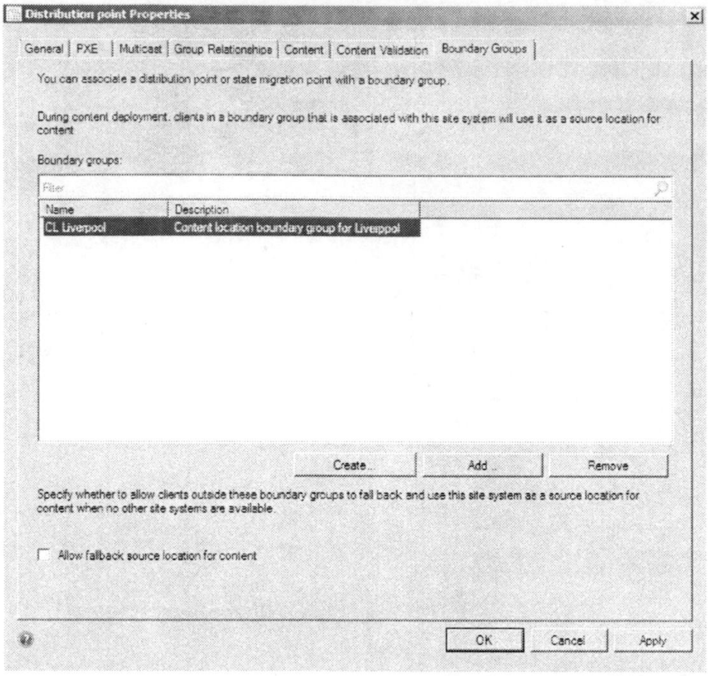

Configuring the distribution point to be protected.

Useful Log Files

You can use the log files in the following table to track activity related to the secondary site installation process.

Log File	Description	Location
Hman.log	Gives you information about running the prerequisites check on the secondary site server	Parent site server default log location
ConfigMgrPrereq.log	Gives you detailed information about running the prerequisites check on the secondary site server	Parent site server default log location
ConfigMgrSetup.log	Gives you detailed information about the secondary site server installation	Secondary site server in the root of C:\
SiteComp.log	Gives you information about installing the site system components.	Secondary site server default log location

Log File	Description	Location
Sender.log	Gives you information about sending content data between the sites	Secondary site and primary site server default log location
Despool.log	Gives you information about receiving content from another site	Secondary site and primary site server default log location
Rcmctrl.log	Gives you information about the SQL replication between the sites	Secondary site and primary site server default log location

Appendix G Migrating from ConfigMgr 2007

Unlike previous versions of ConfigMgr, it is no longer possible to do an in-place upgrade of the old version. In order to preserve existing ConfigMgr 2007 objects, you need to use the built-in migration tool in ConfigMgr 2012. You can migrate several primary ConfigMgr 2007 sites into a single ConfigMgr 2012 site.

Planning for Migration

When migrating from ConfigMgr 2007 to ConfigMgr 2012, you need to be sure to plan the migration correctly. First of all, you need to prepare your environment so that you can migrate the objects to the new ConfigMgr 2012 environment:

1. Service Pack 2 for ConfigMgr 2007 needs to be installed on all site servers. It doesn't matter if R2 or R3 is installed.
2. There is no support for users and devices in one collection. Create separate collections for users and devices.
3. Collections with more than one query rule are not supported.
4. A site code is a unique entity. Use a new site code in your ConfigMgr 2012 environment.
5. Upgrade your branch distribution points to Windows 7.
6. Be sure that your package source is always a UNC path. Local paths will not work when migrating the objects to a new ConfigMgr 2012 server.

Preparing the Configuration Manager 2007 Environment

To be able to use the migrated packages, you must be sure that all packages are using an UNC path to point to the package source. In this example, CM2007 is the name of the ConfigMgr 2007 site server. The site server has been used to store the package source files locally in D:\Sources\Software. The location has also been shared as \\CM2007\Sources$.

Check Package Source Locations from ConfigMgr 2007

1. Log on to the ConfigMgr 2007 server (**CM2007**).
2. Open the **ConfigMgr console** and navigate to **Computer Management, Software Distribution, Packages**. Open the **package properties** for **Adobe Reader 9.3** (for instance) and select the **Data Source** tab. You can right-click the package and select Properties to open the package properties. Notice the source directory.

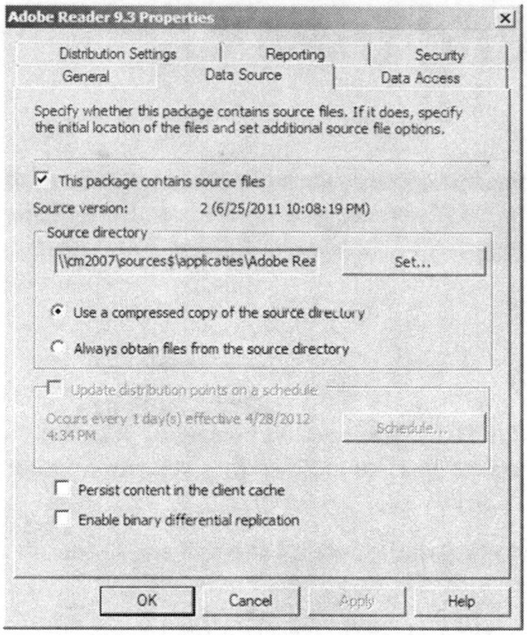

Package with an UNC source path.

3. Click **OK** to close the properties.
4. Open the **package properties** for **Adobe Reader 7.0** and select the **Data Source** tab. Notice the source directory.

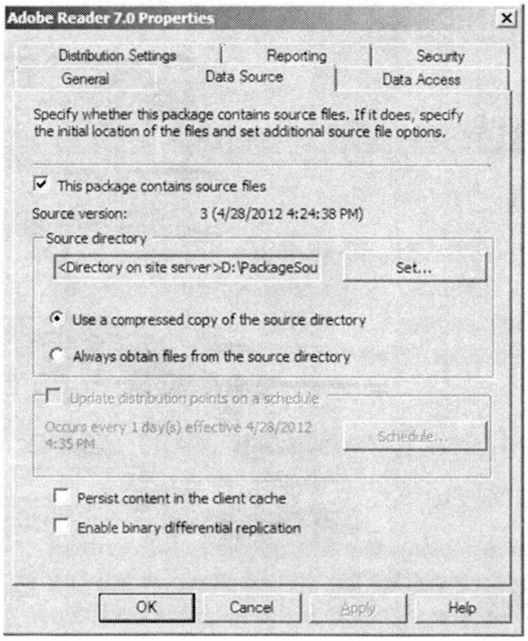

Package with a local source path.

5. Click **OK** to close the properties.

Install and Configure the Package Source Change Utility

One of the community tools mentioned earlier in this book is the Package Source Changer that can be downloaded from http://blog.coretech.dk/jgs/coretech-package-source-changer-0-3-0-0/. The tool is also part of the book sample files.

1. Run **PackageSourceChanger.exe** with administrative privileges.
2. Accept the license terms and click **Configuration**.
3. In **Configuration**, you need to type the name of the ConfigMgr site server; type **CM2007** and click **Save**.

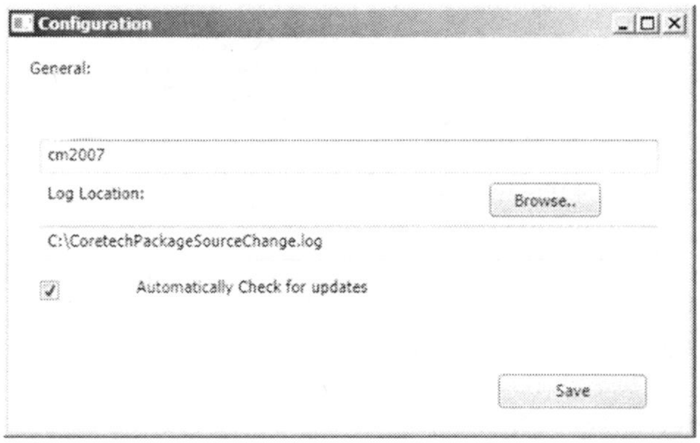

Configuring the utility to connect to the CM2007 server.

4. In **Find**, type **\\CM2007\Sources$\Software** and click **Verify location**.
5. In **Replace**, type **\\CM01\Sources$\Software** and click **Verify location**.
6. Select **Copy content from Old to new source**.
7. Click **Select Packages**. Select the applications that you want to move from the list and click **Save**.

Selecting the packages for which you want to change the package source.

8. Click **Start** to start the package source update process.

Package sources are changed and the source is copied to the new CM01 server.

9. Repeat the step again for every different package source, for instance **d:\sources**.
10. Back in the ConfigMgr console, open the **Adobe Reader 7.0** package properties and select the **Data source** tab.

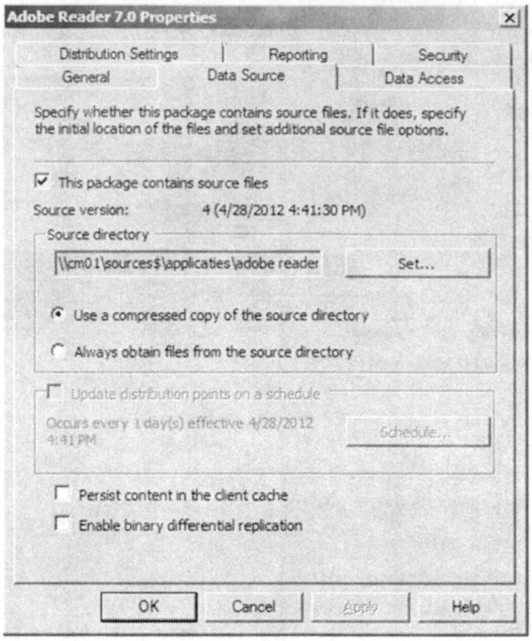

Checking the source of the package.

11. Verify that the source is correct and click **OK**.

Remove Boundaries

1. Open the **ConfigMgr console**.
2. Navigate to **Site Database**, **Site Management**, **Site Settings**, **Boundaries**, and delete all boundaries.

Migrate from CM2007

Configure the Data Source Hierarchy

1. Log on to **CM01** and open the **ConfigMgr console**.
2. Select the **Administration** workspace.
3. Navigate to **Overview**, **Migration**, **Active Source Hierarchy**.
4. Click **Specify Source Hierarchy** on the ribbon.
5. In **Top-Level Configuration Manager 2007** site server, type **cm2007.corp.viamonstra.com**.

6. In **Source site access accounts,** click **Set, New Account, Browse**; type **corp\administrator.** Click **Check names** and click **OK**.

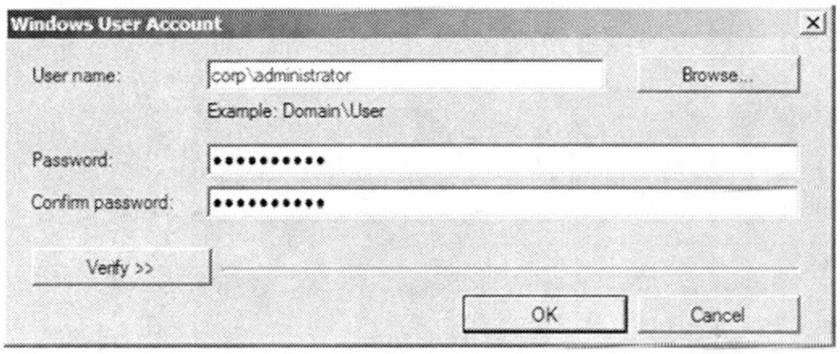

Supplying account information to connect to CM2007.

7. Type **Password01** as the password and click **OK** twice. This starts the gathering process and collects metadata from the CM2007 hierarchy.
8. The gathering process can take a few minutes. Open **migmctrl.log** and monitor the process.
9. Click **Close** when the gathering process is finished.

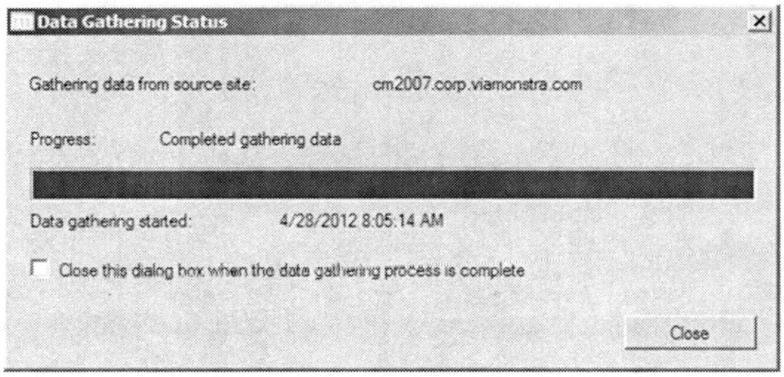

The data gathering process gathers information about your CM 2007 environment.

Migrate Software Packages

After the source hierarchy is configured and the gathering process is finished, you are able to migrate ConfigMgr objects like packages:

1. Select the **Administration** workspace.
2. Navigate to **Overview**, **Migration**, **Migration Jobs**.
3. Click **Create Migration Job** on the ribbon.
4. In **Name**, type **Packages**.

5. In **Job type**, select **Object migration** and click **Next**.

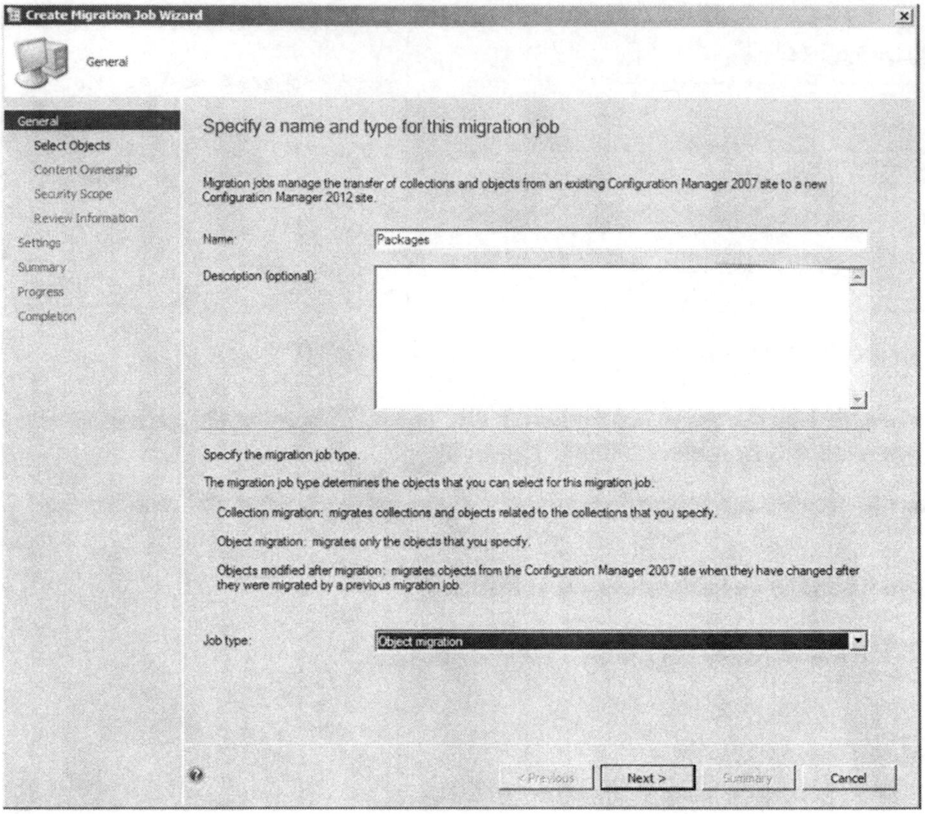

Creating an object migration job.

6. Select **Software Distribution**, select the packages you want to migrate, and click **Next**.

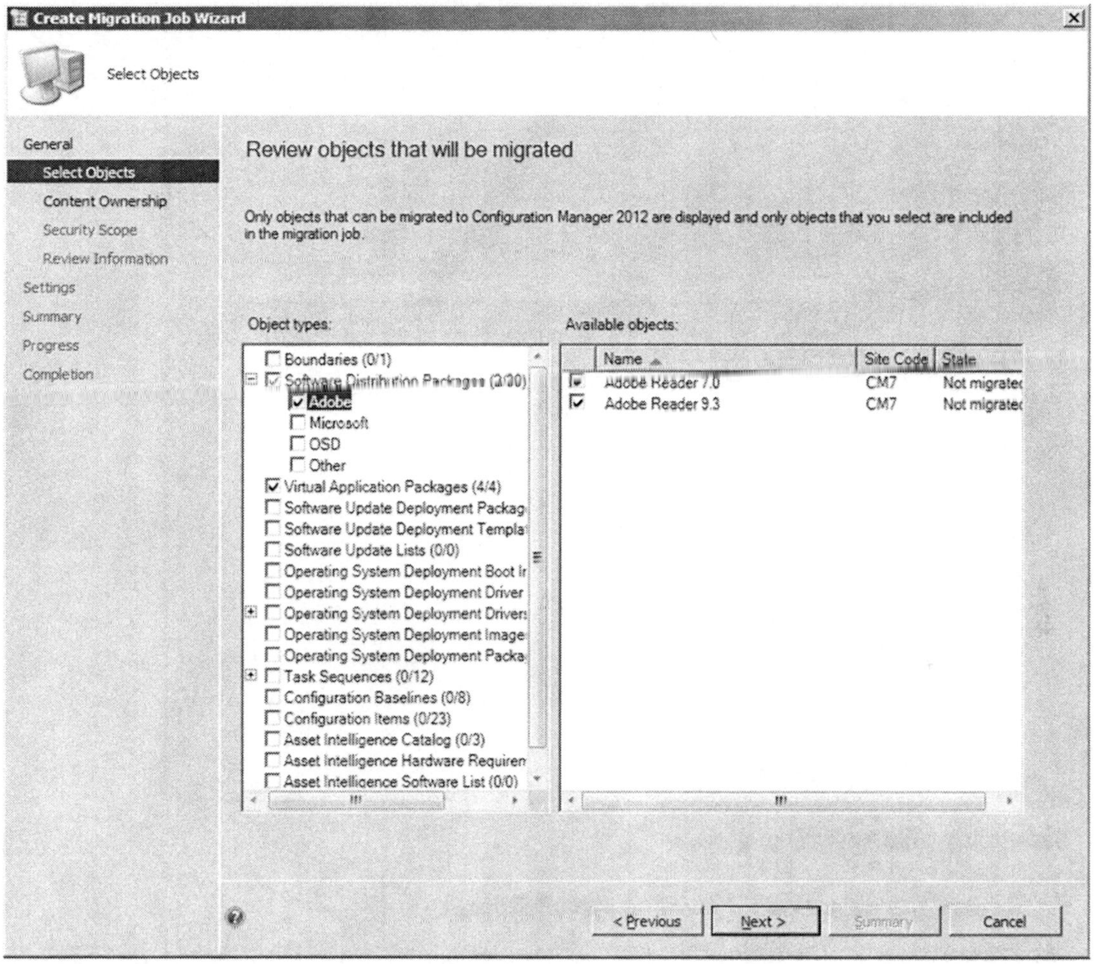

Selecting the packages you want to migrate.

7. On the **Content Ownership** page, click **Next**.
8. Select the **Default** security scope and click **Next**.

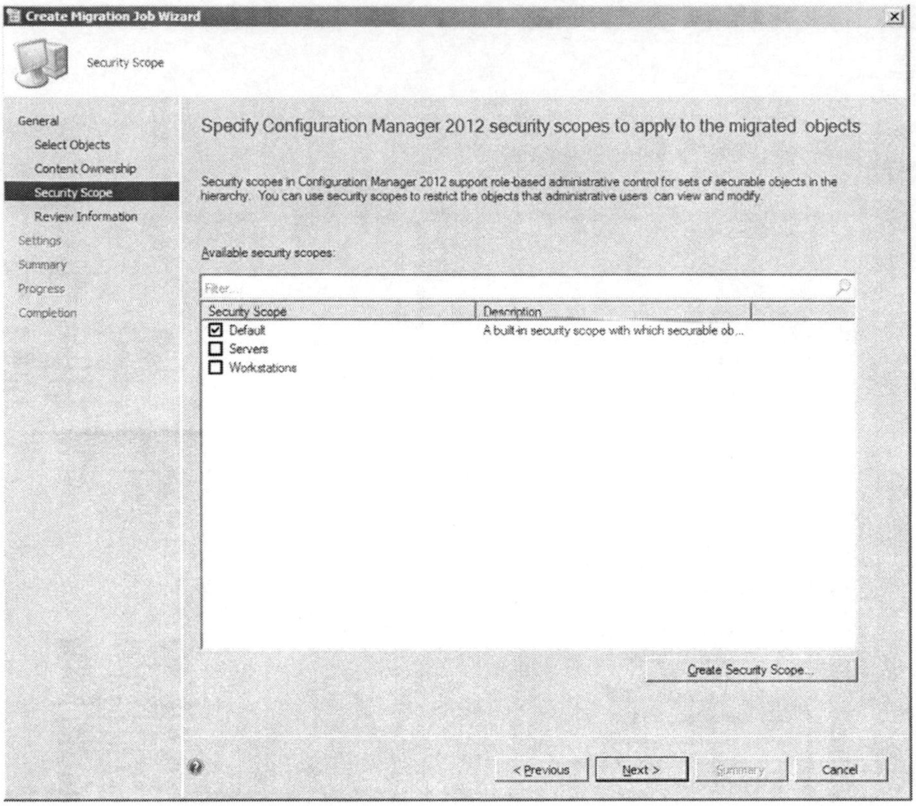

Selecting the security scope.

9. Review the migration information and click **Next**.
10. Click **Schedule the migration job**, assign a schedule for the job to begin, and click **Next**.
11. Click **Next** and **Close**.
12. After the job has started, go back to the **ConfigMgr console**. You are able to see a job status of **Running**.

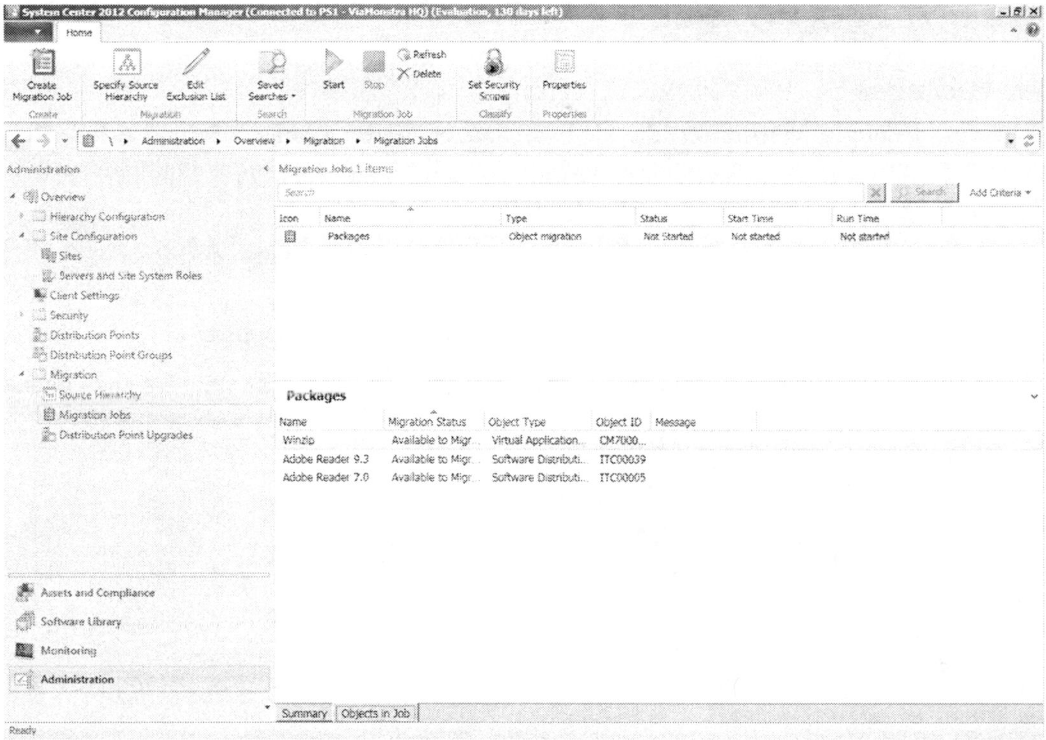

Monitoring the migration of the objects.

13. After the job is complete, refresh the view in Migration Jobs and the status should display **Migrated**.

The Package Conversion Manager

The package conversion manager is a utility from Microsoft that can assist you in converting traditional packages into the application model. The utility integrates into the ConfigMgr console and adds extra options to the Software Library workspace.

Install the Package Conversion Manager

1. Close the **ConfigMgr console**.
2. Download the **Package Conversion Manager** from **http://www.microsoft.com/en-us/download/details.aspx?id=29265**.
3. Run **PCMRTWSetup-English.exe** with administrative privileges from your download location.
4. Click **Next**, **Accept the License terms**, and then click **Next**.
5. Click **Install** and **Finish**.

6. Restart the **ConfigMgr console**.

Convert Packages

In the following example, you convert the MSI versions of Adobe Reader 9.30 and Adobe Reader 7.0. Not all packages can be converted automatically, but the wizard provides you with readiness information for each package that has been analyzed.

1. Select the **Software Library** workspace and navigate to **Packages, Adobe**. Right-click the columns above the packages and select **Readiness.**
2. Select the **Adobe** packages and click **Analyze Package** on the ribbon.

   After analyzing the packages, ConfigMgr 2012 lists the Readiness state for each package.

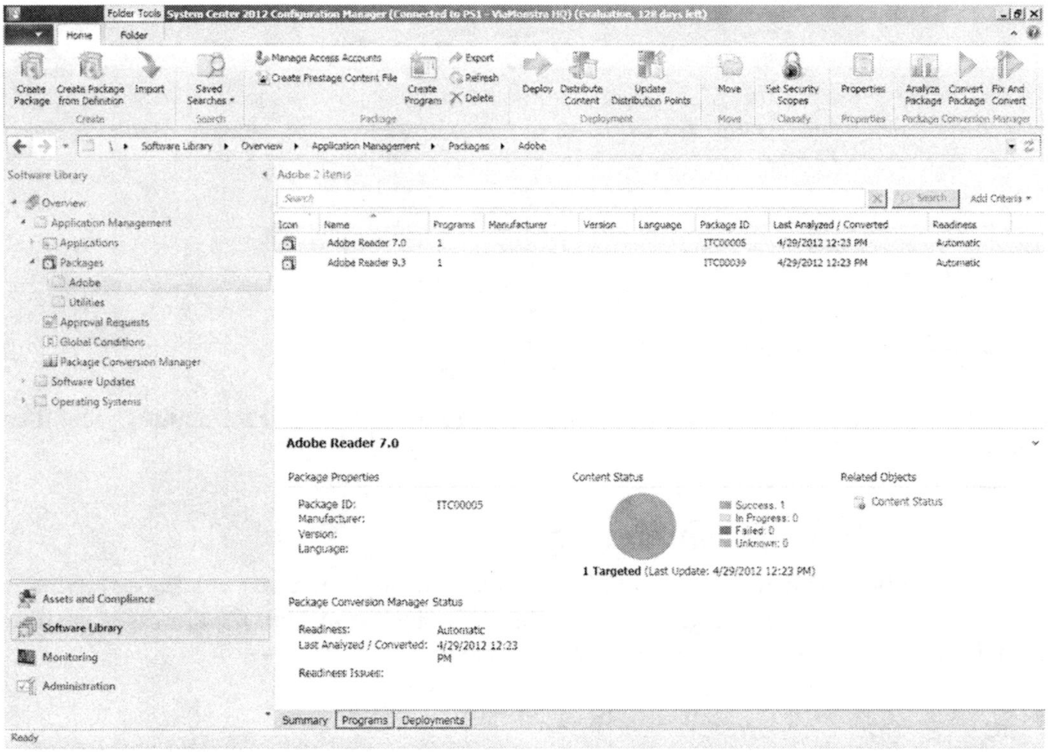

See the readiness state of the packages.

3. Select both **Adobe Reader** packages, right-click the packages, and select **Convert Package**.
4. Click **OK**.

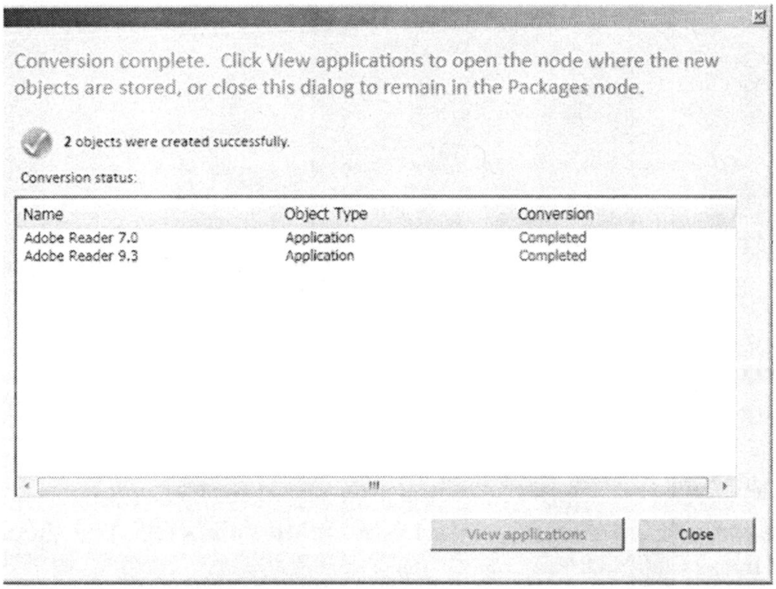

The package conversion completed.

5. Click **Close**.
6. Navigate to **Applications**. After a console refresh, you should be able to see the two new applications.

Distribution Point Sharing

Distribution point sharing is a feature used while the migration is in progress and you have a mix of ConfigMgr 2007 and ConfigMgr 2012 clients. It allows the ConfigMgr 2012 clients to make use of a ConfigMgr 2007 distribution point. It's not a feature you implement for long, only long enough to ensure that all clients have been successfully migrated to ConfigMgr 2012. After that's done, you upgrade the distribution point to a ConfigMgr 2012 distribution point.

1. Select the **Administration** workspace.
2. Navigate to **Overview**, **Migration**, **Active Source Hierarchy**.
3. Click **Share Distribution Points** on the ribbon.
4. Select **Enable distribution sharing for this Configuration Manager 2007 site server** and click **OK**.

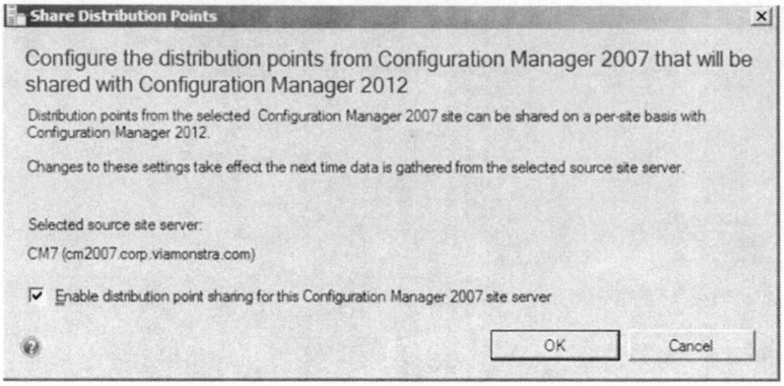

Sharing the distribution points.

5. Click **Close** after the gathering process is finished.
6. While still in **Active Source Hierarchy**, select the **Distribution Points** tab. You should be able to see a list of the available DPs.

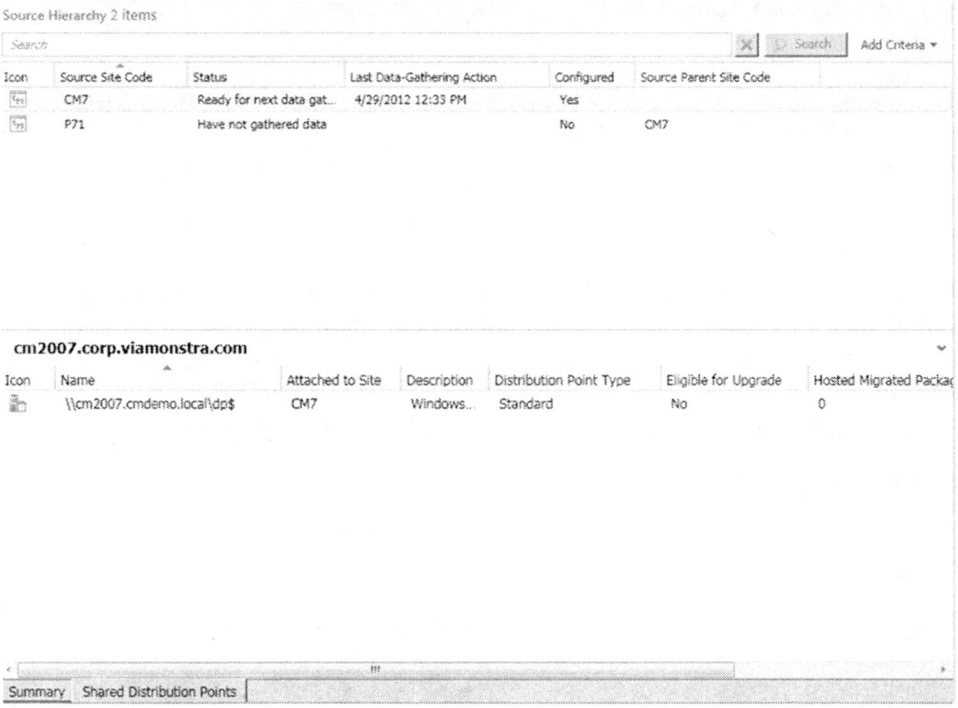

The shared distribution points are listed.

Upgrade the Distribution Point

1. Select the **Administration** workspace.
2. Navigate to **Overview**, **Migration**, **Active Source Hierarchy**.
3. Select **Distribution Point Upgrades** and select **Upgrade Distribution Point** on the ribbon.
4. Click **Browse** and select **CM2007.**
5. In **Site Code**, select **PS1** and click **Next**.
6. Select **Install and configure IIS if required by Configuration Manager** and click **Next**.
7. In **Drive Settings**, configure **D:** as the **Primary content library** and click **Next**.
8. On the **PXE Settings** page, click **Next**.
9. On the **Content Validation** page, click **Next**.
10. On the **Boundary Groups** page, click **Next**.
11. On the **Content Conversion** page, notice the number of packages that will be converted and click **Next**.
12. Click **Next** and **Close** to start the Upgrade process.

Migrate Collection

Another way of migrating your content is migrating the collections with all related objects:

1. Select the **Administration** workspace.
2. Navigate to **Overview**, **Migration**, **Migration Jobs**.
3. Click **Create Migration Job** on the ribbon.
4. In **Name**, type **Collections**.
5. In **Job type**, select **Collection migration** and click **Next**.

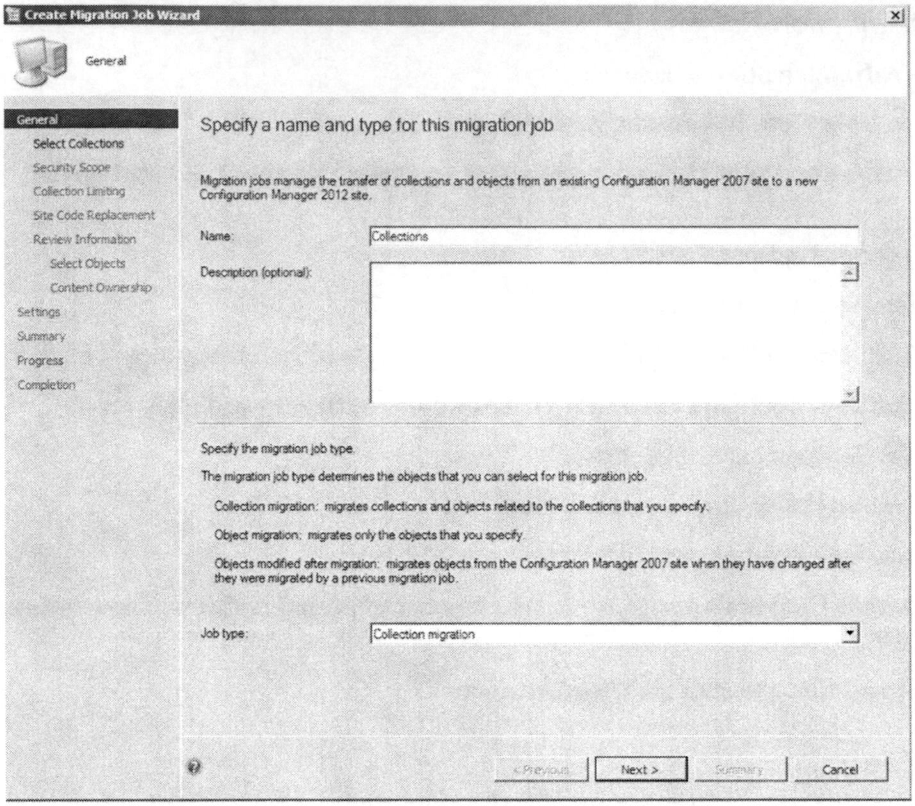

Configuring the migration job type.

6. Select the collections you want to migrate and click **Next**.

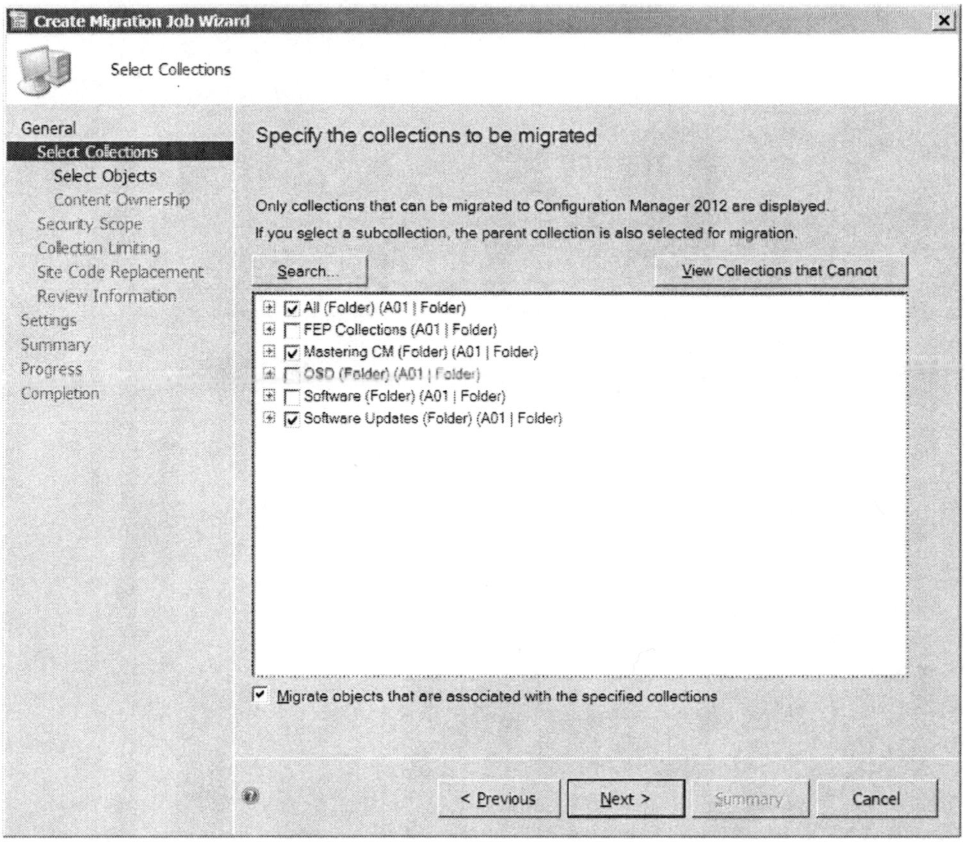

Selecting a list of collections.

7. Notice the list of objects, advertisements, packages, and task sequences. Those are all objects related to the collections you selected. Click **Next** to migrate the associated collections.
8. Select **Security Scope** and click **Next**.
9. Select **Collection Limiting** and click **Next**.
10. On the **Site Code Replacement** page, a list of collections will be shown if those collections contained a hardcoded site code in ConfigMgr 2007. Since ConfigMgr 2012 has another site code, you are able to select that new site code from the drop-down box.

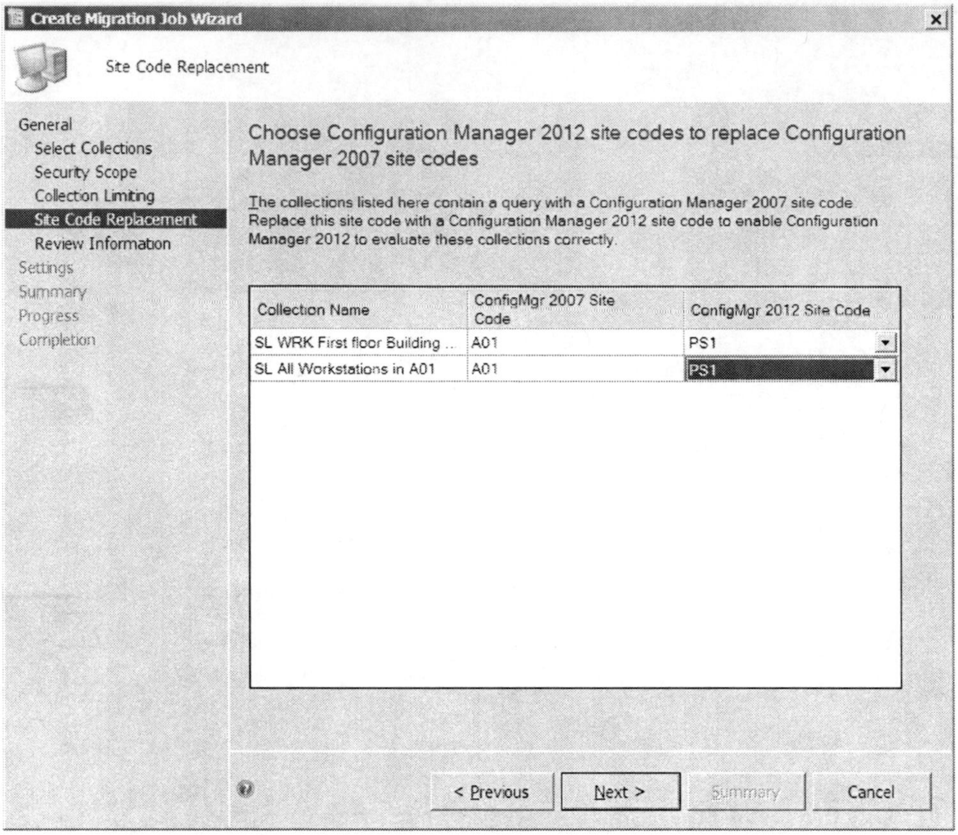

Replacing a hardcoded site code in a collection query.

11. Click **Next** to run the migration job now.

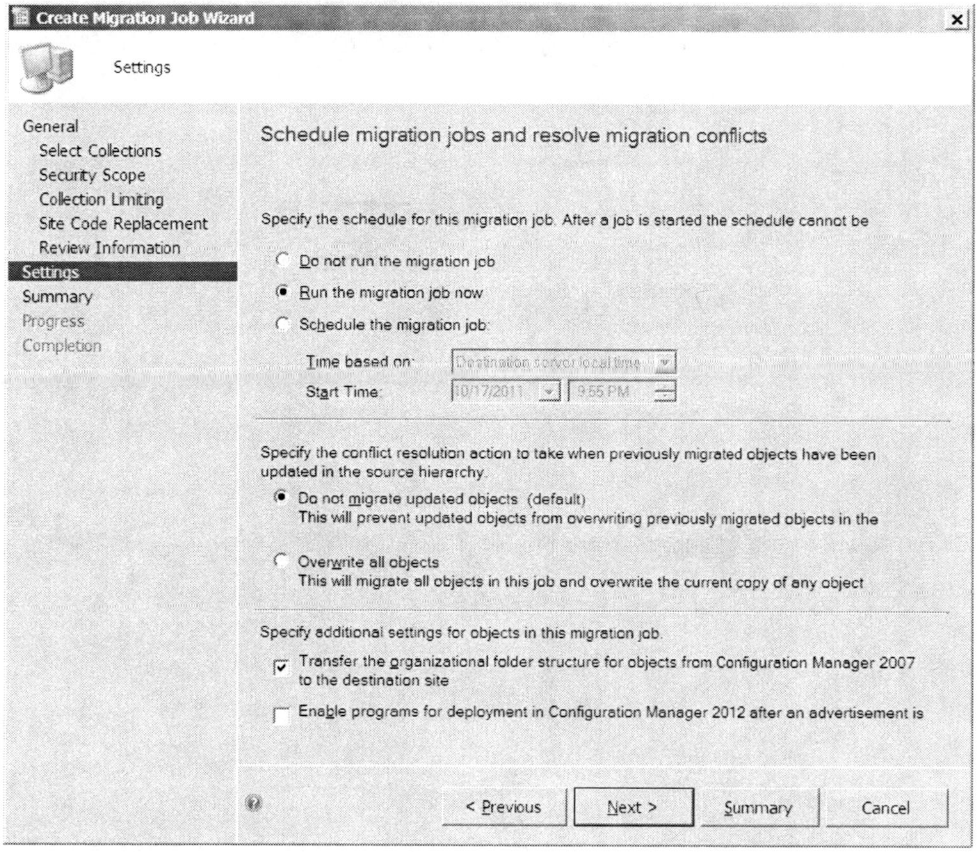

Scheduling the migration job.

12. Click **Next** and **Close**.
13. Monitor the **migmctrl.log** file; it will contain information about the migration process.

Monitor the Migration Process

1. Open the **Monitor** workspace and select **Reporting, Reports**.
2. In **Search,** type **Migration** and press **Enter**. You should see five reports in the Migration folder.

Appendix H Naming Standards

Throughout this book, I have created several different objects like collections, packages, applications, deployment types, update groups, and so forth. The tables in this appendix list the naming standards that I have typically followed.

Naming Conventions for Collections and Folders

Object	Naming Convention
Collection	Collection prefix + Description SUM Workstation Production

Naming Conventions for Software

Object	Naming Convention
Package	Manufacturer Application Version Optional Language Optional **Microsoft Visio 2010**
Program	Application Action Architecture **Visio Install x86**
Deployment	Application Action **Visio Install**
Application	Manufacturer Application Version **Microsoft Office 2010**
Deployment type	Application Version Architecture Language **Office 2010 x86**

Naming Conventions for Software Updates

Object	Naming Convention
Update Group	Year Month value Month name **2012 06 June**
Templates	(WRK/SRV) Description **WRK Production**

Object	Naming Convention
Deployments	(WRK/SRV) Year Month number Month name Target Vendor (Optional Type) **WRK 2012 06 June Pilot 1**
Deployment Packages	Year First/Second half Vendor (Optional Type) **2012-1**
Automatic Deployment Rules	Description **Patch Tuesday**

Naming Conventions for Operating System

Object	Naming Convention
Driver categories	OS Architecture Make Model **Windows 7 x64 Lenovo W510**
Driver packages	OS Architecture Make Model **Windows 7 Lenovo x64 W510**
Task Sequences	Descriptive name OS Architecture **Build and Capture Windows 7 Enterprise x64**
Boot images	Descriptive name Architecture **MDTBoot Image x64**
Images	Descriptive name OS Architecture Version **Win7SP1_x64_Ent_v1**

Index

D

E

F

G

H

I

J

K

L

Beyond the Book – Meet the Expert

If you liked the book, you will love to hear him in person.

Live Presentations

Kent Agerlund frequently speaks at conferences like Microsoft Management Summit (MMS) and TechEd around the world. You also can find Kent at infrastructure tours and local events like Microsoft Campus Days/TechDays, the Nordic Infrastructure Conference (NIC), and user group meetings around the globe.

For current tour dates and presentations, see http://blog.coretech.dk/kea.

Video Trainings

For video-based training, see the following sites:

- www.truesec.com
- www.deploymentartist.com

Live Instructor-led Classes

Kent Agerlund presents scheduled instructor-led classes in the US and in Europe. For current dates and locations, see the following sites:

- www.coretech.dk
- www.truesec.com
- www.labcenter.se
- www.teknologisk.dk
- www.inmetacrayon.com
- www.benchmarklearning.com

CPSIA information can be obtained at www.ICGtesting.com
Printed in the USA
LVOW090824131112
307094LV00001B/1/P

9 789197 939041